THE HUMAN COUPLE IN THE FATHERS

Visit our web sites at
WWW.ALBAHOUSE.ORG
or
WWW.PAULINE.ORG

The Human Couple in the Fathers

Introduction and Notes by
Giulia Sfameni Gasparro, Cesare Magazzù,
and Concetta Aloe Spada

English Translation by
Thomas Halton

ST PAULS

BOOKS & MEDIA
BOSTON

Italian language edition published by Edizioni Paoline under the title
La Coppia nei Padri (copyright 1991, Figlie di San Paolo, Milan).

The Pauline Patristic Series is a joint project of Pauline Books and
Media (Daughters of St. Paul) and Alba House (Society of St. Paul).

Library of Congress Cataloging-in-Publication Data

Coppia nei padri. English.
   The human couple in the fathers / introduction and notes by
Giulia Sfameni Gasparro, Cesare Magazzu and Concetta Aloe Spada;
English translation by Thomas Halton.
      p.   cm.
   Includes bibliographical references.
   ISBN: 0-8189-0803-3
   1. Marriage — Religious aspects — Christianity — History of
doctrines — Early church, ca. 30-600. 2. Early literature,
Christian. I. Sfameni Gasparro, Giulia. II. Magazzu, Cesare.
III. Aloe Spada, Concetta. IV. Halton, Thomas P. (Thomas Patrick)
V. Title.
BT706.C6613   1998
261.8'3581'09015 — dc21   97-33436
                         CIP

Produced and designed in the United States of America by the
Fathers and Brothers of the Society of St. Paul,
2187 Victory Boulevard, Staten Island, New York 10314,
as part of their communications apostolate.

ISBN: 0-8189-0803-3 (Society of St. Paul)
ISBN: 0-8198-3378-9 (Daughters of St. Paul)

Printing Information:

Current Printing - first digit   1   2   3   4   5   6   7   8   9   10

Year of Current Printing - first year shown

1999   2000   2001   2002   2003   2004   2005   2006   2007   2008

For Beverly and Michael Heneghan
Silver Jubilarians
1972-1997

TABLE OF CONTENTS

PREFACE TO THE ITALIAN EDITION

The experts who collaborated in the editing of this volume, while agreeing on the methodology chosen and in the general outline of the problems to be confronted, have felt it best to distinguish between the respective contributors. Thus, while concurring in the selection of the texts judged most significant for the purpose of illustrating the themes under consideration, the translation of these — made from the most accredited critical editions — was done by C. Aloe Spada (St. John Chrysostom) and by C. Magazzù (all the other authors), who also wrote the relative introductory profiles and the notes to the texts with the sole exception of those pertaining to Origen, whose introductory profile along with the notes to the text were done by G. Sfameni Gasparro, who also handled the General Introduction.

In those cases where the same documentation was used in the Introduction and in the Individual Profiles, to facilitate the readers' access to the bibliographical data it was felt that it would be convenient to repeat in the notes of the latter the complete citations of the most significant works.

BIBLIOGRAPHICAL ABBREVIATIONS

AAST	Atti della Accademia delle Scienze di Torino, II Classe di Scienze Morali, Storiche e Filologiche.
ACW	Ancient Christian Writers.
AFLM	Annali della Facoltà di Lettere e Filosofia dell'Università di Macerata.
Annales ESC	Annales. Économie, Sociétés, Civilisations, Paris.
ANRW	Aufstieg und Niedergang der römischen Welt, Berlin-New York.
BA	Biblioteca Ambrosiana, Milan-Rome.
BAug	Bibliothèque Augustinienne, Paris.
BEFAR	Bibliothèque des Écoles Françaises d'Athènes et de Rome.
BP	Biblioteca Patristica, Florence.
CBQ	The Catholic Biblical Quarterly.
CCC	Civiltà Classica e Cristiana, Genoa.
CCSG	Corpus Christianorum, Series Graeca, Turnhout.
CCSL	Corpus Christianorum, Series Latina, Turnhout.
CSEL	Corpus Scriptorum Ecclesiasticorum Latinorum, Vienna.
CTP	Collana di Testi Patristici, Rome.
DACL	Dictionnaire d'Archéologie Chrétienne et de Liturgie, Paris.
DB	Dictionnaire de la Bible, Paris, 1922-1928.
DB Suppl.	Dictionnaire de la Bible, Supplément, Paris, 1928f.
DPAC	Dizionario Patristico e di Antichità Cristiane, Casale Monferrato.
DSp	Dictionnaire de Spiritualité ascétique et mystique, Paris, 1937f.
FOTC	Fathers of the Church, Washington, D.C.
GCS	Die griechischen christlichen Schriftsteller der ersten (drei) Jahrhunderte, Berlin.
GLNT	Grande Lessico del Nuovo Testamento, Brescia.
HTR	Harvard Theological Review, Cambridge, Mass.

JECS	Journal of Early Christian Studies.
JEH	The Journal of Ecclesiastical History, London.
JQR	The Jewish Quarterly Review, London.
JTS	The Journal of Theological Studies, Oxford.
MélScRel	Mélanges de Science Religieuse, Lille.
NBA	Nuova Biblioteca Agostiniana, Rome.
NHS	Nag Hammadi Studies, Leiden, 1971f.
NRTh	Nouvelle Revue Théologique, Louvain.
N.S./n.s.	Nuova Serie.
NTS	New Testament Studies, Cambridge.
OChrPer	Orientalia Christiana Periodica, Rome.
OECT	Oxford Early Christian Texts.
PG	J.-P. Migne, Patrologiae cursus completus, Series Graeca, Paris.
PL	J.-P. Migne, Patrologiae cursus completus, Series Latina, Paris.
PSV	Parola Spirito Vita, Rome.
PW, RE	A. Pauly-G. Wissowa, Realencyclopädie des classischen Altertumwissenschaft, Stuttgart, 1893f.
RAC	Reallexikon für Antike und Christentum, Stuttgart, 1950f.
RAM	Revue d'Ascétique et de Mystique, Toulouse.
RB	Revue Biblique, Paris.
RCCM	Rivista di Cultura Classica e Medievale, Rome.
REA	Revue des Études Anciennes, Valence.
REAug	Revue des Études Augustiniennes, Paris.
RechAug	Recherches Augustiniennes, Paris.
REL	Revue des Études Latines, Paris.
RevHistSpir	Revue d'Histoire de la Spiritualité (previously RAM), Paris.
RevPhil	Revue de Philologie, Paris.
RevSR	Revue des Sciences Religieuses, Strasbourg.
RHL	Revue d'Histoire et de Littérature Religieuses, Paris.
RHR	Revue de l'Histoire des Religions, Paris.
RIL	Rendiconti dell'Istituto Lombardo, Milan.
RivBibi	Rivista Biblica, Rome.
RScPhTh	Revue des Sciences Philosophiques et Théologiques, Paris.
RSLR	Rivista di Storia e Letteratura Religiose, Florence.

RSR	Recherches de Science Religieuse, Paris.
RThL	Revue Théologique de Louvain, Louvain.
SC	Sources chrétiennes.
SDHI	Studia et Documenta Historiae et Iuris, Rome.
SPM	Studia Patristica Mediolanensia, Milan.
StPat	Studia Patristica.
TU	Texte und Untersuchungen zur Geschichte der altchristlichen Literatur, Leipzig and Berlin, 1882f.
VetChr	Vetera Christianorum, Bari.
VigChr	Vigiliae Christianae, Amsterdam.
YClS	Yale Classical Studies, New Haven, Conn.

Biblical Abbreviations

OLD TESTAMENT

Genesis	Gn	Nehemiah	Ne	Baruch	Ba
Exodus	Ex	Tobit	Tb	Ezekiel	Ezk
Leviticus	Lv	Judith	Jdt	Daniel	Dn
Numbers	Nb	Esther	Est	Hosea	Ho
Deuteronomy	Dt	1 Maccabees	1 M	Joel	Jl
Joshua	Jos	2 Maccabees	2 M	Amos	Am
Judges	Jg	Job	Jb	Obadiah	Ob
Ruth	Rt	Psalms	Ps	Jonah	Jon
1 Samuel	1 S	Proverbs	Pr	Micah	Mi
2 Samuel	2 S	Ecclesiastes	Ec	Nahum	Na
1 Kings	1 K	Song of Songs	Sg	Habakkuk	Hab
2 Kings	2 K	Wisdom	Ws	Zephaniah	Zp
1 Chronicles	1 Ch	Sirach	Si	Haggai	Hg
2 Chronicles	2 Ch	Isaiah	Is	Malachi	Ml
Ezra	Ezr	Jeremiah	Jr	Zechariah	Zc
		Lamentations	Lm		

NEW TESTAMENT

Matthew	Mt	Ephesians	Eph	Hebrews	Heb
Mark	Mk	Philippians	Ph	James	Jm
Luke	Lk	Colossians	Col	1 Peter	1 P
John	Jn	1 Thessalonians	1 Th	2 Peter	2 P
Acts	Ac	2 Thessalonians	2 Th	1 John	1 Jn
Romans	Rm	1 Timothy	1 Tm	2 John	2 Jn
1 Corinthians	1 Cor	2 Timothy	2 Tm	3 John	3 Jn
2 Corinthians	2 Cor	Titus	Tt	Jude	Jude
Galatians	Gal	Philemon	Phm	Revelation	Rv

THE HUMAN COUPLE IN THE FATHERS

I

THE MAN/WOMAN RELATIONSHIP:
THE COORDINATES OF THE PROBLEM

An investigation into the various positions assumed by the Christian writers of the first centuries, conventionally called the Fathers of the Church,[1] on the theme of the human couple, would seem at first approach to be proposed as a sort of "variation" on the obviously connected theme of marriage. In fact, for all the authors in question the couple is none other than what results from the union of man and woman in the marriage bond, with all the prerogatives and the web of rights and duties which this envisages.

However, our inquiry is less concerned with and directed to the formal and institutional aspects of marriage, than to the whole series of data offered from the documentation relative to the Christian life of the first centuries[2] and the numerous patristic formula-

---

[1] For the origin of naming Christian writers of the first centuries as "Fathers" and a rapid but richly documented presentation of this sector of historical research cf. J. Quasten, *Patrology*, 1, 1950, rp. 1986, Westminster, MD, 9-12.

[2] The bibliography on the theme is so notoriously extensive that it would be impossible to offer here anything but a summary review. It suffices to mention for the New Testament context, apart from the observations of W. Rordorf, 'Marriage in the New Testament and in the Early Church,' *JEH* 20 (1969), 193-210, Fl. Baltensweiler, *Il matrimonio nel Nuovo Testamento. Richerche esegetiche su matrimonio, celibato e divorzio*, Brescia, 1981 (ed. orig. Zurich, 1967) and, for the 2-5th centuries, the contributions of Ch. Munier, 'L'Église et cité,' in G. Le Bras-J. Gaudement (edd.), *Histoire du Droit et des Institutions de l'Église en Occident, 11, 3. L'Église dans l'Empire Romain (IIe-IIIe siècles)*, P.IIIe, Paris, 1979, 3-71 and J. Gaudement, *ibidem*, III, 'L'Église dans l'Empire romain (IVe-Ve siècles),' Paris, 1958, 514-591. See also Ch. Pietri, 'IV-V secolo. 11 matrimonio cristiano a Roma,' in J. Delumeau (ed.), *Storia vissuta del popolo cristiano*, Turin, 1985 (orig. ed. Paris, 1979), 93-121; C. Burini-E. Cavalcanti, *La spiritualità della vita quotidiana negli scritti dei Padri*, Bologna, 1988, 97-132, and 155-175. An ample view of the problems, with special attention to ritual, and liturgical aspects, is presented in K. Ritzer, *Le mariage dans les églises chrétiennes du Ier au XIe siècle*, Paris, 1970 (ed. orig. Münster, 1962). A recent history of matrimonial institutions in the western world is

tions[3] with regard to the modality and significance of intersecting relations between man and woman, at the center of which the matrimonial bond is placed in a new situation of peculiar interpersonal relationships.

Such a bond in large measure transcends the single and distinct individual conditions of man and woman, to constitute a new existential reality, precisely that of "couple," in the equilibrium and complementarity of its components.

There is question, then, of circumscribing, at the center of the patristic discourse on the fundamental, human institution of marriage in all its complex social, cultural and religious implications to which the attention of these same authors is especially directed, a particular sphere, more intimate and restricted, but nonetheless essential for the understanding of the value and significance assigned to the same institution.

We refer to the level in which the protagonists themselves are called to act in their respective roles, one on one, each assuming the function which, in the view of the Fathers, are the normative principles of ethics and of Christian anthropology.

In fact it is said that the patristic view of the man/woman relationship *qua* married couple, despite different emphases of tone given in greater or less degree to one or the other partner, presents a substantial homogeneity and remains structured on some fundamental directives which, apart from norms of ethical behavior, imply a direct involvement of anthropology, attaining then to ontological assumptions of the conception of man.

Put differently, the discourse of the Fathers on the respective roles and the modality of the mutual relations of the man/woman

---

in J. Gaudemet, *Il matrimonio in Occidente*, Torino, 1989 (ed. orig. Paris, 1987). A rich anthology of texts is offered in Ch. Munier, *Mariage et virginité dans l'Église ancienne (Ie-IIIe siècles)*, Bern, 1987. [See now: D.G. Hunter, *Marriage in the Early Church*, Minneapolis, 1992.]

[3] Apart from specific studies on individual authors, listed under each, an ample treatment will be found in G. Oggioni, *Matrimonio e verginità. Saggi di Teologia*, Venegono Inferiore 1963, 189-193 and in C. Tibiletti, 'Verginità e matrimonio in antichi scrittori cristiani,' *AFLM* 2 (1969),11-217 (rp. Rome, 1983). Both these works, like all the other treatments of the theme, confirm that the Fathers' doctrine on matrimony cannot be examined without an adequate consideration of their respective positions on the other, complementary, theme of continence and virginity.

union is constructed on an articulated web of elements which, at the ethical level, where for various reasons, Jewish and pagan traditions converge, especially of Stoic inspiration, in addition, naturally, to new principles of the Christian message, appeals to the anthropological picture. The latter, in turn, inspired by the biblical postulate of the creation of humankind on the part of God, on which all the Fathers base the inalienable foundation of the substantial goodness and positivity of the entire natural human sphere, is defined in relation to two fundamental parameters.

On the one hand are placed the data contained in the double narrative in Genesis of the formation of the first human couple and of the event which brought about a passage from a primitive state of felicity to a state of decadence, with toil, sorrow, death, homologous to that of actual humanity.

On the other hand, to condition in a particular direction the interpretation of these data, are placed, on the one hand, the exegetical traditions already worked out in a Jewish ambience such as — present if only by brief references in the canonical scriptures — were expressed in the rich apocryphal inter-testamental literature and the work of Philo Judaeus of Alexandria, on the other hand, their utilization in the epistles of Paul which is brought to the attention of Christian authors as the authoritative depository of the Gospel message and of its actual practice.

To this finally is joined the particular and variously constructed cultural backgrounds of individual Fathers and the respective exegetical options which, in the utilization of the data offered issue in diverse anthropological formulas and yet in the presence of some common directives and analogous structural bases.

Such anthropological formulas result in large measure founded on a protological scenario[4] that is, on a complex of elements relative to the first events of history. The nature of human existence, in its peculiar sexually differentiated consistency, the prerogatives with respect to male and female, and the modality of their relationships, defined on a basis of the primordial events. They contemplate not

---

[4] On the notion of protology as the treatment of the first events (*ta prōta*) of cosmic and human history cf. U. Bianchi-G. Sfameni Gasparro, *DPAC* coll. 2929-2941.

only the coming into existence of man and woman through the effect of a creative act on the part of God, which has constituted them
in their ontological structure, but also a series of behavioral activities on the part of the same original couple, which, because of the
transgression of a divine commandment, suddenly produces notable
changes in the negative sense in respect to its primitive existential
situation.

II

THE BIBLICAL DATA:
THE PROTOLOGICAL SCENARIO AND ITS
INTERPRETATION

As is known, the biblical text relating to the creation of man is composed of two narratives, which, while belonging to two different epochs and two different authors, nevertheless end up joined together in a continuous sequence. The ancient exegetes, who naturally were strangers to the modern problematic of textual criticism, when confronted with such a problem, proposed various solutions which were already current in Jewish circles. In particular, Philo of Alexandria, on the basis of his own Platonic presuppositions, had distinguished the "creation in the image" as related to the "heavenly" man, the ideal model of the "phenomenal" man, or the spiritual component (=intellect) of the latter,[1] the *plasmatio* of Adam, the earthly man, in his twofold components, physical and spiritual.[2]

Among Christian exegetes Origen, and some other authors who

---

[1] Cf. J. Giblet, 'L'homme image de Dieu dans les commentaires littéraux de Philon d'Alexandrie,' *Studia Hellenistica* 5 (1948), 93-118.

[2] On the teaching of Philo (on double creation of man) see Ch. Kannengiesser, 'Philon et les Pères sur la double création de l'homme,' in Aa.vv., *Philon d'Alexandrie*, Lyon, 11-15 septembre 1960 (Colloques Nationaux Centre National de la Recherche Scientifique), Paris, 1967, 277-296; A.M. Mazzanti, 'L'aggettivo meqorio e la doppia creazione dell'uomo in Filone di Alessandria,' in U. Bianchi, ed., *La doppia creazione dell'uomo negli Alessandrini, nei Cappadoci e nella gnosi*, Rome, 1978, 25-42. This teaching is enunciated in numerous contexts, and elaborated in particular in *De creatione mundi* and *Legum allegoriae*, both treatises available in *Philo*, Loeb Classical Library, vol. 1. See also G. Reale and R. Radice, *Filone di Alessandria. La filosofia mosaica*, Milan, 1987. For the balance components between Platonic and biblical elements in the thought of Philo cf. R. Radice, *Platonismo e creazionismo in Filone di Alessandria*, Milan, 1989. [Engl. ed. see now: D. Runia, *Philo and the Church Fathers: a collection of texts*, Leiden, 1995.]

5

were inspired in various degrees by him, elaborated along Philonian lines a complex theory of a "double creation" whose various implications and significations it is not possible to illustrate within the present compass.[3]

Outside the lines of interpretation inspired by Philo and Origen, Christian writers of the first centuries generally assumed that the two biblical accounts formed a unified sequence, from which they deduced the constitutive elements of an anthropological conception, making light of essential data from the protological scenario.

First and foremost, the motive of creation "in the image and likeness of God" as it was announced in Gn 1:26-27,[4] which the Fathers variously interpreted,[5] sometimes retaining both prerogatives of the original constitution of man as it had emerged from the creative act, sometimes, however, on the basis of v. 27, which mentions only the "image" (*eikon*) and is silent on the "likeness" (*homoiosis*), depicting a more complex perspective in which emphasis is placed on the ethical tension which should guide man in the movement of assimilation to God.

In such a case it is stated that the effort in every religious ac-

---

[3] For the notion of "double creation," which implies various possibilities including that of two creators (as, for instance, in the gnostic systems) or of a single creator in two successive and diversely motivated moments of a single creator (in Philo and in Origen) cf. U. Bianchi, 'La "doppia creazione" dell'uome oggetto di ricerca storico-religiose,' in *Idem* (ed.), *op. cit.*, 1-23. On the peculiar modality of this conception in Origen, on which we will see more later, see the studies collected in Sfameni Gasparro, *Origene. Studi di antropologia e di storia della tradizione*, Roma Nuovi Saggi, 90, 1984. On Gregory of Nyssa, see contributions of U. Bianchi, 'Presupposti platonici e dualistici nell'antropogonia di Gregorio di Nissa,' in *Idem* (ed.), *op. cit.*, 83-115; *Idem*, 'L'intention du Colloque. Analyse historico-religieuse' in Aa. vv. *Arché e Telos. L'antropologia di Origene e di Gregorio di Nissa. Analisi storico-religiosa, Atti del Colloquio di Milano, 17-19 maggio 1979*, U. Bianchi-H. Crouzel, eds., Milan, 1981, 9-27.

[4] On the significance of such a notion in the biblical text cf. J.F.A. Sawyer, 'The Meaning of "In the Image of God" in Genesis I-XI,' *JTS*, N.S. 25 (1974), 418-426; R. Hinschberger, 'Image et ressemblance dans la tradition sacerdotal GN 1. 26-28; 5,1-3; 9,6b,' *RevSR* 59 (1985),185-199; G.A. Jonsson, *Image of God. Genesis 1:26-28 in a Century of Old Testament Research*, Lund, 1988.

[5] Apart from specific studies on the theme in individual authors and already in Paul, see R. McL. Wilson, 'The Early History of the Exegesis of Gn 1:26,' in F.L. Aland (ed.), *Studia Patristica* I (TU 63), Berlin, 1957, 420-437; J. Jervell, *Imago Dei. Gn 1:26f. im Spätjudentum, in die Gnosis und in den paulinischen Briefen*, Göttingen, 1960; P. Schwanz, *Imago Dei als christologisch-anthropologisches Problem in der Geschichte der Alten Kirche von Paulus bis Clemens Alexandrini*, Göttingen 1979; G. Visonà, 'L'uomo a immagine di Dio. l'interpretazione di Genesi 1,26 nel pensiero cristiano dei primi tre secoli,' *Studia Patavina* 27 (1980), 393-430.

tivity of the Christian should consist in realizing to the full the faculty innate in his nature of "image" to unite with the quality of "likeness" for which his Creator has destined him.[6]

To the notion of the image the biblical text links, as a characteristic human prerogative, that of exercising dominion over the entire rest of creation. It is, in fact, invoked in the words of Gn 1:26, which announce the creative project, while in the divine blessing on the first couple which follows (Gn 1:28), together with the invitation to populate the earth, is joined the precept to hold dominion over every creature.

However, in regard to both of these prerogatives, which represent throughout the entire Christian exegetic tradition the very foundations of the anthropological discourse, by locating in the quality of "image" sovereign dominion over creation, the very essence and distinctive character of man in his mysterious relation of affinity with the Creator represent a problematic which introduces a more or less profound disequilibrium between the two components of the human couple.

In fact, while of course such prerogatives in the various exegetes define the ontological status of the male human being, opinions frequently diverge on the equal pertinence of them to the female, although the Greek version of the biblical text to which all the authors go back in Gn 1:26 at first is the singular *anthropos* (=human

---

[6] The distinction between the "image" conferred on man by the Creator and "likeness" acquired through ethical commitment occurs frequently in Origen (cf. H. Crouzel, *Théologie de l'image de Dieu chez Origène*, Paris, 1956), while Gregory of Nyssa affirms the contextual presence of these two prerogatives in man which results in the initial creative act of God (cf. R. Leys, *L'image de Dieu chez Saint Grégoire de Nysse. Esquisse d'une doctrine*, Brussels-Paris, 1951). The complex position of the Nyssene on the theme marriage-virginity does not affect the focus of the present research since the author is interested especially in the ontological and protological foundations of the problem, on the one hand, and the practice of asceticism, on the other, while barely glancing at the aspect of the concrete life of the couple of which we intend to treat. On this position see P. Pisi, *Genesis e phthora. Le motivazioni protologiche della verginità in Gregorio di Nissa e nella tradizione dell'enkrateia*, Rome, 1981. Cf. also the observations of G. Sfameni Gasparro, *Enkrateia e antropologia. Le motivazioni protologiche della continenza e della verginità nel cristianesimo dei primi secoli e nello gnosticismo* (Studia Ephemeridis Augustinianum 20), Rome, 1984, 235-244 and, for the special connection between the theme of creation and image and the distinction between the sexes see G. Sfameni Gasparro, 'Image of God and Sexual Differentiation in the Tradition of Enkrateia: Protological Motivations,' in K.E. Borresen, (ed.), *The Image of God and Gender Models in Judaeo-Christian Tradition*, Minneapolis, 1995.

being) ("let us make man"), but straight away, on the basis of the collective Hebrew *adam*, they utilize the plural form of the verb "to command" ("they have dominion").

The next verse, for its part, after having presented the creation event of the human being (*anthropos*) in the image of God, in Gn 1:27b evokes in an explicit manner the sexual distinction which defines them in their ontological constitution: "male and female he created them."[7]

However, a sizeable patristic tradition would tend to deny the quality of "image" to the female on the basis of various arguments, among which, on the one hand, the decisive one would be a particular and well-consolidated exegesis of the Pauline text, 1 Cor 11:7-10, which will be treated at length later, and, on the other, the connection between such a quality and the faculty of dominion. This latter in fact appears to be typically extraneous from the woman inasmuch as she is fixed in a status of definite subordination defined in relation to a series of data in part still taken from the protological scenario in a context of an interpretation on which some elements offered in the Pauline corpus[8] exert a strong influence.

---

[7] For the significance of such a statement in the Hebrew text cf. Ph. A. Bird, '"Male and Female He Created Them": Gn 1:2-7b in the Context of the Priestly Account of Creation,' *HThR* 74 (1981), 129-159. The question of the pertinence to the woman of the faculty of "image" had been already raised in the Jewish tradition prior to the Christian. See in this regard M. C. Horowitz, 'The image of God. Is Woman Included?', *HThR* 72 (1979), 175-206. For the various positions of the Fathers on the theme see G. Sfameni Gasparro, 'La donna, l'esegesi patristica di Gn I-III,' in U. Mattioli (ed.), *La donna nel pensiero cristiano antico*, Turin (1994). The doctrine of Augustine on the theme has been acutely analyzed in K.E. Borresen, *Subordination and Equivalence. The Nature and Role of Woman in Augustine and Thomas Aquinas,* Nouvelle éd., Kampen, 1995 (original ed., Oslo, 1968). Cf. *eadem*, 'Imago Dei, privilège masculin? Interpretation augustinienne et pseudo-augustinienne de Gn 1:27 et 1 Cor 11:7,' *Augustinianum* 25 (1985), 213-234; R.J. McGowen, 'Augustine's Spiritual Equality: the Allegory of Man and Woman with Regard to the Imago *Dei*,' *REAug* 33 (1987), 255-264.

[8] The refusal to recognize in the female the quality of image of God occurs in many exegetes in the Eastern church. See S. Zincone, 'Il tema dell'uomo/donna immagine di Dio nei Commenti paolini ca Gil cli area atitiochena (Diodoro, Crisostomo, Teodoro, Teodoreto),' *Annali di Storia dell'esegesi 2* (1985), 103-113. In the West analogous positions were maintained by Ambrosiaster in his *Commentarius ad Epistolam ad Corinthios* (11,7,1: CSEL 81,2, p. 121s.; I 1, 10, p. 122 s,) and in various places in *Quaestioni de Veteri et Novo Testamento* (XXI: CSEL 50, 47 s.; XXIV, p. 51; XLV,2- 3, p. 82 s.; CVI,17, p. 243 s.). [Engl. ed. See D. Hunter, *HThR* 82 (1989), 283-299] In his Commentary on the Epistle to the Colossians, the author, while reaffirming such notions (3, 11, 4, 5: CSEL 81,3 p. 196 s.), recognizes the full equality of man and woman on the level of redemption, in which the woman also possesses the faculty of "image" which she derives from knowledge of the Savior. See D.G. Hunter, 'The paradise of patriarchy. Ambrosiaster on woman as (not) God's image,' *JTS* 43 (1992), 447-469; *idem, HThR* 82 (1989), 283-299.

Such a scenario, in fact, contemplates, in the ample account of Gn 2-3, which takes up again the theme of the creation of the first couple and articulates it with the illustration of its original condition and of the first events in its historical existence, the motive of the "construction" of Eve from the rib taken from the side of the sleeping Adam.

As has been noted already, the patristic tradition, apart from the exegetical line which distinguishes a "first creation" (Gn 1:26-27) variously understood, gives a second creative act which places in being "phenomenal" man (Gn 2:7), even when it attributes the faculty of *eikon* to the spiritual intellectual part of man, which is conjoined with a corporeal element, whose *plasmatio* is described in the second Genesis account, generally reads the latter as a continuation of the former. And that in the sense that it would furnish the details of that creative work which had been evoked at the outset in its globality.

From such a unitarian reading emerges a scene rather important for the definition of the relations between the two members of the original human couple, prototypical and paradigmatic of those which regulate the equilibrium of all actual couples. Appearing decisive in this are the notions of Eve, created as a "helper" like to Adam, and the nuptial relationship as was proclaimed in the exclamation of the first one created at the sight of the woman. Adam's words also contain an explicit reference to her being "derived" from his own body, representing the matrimonial union as a sort of return to original unity (Gn 2:23-24). A significant detail at the end of the definition of the value and modality of the physical relationship which characterizes the interpersonal relationship will cover up in the patristic tradition the nudity of the first-formed and the absence of "shame" which qualified their original situation in the garden of paradise (Gn 2:25).

In fact, as is known, the biblical text locates the account of the transgression of the divine precept after the account of the creation, subjecting both the protoplasts and the whole of humanity to a series of decisive modifications in the negative sense. The narrative sequence is very familiar: the prohibition against eating of the fruit of the tree of knowledge of good and evil, already uttered by

God to Adam (Gn 2:16-17) is broken by the temptation of the serpent, "the most astute of all the animals" in the confrontation with Eve, who offers to Adam the fruit from which they both ate. Next follows the motif of the opening of the eyes, with the consequent recognition of their own nudity and the covering with a fig leaf (Gn 3:1-7).

The divine sanction implies the condemnation of the serpent, the announcement to Eve of the sufferings connected with childbirth, and the dominion to be exercised over her by her husband, to whom she submits, while, in the case of Adam, there is the burden of toilsome work and the threat of death.

The protological scenario, here briefly evoked in its outlines and peak moments, represents one of the principal, if not the essential, parameter of reference of the Fathers for the definition of the ontological and existential state of the human couple. The image of being, and the connected interpretation of the man/woman relationship, in that it constitutes the marriage couple, moreover finds further and other decisive conditions in a series of passages from the epistles of St. Paul, some of which equally evoke, by echoes more or less explicit, this same scenario.

In short, certain peculiar aspects of the socio-cultural climate and of the spirituality of the time emerge as equally important. On the one hand, we refer to the institutional structures of marriage and to the whole complex of conceptions relative to the man/woman relationship and to the prerogatives with respect to the two sexes which represent within the ambit of Greco-Roman society and culture, on the one hand, and to the Jewish, on the other. The various authors experience the effects of such notions, in fact, and in various ways. Despite the "novelty" of the Christian message in which they have their being, they do not cease to be men of their own time, participating in certain mental structures and in determinate expressive formulae typical of such a cultural context.

On the other hand, conditioning in a more or less emphatic manner the positions of the Fathers on the problematic in question, there intervened the particular relationship which the matrimonial theme invested appeals of sexual continence, variously gradated and motivated, which permeated large sections of primitive Christianity in configuring that tradition of *enkrateia* which the present writer has dealt with in greater detail elsewhere.[9]

For a correct historical comprehension, then, of the treatment of the Fathers of the theme under consideration, it is necessary then to take account of the convergence and equilibrium of all the elements mentioned, to avoid either the superficial judgments on respective positions, sometimes barely compatible with, if not totally at variance with, modern sensibility, or improbable "actualizations" of some aspects of the same, too tied to a certain epoch or to relative cultural conditions to find space in a diverse spiritual climate.

It is useful, then, to examine, if only rapidly, the complex of factors which in various ways occurred in the patristic context in the various articulations of its natural prerogatives and functions and in the reciprocity of a relationship which at the same time qualifies and conditions the very existential and religious status of the human being of either sex and determines the particular conception of the entire social and ecclesiastical community.

If in fact the matrimonial union constitutes the nucleus and foundation of the first, and in the second is placed such a more common condition on the more common choice of celibacy on the part of individuals, all that which concerns it, in its internal articulation and in the value attributed to it, is reflected on the image itself of society and of the church reflected on the patristic horizon.

---

[9] See *Enkrateta e antropologia*, cited above in note 6. For a full and nuanced discussion on the theme cf. U. Bianchi (ed.), *La tradizione dell'enkrateia. Motivazioni ontologiche e protologiche, Atti del Colloquio Internazionale Milano 20-23 Aprile 1982*, Rome, 1985. Important contributions on the problem of sexuality in early Christianity are offered in R. Cantalamessa (ed.), *Etica sessuale e matrimonio nel Cristianesimo delle origini* (SPM 5), Milan, 1976. The recent study of P. Brown, *The Body and Society. Men, Women and Sexual Renunciation in Early Christianity*, New York (1988) offers a lively and profound analysis of various attitudes on the theme in late-pagan and Christian ambiences. [Engl. ed. See four reviews in *RSLR* 28 (1992), 105-125.] E. Pagels, *Adam, Eve and the Serpent* (New York, 1988) is dedicated to the proposition to go back "to the origins of Christian sexual morality" through an examination of the exegesis of the biblical account of creation. In her work, which singles out in this exegesis the expression of a profound quest for moral liberty characteristic of various sectors of primitive Christianity down to Augustine, with whom, by contrast, the perspective would change in a radical manner. She presents many interesting interpretative points; however, all the contributions published in recent years on the theme of *enkrateia*, which the results of the Colloquio internazionale di Milano would seem to be fundamental are conspicuous by their absence. Evidently for Pagels the dictum so in vogue in countries of Anglo-Saxon tradition: *Italicus est, non legitur!* still holds.

The first and decisive element of mediation between the protological picture delineated in Genesis and the patristic interpretation of it is constituted, as already indicated, in certain places in the Pauline epistles. However, the importance should not be neglected of the equally fundamental Gospel text of Mt 19:1-15, with its synoptic parallels (Mk 10:1-16; Lk 16:18). These relate to the possibility of divorce, something admitted in the Mosaic law and rejected in turn by Jesus.[10] As is well known, He, when questioned by the Pharisees on the liceity of the spouses separating, replied by evoking the protological perspective of the creation of male and female as is enunciated in Gn 1:26 and adduces the declaration of Adam (here attributed to the Creator himself) on the union of the two "in one flesh."

The sexual distinction results in this way finalized in a nuptial union represented as unbreakable in virtue of its being established on a base both ontological (the creation of human beings, *qua* masculine and feminine) and protological (divine sanction of the union).

On this basis in the Gospels, to which Paul himself refers in his own way in 1 Cor chapter 7, in the whole patristic tradition, as in the entire sweep of the official teaching of the Church, the inalienable principle of the indissolubility of marriage is affirmed, which appears as one of the motives qualifying the relation of the couple.

The purpose of this anthology collection and of the research devoted to it — as we have already explained — is not so much to isolate and recover the lines of formation and the development of the Christian teaching on matrimony, or of the institution of matrimony as such. Attention is rather directed to characterize at its center the peculiar modality of the relationship between the two subjects in which it is concretely realized. Moreover the inevitable interference between them is evident which can define the institutional,

---

[10] From the extensive bibliography relative to the Gospel pericope in which the motive occurs of "becoming a eunuch for the kingdom," which proposes the question of virginity and of continence on which we will see more later, it suffices to cite J. Dupont, *Mariage et divorce dans l'évangile. Matthieu 19:3-12 et parallèles*, Bruges, 1959. Cf. also B. Proietti, 'La scelta celibitaria alla luce della S. Scrittura,' in Aa. vv., *Il celibato per il Regno*, Milan, 1977, 7-75 and in particular 25-40, with full bibliography.

normative and structural aspects, pertaining to the interpersonal relations between the partners of the union.

We should also emphasize in a preliminary way that, in the patristic literature, the first greatly surpass the second, once the interest of the authors becomes more strongly and more frequently focused on the institution, its nature and its social and religious value, which no other sphere of experience directly involves both man and woman together. This sphere transpires only fleetingly and in rapid strokes in the discourse of the Fathers; generally it should rather be reconstructed through the grid of references to institutional structures and to the modality of conceiving, at its center, the reciprocal relations of the two components of the couple.

That holds good for the theme of the indissoluble validity of the matrimonial bond which, forcibly affirmed after the gospel model in all the patristic contexts, represents the most typical novelty of the Christian vision of it in relationship with the usages of the Greco-Roman ambience, on the one hand, and the Jewish, on the other, both of which, with various qualifications and different modalities, were open to the practice of divorce.

This theme, together with that of the perfect reciprocity and equality of the spouses in their rights of access to the bodies of each other, recurs in 1 Cor 7, which represents one of the most solid of the parameters to which the various Fathers appeal, when they are about to trace a chart of the rights/obligations of the spouses. The interpersonal relationship between them, insofar as it pertains to the sphere of sexual activity, which defines the specificity facing whatever other type of relations between man and woman is represented, in fact, on a plane of parity. This, in the sense, explicitly enunciated in the text of Paul, of the equal rights of both in the exercise of the practice of marriage, that by which the "debt" can be asked for with equal legitimacy by each of them, and in which they are equally bound by the obligation of mutual fidelity.

The Fathers, in fact, as we shall see, strongly insist on this principle which contradicts a practice and the connected well-rooted mentality of the contemporary cultural ambience, Greco-Roman and Jewish, which showed a notable tolerance for male infidelity, coupled with extremely severe sanctions for female infidelity. Chapter seven of 1 Corinthians, with the dense pregnancy of its reasoning, touches on a problem of quite broad dimensions, which reflects the concrete situation in the community to which it refers and, as it is legitimate to deduce, to other Christian communities of the time also, but clearly transcends the limits of the historical circumstances of its formulation. The teaching therein expressed, interpreted variously in different ambiences in relationship with presuppositions more or less rigorous of exegetes, will exercise in fact a decisive influence not only on the Christian view of marriage but also on the determination of its role and value in the complex picture of the religious life of the Christian. And this, in relation especially to the alternative choice of virginity, that is, of continence within the realm of marriage itself or of widowhood.

We will return then to this Pauline text, basic for the understanding of the patristic positions on the theme under examination, when we undertake to illustrate the incidence which the problematic of *enkrateia*, so essential in the Christianity of the early centuries, has had in the definition of the essential lineaments of the relation of the couple in its specific sexual validity.

Here we intend rather to evoke briefly those passages in the epistles of Paul to which the Fathers appeal with significant insistence to illustrate the respective roles of husband and wife. Such texts, in their more or less explicit reference to the protological picture, propose an anthropological vision articulated on notions of a diversity of existential status and functions between male and female, which will condition in a decisive manner the patristic exegesis of the opening chapters of Genesis and the image of the actual couple, in large manner determined by its protological model.

There is question of the well-known *loci* of 1 Cor 11:3-16, and 14:33b-35, Col 3:18, Eph 5:21-33 and 1 Tm 2:9-15, around which scientific debate has largely turned, whether in regard to the question of Pauline authenticity or of their correct interpretation for some still controverted aspects.

It suffices to recall the exegesis of the terms *doxa* and *exousia* which turn up in the argumentation of 1 Cor 11:7-8 and 10, connected respectively with *eikon* in relation to the man, defined as "image and glory of God" (v. 7), while woman is only called "*doxa*, glory of man."

In vv. 5-7 there is question of the veil, recognized as the indispensable complement of a woman who prays and prophesies in the congregation. In v. 10 it is said that the woman ought to have an *exousia* on her head, "because of the angels," proposing in this an unquestionable equivalence between the veil on the woman's head and this *exousia*.

This is not the place to evoke in detail the modern exegetical debate on these terms.[11] It is of greater interest to us to note that in the patristic tradition the term *doxa* is constantly understood in its more obvious sense as "glory," while the placing on the woman's head of the veil is felt to be an unequivocal sign of her submission to man.

We touch here on a motif which, without variations or exceptions, pervades the entire vision of the relations of the couple in the patristic literature, that is, one of submission of the female component to the masculine, on the basis of varied, but converging, motivations. The exegesis of the biblical account of creation on Paul's part appears in fact to be solicitous to underline the subordination of the woman not only on the Genesis theme of "dominion" of the male, inflicted as a penalty for sin, but also, and especially, granted the authoritativeness of the sources, of the clear hierarchicalization of the man-woman relationship affirmed in the epistles of Paul. All the more decisive, in fact, emerges the influence of this model in proportion to the husband/wife hierarchy being sanctioned under the religious specifically Christian profile of the double typological parallel of God the Father/Christ and Christ/the Church.

It is neither possible nor useful for us to enter upon the merits of the complex interpretative question relative to the vision of the Apostle, for the correct understanding of which it is necessary to evaluate the entire range of converging elements under the theo-

---

[11] Cf J.A. Fitzmyer, 'A Feature of Qumran Angelology and the Angels of I Cor XI, 10,' *NTS* 4 (1957), 48-58; M.D. Hooker, 'Authority on Her Head: an Examination of I Cor XI, 10,' *ibidem* 10 (1964), 410-416; A. Jaubert, 'Le voile de la femme (I Cor. XI,2-16),' *ibidem* 18 (1972), 419-430.

logical, anthropological and ecclesiological profile. Nor is this the place to address the arduous and debatable exegetical problems pertaining to the attribution of individual epistles, and as a result of the Pauline authenticity of conceptions therein expressed. Suffice it to note that if the critical and by now substantially unified agreement to recognize in 1 Timothy and the other Pastoral Epistles works of "Pauline ambience,"[12] but not directly ascribable to the Apostle, an analogous judgment has been formulated by many scholars on Ephesians, even though upholders of authenticity in the matter are not lacking.[13] Similarly controversial is the Epistle to the Colossians.[14]

On the passage now under examination, 1 Cor 11:3-16, a debate has opened up, which sees opposing views in contention, not only on the merits of its Pauline authorship, but also on the significance of the doctrine contained in it. This excerpt, which calls to judgment the image and role of the female whether on the exquisitely religious plane which in her relations with her male counterpart in the actual picture of criticism and biblical theology which carefully safeguards everything pertaining to the feminine sphere of the studies of social, cultural and religious history appear to some analysts particularly "compromising" for the purpose of evaluating the complex attitudes of the Apostle on the problem of the female.

We limit ourselves to noting that on the part of those exegetes who regard the passage as the authentic expression of Pauline thought, some judge the position delineated there as "anti-feminist" insofar as it would reveal a certain depreciation of the woman according to the canons — converging on this theme — of contemporary Jewish and pagan thought. Other scholars, with arguments which are not completely persuasive, on the contrary, would read it

---

[12] On this hotly debated theme, see the recent corrective of R. Fabris, 'Il paolinismo delle lettere pastorali,' *RivBibl* 34 (1986), 451-470.

[13] A clear and balanced review of the various positions in R. Penna, *La lettera agli Efesini. Introduzione, versione, commento*, Bologna, 1988.

[14] For the *status quaestionis* cf. E. Lohse, *Le lettere ai Colossesi e a Filemone* (CTNT XI/1), Brescia, 1979 (orig. ed., Göttingen, 1968); J. Ernst, *Le lettere ai Filippesi, a Filemone, ai Colossesi, agli Efesini*, Brescia, 1985 (orig. ed., Regensburg, 1974).

as a positive judgment on woman and an affirmation of her dignity.[15]

A third line of interpretation, on the other hand, refuses to attribute to the Apostle Paul this passage which (like 1 Cor 14:33b-35 in which silence in the assembly is imposed on the woman, affirms their submission "as the Law prescribes," maintaining that they could ask for explanations from their husbands at home) could have been the act of a redactor of traditionalist Jewish-Christian inspiration. This redactor could have taken the same position as the author of 1 Timothy who similarly forbade the woman to speak in liturgical assemblies. When these contexts, and the passage in Eph 5:21-33 in which an analogous hierarchical scheme in the relations of the couple is delineated, are eliminated from the picture, Paul's position, for these interpreters, far from representing a retreat in the traditionalist sense from the relatively open positions of Jesus in confrontation with the feminine world, would be in perfect continuity with these same positions.[16]

This rapid account of an exegetical and theological debate of such dimensions, is meant only to reflect the scientific awareness of the existence of a vast and complex problematic rotating around the significance of the statements on the theme contained in the Pauline epistles. However, such a problematic does not directly affect the question confronting us in this context since it was totally extraneous to the Christian writers of antiquity.

For our purposes, in fact, it is of more interest to underline the decisive weight which the clear hierarchicalization of the man-woman relationship at the center of the couple-schema — as is expressed in 1 Cor 11:3-16, and in various ways confirmed in Eph

---

[15] So A. Feuillet, 'L'homme, "gloire de Dieu" et la femme "gloire de l'homme" (1 Cor. XI, 7b),' *RB* 81 (1974), 161-182; *idem,* 'La dignité et le role de la femme d'après quelques textes pauliniens: comparaison avec l'Ancien Testament,' *NTS* 21 (1975), 157-191. An analogous position is maintained by M. Adinolfi, 'Il velo della donna e la rilettura paolina di 1 Cor. XI, 2-16,' *RivBibl* 23 (1975), 147-173.

[16] C.W. Trompf, 'On Attitudes Towards Women in Paul and Paulinist Literature: 1 Corinthians XI, 3-16 and Its Context,' *CBQ* 42 (1980), 196-215. For a rapid synthesis on the problem of the evaluation of woman in the literature of the New Testament cf. E. Corsini, 'La donna nel Nuovo Testamento,' Aa. vv., *Sponsa, Mater, Virgo. La donna nel mondo biblico e patristico,* Genoa, 1985, 21-39.

5:21-33 and Col 3:18 — has exercised in the definition of the image of the couple itself and of the existential status of the woman in the ambience of the patristic tradition.

As can be ascertained from an examination of the texts in the present anthology which exemplify the various positions of the authors, the excerpts in question have been taken from the Fathers on the unquestionable authority of the Apostle to whom they have been attributed to support an image of the woman as a "helper" of man because of her chronologically later creation than man, because of her physical derivation from man himself, and finally from her condemnation to subjection to the latter in consequence of the sin in which Eve took the first step, bear the indelible connotations of an ontological, and not just a hierarchical, subordination.

In 1 Cor 11:3, to justify the different religious status of man and woman in the Christian community, it being imposed on the one to pray and prophesy with head uncovered, and, on the second, to wear a veil, in that it would be "shameful" for a woman to be without a covering on her head, there is represented a clear division of levels in which the two are placed respectively. In fact, in order to establish such a status and the hierarchical man-woman relationship, the Christ/God the Father relationship is invoked and is distinguished from the man/Christ from the corresponding woman/man: *the head of every man is Christ and the head of the woman is her husband, and the head of Christ is God the Father.*

The distance of the woman from Christ and from the Father is further accentuated in what the text goes on to say, in which there is an explicit reference to the protological picture, the theme being evoked of creation in the image and that of the woman's derivation from the man in whom she would be finalized.

In the Pauline text, in fact, the Genesis modalities of the formation of the woman are assumed at the basis of an anthropological vision articulated at two levels. In the case of the male an axiological pre-eminence in the order of creation is recognized, he being placed in a direct and privileged relationship with the Creator: he is the *eikon* (image) and *doxa* (glory) of God, while man/woman is represented not only in a relationship of hierarchical subordination vis-a-vis the man, her "head," but also of ontological inadequacy, insofar as the woman is not seen as subsisting in her own right and for God but rather, in this context, in function of the man: *A man, in fact,* the text says, *ought not to cover his head, because he is the image of God and a reflection of his glory. Woman, in turn, is the reflection of man's glory. Man was not made from woman, but woman from man* (1 Cor 11:7-8).

The reduction of the two accounts in Genesis into a unitarian picture is clear here, since the motive of creation in the image of God and of the formation of Adam is evoked as a continuous sequence with the consequent "extraction" of the rib, as a result of which Eve was "constructed."

The essential data of the Pauline discourse, which will exercise a decisive influence in determining the image of the couple in the patristic tradition, represent at the same time specific interpretations of what is stated in Genesis. Before all else one should recognize, despite the attempts of modern exegetes to limit the import of the Pauline expression,[17] that the latter assumes the quality of *eikon* as an exclusive prerogative of man the male. Such a quality in relation to the male is accompanied by *doxa* which is only mentioned by way of defending the status of the female, which is distinguished in relation to the male himself in his particular role of husband to which the woman is the "glory," according to a notion which the commentators single out as peculiar to the Jewish tradition.

However, apart from the precise significance of this "*doxa,* glory" which is still a matter of discussion and for the exact understanding of which it is necessary to direct the investigation in the direction of the Jewish-rabbinic terrain of the intellectual formation of the author of the quotation, be it Paul himself or one of his followers, the resonance of this discourse remains decisive in the ensuing Christian tradition.

In a wide sector of this tradition, especially in the East, authors in the Antioch area, among them John Chrysostom himself, the problematic of the couple assumes large proportions and presents an intricacy of themes of which we will see more later. Here the woman

---

[17] Cf. *supra*, n. 15.

is profiled as excluded from the quality of "image of God." In the West this notion is affirmed in clear-cut tones in the *Commentaries on Paul* of Ambrosiaster which use it as a basis for underlining female subordination.[18]

With this begins a clear disequilibrium in merit and even ontological validity itself between the two members of the human couple at the center of which the woman was situated at a considerable distance from the Creator, while the man is placed as the intermediary and mediating influence, inasmuch as the Creator is "head" in relation to Christ, who, in his turn, is "head" of man. The "dependence" of the woman, in terms of hierarchical level but also of value, is indicated on the basis of the biblical notion of Eve as "helper" of man and creature drawn from his body.

The report of her chronologically later creation and her physical derivation, apart from the motivation[19] given in Gn 2:18-20, to the formation of the woman result in converging ways in a portrait of "subordination" which, based on the authority of the Apostle,[20] is imposed in a more or less decisive way in the Fathers. These, in fact, as the extracts published here can testify, frequently appeal to Paul for their delineation of the image of the Christian couple.

Other texts in the epistles of Paul, which confirm and reinforce this picture, occur with great frequency in the patristic arguments on the theme. In the first place, there is question of the well-known quotation from Eph 5:21-33, where the woman/man subordination in connection with the quality proper to the latter of being "head" (*kephale*) of the wife is reintroduced. Such a hierarchical scheme is

---

[18] Cf. *supra*, n. 8.

[19] On exegetical developments connected to the biblical theme of the derivation of Eve from the rib of Adam in Greek and Latin patristic tradition see P. Termes Ros, 'La formación de Eva en los Padres Griegos hasta San Juan Crisóstomo inclusive,' in *Miscellanea Biblica B, Ubach* (Scripta et Documenta 1), Montserrat, 1953, 3-18; *idem*, 'La formación de Eva en los Padres Latinos hasta San Agustín inclusive,' in *Estudios Eclesiásticos* 34 (1960), 421-459.

[20] The section in question contains moreover, at vv. 11-13, the affirmation, equally decisive as the preceding, of the necessary and inseparable complementarity of function of the two in their mutual rapport and in their relation with God: "Yet in truth in the Lord the woman is not independent of the man, nor the man of the woman. In fact in the same way that woman was made from man, man was born from woman; and all is from God." Note moreover that these words are faintly echoed in patristic contexts under examination.

elevated to a theological parameter through the parallelism established with the mysterious Church/Christ relationship.[21]

Apart from the complex ecclesiastical and soteriological values of the Pauline discourse which we do not here intend even to touch upon, there remain all the weight which redounds on the husband/wife relationship from this parallelism. In fact, the man, "head" of the "body" which is the woman, assumed as corresponding to Christ/ head of the Church which He loves as His own body, is represented as one who retains a privileged and unquestioned authority, based not only on hierarchical supremacy, but also on an axiological basis in virtue of the dignity of the model which is reflected by, at least partially, the function.

Paul's discourse, in the excerpt in question, takes its beginnings from the notion of the subjection of the wife to the husband, founded and legitimated on the exemplar model, Christ/Church. The Scripture says: *Let wives be subject to their husbands as to the Lord* (Eph 5:22), and *just as the Church is subject to Christ, so also let wives be to their husbands in all things* (v. 24).

The Apostle's arguments develop at some length the great themes of the love of Christ for the Church and of His redemptive action in His relations with this "body" of His, in which the first is presented as the exemplar of the husband/wife relationship itself. In fact husbands are exhorted to love their own wives, in this imitating Christ Himself, solicitous for the integrity and salvation of the Church. They are recommended to have an affectionate concern for their spouses "as for their own bodies" and their own flesh, being the three images of *soma*, *sarx*, and "the self," expressions of a profoundly personal reality to which is equated the feminine counterpart in the marriage relationship.

The discourse develops then in the utilization of nuptial sym-

---

[21] [Engl. tr. On *kephale*, see Perriman, A.C., 'The Head of a Woman: the meaning of *kephale* in 1 Cor 11:3,' *JThS* 45 (1994), 602-622.] On the Christ/ Church rapport, amply illustrated by the commentators, see the observations of R. Batey, 'The *mia sarx* Union of Christ and the Church,' *NTS* 13 (1967), 270-281. The reflections of this Pauline theme on the notion of matrimony in early Christianity have been underlined by E. H. Pagels, 'Adam and Eve, Christ and the Church: A Survey of Second Century Controversies Concerning Marriage,' in A.H.B. Logan-A.J.M. Wedderburn (edd.), *The New Testament and Gnosis. Essays in honour of R. McL. Wilson*, Edinburgh, 1983, 146-175.

bolism, with the explicit citation of Gn 2:24 (=Eph 5:31), to express the mystery of the union of Christ and the Church such as transcends the plane of human reality. The Fathers do not neglect the properly religious dimension of the Pauline affirmations, for the purpose of characterizing the interpersonal male/female relationship. This does not however cease to be articulated according to a clearly defined hierarchical scheme, sacralized and fixed in an immutable manner by its exemplary Christ/Church reference.

In Col 3:18, without alluding to this reference, the Apostle repeats the notion of the wife's submission to the husband "as is becoming in the Lord," by proposing therefore once more a context exquisitely religious as that in which the relationship between the two should be placed.

The submission, then, albeit stripped of the constrictive characteristics of a servile dependence, still once more religiously sanctioned, tends to be depicted as a precise and unquestionable moral obligation and an inescapable connotation of the existential and religious status of the female. As such, in fact, Paul's statement in this and in parallel passages will be assumed in the vision of the Fathers relative to the human couple.

In the same context of Col 3:18, love and the absence of bitterness in his dealings with his wife is recommended to the husband, while the role of the wife, in the precept of submission, tends to be characterized in a passive sense.

Finally, another text equally important for the definition of the image of the couple and of the respective roles of each of its members which crops up in the Fathers is undoubtedly that of 1 Tm 2:9-15, whose authority and Pauline paternity are not called in doubt. In its portrait of the various precepts of behavior directed toward the Christian community, together with modesty in behavior and decency in dress, the woman is told to "learn in silence with all submission."

Repeating the injunction of 1 Cor 14:34-35, it is prescribed in fact forcibly that women should keep silence in the assembly of the faithful. The prohibition against her teaching the male is motivated on precise protological bases: *For Adam was formed first, then Eve. And Adam was not deceived, but the woman was deceived and was in sin. Yet women will be saved by childbearing, if they continue in faith and love and holiness with modesty* (1 Tm 2:13-15).

To the theme of Adam's chronological priority in creation, perceived as a sign of superiority in the order of value and dignity with respect to Eve, such as was announced in 1 Cor 11:3-16, there is joined in the text of 1 Timothy, in the evocation of the scenario of the transgression in paradise, a clear judgment on the responsibility with respect to the two protagonists in the event. In fact, to an Adam who did not endure any "seduction" there is counterposed Eve, subject to "jealousy" and established in her culpability.

It should be noted how the "Pauline" argument bypasses without solution the continuity from protological parameters to actuality. The welding between the two levels is given in the equivalence Eve-woman, in the sense that the first is seen as prototype and representing the second as such. The movement of the discourse, in fact, alternates between the image of the Christian woman to whom it is not granted "to teach," and that of Eve, "seduced" and "seducer" being the negative rule of this last foundation and the motivation of the prohibition imposed on the first.

Then, in the mention of the fall in paradise, Eve becomes again the woman by antonomasia. By this, in fact, is proclaimed the possibility of a salvation which, according to the biblical statement, could come only from her typically maternal function. Such a function, moreover, ought to be accompanied by unexceptionable ethical and religious behavior which is illustrated exactly in the exhortations developed by the authors. This perspective, which by radicalizing the data of the Genesis narrative, caused the greater weight of the fault to be borne by Eve almost to the point of absolving Adam whose figure tended to be characterized in positive terms, has a clear Jewish matrix as has been amply underlined by the interpreters.

Without being able to describe in all its detail the problematic relative to the various conceptions elaborated within Judaism on the protological theme,[22] it may suffice to note that in the ca-

---

[22] Cf. J.-B. Frey, 'L'état originel et la chute de l'homme d'après les conceptions juives au temps de J.-C.,' *RSPhTh* 5 (1911), 507-545.

nonical literature the protoplast event finds a reduced space showing then that in the most ancient traditions of Israel the account in
Genesis has had a meager resonance.

Some fleeting references to the first sin occur in Sirach where
there is a reference to Eve's fault: *in woman was sin's beginning, and
because of her we all die* (Si 25:23).[23] The first woman appears as the
one who has inaugurated the series of human transgressions while a
specific causality in originating the actual condition of mortality is
attributed to her sin.

The book of Wisdom contains two significant allusions to the
fall of our first parents. In Ws 2:23-24, evoking the decisive motive
of creation in the image of God, in which is indicated an exclusive
privilege of the human being created "for immortality," the introduction of death is attributed to the "envy" of the devil. Further on,
the "sin" of Adam is mentioned (Ws 10:1) from which Wisdom has
rescued the protoplast.[24]

It can be stated, therefore, that canonical literature recognizes,
if only in less developed texts, all three protagonists in the Genesis
account as responsible in various ways for the transgression and its
doleful consequences.

In the rich apocryphal literature which flourished in the
intertestamental period, the theme of the original corruption of humanity especially with the episode of our first parents is most frequently connected with that of the marriage contracted between the
"sons of God" and the daughters of men as recounted in Gn 6:1-4.
Such an episode has been the object of frequent elaborations, especially within the ambit of the literature which flourished around the

---

[23] For an analysis of these statements and, more broadly, on the attitudes of Sira toward women see M. Gilbert, 'Ben Sira el la femme,' *RThL* 7 (1976), 426-442; W.C. Trenchard, *Ben Sira's View of Women: A Literary Analysis* (Brown Judaic Studies 38), Chico, 1982. On the author's attitude in the general context of the problematic relative to original sin, cf. F.R. Tennant, 'The Teaching of Ecclesiasticus and Wisdom on the Introduction of Sin and Death,' *JTS* 2 (1901), 207-223; *Idem, The Sources of the Doctrine of the Fall and Original Sin,* Cambridge, 1903, 106-121; A. Buchler, 'Ben Sira's Conception of Sin and Atonement,' *JQR* 13 (1922-23), 303-335; 461-502; 14 (1923-24), 53-83; T. Gallus, 'A muliere initium peccati et per illam omnes morimur,' *Verbum Domini* 23 (1943), 272-277.

[24] On the figure of Adam in this work cf. J. Dupont-Sommer, 'Adam "père du monde" dans la Sagesse de Salomon (10,1-2),' *RHR* 119 (1939), 182-203.

name of Enoch, the "sons of God" of the biblical text being identified with the angels.[25]

In other contexts there is an ever stronger tendency to exalt the figure and the role of Adam, devolving greater responsibility on Eve for the transgression.[26] In the various renderings of the *Life of Adam*, from diverse backgrounds frequently difficult to define, but which seem to stem from a pre-Christian Hebrew background,[27] Eve's culpability is insisted upon in a fairly general manner, and likewise her intrinsic "weakness" and proclivity to seduction by the devil, especially in relation to her "solitude" and separation from Adam which the serpent astutely seizes upon to induce her to transgress the divine commandment.[28]

---

[25] Developed especially in the *Book of Enoch* and accepted also in the patristic literature, this theme has been the object of numerous researches among which it suffices to cite J. Turmel, 'Histoire de l'angélologie des temps apostoliques à la fin du Ve siècle,' *RHLR* 3 (1898), 295-300; A. Lods, 'La chüte des anges. Origine et portée de cette spéculation,' *RHPhR* 7 (1927), 295-315; B.J. Malina, 'Some Observations on the Origin of Sin in Judaism and St. Paul,' *CBQ* 31 (1969),18-34; M. Delcor, 'Le mythe de la chute des anges et l'origine des géants comme explication du mal dans le monde dans l'apocalyptique juive. Histoire des traditions,' in *RHR* 190 (1976), 3-53: D.R. Schultz, 'The Origin of Sin in Irenaeus and Jewish Pseudepigraphical Literature,' *VigChr* 32 (1978), 161-190. The reflections of such a tradition on the definition of the image of woman in late Judaism and in primitive Christianity are emphasized by B.P. Prusak, 'Woman: Seductive Siren and Source of Sin? Pseudepigraphical Myth and Christian Origins,' in R. Radford Ruether (ed.), *Religion and Sexism,* New York, 1974, 89-116. The apocryphal literature of Late Judaism is easily accessible in Italian translation, with ample critical introductions and rich bibliographical documentation: P. Sacchi, *Apocrifi dell'Antico Testamento, I-II,* Turin, 1981-1989.

[26] Cf. U. Bianchi, 'La rédemption dans les livres d'Adam,' *Numen* 18 (1971), 1-8; rp. in *idem, Selected Essays on Gnosticism and Mysteriosophy* (Suppl. *Numen* XXXVIlll), Leiden, 1978, 351-358; *Idem,* 'Adamo e la storia della salvezza (Paolo e i Libri di Adamo),' in Aa.vv. *L'uomo nella Bibbia e nelle culture ad essa contemporanee, Atti del Simposio per il XXV dell'A.B.I.,* Brescia, 1975, 209-223 rp. in *idem, Prometeo, Orfeo, Adamo. Tematiche religiose sul destino, il male, la salvezza,* Rome, 1976, 242-258. See further M. Simon, 'Adam et la rédemption dans la perspective de l'Église ancienne,' in Zwi R.J. Werblowsky-C.J. Bleeker (edd.), *Types of Redemption,* Leiden, 1970, 62-71.

[27] J.-B. Frey, art. 'Adam (Livres aprocryphes sous son nom),' *DB, Suppl.* I, Paris, 1928, coll. 101-106. On the entire literature of "cycle of Adam" ibid., coll. 106-134 and, more recently, A.-M. Denis, *Introduction aux pseudépigraphes grecs d'Ancien Testament,* Leiden, 1970, 3-14.

[28] Cf. *Vita Adae et Evae*, 3, ed. W. Meyer, Munich, 1879, p. 37 where Eve, turning to Adam, underlines her own responsibility "because of me the Lord is annoyed with you; because of me you have been expelled from there." Eve is induced to abandon penitence in the waters of the Tigris by Satan who finds her alone (ibidem 9-10, pp. 39-40) the angels being also far from her to carry out their liturgical service (*Apocalypse of Moses,* ed. W. Meyer, p. 53). An opposite conception, tending to diminish or to excuse the culpability of Eve, in the opinion of J.R. Levison, in chpts. 15-30 of the *Apocalypse of Moses,* which could however have been the work of a redactor different from the author of the rest of the work ('The Exoneration of Eve in the Apocalypse of Moses 15-30,' *Journal for the Study of Judaism* 20 (1989), 135-150). For the theme of "separation" of Eve from Adam, elaborated in various registers even in gnosticism, see A. Orbe, 'El pecado de Eva, signo de división,' *OrChrPer* 29 (1963), 305-330.

The Jewish apocrypha underline with notable frequency the motive of immediate "seduction" on the part of the first woman, with intellectual jealousy motivated by her intrinsic weakness, which *astheneia* ("weakness") indicated in the Jewish, as likewise in the Greco-Roman, world and then also in large sectors of the Christian tradition, as a special connotation of the nature of the female.[29] There exists moreover an encratitic and gnostic interpretation, attested in the rabbinic literature, and known also in Christian circles, which sees in such "seduction" a true and proper physical contamination on the part of the serpent-devil.[30]

We have here only evoked by rapid strokes[31] what is in fact a dense stratum of ideas already circulating widely in the time of Paul and the Pastorals in various Jewish circles and soon consolidated in a series of writings to which also the Christians had recourse to elaborate their exegesis of the sacred texts and the anthropological vision which is at its basis.

The Jewish traditions, in representing a certain image of the first human couple, and of the respective functions and roles of the two partners, have constituted one of the parameters of reference in the elaboration of positions on the theme on the part of the first Christian authors variously interested in these traditions.[32] The same interpretations of the protological event and, more broadly, of the relationship of the couple present in the Epistles of St. Paul, which largely conditioned the patristic formulations, in their turn reflect in various ways the positions of late Judaism.

---

[29] A perceptive analysis of this motive in U. Mattioli, *Astheneia e andreia. Aspetti della femminilità nella letteratura classica, biblica e cristiana*, Rome, 1983.

[30] For the Jewish tradition cf. V. Aptowitzer, *Kain und Abel in der Agada, den Apocryphen, der hellenistischen, christlichen und mohammedanischen Literatur*, Wien-Leipzig 1922; L. Ginzberg, *The Legends of the Jews*, vol. I, Philadelphia, 1937 (12 ed.), 105-106; vol. V, 133-134, notes 3-4. The theme, encountered in the Christian apocryphon, *Protoevangelo di Giacomo* (cap. 13,1, ed E. De Strycker, *La forme la plus ancienne du Protévangile de Jacques*, Brussels, 1961, 122-125), is amply elaborated at the center of the dualistic schemes of gnosticism where frequently the rejection of marriage and generation, while founded on peculiar ontological bases, anti-cosmic and anti-somatic proper to the movement, find an ulterior protological motivation in the notion of Eve contaminated by the Demiurge and his archons. Cf. G. Sfameni Gasparro, *Enkrateia, op. cit.*, 115-139.

[31] For more extensive information see *Enkrateia, op. cit.*, 341-365.

[32] Cf. F. Gori, 'Gli Apocrifi e i Padri,' in A. Quacquarelli, ed. *Complementi interdisciplinari di Patrologia*, Rome, 1989, 223-272.

Naturally, then, recognizing the other essential side of the thought of the Apostle on the same protological theme must not be passed over, which, centered on the opposition between the first and second Adam, neatly focused the decisive role of our first parents as representing the whole of humanity in the definition of this state, decadent and culpable, before and apart from the redemption brought about by Christ.

III

WOMAN AND MARRIAGE IN THE
JEWISH AND GRECO-ROMAN TRADITIONS

Another New Testament text to which the Fathers refer with great frequency to define the modality of the relations between the spouses is that of 1 Peter 3:1-7. In it, the author, along Pauline lines, first and foremost proclaims the submission of the wife, here religiously finalized to procure spiritual advantages even for non-believing husbands. The action of the wife is characterized in the sense of an exemplary chaste conduct, carried out in fear, the man living with her.

Peter admonishes the wife to avoid luxury and material ornaments in order to grant precedence to the beauty of the "interior person" and adduces the biblical example of Sarah, subject to Abraham, who will become a recurring motive in the patristic literature as a model of female conduct, who in docile submission to her husband fully realizes her status as wife. Equally paradigmatically, especially in the teaching of Chrysostom, will be the invitation of Peter to husbands that they honor their wives bearing in mind their "fragility" and the equality of their religious vocation.

The paranesis developed in 1 Peter 3:1-7, together with the teaching formulated in texts like Col 3:18-20, Eph 5:21-33, and 1 Tm 2:9-15, is included in the context of those "household codes" (*Haustafeln*) which modern New Testament criticism has located in the Epistles of Paul,[1] pointing to reflexes also in some of the Apostolic Fathers,[2] a sort of statute of behavior of the primitive Church.

---

[1] To the texts cited add Tt 1:7-9; 2:1-10 and 3:1-3.

[2] Cf. *Didache* 4,9-11; *Epistle of Barnabas* 19,5-7; Ignatius, *Epistle to Polycarp* 4,2-6,3; *1 Epistle Clement* 21,6-9; and Polycarp, *Epistle to the Philippians* 4:2-6:1.

The problem of the significance and origin of such norms is quite controverted. Here it suffices to note that interpreters tend at times to underline analogies with ethical canons and forms of family organization coming from a Jewish ambience, at other times, from a Greco-Roman ambience, pointing to one or other of them as the original source of these same "household codes" without of course disregarding the undoubted Christian connotation which these norms of behavior assumed once they were transposed into the New Testament context.

Other scholars, focusing on the presence of such a Christian ethos, consider the Pauline and Petrine *Haustafeln*, with their parallels in the apostolic authors, as a creation of the new religious ambience.[3] This is certainly not the place to enter into a discussion of the merits of the case which besides is of interest only for the part which concerns the influence, moreover quite noteworthy, exercised by these "codes" on the various positions of the Fathers with regard to the mutual relations at the center of the matrimonial union. Let us observe only that the same contrasting interpretations of scholars brings to light an aspect, in our view extremely significant, to be precise, the convergence, in the models of behavior assumed in the apostolic literature, of elements and notions which precisely because individually recognizable as of possible Jewish or of gentile matrix, emerge as substantially common, at least for some important aspects, to the two ambits in question.

In other words, the supporting lines of ethics which regulate the interpersonal man/woman relationship within the ambit of the family, such as are expressed in the "family codes" in question, reflect a cultural and spiritual climate, a mind set, and a behavioral model, in which, in fact, both the Jewish and the Greco-Roman traditions substantially converge.[4]

---

[3] See Col 3:18-4:1; Eph 5:22-6:9; 1 Tm 2:8-15; Tt 2:1-10; 1 P 2:13-3:12. A clear presentation of the *status quaestionis* is to be found in E. Bosetti, 'Codici familiari: storia della ricerca e prospettive,' *RivBibl* 35 (1987), 129-179. [Engl. tr. See also D.F. Balch, 'Neopythagorean Moralists and the New Testament Household Codes,' *ANRW* II, 26, 1, Berlin/New York, 1992, 380-411, esp. 392f.]

[4] Numerous parallels between the "Household codes" of Paul and the relative norms of behavior in late Judaism and the Greco-Roman world are underlined in S. Zedda, *Relativo e assoluto nella morale di San Paolo*, Brescia, 1984, 121-245. The results of this investigation which is conducted on strongly traditional presuppositions with regard to the female condi-

It is certainly not possible to trace an outline, even in the most general terms, of the matrimonial institutions at the heart of such traditions nor of the connected problematic relative to the condition and role of the woman, themes that are strictly interdependent, since the first constitutes one of the most significant parameters for checking the definition of the second, which in their turn determine in relation to the multiplicity of planes — political, socio-economic, juridical, cultural and religious — to which they are contextually related.

The literature on the theme, by now quite substantial even though of uneven scientific value,[5] frequently appears conditioned by the respective theoretical positions of scholars, tending at times to emphasize the negative aspects of the status of women and the misogynous attitudes of the cultural traditions under examination, or at other times to minimize, with greater or less emphasis, especially in the case of the biblical context, both Old and New Testaments,[6] failing to avoid the risks of an "apologetic" agenda, of which

---

tion, in our view are compromised by a failure to distinguish between what in the Epistles is a definite expression of the thought of the Apostle and what is to be referred rather to the "Paulinist" tradition which is expressed in the Pastorals and in letters of uncertain attribution. A careful comparison with expressions in Plutarch made in another article by the same author, contributes useful elements to the discussion: S. Zedda, 'Spiritualità cristiana e saggezza pagana nell'etica della famiglia: affinità e differenze tra S. Paolo e i *Coniugalia Praecepta* di Plutarco,' *Lateranum* N.S. 48 (1982), 110-124.

[5] For a general orientation on studies relative to the situation of the female in the social and religious context of the ancient world cf. P. Goodwater, *Women in Antiquity: An Annotated Bibliography,* Metuchen, NJ, 1976 [S.B. Pomeroy, 'Selected Bibliography on Women,' *Antiquity: Arethusa* 6 (1973), 125-157]. See *Histoire mondiale de la femme,* P. Grimal, ed., Paris, 1965, v.I, and the synthesis of K. Thraede, "Frau," in *RAC* VIII (1972), 197-269. An articulated presentation of the modality by which the image of the woman in Hebrew culture, in Greco-Roman culture, and in Christianity in the early centuries, is defined, which however tends to radicalize the significance of the contexts examined, is P. Gramaglia, 'Personificazioni e modelli del femminile nella transizione dalla cultura classica a quella cristiana,' in G. Galli (ed.), *Interpretazione e Personificazione. Personificazioni e Modelli del Femminile. Atti del Nono Colloquio sulla Interpretazione (Macerata 6-8 Aprile 1987),* Genoa, 1988,17-164.

[6] Such seems to be the case in a work like M. Adinolfi, *Il femminismo della Bibbia* (Spicilegium Pontificii Athenaei Antoniani 22), Rome, 1981. See, by the same author, '"Ab initio autem fuit sic." Osservazioni sulla problematica della coppia in Gn 1-3,' *RivBibl* 18 (1970), 357-378; *idem,* 'La donna e il matrimonio nel giudaismo ai tempi di Cristo,' *ibidem,* 20 (1972), 369-390. On analogous positions see P. Grelot, *La coppia,* Milan, 1968 (orig. Paris, 1964), A. Tosato, *Il matrimonio nel giudaismo antico e nel nuovo testamento,* Rome, 1976, and the brief, rather superficial, study of S. Sierra, *La donna nel mondo ebraico biblico,* in aa.vv. *Sponsa Mater, Virgo, op. cit.,* 9-20.

the truth of the facts, if pursued with a balanced critical sense, should have no need.

For our purposes it could be useful to single out some fundamental directives on the theme in question at the center of the Jewish and the Greco-Roman worlds in the same time period as that of the composition of the Pauline epistles to situate in their cultural context the so-called "household codes" for the part relating to the husband-wife relationship, in so far as the modality of such a relationship has constituted a model more or less decisive in the patristic vision which is chiefly what interests us. This vision is elaborated moreover, by way of influence or reaction, by contact with the positions on problems contemporary with the various authors, such as naturally feel the effects of the respective cultural contexts which from the 2nd to the 5th century underwent an evolution on the theme in question, in continuity or in partial transformation with respect to the ideological and socio-economic structures already consolidated in the age of the Apostle.

One of the essential components of these structures is undoubtedly represented by a system of subordination, more or less accentuated in individual instances, of the wife to the husband, founded on a presupposition, explicit or implicit, of natural inferiority of the former to the latter. This motive, even if it should be situated in the distinct cultural contexts in question, considered in the complexity of their various respective *facies* and their relative processes of formation, more than in the interference of numerous elements which concur and determine the entire picture, appears in fact one of the important axes of the general structure of interpersonal relations between the two sexes, both in the broadest sphere of society and in the special ambit of the couple in the two traditions under discussion.

An image of matrimonial usages and of the value attributed to the same in Judaism in the first century A.D. is provided by Flavius Josephus in his work, *Against Apion*, which is a reflection of the ancestral norms established in the Mosaic Law and in polemic against the sexual practices of the pagan world which left open a more or less large area for homosexuality and connived at adultery and divorce. Only one legitimate form of union is recognized as "second nature" for man and woman, finalized in the procreation of children. Marriages should not be contracted out of greed for the dowry nor with violence or deceit, requiring to receive the bride in a legitimate manner from the one who holds control over her. "The woman — according to what the Law says — is in everything inferior to the man. Therefore she ought to obey, not for her own humiliation but because she can be guided. For God in fact has given the power to the male."[7]

In these affirmations of Flavius Josephus the hierarchical system of a subordination of the wife within the marriage ambit clearly emerges, motivated by laws religiously sanctioned by the Mosaic Law and the recognition of the faculty of dominion (*kratos*) which is an exclusively male prerogative. The peculiar power of "dominion" exercised by the husband over the wife is, however, defined in terms of *arche* (head, guide), and not of *hybris* (arrogance), the coercive and violent aspect being, as it were, muffled, and the emphasis placed rather on protection of a person constitutionally recognized as inferior and incapable of managing her own affairs independently.

In the case of the husband, the obligation is recognized of remaining united to one wife only, and of not seducing the wife of another; violence to a betrothed girl and the seduction of a married woman were punishable by death. In the enunciation of this legal precept which safeguarded the integrity of marriage, the author insists exclusively on the active role of the male, the notion of the inviolability of the right of the engaged groom being essential, or of the married man against whom the man who waylays the woman belonging to the one or the other.

The information in Flavius Josephus is only one stroke in a large profile which, structured on patriarchal principles, have relegated a very attenuated space to the social, cultural and religious activity of the female component. It is well known, in fact, how very limited were the civil and juridical rights of the Hebrew woman, subject at

---

[7] *Contra Apionem,* 11, 24,199-203 ed. H. St. J. Thackeray, *Josephus, I,* Cambridge, MA, 1961, rp. 1976, 372-375. Cf. also *Antiquitates iudaicae* 23, ##244-259, ed. Thackeray IV, 592-601. On the literary production of the author see G. Ricciotti, *Flavio Giuseppe tradotto e commentato,* Turin, 1937. [See also L.H. Feldman, 'Origen's *Contra Celsum* and Josephus *Contra Apionem,*' *VigChr* 44 (1990), 105-135.]

first to the authority of her father, who picked out her husband for her, and then to her husband who administered whatever goods they might have, and, while having the obligation to maintain her in a worthy fashion, had plenty of scope to limit by prohibitions and impositions her private and public life.[8]

If even in the sphere of matrimony the disparity of value is heavily reflected between man and woman, since, apart from exceptional cases, only the man could decide on getting a divorce, sometimes for quite frivolous reasons, by sending to the wife a bill of repudiation, there is also the criterion of a strong discrimination between the two in the religious sphere, which operates in a rather clear-cut way.

Although women, as essential components of the national community, were regular members of the Covenant and as such bound to the observance of ethical precepts and also legal prescriptions not connected to precise calendar dates, they remained exonerated from the observance of all those religious obligations pertaining to feasts and rites connected with a definite period of the year as, for instance, the pilgrimage to Jerusalem.

Women were above all strictly excluded from an active role in cult activity, being forbidden to offer sacrifice, or to perform other rites in their own person; in particular, they did not participate in teaching the Torah. Although the positions of rabbis in this regard were not altogether in agreement, and there were some well-known

---

[8] On the condition of women and the institution of matrimony in Judaism see also, apart from the works of M. Adinolfi and A. Tosato cited above in note 6, A. Tosato, *Il matrimonio israelitico*, Rome, 1982. Cf. J. Bottero, 'La femme dans l'Asie occidentale ancienne: Mésopotamie et Israél,' in P. Grimal (ed.), *op. cit.*, 1, 224-247; J. Pirenne, 'Le statut de la femme dans la civilisation hebraïque,' in *Recueils Jean Bodin XI, La femme, 1,* Brussels, 1959, 107-126; L. Swidler, *Biblical Affirmation of Woman*, Philadelphia, 1979. A useful anthology of biblical texts, including New Testament sources, on the situation of the female is presented in M. J. Evans, *Woman in the Bible. An Overview of All the Critical Passages on Women's Roles*, Devon, 1983. Judgments that are frequently very radical on the image of woman in the Old Testament are formulated in K. Harris, *Sex, Ideology and Religion. The Representation of Women in the Bible*, Brighton-Totowa, 1984. Some contributions are dedicated to the theme of conjugal relations and its symbolic utilization on the religious plane such as occur in the O.T. are to be found in vol. 12 (*Lo sposo e la sposa*) of *Parola Spiritu Vita* (1986/1), where the same theme in the N.T. and the continuing Christian tradition is also examined.

On the anthropological vision of rabbinical Judaism, justifying the positions on the theme of sexuality and marriage, see the analysis of E. Stiegman, 'Rabbinic Anthropology,' in *ANRW* 11, 19, 2, Berlin-New York, 1979, 187-579.

cases of women who gave instruction in the Sacred Scriptures, normally such knowledge was regarded as not suitable, or certainly not necessary, for women. She was, then, excluded from the teaching of religion as a passive subject and, even more so, in her own right.[9]

It is easy, then, to assess the weight which such a situation could have exercised in the definition of positions like those of 1 Cor 14:34-36 and 1 Tm 2:11-12, which ordered the woman to keep silent in the Christian assembly, prohibiting her any teaching role in the presence of men.

Without attributing an absolute value to the noted formula of benediction of Rabbi Juda who had prescribed its recital by a man three times a day ("Blessed be the One who has not made me a gentile, or a woman, or an ignoramus") one cannot minimize, as far as evaluating the man/woman relationship in the context of Jewish tradition, the strong qualitative difference between the two members of the couple in the entire spectrum of levels (ideological, religious, socio-economic, juridical and political) constituting the relative cultural *facies*.

Naturally we have not reviewed all the elements of a positive value in the role of the female present in this tradition, such as the exaltation of female fecundity, the recognition of the capacity of realizing ethical and religious values in conformity with the requirements of the Law, of the ability to conduct family life, such as correspond to the requirements at the heart of Sacred Scripture in relation to certain female figures as, for example, the wives of patriarchs, or the personality of heroines endowed with prophetic charisms, or invested with "political" roles at exceptional moments of Hebrew history. We might think also of that glorification of the "wise woman" elaborated in Pr 31:10-31[11] which sheds light on the modality and positive effects of a female identity realized according to the ethical and behavioral norms handed down by the tradition.

---

[9] Cf. K. H. Rengstorf, art. 'Mathetria,' in *GLNT* 6 (1970), col 1236-1237; L.J. Archer, 'The Role of Jewish Women in the Religion, Ritual and Cult of Greco-Roman Palestine,' in A. Cameron-A. Kuhrt (edd.), *Images of Women in Antiquity*, Detroit, 1983, 273-287.

[10] Berakot T. 7,18 in J. Bonsirven, *Textes rabbiniques des deux premiers siècles chrétiens pour servir a l'intelligence du Nouveau Testament*, Rome, 1955 n. 493.

[11] Cf. A. Bonora, 'La donna eccellente, la Sapienza, il sapiente (Pr 31:10-31),' *RivBibl* 36 (1988), 137-163.

These data, however, do not substantially modify that basically hierarchically gradated structure which could result in the inclusion of woman in the same category as slaves and freedmen as the subjects of so limited, if not non-existent, juridical capacity and of the substantial irrelevance of a certain religious activity such as, for instance, giving the blessing after a meal, obligatory whenever three men were present, not included in the number, "women, children or slaves."

Finally, in proof of the profound imbalance in value between the two sexes, in their respective functions and specific roles, as the qualifying motif of the cultural physiognomy of Israel, notwithstanding the Genesis theme of creation in the image as a contextual creation of human beings male and female, one can record the peculiar typification of male/female in Philo of Alexandria. It is, in fact, well known that this 1st century author, who has profoundly influenced a large segment of the patristic tradition with his allegorical interpretation of scripture, nurtured on philosophical presuppositions of a Platonic or Stoic imprint, had assumed the categories of male and female as modules expressive of values, respectively positive and negative, or at least dangerous and ambiguous, at levels whether ontological or ethical.[12]

In this Philo, on the one hand, reflects a mentality well-grounded in his own ambience, and also in that Greek culture in which he was well versed, and, on the other hand, has contributed to fix a model of classification by articulating on the level of metaphor the terms, respectively positive and negative, of the same model.

If the cultural tradition and the models of behavior of the Jewish world, as well, naturally, as its religious presuppositions, have exercised an important role in the definition of the man/woman relationship at the center of the marriage union as it is represented in the letters of St. Paul and, stemming from there, in the patristic tradition, no less relevant, especially in relation to the latter, resulted the positions on the theme in the Greco-Roman ambience, to which the Christian message was addressed and with whose social and cul-

---

[12] Cf. R.A. Baer, Jr., *Philo's Use of the Categories Male and Female*, Leiden, 1970, esp. 40-44.

tural structures, apart from its intrinsic religious "newness," it was confronted and involved.

For the correct historical understanding of these positions it is necessary to bear in mind the long and differentiated evolutionary process of the customs and the relative ideological supports which characterize the respective contexts, Greek and Roman, and in the first ages of the Christian era, while maintaining some peculiar characteristics of their different cultural physiognomies, converge substantially on common ground at the heart of the Empire where an ideological and cultural symbiosis among the different traditions is already amply attested in the Hellenistic age.

Only a careful analysis of the different socio-political, economic, juridical, literary and religious ambits could bring about the emergence in their complex articulation of the web of relations among the two spheres of the male and female, whose variously graduated complementarity remains the ineluctable constant, even though frequently kept silent about or relegated to the margins of historical discourse, of the values of every human society.

Unable to proceed further in this direction, and content merely to give a reference to a literature already rich and plentiful, and of good scientific quality, on the theme of women and marriage in Greece and Rome,[13] it suffices to say here that basically two parameters remain essential for the definition of the picture. We refer first to the institutional aspect which is reflected in the procedure, more

---

[13] From the extensive bibliography on the theme (cf. *supra,* note 5) we might mention as points of entry to the problem: S.B. Pomeroy, *Women in Athens and Rome,* New York, 1975; E. Cantarella, *L'ambiguo malanno. Condizione e immagine della donna nell'antichità greca e romana,* Rome, 1981 (2ed. 1983). On the Greek world, see, in particular, the useful collection of texts, with ample introductions in I. Savalli, *La donna nella società Grecia antica,* Bologna, 1983 and G. Arrigoni, ed., *Le donne in Grecia,* Bari, 1985. On the Roman world, P.V.D. Balsdon, *Roman Women. History and Habits,* London, 1962. The Associazione italiana di cultura classica have organized two Conventions of which the *Atti* offer excellent contributions on the problematic in question: R. Uglione (cur.), *Atti del Convegno nazionale di studi su "La donna nel mondo antico."* Torino 21-22-23 Aprile 1986, Turin, 1987; idem, *Atti del II Convegno nazionale di studi su "La donna nel mondo antico." Torino 18-19-20 Aprile 1988,* Turin, 1989. See further *A History of Women in the West I. From Ancient Goddesses to Christian Saints,* P. Schmitt Pantel, editor, A. Goldhammer, tr. Cambridge, MA, 1992, which contains, among other studies on the Greco-Roman world, a contribution by M. Alexandre, 'Immagini di donne ai primi tempi della cristianità.' [Engl. ed. Add: AA.-vv. *La donna nel pensiero cristiano antico,* edited by U. Mattioli, introduction by M. Simonetti (Teologia. Saggi e ricerche), Marietti, Genoa, 1992 (Table of contents in *REAug* 41,1 1995, 168).]

or less rigidly codified, of matrimonial rights and the juridical status of the woman in the social community, and secondly to the ideological, which is expressed at the literary and philosophical level and more fully in the various ambiences of cultural life.

Both these parameters, in the era that interests us, present themselves as the fruit of a long historical evolution which, despite some rather noteworthy changes of certain positions, present an undeniable continuity with older institutional forms, on the one hand, and with ideological impositions already formulated in the classical and hellenistic age, on the other.

As regards the Greek world it is known that the juridical condition of the woman and the modality of the institution of marriage reveal, at the end of the classical age, a peculiarly subordinate status with respect to her male counterpart, whether within the ambit of the family or in the wider range of society.[14]

Although, as has been emphasized in its proper place,[15] it would be necessary to make distinctions between the different situations in various centers of the Greek world so that the resulting female condition characterized in the sense of a greater or less social and juridical autonomy, depending on individual cases, one can recognize as a common and defining characteristic of the whole Greek world, the exclusion of woman from active participation in the political life, and a strong limitation on the juridical plane in relation to males.[16]

In particular, the Athenian woman was deprived of the fac-

---

[14] For the oldest institutions of matrimony see H.J. Wolff, 'Marriage Law and Family Organization in Ancient Athens,' *Traditio* 2 (1944), 43-95; J.-P. Vernant, 'Il matrimonio nella Grecia arcaica,' in *idem, Myth and Society in Ancient Greece,* Cambridge, MA, 1988, rp. in a collection of studies titled *L'amore in Grecia,* C. Calamo, ed., Milan, 1983, 21-39, in which there are also other contributions useful for the definition of the relations between the sexes in the Greek world. A picture of the condition of women in ancient Greece, for whom the family sphere constituted the essential nucleus, is traced with good documentation, even though the methodology has been superseded, in U.E. Paoli, *La donna greca nell'antichità,* Florence, 1955.

[15] See the arguments of G.P. Arrigoni, 'Le donne dei "margini" e le donne "speciali,"' in *eadem, op. cit.,* pp. XI-XXVIII. Cf. *eadem,* 'Tra le donne dell'antichità: considerazioni e ricognizioni,' in R. Uglione (cur.), *Atti del Convegno nazionale, op. cit.,* 39-71.

[16] Cf. I. Savalli, *op. cit.,* 37-70. A synthesis of family structures in the Greek world is presented also in M. Pohlenz, *L'uomo greco,* Florence, 1947 (ed. orig. Göttingen, 1947), 713-743. [See now B.S. Strauss, *Fathers and Sons in Athens,* Princeton, NJ, 1993.]

ulty of performing any juridical act without the assistance of a *kyrios* ("lord"), and through the practice of the betrothal *(engyesis)* became transferred from the authority of the father to that of the husband. The latter, moreover, acquired such status and the full rights over his wife only with the subsequent handing over *(ekdosis)* of her and the start of a life in common without which the marriage was not valid.

At the same time, only the previous betrothal *(engyesis)*, with the remittance of the dowry on the part of the father of the bride to the husband, rendered marriages legal and this conferred on the woman the status of legal wife.

In the rigorous separation of tasks, domestic in the woman's case, public in the man's, the relation between the two was strongly affected by the decisive circumstance that the matrimonial union was not the fruit of a free choice of the two, but rather of an accord between the *kyrios* of the woman, who was usually the father, or in his absence the next parent, and the future spouse. Another factor affecting the relationship was the more or less considerable age difference between the spouses, the woman being usually much younger than the man. Stood surety for in various ways by the integrity of the dowry received from the bride's father, which had to be returned to him in case of divorce, the woman was obliged, on the one hand, to a more or less rigid form of segregation within the walls of the home, and the higher their social status the more rigorous it was, women of the lower classes being granted greater freedom of movement if only for reasons of economic necessity.

Kept at a distance from the social life of her husband, and not allowed to participate with him even at banquets, the wife was bound to a rigorous observance of conjugal fidelity while the conduct of the male could be more lax, the legitimacy of his extra-marital relationships of various kinds being broadly connived at, if not downright recognized.[17]

---

[17] As is known, homosexual relations were very widespread and were in Sparta institutionalized within the ambit of the social structure with the aim of educating the youth. Cf. W. Jaeger, *Paideia: the Ideals of Greek Culture*, Oxford University Press, 1960,[3] v. 1, ch. 5: 'State-Education in Sparta'; H.-I. Marrou, *History of Education in Antiquity*, London, 1966 (ed. orig 1948, 1964[6]), Vol. 1, 55-67.

The woman's primary function within the ambience of the union was undoubtedly a reproductive one, to ensure a legitimate line of succession for the husband's family, and at the same time the custody and safe management of domestic affairs.[18]

In contrast with such a restricted role in the socio-economic life, the participation of women in religious life was fairly extensive and articulated. But in the realm of the essential cult activity in the city, blood sacrifices, and the subsequent dismembering of the animal flesh, the woman continued to hold a secondary role compared to the man,[19] while in the rest of religious activity her role was apparently one of substantial parity. Numerous public priesthoods were, in fact, accessible to women, or even reserved for them, while various forms of cult were exclusively feminine, and emphasized the essential role of woman in her civic role as spouse and mother of citizens, for the correct functioning of civic life. So, for instance, the cult of Thesmophoria, devoted to the great goddess Demeter Thesmophorus, was one of the most ancient and widespread in the entire Greek world.[20]

As regards cultural life, even if there were instances, admittedly rather limited, of women who became famous because of their literary activity,[21] one can undoubtedly recognize that the education of Greek women was generally not very extensive, and was directed toward the development of her primary domestic tasks.[22]

The juridical position of woman in society, and in particular in the family, and the modality of the marriage relationship underwent an evolution in the Hellenistic age in the sense of a greater autonomy of action on the socio-economic and juridical planes, and

---

[18] It suffices to recall the well-known formula of pseudo-Demosthenes: "We have prostitutes for pleasure, concubines for the daily welfare of the body, and wives to beget legitimate sons and to watch dutifully over the domestic welfare" (*Against Naeara*, LIX,122). Cf. R. Flacelière, *L'amour en Grèce,* Paris,1960.

[19] Cf. M. Detienne - J.-P. Vernant, *La cucina del sacrificio in terra greca*, Turin, 1982 (Paris, 1979).

[20] Cf. G. Sfameni Gasparro, *Misteri e culti mistici di Demetra,* Rome, 1986, 223-283. M. Lefkowitz, ed., *Women's Life in Greece and Rome,* Baltimore, MD, 278-281.

[21] See the cases illustrating this in I. Savalli, *op. cit.*, p. 93 which records some other examples of women dedicated to the pursuit of medicine (89-92).

[22] Cf. H.-I. Marrou, *op. cit.*, I, *passim.*

more ample guarantees in marital relations, especially the more correct equilibrium, if not complete parity, of rights and duties with
regard to conjugal fidelity.[23]

If this evolution is more clearly evident in the lives of the
Greeks in Hellenistic Egypt, where a rich store of papyrological documents enables us to know the modality of marriage contracts and to
observe the signs of expansion in the sphere of female activity at the
juridical and economic levels,[24] it is to be observed, however, that
such an evolution embraced to a great extent the entire Greek society during the same period. This led to a new image of the female,
less conditioned by the domestic role, and generally more active at
the center of the couple's relationship, even if the fundamental canons on the pre-eminent authority and the primary socio-political
activity of the man are never in question.

On the more specifically ideological side, apart from the dimension underlying juridical norms, social institutions and the economic
and social structure of the Greek city that emerge in a more or less
explicit and programmatic manner in literary works and in the theoretical formulations of the philosophers, it is possible to characterize a series of positions which are the foundation and motivation of
a strong disparity, in an axiological and functional sense, of the two
sexes in the Greek cultural tradition, or else, in various measures,
could contradict it or in any case strongly limit its legitimacy.

Here, besides a consolidated tendency to misogyny, rooted in
a stereotypical image of the weak, inept woman, inclined to every
kind of vice, intemperate and dangerous, which runs through a large
part of the literature on the subject,[25] we refer to the discussions and
theorizings on the respective nature of male and female, on their
parity in regard to their constitutional prerogatives, or on the substantial diversity, tending to characterize often in a more or less clear

---

[23] See the extensive, well documented analysis of C. Vatin, *Recherches sur le mariage et la condition de la femme mariée à l'époque hellénistique*, Paris, 1970.

[24] C. Préaux, 'Le statut de la femme à l'époque hellénistique, principalement en Égypte,' *Recueils Jean Bodin. XI. La femme*, 127-175.

[25] Apart from the analysis of the theme of "feminine weakness" in the classical world conducted by U. Mattioli (*op. cit.*, 11-20), cf. G. Arrighetti, 'Il misoginismo di Esiodo,' in Aa. vv., *Misoginia e maschilismo in Grecia e in Roma*, Genoa, 1981, 27-48. [D.L. Cairns, 'Off with her AIDOS: Herodotus,' 1, 8-34, *Class. Quarterly*, 46,1 (1996), 78-83.]

manner as natural the inferiority of the woman with regard to the man underneath the ontological and ethical profile.

The reflections of one solution or the other on the characterization of the interpersonal relations between the married couple are evident once the notion of male superiority depicts those relations according to a more or less rigid hierarchical scheme, while the recognition of substantial parity, despite the diversity of roles, tends to characterize them rather in the sense of complementarity.

We should note moreover that even in this second position there is no need to presume the anachronistic admission of a real parity between the two members of the union, in that the model of the man as guide of his partner remains always in one way or another active, and the clear delineation of their areas of competence, domestic and public, that were proper to each of them. Exemplary in this sense is the image of the matrimonial relationship delineated in Xenophon's *Oeconomicus* which was inspired in large measure on the Socratic principle enunciated by the same author in a passage in his *Symposium*,[26] of the substantial equality in nature between man and woman, the latter having a capacity for virtue on the same basis as the man, and at a level to develop equally correctly numerous activities and functions, except that, in the opinion of Socrates, they are characterized by a deficiency of wisdom and strength.

If this latter prerogative of "weakness" is inherent in the physical nature of women, the defect of wisdom is due rather to educational shortcomings and should be corrected by opportune instruction of the wife by the husband.[27] Such educational activity, in fact, is mirrored in the situation of one Isomachus and his young wife, described by Isomachus to Socrates in Xenophon's *Oeconomicus*.[28]

---

[26] Xenophon, *Symposium* 11,9 ed. E.C. Marchant, O.J. Todd, II, Oxford-London 1921². Cf. *Oeconomicus* III,10-16, 386-388. [S.I. Oost, 'Xenophon's Attitude toward Women,' *Classical World* 71 (1977), 225-236.]

[27] *Symposium* 11, 9-10.

[28] *Oeconomicus* VII, 1-43. For a new translation and commentary see S.B. Pomeroy, *Xenophon Oeconomicus*, Oxford University Press, 1994 for a full analysis of the ideology of the *gyne oikonomos* or rather of the woman's domestic role in the entire ambit of archaic and classical Greece. On the husband-wife relationship delineated in the episode of Ischomachus see the observations of R. Just (*Women in Athenian Law and Life*, London-New York, 1989, 114-118) in a larger portrayal of a study on the juridical and social situation of the Athenian woman. [F.D. Harvey, 'The Wicked Wife of Isomachos,' *Echos du Monde Classique* 28 (1984), 68-70.]

In spite of all, the matrimonial relationship, decided between the parents of the child and the betrothed spouse, is presented as the fruit of a search for the "best partner possible for home and for children" (VII, 11).

There is question, then, of a sharing in common of material possessions by the two, but especially of the respective ethical and practical capacity of each for the conduct of the family and the development of the domestic patrimony. All this is possible through the harmonious collaboration of the two spouses whose activities are directed respectively outwardly and inwardly, the husband toward matters in the public forum, and the wife toward everything concerned with the management of the household.[29] "And since both the indoor and the outdoor tasks call for labor and attention, I think that God from the first designed the woman's nature for indoor activity and man's for the outdoor tasks" (VII, 22).

Man's greater physical endurance of fatigue is in fact the proof of this natural destiny of his to public life, while the woman's natural weakness shows her as designed by nature for the care of the household (*oikos*), just as her innate greater tenderness toward the children is a sign of her maternal qualities. Certain typically feminine characteristics also, like less fortitude, are finalized in the domestic role for the woman, while other faculties, like memory and attention, are proper to both sexes, as is the aptitude for virtue and the capacity to exercise control over the passions (VII, 25-27).

Having recognized the diversity of attitudes of the two sexes as characteristic of their nature as it has been intended by the deity, while not possessed of equal intellectual and ethical faculties, Xenophon's discourse culminates in the exaltation of the matrimonial relationship in which the diversity and complementarity of man and woman find their special terrain of actualization, leading to the

---

[29] On the man-woman dialectic as a movement toward the outside and rootedness at the inside of the family residence, see the observations of J.-P. Vernant, 'Hestia-Hermes. Sull'espressione religiose dello spazio e del movimento presso i Greci,' in: *idem, Mito e pensiero presso i Greci. Studi di psicologia storica*, Turin, 1982 (ed. orig. Paris, 1972), 147-200.

procreation of children and the pursuit of blessings for the family in which both concur in their respective functions.[30]

The Socratic notion of the substantial identity of nature between the two sexes stands at the basis of the vision of the ideal state elaborated in Plato's *Republic* in which a utopian community of wives is proclaimed in place of the traditional family scheme and then the need for an equal education of men and women is also proclaimed, both destined for active participation in the life of the city.[31]

The position of the *Laws*, in underlining the obligatory character of marriage as an instrument in perpetuating the human race in general, and the city community in particular, repeats the need that both sexes be involved in the same occupations for the well-being of the entire state, women being recognized as possessing the same essential components and being capable of the same activity as their male counterparts.[32] Male authority remains moreover reaffirmed, on the part of the father or the husband over the woman, according to the common schemata of the Greek social structure, but a new element in the relations of the couple is introduced with the affirmation of the necessity for the marriage partners to know each other carnally before the marriage itself, in order to avoid any subsequent incompatibility between the two.[33]

Sharply juxtaposed to the Socratic-Platonic position is the strongly traditional viewpoint of Aristotle which emphasizes the exclusively domestic role of the woman, who is seen as a dangerous and turbulent element in the order of the city if not adequately kept

---

[30] *Oeconomicus* VII, 28-30: "And just because both are not equally endowed with the same aptitudes, they have the more need of each other, and each member of the pair is the more useful to the other, the one being competent where the other is deficient. Now since we know, dear wife, what duties have been assigned to each of us by the God, we must endeavor, each of us, to perform the duties allotted to us as well as possible. The law moreover approves of them, for it yokes together man and woman. And, as the God has made them partners for the procreation of children, so the law appoints them partners in the domestic sector. And besides, the law declares those tasks to be honorable for each of them wherein God has made the one more capable than the other. Thus, to the woman it is more honorable to stay indoors than to abide in the fields, but for the man it is unseemly rather to stay indoors than to attend to the work outside." (tr. S.B. Pomeroy)

[31] Plato, *Repub.* V, 451c-461e.

[32] Plato, *Laws* VII, 804e-806e. Large sections of Books V-XI of the work are devoted to questions relating to the organization of the feminine component of the state of marriage. On the position of Plato cf. C. Vatin, *op. cit.*, 17-24.

[33] Plato, *Laws* VI, 771e.

in check by the power of the state and subjected in a rigorous fashion to male supervision.

This is founded on a programmatic affirmation of a natural inferiority on the part of the woman. "In the male/female relationships the male is superior by nature, and the female inferior; the one rules and the other is ruled," declares the philosopher[34] who elsewhere explains the superiority and aptitude to command on the part of the male with the recognition of full possession on his part of the deliberative faculty, while the slave possesses it in an inferior fashion and "the woman possesses it but without authority, and the child has it but it is immature."[35] This text, while it relegates the woman in various ways to the imperfect categories of slave and freeman, proposes a gradated scale of values at the ontological level between the male and female, the deliberative faculty (*bouleutikon*) in them being described differently.

The same gradation is established on the ethical level, Aristotle rejecting the Socratic notion of the identity of the sexes in relation to virtue, insofar as temperance, justice and fortitude, like all other virtues, were not equal in them.[36] In this context, citing a verse from Sophocles, *Ajax*, "a woman's decency is silence" (v. 293), Aristotle individuates the typical female virtue in silence which manifests and ratifies in the most exact fashion the relation of insubordination in which the woman, in the perspective of the philosopher and of a

---

[34] Aristotle, *Politics* I (A) 5,1254b. The notion is refuted by the philosopher when he illustrates the diverse modalities of command exercised by men in the domestic ambit. In fact he is the ruler over the slaves as master, over children as father, and over his wife as husband, the two categories of wife and children being made up of freemen. "This authority," declares Aristotle, "differs in the two cases, that over the wife, being constitutional, and that over the children being royal." And he concludes: "the male is by nature more fit for command than the female" (1259 ab).

Such a notion justifies the continuity without alternative of the authority of the husband vis-a-vis the wife, different from that exercised by the head of state over his citizens which envisions an exchange of roles (from governing to being governed).

[35] *Politics* I (A) 13,1260a. On the position of Aristotle cf. C. Vatin, *op. cit.*, 24-29. See further the observations, relative also to Plato, of S. Campese, 'La donna e i filosofi,' in R. Uglione, *Atti del Convegno. op. cit.*, 105-117.

[36] *Politics* I (A) 13,1260a. All three categories participate in virtue, but in diverse ways and in relation to their respective conditions. The philosopher then declares: "consequently it is clear that moral virtue belongs to all of them; but the temperance of a man and of a woman, or the courage and justice of a man and a woman are not, as Socrates maintained, the same thing; the courage of a man is shown in commanding, of a woman in being submissive. And this holds for the other virtues."

large segment of Greek culture, is fixed in respect of man in general
and the married man in particular.

If Aristotle's position was substantially maintained in the succeeding Peripatetic tradition, and Theophrastus affirmed that the
woman's education ought to be exclusively dedicated to her domestic duties,[37] in the ambit of other Greek philosophical currents, also
outside the Socratic-Platonic lines, the fundamental equality of nature was recognized, and of equal predisposition to virtue in the two
sexes affirmed in theory — and the possibility of an equal cultural
formation was sometimes realized in practice. If Pythagoras had already (6th cent. B.C.E.) admitted women to his teaching and such
practices remained in various measures attested in succeeding ages
in the Pythagorean school, Epicurus also (4th cent. B.C.E.) offered
access to his school to women, while the Cynic philosopher,
Antisthenes (5th-4th cent. B.C.E.) recognized that women had an
equal disposition toward virtue as men.[38]

However, it is particularly within the ambit of the Stoic school
that, on the one hand, a high value was attributed to matrimony as
a natural institution whose end is to guarantee the succession of the
human race, a harmonious life in the cosmos, and in the city, and,
on the other hand, there was an insistence on the aptitude to virtue
common to the two sexes inasmuch as it is based on equal natural
faculties. Already in the 3rd century B.C.E. there is a record of a work,
On Matrimony, composed by major representatives of Stoicism.[39] The
work has not survived, except in fragments found of a treatise on
the same theme by Antipater of Tarsus (2nd cent. B.C.E.); it states
that a profound communion of life exists between man and woman
at the center of marriage. This, defined as natural completion of
human life and then due to every human being "of good race and
noble soul," is considered as a profound fusion (krasis) between man
and woman in that it implies the sharing not only of material goods
and children, but also of soul and of body. The marriage union is

---

[37] In Stobaeus, *Anthologia* IV, XXVIII,7, ed. Hense, V, p. 678.
[38] Diogenes Laertius, *Lives* VI,1,12, LCL English trans., M. Lefkowitz, *op. cit.*, #96.
[39] Cf. von Arnim (ed.), *Stoicorum Veterum Fragmenta* (=SVF), 111, Stuttgart, 1903, nn. 253-
254; Perseus of Cyzicus in Diogenes Laertius, *Lives* VII,1,36.

represented as the greatest and most profound *koinōnia* which can exist in human life.[40]

In the 1st century A.D. an analogous vision of the interpersonal relations of the couple, based on explicit theorization on the identity in nature between the two sexes[41] and on their equal predisposition to virtue, the latter being a natural faculty,[42] is expressed in the *Diatribes* of Musonius Rufus, the neo-Stoic philosopher and teacher of Epictetus.[43]

On these presuppositions the author argues at length on the rights/duties of the wife, dedicated to "philosophy," intending by this definition the acquisition of that "knowledge of life"[44] in which knowledge is finalized in practice by the realization of ethically correct behavior which permits man the perfect adherence to the rational principles of his nature.

Recognizing the special competence of the woman in directing domestic affairs,[45] in conformity with the traditional Greco-Ro-

---

[40] In Stobaeus IV, XXII,I,25, ed. Hense, pp. 507-512.

[41] Musonius Rufus, *Diatribe* III. The critical edition of the text, O. Hense, *C. Musonii Rufi Reliquiae*, Leipzig, 1905) is substantially reproduced in E. Lutz, *Musonius Rufus and The Roman Socrates*, YCS 10, 1947, with English translation, commentary and good introduction. There is an earlier Italian translation: N. Festa, *Epitteto.Il "Manuale" Traduzione di Giacomo Leopardi con saggi delle "Dissertazioni" e coi frammenti di Musonio*, Milan, 1913, 149-152. See also the more recent edition, with translation in Italian: R. Laurenti, *C. Musonio Rufo, Diatribe e frammenti minori*, Rome, 1967. On the theme of the natural equality of the sexes cf. A.C. van Gevtenbeek, 'Women's Equal Status in Musonius Rufus and Greek Diatribe,' in *Trans. B.L. Hijmans Jr.*, Assen, 1963, 51-62; C.E. Manning, 'Seneca and the Stoics on the Equality of the Sexes,' *Mnemosyne*, S.IV, 26 (1973), 170-177, who however underlines the presence in the Latin author of judgments that are strongly negative on women, apart from the persistence of consolidated metaphors, female and male, as expressions of values respectively negative and positive (weakness/ fortitude, pusillanimity/courage). In this context see Ch. Favez, 'Les opinions de Sénèque sur la femme,' *REL* 16 (1938), 335-345.

[42] *Diatribe* III, ed. Lutz 36-39: "That man is born with a natural disposition to virtue."

[43] There is a personal profile in G. Reale, *Storia della filosofia antica, IV, Le scuole dell'eta imperiale*, Milan, 1975, 99-104.

[44] *Diatribe* III, ed. Lutz 40-41: "Moreover, not men alone, women too have a natural inclination toward virtue and the capacity for acquiring it; and it is the nature of women no less than men to be pleased by good and just acts, and to reject the opposite of these. If this is true, by what reasoning would it ever be appropriate for men to search out and consider how they may lead good lives, which is exactly the study of philosophy, but inappropriate for women." Cf. also *Diatribe* IV, ed. Lutz, 48-49: "Now in very truth philosophy is training in nobility and nothing else." For a history of the use of the term and notion of philosophy cf. A.-M. Malingrey, *"Philosophia." Étude d'un groupe de mots dans la littérature grecque des Présocratiques au IV siècle après J.-C.*, Paris, 1961.

[45] *Diatribe* III, ed. Lutz 40-41: "In the first place, a woman must be a good housekeeper; that is a careful accountant of all that pertains to the welfare of her house and capable of directing the household slaves."

man cultural models, Musonius shows how the totality of virtues (temperance, justice, fortitude) which the woman can attain with education[46] and the exercise of philosophy is the most suitable instrument to attain this end.

To those who were dubious about his proposal, the philosopher retorts: "If this is true, by what reasoning would it ever be appropriate for men to search out and consider how they may lead good lives, which is exactly the study of philosophy, but inappropriate for women?"

"As for justice would not the woman who studies philosophy be just, would she not be a blameless life-partner, would she not be a sympathetic help-mate, would she not be an untiring defender of husband and children, would she not be entirely free of greed and arrogance?"[47]

It is easy to perceive in each of these affirmations of the author the definition of "quality," especially of the wife who, recognized as "a life companion," in a picture of harmonious concord has as her primary scope the cares of the family, by being rid of those defects (greed for wealth and arrogance) which appear to be the most insidious enemies of domestic concord.

It is important to note how these traits turn up frequently in the images of married life delineated in the literature of the Fathers, beginning with an author like Clement of Alexandria who, with greater depth than the other Fathers, reveals a cultural background of a philosophical stamp in which — in accordance with the schemes common in the intellectual *koiné* of the time — Platonic and Stoic elements converge.

The image of the woman "philosopher" in Musonius bears a distinct resemblance to certain arguments elaborated in the *Paidagogos*[48]: "So it is that such a woman is likely to be energetic, strong to endure pain, willing to do things which some would con-

---

[46] *Diatribe* IV, ed. Lutz 42-49, is dedicated to the theme of imparting equal education to the youth of both sexes. Also it is underlined in this context, how, on the basis of the same moral formation and practical virtue, the roles remain distinct, the domestic being proper to the woman, and the socio-political proper to the man.

[47] *Diatribe* III, ed. Lutz 40-41.

[48] Cf. *infra.*, text n. 11, 210-211.

sider no better than slaves' work, Would not such a woman be a great help to the man who married her, an ornament to her relatives, and a good example for all who know her?"[49]

Although the educational principles intended to procure the attainment of virtue ought to be available in common to both sexes, the Stoic philosopher does not fail to underline the difference in roles and, taking up the well-established theme of the "weakness" of the female sex,[50] indicates that the woman's special province resides in the performance of household tasks. However, to mitigate this perspective that, on the basis of an undeniable biological difference, seems to restrict the female role within the sphere of the family, he goes on to say that no tasks are appointed for either one exclusively, but that some tasks are more suited to the nature of one, some to the other, and for this reason some are called men's work, and some women's. He concludes: "For all human tasks, I am inclined to believe, are a common obligation and are common for men and women, and none is necessarily appointed for either one exclusively; except that some pursuits are more suited to the nature of one, some to the other, and for this reason, some are called men's work, and some women's."[51]

In these affirmations in which the author's ideological presuppositions are balanced in various ways, implying the perfect natural parity between the sexes, and the common canons of ancient society hierarchically structured, founded on a rigid differentiation of roles in the couple, one can detect one of the high points in the evolutionary process, certainly not univocal or uniform, which characterizes the conception of the woman and of the relations between the sexes in the ancient world.

To these relationships the attention of Musonius Rufus himself was directed, who, in harmony with the principles of Stoicism, enunciated a definition of matrimony in its peculiarly sexual dimension, which binds it strictly to the sphere of pleasure, which emerges in large measure in conformity with patristic formulations on the

---

[49] *Diatribe* III, ed. Lutz 42-43.
[50] *Diatribe* IV, ed. Lutz 46-47.
[51] *Ibidem*, ed. Lutz 46-47.

theme. "Men who are not wantons or immoral," he proclaims, "are bound to consider sexual intercourse justified only when it occurs in marriage and is indulged in for the purpose of begetting children, since that is lawful, but unjust and unlawful when it is mere plea-sure-seeking, even in marriage."[52]

By such a peremptory affirmation matrimonial copulation is tied exclusively to the finality of reproduction and is excluded en-tirely from the realm of pleasure which is not so strictly dependent on this stated finality. This perspective is proposed as one of the can-ons in the Christian ethics of matrimony formulated in the Fathers, from Clement to Augustine.

A significant discussion on the rights/duties of the spouses in the matter of reciprocal fidelity accompanies this affirmation. Musonius, in fact, heavily underlines the position of total parity of both members of the couple in this regard with arguments which, focusing on the motive of equal obligation and duty of man and woman in the exercise of virtue,[53] is revealed to be in sympathy with the analogous position of the Fathers, in whom, in addition to the basic ethical motivation, there is also added a properly religious one in the appeal to equal dignity of the faithful ransomed by Christ and to the Pauline imperative of the reciprocal and inalienable right of each marriage partner to the other's body.

Also present in Musonius is a highly positive image of the mat-rimonial couple in which are underlined the values outstanding be-yond all others that characterize the correct human and social rela-tions, of a profound communion between the spouses at the affec-tive level,[54] physical and material: the blessings, in fact, are in com-

---

[52] *Diatribe* XII, ed. Lutz 86-87.

[53] *Diatribe* XII, ed. Lutz 86-89. After arguing that adulterous unions are equally grave for both he continues: "And yet surely one will not expect men to be less moral than women, nor less capable of disciplining their desires, thereby revealing the stronger in judgment inferior to the weaker, the rulers to the ruled. In fact, it behooves men to be much better if they expect to be superior to women, for surely if they appear to be less self-controlled they will also be baser characters." It is easy to note how persistent in the argument are the motives of fe-male "weakness" at the intellectual level and of subjection to the man, to whom the faculty of commanding belongs.

[54] *Diatribe* XIII A, ed. Lutz 88-89. With an argumentation which will find a significant correspon-dence in analogous positions of Augustine, the Stoic philosopher, while indicating that pro-creation of children is the primary purpose of marriage, does not intend to identify the latter

mon, the bodies and the sentiments[55] are in common in an effort at harmonizing two individuals in whom the element characterizing the union of matrimony is indicated.

Neither riches, nor good looks, nor social status should influence the choice of a partner, where the decisive factor should be the quality of soul which one should expect to be "habituated to self-control and justice, and, in a word, naturally disposed to temperance, honesty and virtue in general."[56]

An attitude substantially analogous to that of the Stoic Musonius in his dealings with marriage and women characterizes the position of the Platonist, Plutarch of Chaeroneia (1st-2nd century, A.D.)[57] who with firm conviction proclaimed the principle of equality of disposition to virtue in the two sexes and dedicated a work to demonstrate this proposition by means of a gallery of female portraits who, in the Greek, Roman and "barbarian" ambience, exemplify the capacity of the female to realize, even in the exercise of activity that is typically associated with men, a high ethical ideal.[58]

In the dialogue *On Love*, elaborated on the model of Plato's *Symposium*, a debate concerning the modality and the values of *erōs*, Plutarch exalts — against the image of the homosexual relationship — a widely diffused practice in the Greek tradition and theorized at the philosophical level as an occasion for an educational activity,

---

with the pure reproductive function. "The birth of a human being which results from such a union is, to be sure, something marvellous, but it is not yet enough for the relation of husband and wife, inasmuch as, quite apart from marriage, it could result from any other sexual union, just as in the case of animals." "In fact," he continues, in pointing to the bond of affection and community of life that characterize the intimacy of the union of the couple, "in marriage there must be above all perfect companionship and mutual love of husband and wife, both in health and in sickness and under all conditions, since it was with desire for this, as well as for children, that both entered upon marriage."

[55] *Ibidem*: "Where, then, this love for each other is perfect and the two share it completely, each striving to outdo the other in devotion, the marriage is as it should be and worthy of envy, for such a union is ideal."

[56] *Diatribe* XIII B, ed. Lutz 90-91: The primary foundation of matrimonial *koinōnia* is indicated in the concord which is born from equal diligence in the practice of virtue.

[57] On the personality and works of Plutarch it suffices to refer to the monograph of K. Ziegler, 'Plutarch,' in Pauly-Wissowa, *RE* XXI,I, 1951, coll. 636-962.

[58] This is the treatise, *De mulierum virtute*, *On the Bravery of Women*, for which cf. *Plutarch Moralia, III*, Loeb Classical Library, Cambridge, MA, 1936, 474-581. Frequent references to women are also found in the *Parallel Lives*, on which see F. Le Corsu, *Plutarque et les femmes dans les Vies parallèles*, Paris, 1981.

on the part of youth and a foundation for spiritual and intellectual friendship,[59] that of the love of the married couple.[60]

After having reaffirmed the presence even in the woman of the basic virtues (temperance, prudence, fidelity and justice as well as fortitude and magnanimity),[61] the author recognizes in her a profound tendency to "friendship" (philia). Still, he asserts, "they show love for their children and spouses and the power of their affections, enriched with charm and grace, which always form the basis of their person like a fertile field, prompt to receive the seed of friendship."[62]

In marriage erōs finds its most appropriate location, since in that state it is better to love than to be loved, in an attitude of total availability which prevents any action that can disturb the union. He also presents the image of marriage as a total fusion (krasis) effected by love: no union, in fact, is so complete as that which erōs realizes in the matrimonial union (gamikē koinōnia[63]). In fact there are no other relationships in which mutual friendship can produce greater joy and better advantages, it being the foundation for a harmonious life in common and for the procreation of children.

This erōs which keeps the spouses united, a divine principle which rules the life of the universe in its totality, is at the same time a guarantee of stability, since it nourishes a union destined to accompany the whole of human life.[64]

In Advice to the Bride and Groom, dedicated to a couple of friends, the author furnishes a sort of decalog on conjugal harmony and happiness, indicating the parameters of behavior to which man and woman ought to conform in order to reach that communal ideal of life in which, in his view, marriage itself consists.

Without going into a detailed analysis of the work of Plutarch, let us say that it, totally articulated on the motive of harmony as the golden rule for relations between the couple, intends to show that it

---

[59] Cf. K.J. Dover, Homosexuality in Ancient Greece (London, 1978).

[60] On Love, 23,768D-769E, LCL, edd. E.J. Minar Jr.,/F.H. Sanbach/W.C. Helmbold, London-Cambridge, 1961 424-431. In Italian see V. Longoni, tr.; intro., by D. Del Corno, Plutarco Sull'amore, Milan, 1986, 99-103.

[61] Ibidem 769B-C, pp. 428-429; trans. Longoni 101-102.

[62] Ibidem 769C, pp. 428-429; trans. Longoni 102

[63] Ibidem 24,769F, pp. 430-432; trans. Longoni 103.

[64] Ibidem 769D-770C, pp. 430-434; trans. Longoni 102-105.

is founded on ethico-spiritual values, while the purely physical and passionate component is relatively marginal and in any case substantially ephemeral.[65]

With the recommendation of great temperance in the relationship, in which the manifestation in public of mutual affection is considered inappropriate (*Advice*, 13) and having admonished the husband to behave with moderation in his relations with his wife (*Advice*, 47), he insists on the motive of profound physical and spiritual communion between the spouses (*Advice*, 34) which extends to community of goods (*Advice*, 20) and obligates both to fidelity (*Advice*, 44).

In this harmonious relationship between the two, the well-known model, however, of the supremacy of the male as the source of authority and wisdom remains operative. It is his task to teach his wife (*Advice*, 48), according to a model of behavior which, motivated by her extreme youth and the rudimentary nature of the education she received, runs through the entire Greco-Roman tradition, and, already given expression in Xenophon's *Oeconomicus*, finds numerous exemplifications even in the documentation of epigraphy and the monuments.[66]

In the family — he asserts — every business is carried out with the agreement of both spouses, but, however, the authority of the husband was higher (*Prec. cong.* 11). The woman, in her role of companion, is the participant in the distractions and occasions of joy of the husband (*Prec. cong.* 14) and should be allowed to join him at table (*Prec. cong.* 15) according to a conception which the Greek Plutarch reflects rather the usages of Roman society, which allowed the woman a greater liberty of movement and made her a participant in the social life of her husband, unlike the Greek world.

Insisting on the principle of community between the two, the author asserts that their habits should be shared in common, their friendships and their religious beliefs, bringing the wife into total

---

[65] *Advice to Bride and Groom* 1-7, ed. F.C. Babbit, London-Cambridge, 1962, 300-305.

[66] Cf. P. Brown, *The Body and Society: Men, Women and Sexual Renunciation in Early Christianity*, New York, 1988, 13-14. [See four interesting reviews of this work in *Rivista di Storia e Letteratura Religiosa*, 28 (1992), 105-125.]

uniformity with the habits of the husband. This remains therefore the constant parameter of reference, according to which graduated scheme, notwithstanding everything, all the relationship persists. The ethical responsibility, however, of the man is underlined; if he is vicious he will make his wife likewise, but if temperate he will educate her to be wise and modest (*Precepts*, 17).

The model of subordination is announced in significant terms which evoke, *mutatis mutandis*, those operating in the epistles of St. Paul, which are proposed as decisive in the view of the Fathers. Wives, he affirms, will win praise if they submit to their husbands. It is in fact inconvenient for the woman to presume to exercise power over the man. "But control ought to be exercised by the man over the woman, not as the owner has control over a piece of property, but as the soul controls the body by entering into her feelings and being knit to her through goodwill. As therefore it is possible to exercise care over the body without being a slave to its pleasures and desires, so it is possible to govern a wife and at the same time to delight and gratify her" (*Advice to the Bride and Groom*, 33, Loeb tr., *Moralia*, v. 2, 142).

We have lingered over evoking the positions of Musonius Rufus and Plutarch because they largely converge on some characteristic themes such as the recognition of the complete aptitude of the woman for virtue, the notion of matrimony as a profound communion of sentiments and of behavioral patterns as well as just material possessions, and the sole legitimate place for sexual activity mainly or exclusively finalized in procreation, illustrating an attitude of cultivated pagans of the 1st and 2nd centuries, A.D. which shows significant parallels with some aspects of the patristic tradition.

Without being able to measure in breadth and depth the influence exercised of the theoretical formulations at the ideological and ethical level, of Stoic and Platonic imprint, of which these authors are spokespersons, the very fact of their existence is a significant indication of a mentality open to recognize in the woman the status of a person ethically responsible on the same terms as a man. The relationship of the couple, granted the traditional differentiation of functions, namely, in the house and in public, and maintaining the guiding role of the man, is represented as being on a plane of

equal dignity, especially in what pertains to moral obligation of reciprocal fidelity.

At the same time a sense of a profound spiritual community is
affirmed, beyond the physical and economic, as a peculiar element
of the marriage relationship, an expression of a spiritual climate more
attentive to the private sphere of personal contacts and sentiments.
Such a mentality appears a common patrimony, even if hard to quan-
tify, in diffusion and incidence at the level of concrete experienced
life of the pagan world including that Roman ambience to which
Musonius Rufus belongs. Such an ambience naturally merits equal
attention to that bestowed on the Greco-Hellenistic one for the purposes of the present problematic.

Returning to the specific literature on the argument, which is
sufficiently rich and valid, especially as far as concerns the institutional aspects of marriage,[67] here let us say merely that the Roman
woman, equally excluded as her Greek counterpart from political life,
and subject within the ambit of the family first to the authority of
her father and then after marriage to that of her husband, nonetheless enjoyed much more juridical safeguards and especially guarantees concerning patrimony. While still in the traditional domestic
and maternal role, as already indicated, she had at her disposal con-

---

[67] Apart from works already cited (cf. note 5 p. 44 and note 13 p. 52) which analyze the condition of the woman in both Greece and Rome and the related matrimonial practices, it suffices to recall R. Villers, 'Le statut de la femme à Rome jusqu' à la fin de la republic,' in *Recueils
Jean Bodin, XI, La femme, op. cit.*, pp. 177-189; J. Gaudemet, 'Le statut de la femme dans
l'Empire romain,' *ibidem*, pp. 192-222; P. Veyne, 'La famille et l'amour sous le Haute Empire
romain,' in *Annales ESC* 33 (1978), 35-63. Strong reservations, however, can be expressed
about this author's thesis, which attributes to exclusively psychological motivations (attention to the "private sphere" as a mechanism due to a loss, on the part of men, of competi-
tiveness and aggressiveness in the public sphere); the transformation of sexual and family
customs at Rome between the late Republic and the first generations of the Empire while at
the same time maintaining that the new morality of marriage, more attentive to the values of
the couple, is an acquisition of that transformation of all things similar to the Christian position on the theme. [See P. Veyne, 'The Roman Empire' in *A History of Private Life, 1. From
Pagan Rome to Byzantium*, P. Veyne, ed, Harvard U. Press, 1987, 5-233, esp. 9-93.] For a
more balanced presentation of the problem cf. R. Saller, 'I rapporti di parentela e
l'organizzazione familiare,' in E. Gabba-A. Schiavone (cur.), *Storia di Roma, IV Caratteri e
morfologie*, Turin, 1989, 515-555; cf. also E. Cantarella, 'La vita delle donne,' *ibidem*, 557-
608. See also J.F. Gardner, *Women in Roman Law and Society*, London-Sydney, 1986, and
earlier the part reserved for the role of the female in the lively, albeit in some respects anti-
quated, J. Carcopino, *Daily Life in Ancient Rome*, 1940. [Add: B. Rawson, ed. *Marriage,
Divorce and Children in Ancient Rome*, Oxford, 1991.]

siderable freedom in her public relations and in various ways participated in the social relations of her husband.

Even with regard to the nuptial bond, this relatively greater autonomy is manifest in the case of the Roman woman; she participated on a basis of equality with her brothers in the paternal inheritance using it as her own patrimony and she could take the initiative in the matter of a divorce. Even her role in the family became more incisive, in being entrusted with the education of the children, at least in their early years.[68]

What seems likely from a quotation from Martial, even the girls went to the same public schools as the boys of their own age, even though frequently a private tutor proved preferable for them.[69] In any case the Roman children enjoyed a better education than their opposite numbers in Greece.

Naturally this picture underwent a profound change from Republican to Imperial times. The general change in the customs and socio-economic structure in the latter period, still did not afford an entrée to woman to political life and more generally to social activity, which was the traditional preserve of the male; however on the economic and juridical planes, as in that of behavioral patterns, a more or less profound transformation occurred in the status of women.[70]

Even though branded rather frequently as an indication of moral depravity and pointed to as a cause of the corruption of society as a whole, especially in the literature of satire shot through with strong misogynous tendencies and in any case very prone to utilize all the stereotypical models of a negative femininity,[71] it is indisputable that there emerged in the Imperial Age a more liberated and independent woman.

---

[68] Cf. H.-I. Marrou, op. cit., II,15-16.

[69] "Quid tibi nobiscum est, ludi scelerate magister, invisum pueris virginibusque caput?" Martial IX,68,2; cf. H.-I. Marrou, op. cit., II, 65.

[70] To the works cited in note 67 p. 72, add R. Scuderi, 'Mutamenti della condizione femminile a Roma nell'ultima etàt-repubblicana,' CCC 3 (1982), 41-84. [See now S. Treggiari, 'Digna condicio: Betrothals in the Roman Upper Class,' Echos de Monde Classique 28 (1984), 419-4511; eadem, 'Putting the Bride to Bed,' loc. cit. 38 (1994), 311-331.]

[71] M. Coccia, 'Multa in muliebrem levitatem coepit iactare (Le figure femminili del Satyricon di Petronio),' in R. Uglione, ed., Atti del II Convegno, op. cit., 121-140.

Even if limited to the socially upper classes, where it was possible to achieve a consistent patrimonial importance and relative social influence on the part of the woman more than a greater cultural preparation, this process of evolution was reflected also in the relations of the couple which do not appear too rigidly bound to the patriarchal hierarchical model.

As far as the bond of marriage was concerned, it should be noted that, while both spouses had an equal right to decide on its dissolution, a notable discrimination continued until a late date on the juridical level, and on that of moral judgment on the question of adultery. Adultery on the part of a woman, daughter or wife, and of the man with whom she was compromised, was subject to the gravest sanctions, while the husband was allowed a great measure of liberty in his behavior, where the term "adultery" was employed only when he committed it with another man's wife. At the same time, as resulted from similar positions in Musonius Rufus or Plutarch, while openly recognizing the values of the female and of the couple, the model of female "submission" remained in large measure operative which was the basis for variously gradated positions of inferiority for the wife in the ambit of interpersonal relations with her husband.

IV

THE IMAGE OF THE COUPLE
IN THE FATHERS AND THE TRADITION
OF ENKRATEIA

A further, fundamental element in the correct evaluation of the various patristic positions on the theme of the couple is constituted by the relationship which is placed in these same authors and in the wider panorama of contemporary Christianity, in theory and practice, between the reality of marriage, to which theme it is tied in a specific manner, and the variously motivated exaltations of sexual continence.

As has already been alluded to, in numerous sectors of the Christianity of the early centuries, there emerged a strong tendency to situate *enkrateia*, in its twofold meaning of virginity and matrimonial continence,[1] as preeminent values or absolutely central directives in the life of the faithful.[2] These, therefore, converged to paint a picture sufficiently homogeneous in the exaltation of this value but the motivations behind such tendencies differ in as many

---

[1] It is known that the term in question, in its primary meaning of "self-control," "temperance," in Greek linguistic usage embraces a wider range of significance than with respect to what relates to the sphere of sexuality, here taken into consideration. Cf. W. Grundmann, art. *Enkrateia* in G. Kittel, *ThWNT* 11, 1935, coll. 337-341; P.Th. Camelot, art. ΕΓΚΡΑΤΕΙΑ (*Continentia*), in *DSp* IV, I, 1960, coll. 357-370; H. Chadwick, art. *Enkrateia*, in *RAC* V, 1962, coll. 343-365. However, although authors like Clement of Alexandria were well aware of the broader meaning of the notion of *enkrateia* as a capacity to exercise control over the passions at all levels of human life (*Stromata* III,VII,57,1-60,4; GCS 52 [15], pp. 222,14-224,9), in Christian ambiences of the first centuries it had come to describe a special relationship with this sphere, so therefore the use of the term to define and circumscribe the positions on the theme of sexual behavior in such an ambience appears historically legitimate.

[2] See also the analysis of P.F. Beatrice, 'Continenza e matrimonio nel cristianesimo primitivo (secc. I-II),' in R. Cantalamessa (ed.), *op. cit.,* 3-68.

ways as the practical behavioral patterns which are derived from them.[3]

In regard to the latter, there was a well defined line between the abstentionist behavior accompanying the condemnation of marriage, on the one hand, and the voluntary renunciation on the part of one partner of the practice of marriage, on the other, recognized as a divine institution and therefore licit for Christians.

However, on the basis of these diverse motivations, we can make a legitimate distinction. There is a radical side in the tradition of *enkrateia* implying at the same time abstention from and condemnation of marriage, which is commonly called encratism, its representatives being defined already as "encratites" in the heresiological language of Irenaeus of Lyons.[4]

Opposed to this is what we call a "moderate" side, in large measure coinciding with the position of the Great Church at the center of which in more or less enthusiastic tones the preeminent dignity of continence had always maintained the biblical principle of the divine origin of the institution of marriage. This then was recognized as a condition of the practical life of the Christian.

However, after this essential distinction on the practical level and the value judgment formulated regarding marriage, there remains the more complex and delicate problem of perceiving and describing the motivations underlying the two different modes of behavior invoked above which constitute the indispensable terms of reference for the historico-religious evaluation of practical behavior in question.

In fact, in the radical condemnation of marriage, persons like Tatian and Julius Cassian[5] converge, and ambiences like those which are so prominent in a large part of the apocryphal literature[6] as well

---

[3] For a broader and well-documented illustration of these affirmations see *Enkrateia e antropologia*, *op. cit.*, *supra*, in note 6, p. 19.

[4] Cf. F. Bolgiani, 'La tradizione eresiologica sull'encratismo. 1. Le notizie di Ireneo,' in *AAST* 91 (1956-57), 343-419.

[5] On these authors see the sources, with relative discussions and bibliographical documentation, in *Enkrateia e antropologia... op. cit.*, 23-79.

[6] Cf. *ibidem*, 87-101.

as numerous anonymous texts inspired by the same encratite ideal,[7] those who maintain the biblical notion of one only God the Creator to which is also referred the salvific action of Jesus, and some gnostic currents, that is to say, movements which, while variously appealing to the Christian message, emerge as upholders of a dualistic ontology.[8]

The discovery of numerous original Gnostic texts in Coptic in the vicinity of Nag Hammadi in Egypt has confirmed the presence at the center of gnosticism of a strong interest in abstensionism at the sexual, and sometimes at the alimentary,[9] level. Among the gnostics the rejection of physical union and consequently of generation found its primary and decisive justification in the intrinsic negativity of matter and of corporeity, in which such activity is based and which constitutes the second "principle" of reality permanently opposed to the sphere of the spiritual and the divine.

Next the encratites, who did not demand the existence of two counterposed "principles" or of a twofold divinity (a God supremely transcendent and an inferior Creator) as the gnostics desired, inter-

---

[7] Among them it suffices to record works like the *Physiologus,* or the treatise, *De centesima, sexagesima, tricesima,* which treats of "three recompenses" looking respectively to the martyr, the virgin, and to the continent, on the basis of the Gospel parable of the sower and the fruits of his work. Cf. *Enkrateia e antropologia... op. cit.,* 101-108.

[8] For the definition of dualism in its historico-religious meaning which contemplates the admission of two principles, which, for different reasons, are the foundation of all reality, see U. Bianchi, *Il dualismo religioso, saggio storico ed etnologico,* Rome, 1958: *idem,* 'Le dualisme en histoire des religions,' *RHR* 159 (1961), 1-4 (rp. in *Selected Essays... op. cit.,* 3-48) where there are numerous other studies on the same theme and on particular dualistic versions of gnosticism. There is a recent discussion on the term in an historico-religious setting in I.P. Couliano, *I miti dei dualismi occidentali. Dai sistemi gnostici al mondo moderno,* Milan, 1989 (ed. orig. Paris, 1987).

[9] Cf. *Enkrateia e antropologia, op. cit.,* 115-166. For information on Gnosticism, object of ample scientific debate in depth, too extensive for coverage here except to refer to a few essential titles, apart from the Proceedings of an international Colloquium which has given a new impulse to research on the thema (I. Bianchi, ed., *Le origini dello gnosticismo, Colloquio di Messina 13-18 aprile 1966,* Leiden, 1967), the bibliographical surveys of D.M. Scholer, *Nag Hammadi Bibliography,* 1948-1969 (Nag Hammadi Studies 1), Leiden, 1971 with annual updates, since 1971, in *Novum Testamentum.* See also such representative fundamental studies as H. Jonas, *Gnosticism,* Boston, 1958, 1967[2]; R.M. Grant, *Gnosticism and Early Christianity,* New York, 1959, 1966 and Ch. Puech, *Sulle tracce della gnosi. I. La Gnosi e il tempo; II. Sul Vangelo secondo Tommaso,* Milan, 1975 (ed. orig. Paris, 1978). See further G. Filoramo, *L'attesa della fine. Storia della gnosi,* Bari, 1983. [Engl. ed. See now W. Foerster, ed. *Die Gnosis. 1. Zeugnisse der Kirchenväter, 2. Koptische und Mandäische Quellen, 3. Der Manichäismus,* Munich, 1995; *idem, Gnosis. A Selection of Gnostic texts in Patristic Exegesis,* tr. R.McL. Wilson, Oxford, 1972.]

posed to found the practice of abstentionism, a series of motivations the respective weight of which it is necessary to evaluate in order to define the ideological picture underlying this same practice.

The exaltation of virginity and of continence at the heart of the Great Church, in its turn, was variously motivated in different contexts. Therefore, apart from the distinction however essential between the radical and moderate forms of *enkrateia*, it is important, under the historical profile, to individuate the theoretical reasons, more or less explicit and elaborated, which intervened in one or the other ambience, to justify the different practical attitudes.

It is possible, then, to perceive, apart from that ontological one of a dualistic-gnostic brand evoked above, at least three major motives, inspired by the tradition of *enkrateia*, which, while interfering sometimes in various contexts and distinguishable in their various physiognomies and validity are, in fact, in their exclusive or prevalent intervention in one or the other picture, of sufficiently homogenous trend in the ambit of this tradition. This identification of different theoretical motivations is a *sine qua non* of any analysis of the historical problem, apart altogether from the important distinction invoked above between radical encratite positions of a programmatic repudiation of marriage as a necessary condition for the realization of the Christian ideal and the moderate positions of the Great Church, where the exaltation, more or less accentuated, of virginity and continence is accompanied by a recognition of the liceity of marriage. To the grand evangelical theme of *eunuchia* for the kingdom of heaven, announced in Mt 19:12, and in its parallels in the Synoptics,[10] which depicts a spirituality of voluntary renunciation of an earthly blessing in view of a religious ideal, in an ascetic tension which transcends the values of the world without despising them, is placed side by side a perspective strongly characterized in

---

[10] Mk 10:2-12; Lk 18:15-17; cf. Lk 16:18. Among the numerous exegetical studies of the Gospel pericope, besides J. Dupont *(op. cit.*, at note 10, p. 25), Q. Quesnell, '"Made Themselves Eunuchs for the Kingdom of Heaven" (Mt 19:12),' *CBQ* 30 (1968), 335-358. It does not however seem to us that the intention of Jesus, expressed in the text in question, was either to propose "continence inside and outside of matrimony," as is maintained in B. Rigaux, 'Le célibat et le radicalisme évangélique,' *NRTh* 94, 1972, 157-17, and so a "spiritual matrimony" as is maintained by P.F. Beatrice (*art. cit.*, p. 59). Cf. *Enkrateia e antropologia*, 16-18.

an eschatological direction. This, inspired by the Pauline exhortation to use with detachment the reality of the world, in pursuing the by now urgent *kairos* of Christian salvation, which is formulated in 1 Cor 7, as decisive for the problematic of *enkrateia* in its multiple formulations, assumes different connotations in different situations, with outcomes sometimes definable in the sense of a "realized eschatology."[11]

There is question, then, in this latter instance, of positions which, by implying the notion of bringing to completion of the salvific event in adhesion through baptism to the death and resurrection of Christ, deduce the opportunity, if not the obligation, for the Christian to cease from the typically "worldly" activity of marriage and procreation. He, in fact, already "risen" with the Savior, ought to adapt to that model of "the angelic life" which does not know marriage or generation, indicated as typical of the eschatological situation of the saved in the celebrated passage in Luke's gospel (Lk 20:34-36).

In any case, the eschatological motivation of *enkrateia* appears well defined in its physiognomy and apt to describe a vast range of positions in the area under examination. However, in some cases, the eschatological valency of the privileged role entrusted to virginity and to continence in the Christian experience is joined to that in which the practice of *enkrateia* represents one of the decisive presuppositions and at the same time the privileged "sign" of the restoration of the initial situation of the human condition, in its turn characterized by the condition of virginity.

Such is the definition of the third peculiar motivation of the tradition under examination, that is, the protological, which inter-

---

[11] Cf. E. Peterson, 'L'origine dell'ascesi cristiana,' *Euntes Docete* 1 (1948),195-204, rp. in *Frühkirche, Judentum und Gnosis. Studien und Untersuchungen,* Rome-Freiburg-Vienna, 1959, 209-220; P. Nagel, *Die Motivierung der Askese in der alten Kirche und der Ursprung des Monchtums* (*TU* 95) Berlin, 1966, 20-55; Ton H.C. van Eik, 'Marriage and Virginity, Death and Immortality,' in J. Fontaine-Ch. Kannengiesser (edd.), *Epektasis-Mélanges patristiques offerts au Cardinal Jean Daniélou,* Paris, 1972, 209-235; J.B. Bauer, *Alle origini dell'ascetismo cristiano,* Brescia, 1983. On the relationship between eschatology and positions on the theme of sexuality see finally B. Lang, 'No Sex in Heaven: the Logic of Procreation, Death, and Eternal Life in the Judaeo-Christian Tradition,' in *Alter Orient und altes Testament* 215 (1985), 237-253.

venes to characterize large sections of it, either in its radical or its moderate form. Such motivations establish a solid and qualitative bond between the beginnings of human history with the decisive and fundamental event of the first couple and the actual condition of the faithful, whose existential choices in the sense respectively of virginity and continence, or of marriage are measured in dignity and value, from reference to the situation of the protoplasts before or after sin. The specificity of the protological motivation results especially from its peculiar implications at the anthropological level. It affirms in fact an unmistakable link between the actual practice of *enkrateia* and the original condition of the first human couple in paradise before they sinned, a condition seen as a state of virginal integrity to which that same sin put an end. The relationship between the original transgression and the virginity/marriage binomial, is configured according to two distinct possibilities. On the one hand, there is the encratite notion, according to which the sin of Adam and Eve consisted in the exercise of marriage. On the other hand, it is held that this exercise, neither necessary nor useful in the state of paradise, has been permitted by God to a humanity already weak and mortal, as a remedy for concupiscence to guarantee, with the generation of children, the propagation of the human race and to bring to realization God's plan of salvation.

This second conception characterizes the position of numerous influential representatives of the Great Church, who, while forcibly proclaiming the liceity of marriage against the encratites and gnostics consider it nevertheless a post-Fall institution.

In this perspective, in both formulations — the radical (marriage = sin) and moderate (marriage = consequence of original sin) the practice of virginity and of continence is defined as the restoration of the integrity that preceded the Fall. This is founded therefore on a specific protological motivation which contextually reveals an anthropology with a "graduated" structure.

In fact, at the very moment in which is affirmed the extraneousness of sexual activity and the generation of children to the original state of humanity as it had been envisaged in the "design" of the Creator, such activities being tied to Adam's transgression as its specific consequence, there is delineated an anthropology modulated in two time zones and at two levels. The second of such levels, in the order of chronology and ontology, is typically linked to an initial degradation. With this is coupled the fact that frequently this second tier of existence, implying marriage and generation, is regarded as "animal" in quality, in profound contrast with the original "angelic" quality of humanity. The quality, which defines humanity in the sense of a profound affinity with the nature of angels, would be fully restored in the eschatological perspective. This is however already realized in the earthly life of the virgin and the continent, in which the beginning (*initium*, arch) of the situation in paradise has been intimately joined with the eschatological end (*telos*).

This complex panorama, in which there is a confluence of diverse and sometimes opposed positions, constitutes the backgrounds in which is situated historically the various patristic formulations on the theme under examination.

The authors, each with his own physiognomy and placed in their respective cultural contexts, participate in strong tensions of contemporary spirituality and seek to overcome with personal solutions in a balanced portrait which respects the biblical principle of the substantial goodness of creation at all its levels and at the same time satisfies the aspirations to full realization of the evangelical ideal, with its eschatological position and its summons to detachment from earthly goods.

The Fathers in their role of influential representatives of the Great Church with all the instruments of polemical refutation conducted a tenacious struggle against the extreme positions of the gnostics and encratites. Those latter, in their unrelenting condemnation of the practice of marriage, defined, in the well-known formula of Tatian, as "fornication and corruption,"[12] were perceived as contradictory with respect to the biblical presuppposition of God's positive creative activity.[13]

---

[12] In Irenaeus, *Contra haer.*, 1, 28,1 [=frag. gr. 21 in Eusebius, *Hist. eccles.* IV,29,2 3], edd. A. Rousseau-J. Doutreleau (SC 264), Paris, 1979, 356-357; *ACW* 55, 92-93, 254.

[13] Already in 1 Tm 4:1-3 the position of those who forbid marriage and prescribe abstention from foods created by God is condemned as apostasy from the faith, inspired by "deceitful spirits and things taught by demons."

In fact, gnostic *enkrateia* sprang from a programmatic admission of a duality of principles at the ontological and theological levels (a transcendent divine world and relative spiritual substance, on the one hand, and, on the other, this material world with its Demiurge who is imperfect or downright malevolent), reflected at the anthropological level in a radical distinction and opposition between the spiritual/divine component, and the element that is corporeal, corruptible, and mortal. The abstentionist behavior of the encratites, for their part, in identifying in the sphere of marriage and genital activity a reality of "animal" type, which, extraneous to the original nature of man, has been set in motion by the first sin consisting in the practice of sex in imitation of the brutes[14] according to Julius Cassian, equally represents an anthropological dualism, by connecting to culpability and decadence a peculiar activity of the existential status of man.

This fundamental convergence of gnostics and encratites in contradicting an essential postulate of the biblical vision is definitely perceived by the Fathers and clearly reflected in the extensive polemical discussion of Clement of Alexandria which unites both types of upholders of "false continence," countering their position with the notion of the intrinsic goodness and legitimacy of marriage and of procreation[15] as the unshakable foundation of the Christian creed.

The defence of such a notion, in fact, runs throughout the entire patristic tradition constituting one of the definitive and constant motives of the literature on the theme. It emerges with particular prominence, apart from Clement, in authors like Tertullian and Origen who were involved in lengthy and intensive polemic against the ideological and ethical positions of the gnostics and encratites. Likewise in Augustine, placed on his guard by his experience of manichaeism and his subsequent strenuous activity of refuting the radical dualism of his former coreligionists[16] against the

---

[14] Clement of Alexandria, *Stromata*, 111,102,1.4: GCS 52 [15], p. 243, 8-20. Cf. *Enkrateia e antropologia, op. cit.*, pp. 70-76.

[15] To it is dedicated the whole of *Stromata* Book III. Cf. F. Bolgiani, 'La tradizione eresiologica sull'encratismo, II. La confutazione di Clemente di Alessandria,' in *AAST* 96 (1961-1962), 537-664.

[16] Cf P. Alfaric, *L'évolution intellectuelle de Saint Augustin. I. Du Manichéisme au Néoplatonisme*, Paris, 1918.

risk of underestimating the weight of any negative or even ambiguous position on the theme of marriage and procreation.

It is well known in fact how, even in his long and extended polemic against Pelagianism which pitted him especially against Julian of Eclanum, while defending with every sort of argument his own thesis on the theme of original sin insofar as it was connected with sexual concupiscence, Augustine never makes any concession on the principle of the intrinsic and original goodness of the practice of marriage.[17]

At the same time the strong ascetical calls and exaltation of the idea of virginity and continence which characterize the Christian spirituality of the first centuries, by configuring such an extensive and articulate "tradition of *enkrateia*" as we have described above, profoundly conditioned the patristic conception of the relationship of the couple in its specific nuptial dimension.

In fact, with the exception of Lactantius, whose particular cultural physiognomy is reflected even in his meager interest in the problematic in question, all the authors who provide materials for this anthology are more or less ample and programmatic in the question of virginity and continence exalted as a higher and more perfect form of realizing the religious ideal of the Christian.

On the basis of 1 Cor 7, which recurs with significant frequency in various contexts, the Fathers are in agreement in recognizing the superiority of the state of virginity and continence, whether in the state of widowhood or in the state of matrimony, in respect to those involved in the marriage state.

Without being able to address all the problems inherent in the Pauline text[18] it suffices to underline the decisive normative function which it has exercised in the patristic literature, whether in its insistence on the liceity and dignity of marriage or in delineating a precise scale of values in which virginity and continence occupy an unrivalled position of superior dignity compared to matrimony. In

---

[17] See further.

[18] For a first approach it suffices to refer to the analysis of S. Prete, *Matrimonio e continenza nel cristianesimo delle origini, Studio Su 1 Cor 7:1-40,* Brescia, 1979, where the *status quaestionis* is presented and the relative bibliography discussed. See also the analysis of some patristic interpretations of the Pauline statement in J. Massingberd Ford, 'St. Paul, the Philogamist (1 Cor, VII in Early Patristic Exegesis),' *NTS* 11 (1965), 326-348.

particular, on the dictate of Paul is based the affirmation, not even mentioned by the Fathers, of the reciprocal and inalienable faculty of married couples to render the marriage "debt" to each other. From that descends, first, the notion of indissolubility of the marriage bond and of the equal ethical responsibility of male and female to the pledge of mutual fidelity, with no concession to the male of any greater sexual freedom and, secondly, the principle of "mutual consent" preparatory to any abstention from sexual relations.

Continence within marriage directed to the purpose of obtaining greater dedication to religious activity, as is proposed in the Pauline text itself, and which in the subsequent tradition had been frequently emphasized to the point of establishing a tension, if not a genuine opposition, between the exercise of marriage and the religious practice of the Christian,[19] remains however always a value which, while remaining such, should spring from the voluntary agreement of the marriage partners.

This theme, recurring with significant frequency in the patristic problematic, assumes a decisive role especially between the end of the 4th and the beginning of the 5th centuries, when, with the consolidation of the monastic movement, the tendencies to institutionalize virginity became stronger. These expressed themselves, among other ways, in the flourishing of a widespread production of treatises, On Virginity,[20] and on the diffusion of the practice of continence within marriage.

If the Epistle to Apro and Amanda of Paulinus of Nola exalts the full realization of this ideal in that it is entered into with the mutual consent of the two partners, the Letter to Celantia, of the anonymous author, whom we still prefer to designate as Pseudo-Jerome although

---

[19] Cf. Tertullian, De exhortatione castitatis, X,2: CCSL 2,2, pp. 1029-1030: from the necessity of "temporary purification," implying abstention from matrimonial relations which the Apostle recommends so that the couple may be dedicated to prayer, the author deduces that, since the uninterrupted practice of prayer is useful to man, continuous continence is equally indispensable. This theme recurs with particular relevance in Origen. Cf. frag. III in Rom. ed. A. Ramsbotham, 'The Commentary of Origen on the Epistle to the Romans,' JTS 13 (1911-1912), pp. 213,5-214,6. In frag. XXXIV on 1 Cor. ed. C. Jenkins, 'Origen on 1 Cor.,' JTS 9 (1907-1908), p. 502, 11-15 affirms as a condition of reception of the Eucharist, the necessity of abstention from conjugal relations as also of prayer and fasting (ibid. p. 502, 32-33).

[20] Cf. P.Th. Camelot, 'Les traités De Virginitate au IVe siècle,' in Mystique et continence. Études carmelitaines 31 (1952), 189-197.

there is considerable scholarly consensus[21] for identifying him with Pelagius, and Epistle 262 of Augustine, both show the manifold risks which, under an ethical profile, such an ideal could produce for those (generally the wife), while united by the marriage bond, would presume to withdraw from the obligations of the marriage "debt" without the prior consent of the other marriage partner.

The role exercised in the patristic perspective by 1 Cor 7 remains, however, essential in defining that unquestionable graduality of value between, on the one hand, virginity and continence and, on the other, which characterizes such a perspective. To this rather frequently is joined, to emphasize this gradualness there intervenes a patristic interpretation of the expression of Paul in v. 6 according to which the preceding expressions on abstention from marital relations for the purpose of prayer and the subsequent return to the *status quo*, "that Satan may not tempt you through your lack of self-control," have been pronounced "by way of concession and not as a command." The Apostle's "counsel" in fact is frequently understood as referring to the nuptial practice itself, which would then be the fruit of a concession made to the "weakness" of man, incapable of maintaining perfect continence. This interpretation tends to find support in succeeding statements of Paul who, when he turns to the unmarried (*agamoi*) and widows, recognizes that it is good to remain in that same condition. "However," he continues, "if they cannot exercise self-control, they should marry. It is better to marry than to be on fire" (v. 9).

From these words of the Apostle numerous authors, including Tertullian[22] and Origen,[23] draw out arguments to connect the choice

---

[21] See the titles cited in the relevant Introductory Profile.

[22] Cf. *To his Wife*, I,III,2-3: *CCSL* II,I, 375; ed. Ch. Munier, *Tertullien A son épouse*, SC 273, Paris, 1980, 98-99. For the interpretation of Tertullian of the Pauline passage see A. D'Alès, *La théologie de Tertullien*, Paris, 1905², p. 252 and R. Braun, 'Tertullien et l'exégèse de 1 Cor 7,' in J. Fontaine-Ch. Kannengiesser (edd.), *Epektasis, op. cit.*, Paris, 1972, 21-28.

[23] The theme is developed especially in his *Commentary on the Epistle to the Corinthians,* fragments of which have survived in exegetical *Catenae* and edited by C. Jenkins, *JTS* 9 (1907-1908) 231-247; 353-372; 500-514; *JTS* 10 (1908-l909) pp. 29-51. In particular, cf. frag. XII, pp. 241,13-242,17; frag. XXIX, pp. 370,1-371,2; and frag. XLIII, pp. 513,37-514,41. It turns up moreover in the entire range of the production of Origen, as one of the characteristic motives revealing the ethical doctrine of the Alexandrian. Among numerous examples it will suffice to cite an affirmation in *Contra Celsum*: "God permitted all those who were incapable of comprehending the supreme good of absolute purity to take many wives" (VII,55 ed. M. Borret, SC 150, Paris, 1969, 300-301).

of marriage with man's incapacity to practice the rigorous ideal of *enkrateia* and as a result to depict such a choice, licit for the Christian, on a plane notably inferior to the same ideal.

A final important element whose weight cannot be ignored in defining the attitude of the Fathers on the theme under examination is given in the eventual presence in them of this protological motivation of *enkrateia* which occurs to make a profound impression on the Christian vision of marriage in the early centuries.

The notion of a causal relationship between the transgression of the divine precept and the beginning of the practice of matrimony, where the condition of the first human union in paradise is defined in terms of virginal integrity, turns up in various modalities in numerous authors.

Without repeating in detail here an analysis which we have conducted elsewhere,[24] we will say only that in Tertullian, Origen, Ambrose and Jerome one can grasp the profound incidence of the peculiar connection which these authors recognize between the loss of original perfection of humanity because of the sin in paradise and the beginning of the regimen of the nuptial union and procreation, bound in a manner not to be ignored to the cycle of death and corruption which characterize actual human existence. Although, in the texts which we have chosen as particularly expressive of the modality of the marriage relationship in each of these authors, the connection between the sin of Adam and the inauguration of the practice of marriage does not appear explicitly, the presence of this motive qualifying the entire portrait of their spirituality and their related anthropological vision cannot be avoided.

Clement of Alexandria, for his part, makes the maximum concession to the radical formulas of the encratites and gnostics when he recognizes the content of Adam's sin. However, he distinguishes carefully from this formula so that he indicates in the same marriage and in consequent physical regeneration a constitutive element in man's existential regimen which has been prearranged in God's creative plan. The fault of Adam and Eve was only to have anticipated

---

[24] Cf. *Enkrateia e antropologia, op. cit.*, pp. 167-322.

the time of their marriage when, while still children[25] they would not be adapted to such activity.[26]

For this solution of his he distinguishes other patristic positions which motivate on a protological basis the practice of continence and of virginity by establishing a strong disparity of values between such practice and the exercise of sexuality, only within the context of matrimony. The latter, in fact, according to these positions, was retained outside the original plan of the Creator as the fruit of a benevolent "concession" of his.

In Augustine, after a preliminary period of adhesion to a formula which closely connected, as cause to effect, the transgression of Adam to the institution of marriage, and a later period of uncertainty between the different solutions to the problem, as the text in no. 26 testifies, there is a clear affirmation of a specific pertinence of the physical union and the connected procreation to the ontological structure of man, defined from the creative act which brings the sexual distinctions into being.

This conception, on which there would be no more further changes of mind nor uncertainty, characterizes Augustine's vision of the relations of the couple and also exercised a very decisive role in the broader and more complex picture of the problematic of original sin.[27]

---

[25] The theme of the "childhood" of the protoplasts as motivation of their transgression of the divine precept intervenes in a characteristic manner in the perspective of Irenaeus where the sexual dimension with its related "shame" is linked to the relation between the same transgression and the discovery of it on the part of the two. On this theme, cf. G. Sfameni Gasparro, 'La vergogna di Adamo e di Eva nella riflessione dei Padri,' in *PSV* 20 (1989), 253-270. On the anthropological doctrine of Irenaeus cf. A. Orbe, *Antropologia de San Ireneo*, Madrid, 1969.

[26] *Protreptic* XI,III, 1, ed. C Mondésert (SC 2 bis), Paris, 1949, p. 179; *Stromata* III, XIV,94,3: GCS 50 [15], p. 239,16-21. FOTC 85, tr. J. Ferguson. In the same argument (*Stromata* III,XVII,103,1: GCS 50 [15], p. 243,23-25, FOTC 85) Clement does not repudiate the encratite hypothesis of an imitation of the irrational animals but affirms that the two sinned by completing nuptials prematurely, being still young, because of the jealousy of the devil. For an analysis of Clement's position, within the broader picture of the earliest formulations on the theme, marriage-original sin, see A. Orbe, 'El pecado original y el matrimonio en la teologia del s. II,' *Gregorianum* 45 (1964), 449-500 (esp. 468-481).

[27] See further P.F. Beatrice, *Tradux Peccati. Alle fonti della dottrina agostiniano del pecato originale*, Milan, 1978, 90-149.

V

THE HUMAN COUPLE IN THE FATHERS

Taking account of this complex articulation of elements which, in proportions which vary according to individual instances, go to make up the terrain in which the various patristic formulations are rooted and take shape, analysis of them reveals, along with the frequency of certain typical themes, a variety of tones and a broad range of nuances to match the different physiognomies of different authors, and the historical circumstances and cultural settings in which each of them operated.

We should not, in fact, neglect to evaluate the weight of such data for the correct understanding of the different positions on the theme, just as it also appears indispensable to pay attention to the specific context in which the excerpts examined are situated. In fact it is necessary to avoid the risk, always present in an anthology, of not appreciating fully the significance of certain affirmations isolated from their general frame of reference, that is, of the work from which the excerpt is taken and more generally of the entire problematic of the author.

A separate question, also necessarily connected with the subject under investigation, is that of the attitude of the Fathers in their dealing with women, in the specifics of their anthropological, social and religious status. This aspect of the problem, the subject of many specialized studies,[1] cannot be addressed in the present context, in

---

[1] For a rapid overview of the patristic attitudes with regard to woman, apart from the earlier work of A. Castiglioni, 'La donna nel pensiero Padri della Chiesa greca del IV secolo,' *La Scuola Cattolica* 46, (1918), 29-51, 131-146; 212-233; 353-365; 439-466, (rp. in book format, Monza, 1919); see also C. Scaglioni, 'La donna nel pensiero dei Padri,' *Vita e Pensiero* N.S. 58 (1975), 28-50, which however too frequently minimizes the significance of some judg-

the articulated complexity of its relationships and must be situated in the wider context of the role of the woman in the Christian life of the early centuries which emerges from the entire spectrum of the relative documentation[2] to make reference to the part which regards more directly the discourse on the couple, the latter being inevitably conditioned by the image of the role and function of the wife at the center of the matrimonial bond.

The individual introductions to the chosen passages are meant to provide in rapid synthesis the essential features of the biography and literary activity of the Fathers to situate them in their historical-cultural ambiences. Here we will sketch the principal lines of the discourse elaborated by each of them on the theme of the personal relationship of the two participants in the couple relationship, centered on their respective positions on the system of values pertaining to the matrimonial condition in which such a relationship is brought to realization.

---

ments formulated by authors on the status of women. The interpretation of U. Mattioli, 'La donna nella pensiero patristico,' in R. Uglione (ed.), *Atti del Convegno, op. cit.*, 223-242 seems more balanced and correct. Cf. also A. Pastorino, 'La condizione femminile nei Padri della Chiesa,' in Aa. vv., *Sponsa, Mater Virgo, op. cit.*, 109-122 and the apt observations of M.G. Mara, 'I Padri della Chiesa e la donna,' in *Parole di Vita* 30, 6 (1985), 11-18 (=411-418). A collection of texts on the theme is found in F. Quère-Jaulmes, *La femme. Les grandes textes des Pères de l'Église*, Paris, 1968 and more recently E.A. Clark, *Women in the Early Church* (Message of the Fathers of the Church 13), Wilmington, DE 1983. [Add: M. Veggeti, D. Lanza, *La Donna Antica*, Turin, 1982; A.M. Vérilliac, éd., *La femme dans le monde méditerranéen 1. Antiquité*, Lyon, 1985.]

[2] From the extensive bibliography on the problem it suffices here to refer to the recent work of C. Mazzucco, *"E fui fatta maschio" La donna nel cristianesimo primitivo (secoli I-III)*, Florence, 1989, with good documentation. However it seems that the results of this study of the female condition in the early centuries is weakened by the almost total silence of the author on the problem of encratite currents and more generally of manifold rigorist tendencies in the matter of sexual continence which strongly conditioned the image and the role of woman in the picture of Christian spirituality of the time. Cf. also *eadem*, 'Figure di donne cristiane: la martire,' in R. Uglione (ed.), *Atti del II Convegno. op. cit.*, 167-195; A.V. Nazzaro, 'Figure di donne cristiane: la vedova,' *ibidem*, 197-219. An extensive and balanced discussion on the theme in E.A. Clark, 'Devil's Gateway and Bride of Christ: Women in the Early Christian World,' in *eadem, Ascetic Piety and Women's Faith. Essays on Late Ancient Christianity*, New York-Toronto, 1986, 23-60, For the 4th-5th centuries apart from E. Giannarelli, *La tipologia femminile nella biografia e nella autobiografia cristiana del IV secolo*, Rome, 1980; *eadem* (ed.), *S. Gregorio di Nissa, Vita di S. Macrina*, Milan, 1988, cf. F.E. Consolino, *Modelli di comportamento e modi di santificazione per l'aristocrazia femminile di Occidente*, in A. Giardina (ed.), *Società romana e impero tardo-antico, I, Istituzioni, ceti, economie*, Bari, 1986, 273-306 and 684-699 (notes); L. Cracco Ruggini, 'La donna e il sacro, tra paganesimo e cristianesimo,' in R. Uglione (ed.), *Atti del II Convegno, op. cit.*, 129-179. [Engl. ed. Add: J. Bremmer, 'Why did Early Christianity attract Upper class Women,' in *Fructus centesimus, Mélanges. G.J.M. Bartelink*, Steenbrugis, 1989, 37-47.]

Such a system of values in the early Christian centuries is linked more or less strictly by distinction or absolutely by contrast with what relates to the condition of celibacy in its double aspect of virginity or widowhood, or even to voluntary continence within the state of marriage itself. It should be stressed finally that the image of the couple is generally strongly conditioned by certain postulates characteristic of the tradition of *enkrateia* described above.

(I) TERTULLIAN

This conditioning is clearly perceptible in Tertullian, who, in the eschatological tension of his religious experience, which emerged acutely during his Montanist phase, and in the ethical rigorism which characterized his faith, with its uncompromising adhesion to the newness of the gospel, represents one of the most significant testimonies of this tradition.

Within it, he is located on the moderate side because of his recognition — against the gnostics and Marcionites — of the liceity of the practice of marriage, reaffirmed even in the Montanist phase of his spiritual odyssey.

However, the peculiar traits of his acerbic temperament and of his rhetorically constructed language frequently translate into arguments extremist in tone which cast long shadows on the sexual reality connected with desire and pleasure,[3] and describe the prac-

---

[3] In Ad *uxorem* is seen the strict, if not exclusive, conjunction established between the regime of matrimony and the *concupiscentia carnis* apart from *concupiscentia saeculi* (I,IV,2: SC 273,102-103 and the entire discussion is developed in ##3-8, 102-107). Full discussion on these themes in the well documented commentary in the Italian translation of this and other works on matrimony of the African author in P.A. Gramaglia, *Tertulliano II matrimonio nel cristianesimo preniceno*, Rome, 1988. Cf. also M. Turcan, 'Le mariage en question? Ou les avantages du célibat selon Tertullien,' in *Mélanges de philosophie, de littérature et d'histoire ancienne offerts à Pierre Boyancé*, Rome, 1974, 711-720; R. Uglione, 'Il matrimonio in Tertulliano tra esaltazione e disprezzo,' *Ephemerides liturgicae* 93 (1979), 479-494. On the ethics of Tertullian see M. Spannuet, *Tertulien et les premiers moralistes africains*, Paris, 1969. [Engl. ed. Add: C.B. Daly, *Tertullian the Puritan*, Dublin, 1994 =*Irish Ecclesiastical Record* 69 (1947) 693-707, 815-821; 70 (1948) 731-746, 832-848]; S. Heine, *Women and Early Christianity. Are the Feminist Scholars Right?* London, 1987 (German orig. Göttingen 1986).

tice of marriage in terms and images that are frankly disparaging.[4] At the same time the presence of protological motives in virginal *enkrateia*, connected with the state of integrity of our first parents, is pointed to as a privileged instrument for the anticipated realization on the part of the Christian of the eschatological condition with the acquisition of "angelic likenesses" which he notes the Gospel text (for they are equal to the angels: Lk 20:34-36) reserves to the risen,[6] defines a scenario in which the matrimonial sphere emerges as "second" and "secondary" in the religious perspective on the basis of the particular exegesis of the statement of Paul in 1 Cor 7:6, a "concession" of the Creator to mankind by now decadent.[7]

To connote this sphere in an ambiguous sense, there frequently intervene then attitudes quite acerbic, though sometimes it is the rhetorical ardor of his discourse that determines the derogatory tone in confronting the feminine component of the couple, on the role attributed to whom depends in large measure the evaluation of the relationship begun in it.

The motif in Tertullian of the peculiar connection of Eve and through her of actual women with sin,[8] is well known, underlining the link between feminine behavior and seduction which finds its exemplary and prototypical model in the context of marriage be-

---

[4] It suffices to mention, in the context of a particular exegesis of Lk 17:27-28 [they ate and drank, they took husbands and wives right up to the day Noah entered the ark] developed in the first book of the treatise *Ad uxorem,* the definition of marriage, together with that of commercial activities. The author, in fact, says: "This is not limited simply to the combination of matrimony and business; when, however, he says: 'they took husbands and wives, they bought and sold' (Lk 17:27-28), is meant to denounce particularly these two vices which are the most vicious, of the flesh and of the world, which have the greatest capacity to alienate from the moral norms enunciated by God, the first with sexual lack of control and the latter with the longing for possessions" (*Ad uxorem suam* 1,V,4).

[5] Cf. *De patientia* V,5-10: CCL 2,1, 303-304; *De carne Christi* XVII,3-6: CCSL 2,2, 904-905. For a more extensive discussion see *Enkrateia e antropologia, op.cit.,* 174-184.

[6] *Exhortation to chastity* XIII,4: CCL 2,2, 1035.

[7] Cf. *supra,* note 22, p. 69.

[8] In particular see *On the Apparel of Women* where the author by referring to the interlocutors as "my dearest sisters" exhorts them to consider their own case in relation to Eve's transgression. From them, in fact, the woman derives a penal inheritance, the ignominy of original sin which has caused the fall of the human race and the death of Christ. However she ought to assume the attitudes of penitence and sorrow. Further, the experience of the sorrows of maternity and of subjection to a husband are the tangible sign of which in Eve has penalized all women (I,1-2: CCL 2,1, 343). For recent editions and commentary see also M. Turcan, *Tertullien La toilette femmes* (SC 173), Paris, 1971 and S. Isetta, *Tertulliano. L'eleganza delle donne De cultu feminarum* (BP6), Florence, 1986.

tween "the sons of God" and the "daughters of men" in Genesis 6:1-4. Tertullian interprets such an event, through the mediation of the *Book of Enoch*, a Jewish apocryphal work, which he recognized almost on a par with that of canonical scriptures,[9] as a union between angels and women to whom they taught magical arts and all sorts of harmful techniques.

In his treatise, *That Virgins should wear Veils*, to affirm the need for all women to wear veils on their heads, Tertullian proposed the motive of the "natural" subjection of the woman,[10] and the related theme of her own finalization through man,[11] on the authority of Paul in 1 Cor 11:8-9.

Without denying to her the quality of "image" of God, the author establishes however on this proposition a sense of values recognizing a "more familiar" image of God in the man, in comparison with whom the woman — in the person of Eve — has acted negatively by inducing to sin.[12]

In consideration of all this, it is not surprising that in the entire literary production of Tertullian only the two selections from *To His Wife* included here could be found as expressing the image of relationship between spouses that characterize the author. But at the same time it should be recognized that, in the entire patristic literature on the theme, these pages are among the most vivid and clear

---

[9] *De virginibus velandis* VII, 2-4: CCL 2,2, 1216. See Italian translation, with introduction and commentary of P. A. Gramaglia, *De virginibus velandis. La condizione femminile nelle prime comunità cristiane*, Rome, 1981, 253-257.

[10] *Ibidem* X, I, 1219, where the obligation of every woman, married or virgin, to wear a veil on her head is justified as follows: "Moreover, it would be sufficiently contrary to normal human life if women who ought to remain in total submission to men, would expect to show in public a distinctive sign to put on exhibition the prestige of their virginity."

[11] *Ibidem* VII, 2, 1216: "If man was not made from woman but woman from man (1 Cor 11:8-9) well then the rib of Adam was first of all a virgin (1 Cor 11:8-9). If the woman ought to carry a sign of submission on her head (1 Cor 11:10), it is still more proper that she be above all a virgin."
    The latter statement is justified in the light of the relationship established by Tertullian between the mention of angels in the Pauline text and the event of the marriage of angels with the sons of men narrated in late Jewish Apocrypha, and in particular in the *Book of Enoch* (cf. *supra*, note 25, p. 25 and note 9, p. 77).

[12] *De virginibus velandis* X,4: CCSL 2,2, 1220. For the judgment of Tertullian on woman, apart from the old work of G. Cortellezzi, 'Il concetto della donna nelle opere di Tertulliano,' in *Didaskaleion N.S.* 1 (1923), fasc. 1,5-29; fasc. 2,57-79; fasc. 3,43-100, see F. Forrester, 'Church, Sex and Salvation in Tertullian,' *HThR* 68 (1975), 83-101 and C. Tibiletti, 'La donna in Tertulliano,' in Aa. vv., *Misosoginia e maschilismo in Grecia e in Roma, op. cit.*, 69-95.

expressions of personal sentiment, from which emerge the aspiration to a total communion, physical as well as spiritual, as distinctive and qualifying traits of the nuptial relationship.

Placing such a relationship under the Christian sign, Tertullian outlines a portrait of complete dedication of one to the other and a common religious ideal in which the man and woman are situated on a perfectly equal plane. The affirmation according to which the two are "brothers and collaborators at the same time, no difference between flesh and spirit" (no. 2) resounds in fact as one of the clearest statements of the dignity of an existential condition which by being described here in existentially religious terms, is not lacking a natural, human basis in which the author, despite the positions taken as mentioned above, shows that he recognizes an intrinsic value.

(II) CLEMENT OF ALEXANDRIA

Clement of Alexandria's position is characterized by a delicate balance in evaluating the diverse aspects of human life and the different spheres, physical and spiritual, which concur in the correct development of personal and social levels. The author's cultural development, deeply rooted in the Greek philosophical tradition, furnished the weapons for an interpretation of the Christian message at the theological and ethical level which, while maintaining the specificity of its contents, utilized structural and formal currents of the contemporary cultural ambiences.

The biblical notion of the positive nature of the whole of creation, and particularly of the practice of marriage, is expressed according to the canons of Stoic ethics of which Musonius Rufus offered a typical exemplification, within the ambit of arguments which insist on the opportunity, indeed the obligation of the wise man, to undertake marriage and to participate, by means of procreation, in the creative work of God.[13]

---

[13] Cf. Texts nn. 3-4. Fundamental on the theme is the work of J.-P. Broudeaux, *Mariage et famille chez Clément d'Alexandrie*, Paris, 1970. See also. M. Mees, 'Clemens von Alexandrien über Ehe und Famile,' *AugR* 17 (1977), 113-131 and, on the problem of second marriage, Y. Tissot, 'Henogamie et remariage chez Clément d'Alexandrie,' *RSLR* 10 (1975), 167-197. For the presence of Stoic elements in the patristic tradition see M. Spannuet, *Le stoïcisme des Pères de l'église de Clément de Rome a Clément d'Alexandrie,* Paris, 1957.

The image of the "true gnostic,"[14] typical of the spiritual horizons of the Alexandrian, that is, of the perfect Christian who combines ethical and intellectual training for the attainment of this "knowledge (gnosis)" which were pursued by so many contemporary movements within the systems of ontological dualism, anti-cosmic and anti-somatic, is analogous to the Stoic model, that of a man who does not practice a radical renunciation of the world but discharges his own social obligations by an internal disposition of distancing himself from the passions, with temperance as one of its special characteristics.

Into this perspective re-enters the practice of marriage from which is excluded all passionate irrational elements (nn. 5-6), finding its proper end in the legitimate procreation of children (nn. 3-4). Such practice results therefore in Clement, placed on a level pretty much homologous to that of *enkrateia*, once in its ample and nuanced polemic against the opposing extreme positions of the encratite and libertine gnostics in Book III of the *Stromata*, he defends with all the arguments of Christian and Stoic ethics the complete legitimacy of the exercise of sexuality which, at the heart of the institution of marriage, is revealed as a necessary dimension of the social nature of man, inasmuch as it is an instrument to safeguard the structure of the organized civil community, of which the family is the basis, and their perpetuation through the procreation of children.

Also present in Clement, as throughout the entire patristic tradition, is the motif of the superior religious value of virginity and of continence. This, joined to the theme of the exclusive marriage/generation connection, is reflected in the repeated affirmation of the necessity to eliminate every element of passion from the couple's relationship and to terminate sexual relations after childbirth (no.

---

[14] Cf. W. Völker, *Der wahre Gnostiker nach Clemens Alexandrinus* (TU 57), Berlin-Leipzig, 1952. For the convergence in Clement of philosophical interests, on the one hand, and the science of scripture and Christian spirituality, on the other, see P. Guilloux, 'L'ascétisme de Clément d'Alexandrie,' *RAM* 3 (1922), 282-300; C. Mondésert, *Clément d'Alexandrie. Introduction a l'étude de sa pensée religieuse à partir de l'Écriture*, Paris, 1944; P.Th. Camelot, *Foi et gnose. Introduction à l'étude de la connaissance mystique chez Clément d'Alexandrie*, Paris, 1945; S, Lilla, *Clement of Alexandria. A Study in Christian Platonism and Gnosticism*, Oxford, 1971. On the relationship between the notions of faith and of knowledge in the early centuries of Christianity cf. G. Sfameni Gasparro, 'Fede, rivelazione e gnosi nel cristianesimo e nello gnosticismo,' in *eadem, Origene, op. cit.*, 13-99.

7). In this way the sexual union is represented as the privileged condition of encounter and harmonization between two equally cogent exigencies of the conscience of the Christian, on the one hand, the biblical invitation to increase and multiply, and to assume entirely one's proper role in society and, on the other, the religious obligation to an undivided dedication to spiritual realities and the eschatological tensions proper to the Christian message.

Another theme, in which the Christian foundations and the cultural component of the Greek philosophical ascendancy of the Alexandrian, is encountered and well worked out is that of the equality of men and women vis-a-vis virtue and religious activity, on the basis of the common nature of human beings as such (nn. 8-9). Here, in fact, can be seen the convergence of the Pauline statement in Galatians 3:28, according to which, in Christ, together with all other distinctions, that of male and female is abolished, and of the postulates of the Socratic-Platonic and Stoic schools on the equality of aptitude for virtue in both sexes, given their common human nature and their right to equal education.

Our author's affirmation that the woman ought to dedicate herself to "philosophy" on the same level as the male to grasp the knowledge of virtue and practice it, uses that very same term whose meaning was widely accepted in an ethical-practical sense of the knowledge of human nature for the realization of a moral ideal of perfection,[15] already exemplified in Musonius Rufus. This usage confirms the profound incidence of these postulates in the definition of the anthropological vision of Clement.

The notion of the absence of any distinction, on the spiritual level, between male and female, moreover, if connected in a special manner to the identification of the human quality of "image of God" in the intellectual component, the *nous*, a prerogative of being human, apart from sexual differences, on Philonian lines is deftly affirmed by the Alexandrian.[16]

---

[15] Cf. A.-M. Malingrey, *op. cit.*, 129-157.

[16] A. Meyer, *Das Bildgottes im Mensch nach Clemens von Alexandrien*, Rome, 1942, and the very extensive treatment of the theme in the Fathers cf. H.C. Graf, 'L'image de Dieu et la structure de l'ame d'après les Pères grecs,' *La vie spirituelle, Supplément. 22* (1955), 331-

It is significant to note the resonance, in this context, of a motif recurring in various ways in the tradition of *enkrateia* which, by counterposing to the distinction between the sexes an original state of integrity understood also as undivided "unity" and perfect total-ity, indicates in the term "concupiscence" (*epithumia*), typically con-nected with the exercise of sexuality in which such distinction be-comes effective, the factor of rupture and disintegration of this state. Present already in Philo[17] and in encratite and gnostic contexts,[18] this motive underlies Clement's affirmation that (no. 8) "only in this world is the female differentiated from the male. There the reward of a life in matrimony passed in common and sanctified, will not be reserved to male and to female, but to humanity, which is far removed from concupiscence which divides them in two."

The quality of *epithumia* in fact is the basis and moving force of that sexual differentiation which "breaks in two" human beings whose true nature transcends such differences to concentrate com-pletely on the spiritual dimension. The exercise of virtue in the framework of the Christian life, while it has its place for the prac-tice of marriage, is when it has fulfilled its procreative function (no. 7) and especially in the eschatological dimension in which the hu-man being will be liberated from all physical conditions.[19]

It is equally important to indicate how this motive of the abo-lition of sexual distinctions, in the same context is accompanied by that, equally typical, of the transformation of woman into man, by

---

339; P.Th. Camelot, 'La théologie de l'image de Dieu,' *RScPhTh* 40 (1956), 443-471 and in particular, for Alexandrian authors, W.J. Burghardt, 'The Image of God in Man: Alexandrian Orientations,' in *The Catholic Theological Society of America, Proceedings of the Sixteenth Annual Convention,* Ottawa, Ontario, June 19-22,1961, 147-160.

[17] *De creatione mundi* 151-152, ed. R. Arnaldez, Paris, 1961, 242-243; *De alleg Leg.* 11,71-73, ed. C. Mondésert, Paris, 1962, 142-143. For a discussion on these texts and in general on the position of Philo on the problems of sexuality see G. Sfameni Gasparo, *Enkrateia e antropologia, op. cit.,* 323-341.

[18] Cf. *Enkrateia e antropologia, op. cit.,* 56-166. On the theme, already present in the literature of late Judaism on Adam (*ibidem*, 356-358), see also M.V. Cerutti, 'Epithymia e phthora nei testi tardo-giudaici e gnostici (Apocalisse di Mosè e apocalisse di Adamo),' *RivBibl* 36 (1988), 199-227.

[19] On the theme of the abolition of the distinction between the sexes in an eschatological per-spective, apart from the study of B. Lang, cited *supra,* note 11, p. 63 see M. Delcourt, 'Utrumque neutrum,' in *Mélanges d'histoire des religions offerts a H.Ch. Puech,* Paris, 1974, 117-123.

expressing the achievement of perfection through the metaphor of male as preeminent value with respect to the female.[20]

Apart from the metaphor, widely diffused in various ambiences, pagan, Jewish and Christian, it should also be noted that notwith-standing the affirmation of ethical and religious parity between the two members of the married pair, Clement accepts the consolidated scheme of man's superiority to the woman (no. 9), who, according to the formula of Genesis, is seen in the peculiar role of "helper," (nn. 4 and 10) and, on the authority of Paul, invited to be submis-sive. In particular, the obvious biological differences between the sexes, while, on the one hand, being the foundation of the complementarity of the two persons involved in the union, on the other hand, are retained by the author as introduction and founda-tion of a clear distinction of familial and social roles. So, the natural maternal function of the woman is connected to her exclusive do-mestic role (no. 9) according to prevalent contemporary sociologi-cal parameters.

The citation of 1 Cor 11:3 — *the head of a woman is her hus-band* — by confirming this scheme of submission, along with evok-ing the image of man as head and the derivation from him of the woman (11:8) is careful, however, to repeat at the same time the indispensable convergence of the two. He in fact also adduces the concluding v. 11 (*Yet in the Lord woman is not independent of man, or man of woman*) which completes the balanced perspective, which in other authors is almost completely absent with the result of fur-ther underlining the hierarchical relationship.

---

[20] For the history of this notion Philo proves to be one of the most authoritative sources (cf. R. A. Baer, Jr. *op. cit.*, 45-64; 69-71), see K. Vogt, '"Divenire maschio" Aspetti di un'antropologia cristiana primitiva,' *Concilium* 6 (1985), 102-117. The theme is present in various sectors of primitive Christianity, in the literature of the martyrs (*The Passion of Perpetua* 10,7, ed. Beek p. 26,7) in Valentinianism (*Extracts of Theodotus* 21,3, ed. F. Sagnard SC 23bis, Paris, 1970, 90-101; *Extracts of Theodotus* 79, *ibid.*, 202-203; Heracleon fr. 5 in W. Völker, *Quellen zur Geschichte der christlichen Gnosis*, Tübingen, 1932, 65, cf. M. Simonetti, *Testi gnostici cristiani*, Bari, 1970, 140, 229 and 256) and in a text of strong encratite import discovered among the Nag Hammadi codices in the *Gospel of Thomas* (logion 114, edd. A. Guillaumont et al, Leiden, 1959, 56-57; Italian trans. M. Erbetta, *Gli Apocrifi del Nuovo Testamento*, 1,1, Turin, 1975, 282). Cf. M.W. Meyer, 'Making Mary Male: the Categories of "Male" and "Fe-male" in the *Gospel of Thomas*,' *NTS* 31 (1985), 554-570; J.J. Buckley, 'An Interpretation of Logion 114 in the Gospel of Thomas,' *Novum Testamentum* 27 (1985), 245-272; *eadem, Female Fault and Fulfillment in Gnosticism*, Chapel Hill-London, 1986, 84-100.

Finally we should not overlook the considerable space given by the Alexandrian, which in other authors is almost completely absent, to the affective component of the inter-personal relationship, which, from the recognition of a certain affinity of sentiments and mutual consent in the initial choice of a companion (no. 3) touches on the various aspects of the relationship of the couple, even in their exclusively domestic aspects. In this special attention is devoted to the various functions and behavioral patterns of the wife who is frequently urged by Clement to practice temperance, modesty and in general the exercise of Christian virtue.

At the center of the couple, then, to the wife is entrusted, in the concrete circumstances of daily life, a more ample and decisive role in the realization of that ideal of harmony and community of interests in which, for the author, resides the final end of the matrimonial union.

The affirmation of *Stromata* IV, 123, 2 (no. 12) according to which "the temperate woman will first and foremost choose to persuade her husband to be her associate in what is conducive to happiness," that is, in the fulfillment of the religious and ethical imperative, confirms this peculiar aspect of the image of the Christian couple.

(III) ORIGEN

In Origen the problematic relative to the man/woman relationship in its matrimonial dimension is joined, not only, as in other authors, to the general theme of the respective value which the choice of marriage and of celibacy and continence assumed for the Christian, but calls in question the entire complex ideological portrait of the author with his peculiar anthropological and cosmological vision structured around his scheme of "double creation" to which we have already referred.[21] It is, however essential to recall, if only in general lines, the positions of the Alexandrian teacher, on questions relative to sexuality and the practice of marriage to which the theme of the couple is bound in a manner that cannot be ignored.

---

[21] See *supra*, notes 2-3, pp. 5-6.

We might also add that this last theme, in its specific validity of interpersonal relations between man and woman and definition of their respective roles, occupies a much reduced space within Origen's horizons.

This is the case although a large part of Origen's literary output, whether made up of homilies devoted to the instruction of the people, or established as the teaching of the author, based on the exegesis of the biblical text read in the Christian liturgy, insists on fundamental ethical parameters which ought to regulate the behavior of the faithful for the attainment of moral purification without studying in depth a parenesis specifically directed to the Christian couple.

Naturally, questions of sexual ethics frequently recur in the broader picture of exhortation on the part of the preacher[22] to practice virtue as in references to the institutional aspect of marriage,[23] but nevertheless the author's reticence with regard to the most intimate aspects of the personal relations of the spouses seems noteworthy.

The directives of the ideological horizons of Origen, rich in intellectual tensions and profoundly marked with ethical, ascetical and mystical requirements are made up first and foremost of solidly founded biblical faith in one only God the Creator and through Christ the Savior with all the corollaries of this which are set forth in the preface to On Principles,[24] together with certain presuppositions originating in Greek philosophy, especially Platonic, which the author drew from the common cultural patrimony of his day with which the breadth and profundity of his intellectual interests had already been familiarized.[25]

---

[22] Cf. A. Monaci Castagno, Origene predicators e il suo pubblico, Milan, 1987, 188-201.

[23] For a careful and balanced analysis of Origen's conception cf. H. Crouzel, Virginité et mariage selon Origène, Paris-Bruges, 1963.

[24] De Princ. Pref. edd. H. Crouzel - M. Simonetti (SC 252), Paris, 1978, 76-89; Italian translation with full commentary: M. Simonetti, I Principi di Origene, Turin, 1968, 76-89.

[25] For information on this and other aspects of Origen's physiognomy, the object of numerous critical studies, it suffices to refer to H. Crouzel, Bibliographie critique d'Origène (The Hague, 1971) with Supplément I (The Hague, 1980); Supplément II, 1996, sv. The ongoing interest in the multiform works of the Alexandrian is obvious from the regular organization of International Colloquia entirely dedicated to the study of this author, for instance in Boston (August, 1989) which had as its theme "Origen and Philosophy" [Engl. ed. For more recent work see H. Crouzel, 'Bibliographie,' Supplément II, Turnhout, 1996, and J.W. Trigg, 'Origen and Origenism in the 1990's,' Religious Studies Review 22 (1996), 301-308.]

In his determination to formulate a rationally coherent explanation of the essential contents of revelation in respect to the common deposit of faith safeguarded in the ecclesiastical tradition, Origen was solicitous about a problem fairly widely debated in Christian circles of the time, and likewise commanding the attention of pagan thinkers, albeit in the diversity of their respective ideological contexts, that is, that of reconciling the divine attributes of goodness and justice, whether in the equilibrium of their theological picture, or more particularly in relation to the governance of the world, and to the widely different conditions of rational beings.

The Alexandrian teacher, like numerous other Fathers, intended to refute solutions of a dualistic nature proposed by gnostic movements. In particular, Marcion and his followers made a distinction between a just God, identified with the Creator revealed in the Old Testament and a good God, known first through the revelation in Jesus.[26] The Valentinians, counterposing the divine *Pleroma* ("world of fullness") at the cosmic level, material shaped and presided over by the Demiurge and his archons, had theorized the existence of three substances, respectively spiritual, psychical (i.e. "animal") and material, corresponding, on the one hand, to that reality (the spiritual *pleroma*, the psychic Demiurge and the material cosmos) and, on the other hand, converging at the anthropological level by humanity being composed of three categories (the spiritual, the psychic, and the material) differing in nature, origin and destiny.[27]

---

[26] Notwithstanding the interpretation of A. von Harnack who made of Marcion "a biblical theologian" on radical Pauline lines (*Marcion. Das Evangelium vom fremden Gott*, Leipzig, 1924), for the most part it has been recognized as legitimate to situate Marcion in a wider context of gnosticism, tied to radical ditheism and especially anti-cosmism and anti-somatism, notwithstanding some original aspects of his positions, that are not reducible to general gnostic parameters. Cf. H. Jonas, *op. cit.*, 153-163; R.M. Grant, *op. cit.*, 134-140; U. Bianchi, 'Marcion: théologien biblique ou docteur gnostique?,' in *idem, Selected Essays, op. cit.*, 320-327. We cannot, however, endorse the recent interpretation of E. Norelli, 'La funzione di Paolo nel pensiero di Marcione,' *RivBibl* 34 (1986), 543-597, which substantially reintroduces the figure of Marcion in Harnack's exegetical schemes. A substantial influence of middle platonic philosophy on the dualism of Marcion and a profound diversity of his thought with respect to gnosticism are affirmed by I.P. Couliano, *op. cit.*, 175-192.

[27] For many aspects of Valentinianism the analysis of F. Sagnard (*La gnose valentinienne et le témoignage de Saint Irénée*, Paris, 1947) remains still valid, and especially that of A. Orbe (*Estudios Valentinianos, I-V*, Rome, 1955-1966), although the research on this important gnostic current has assumed broader dimensions, especially with regard to the discovery of the collection of Gnostic texts in the Coptic codices of Nag Hammadi which in large measure reflects precisely the teachings of Valentinian ambience.

In the face of Marcionite ditheism, and, even more so, the gnostic dichotomy between the divine and demiurgic-archontic levels, in the distinction and juxtaposition between the Old Testament economy and that of the Christian, Origen proposed a solution which, while presented as a personal interpretative "hypothesis," in his view was the only one adapted to maintain in its integrity the biblical postulate of one only God, who was good and just and, at the same time, to justify the profound diversity of the conditions of rational creatures without having to seek recourse in a theory of distinct natures.

In fact, in the eyes of the Alexandrian teacher, as in the eyes of all his contemporaries, be they Christians, Jews or pagans, the world appeared populated with beings endowed with reason, in distinct categories of good and bad. There is question, on the one hand, of angels and demons in the Jewish-Christian tradition, and, on the other, of *daimones* in the pagan tradition, in which there is a confluence of ancient Greek, Roman and Oriental concepts, representing a panorama of quite articulated creatures, yet solidly dominated by the idea of a hierarchical structure of rational beings, active at different cosmic levels and capable of influencing human life.

The Origenian "hypothesis" is articulated on the double postulate of preexistence, clearly derived from Platonism, and of a "double creation" with the related notion of an "antecedent fault." This implies, then, the admission of a primary creative act by God who, in His goodness and justice, placed in existence rational creatures (in Origen's language, *noï, mentes*), all equal by nature and endowed with free-will, in a condition of perfection, which, while contemplating in all likelihood also a form of "ethereal" corporeity which indicates their creaturely condition, is characterized in the sense of spirituality as being exempt from matter and is expressed in biblical terms of participation in the "image" of God.[28]

Such a quality, in fact, inheres in the intelligent creature as a distinctive and qualifying element of its rational nature, an "image"

---

[28] On this theme, apart from the fundamental contribution of H. Crouzel (*Théologie de l'image, op. cit.*); see also the studies in *Origene, op. cit.*, 101-192, where the relative documentation will be found.

of the divine Logos. However, because of a greater or less removal of the "ardor" of the divine love, possible because of the free-will of the creature and motivated by a sort of satiety of goodness, or negligence in adhering to it[29] passing to a condition of soul.[30] In this way, differing in the respective movements of the "fall," they lapse from unity to the original equality in multiplicity and diversity.

A second intervention of God providentially furnishes a material support to creatures who receive a corporeity of differing "heaviness" in relation to the gravity of individual faults.

In this way is realized the creation of the world and is constituted the three categories of angels, men and demons who actually populate it. The first are intelligent beings who have persevered in good, that is, are not alienated in the least degree,[31] and the latter are those who have grave sin, affirming also the responsibility of one of them, Lucifer-Satan of the Jewish-Christian tradition, of having initiated the general process of decadence.

Humanity, then, is made up of rational beings endowed with a material body with physiological and sexually differentiated functions in whom the original intellect persists in the condition of a rational soul (="cool" intellect) seeing that the anthropology of Origen is not constructed in a rigidly systematic manner. It is expressed in fact sometimes in a trichotomous formula — body, intellect, soul — the last-named being the mediating element between the other two. To such constitutive components of man is joined the spirit (*pneuma*) which is a superior faculty, a divine gift through which is accomplished the work of sanctification of the creature,[32]

---

[29] *I Principi*, 11,9,2, trad. Simonetti, p. 318. Cf. M. Harl, 'Recherches sur l'origenisme d'Origène: la "satiété" (*koros*) de la contemplation comme motif de la chute des ames,' *Stud Pat* VIII, Berlin, 1966, 373-405.

[30] *De Principiis* 11,8,2-3, Ital. trans., Simonetti, 305-312. This affirmation is based on a particular etymology, already present in the Greek tradition which connects *psyché* (soul) with *psychrōs* (cold). Cf. Plato, *Cratylus* 399D-E. Aristotle, *De anima* 1,2. Already Philo had put forward such an etymological interpretation *(On Dreams* 1, 30-32).

[31] Some passages in Origen permit the conclusion that, together with those which had come from the soul of Christ, some other intelligent preexisting creatures had no sin. Cf. M. Simonetti, 'Due note sull'angelologia origeniana, II. Sulla caduta degli angeli,' *RCCM* 4 (1962),180-208.

[32] H. Crouzel, 'L'anthropologie d'Origène dans la perspective du combat spirituel,' *RAM* 31 (1955), 364-385; J. Dupuis, *"L'esprit de l'homme." Etude sur l'anthropologie religieuse d'Origène*, Bruges, 1967.

while remaining moreover the essential faculty of free choice inherent in the animal-rational dimension, in which persists the quality of "image" of God constituting the ontological foundation of the creature and the presupposition of his ethical choice.

The material dimension of man is both the sign of that "antecedent fault" which has brought about the downfall of the rational creature and the location of its purification.

Origen in fact insists on the intrinsic goodness of God's second creative act, biblically expressed in the "fashioning" of Gn 2:7, and in its primary providential and salvific function, forcefully rejecting the anti-cosmic and anti-somatic positions of the gnostics.

The world then and the body are intrinsically positive realities, in their ontological consistence and their finality. However they remain equally logically "second" and "secondary" with respect to the preeminent dignity of the rational component of the creature and the sign and place of its decadence.

An essential and qualifying element of Origen's cosmological and anthropological vision turns out to be, as we have shown elsewhere,[33] the notion of a "contaminating" effect exercised on cosmic reality, in as much as it is a theater for creatures who are actually wicked and instigators of evil and of a struggle which man must sustain against being and of the soul-rational component. By contact with this reality the intelligent creature endures "contamination," a quality very different from sin which implies a voluntary violation of an ethical norm. Such contamination however remains profoundly active in defining a state of "impurity" and of imperfection of the same creature who ought to be liberated from this by realizing his own salvation.

In particular, sexual activities render this state of impurity operative and sustaining, which, on the one hand, inheres in the same modality of birth and, on the other, its own efficacious potency in the exercise of such activity.

In Origen besides, to the notion of "antecedent fault" which anthropology binds in an unquestionable manner to a protological

---

[33] G. Sfameni Gasparro, 'Le sordes (*ruphos*), il rapporto genesis-*phthorà* e le motivazioni protologiche dell'*enkrateia* in Origene,' in *eadem, Origene, op. cit.*, 193-252.

scheme gradated in two moments (the "first" and the "second" creation), between which is situated a rupture which defines the second and, to be precise, the corporeal dimension of actual man, with all its physiological functions and sexual differentiations in terms of decadence. To this is joined that of the "historical" sin of Adam joining the common Judaeo-Christian tradition relative to the event in Genesis.

According to the author the first human couple's transgression in its ethical motivation of proud rebellion against a divine precept, is at the same time at the origin of nuptial practice, that protological motivation of continence and virginity intervening which qualified large sectors of the tradition of *enkrateia*.

Origen, in a rather important passage in his *Commentary on 1 Corinthians*, asserts that in God's creative project the finality of the human body, while being sexually differentiated, had no physical union and procreation, but rather a virginal integrity which would have made of it a "temple" of the Spirit in the uninterrupted exercise of prayer and of the soul's tension toward God.[34]

Defined as a protological scenario articulated in successive moments, each of which places a precise mortgage on the significance and value of the practice of matrimony, which, while retaining legitimacy insofar as it is granted as a "concession" to humanity as a remedy for their "weakness"[35] is however tied to a situation of double decadence, that of a creature of pre-existence come in a cosmic and bodily-material dimension, and that of humanity derived from the primal couple who have transgressed a divine precept.

In the picture of decisive ethico-ascetical appeals of the spirituality of Origen which intervene to characterize his notion of virginity and continence, exalted as essential values in the Christian experience, all the weight exercised by the protological motivations which concur to define it should not be overlooked. Such motivations also in fact qualify the image of the couple, whose reality for the author occupies a legitimate post in the Christian life and rep-

---

[34] Fr. XXIX in I Cor, ed. C. Jenkins, *JThS* 9 (1908) 370,1-371,2. Cf. F. Cocchini, *Origene, Commento alla Letters ai Romani*, 1, Casale Monferrato, 1985, 291-292.

[35] Cf. note 23, p. 69.

resent on the contrary the more common condition of the faithful faced with the choice of celibacy and continence of some of them.

In fact, the selections which illustrate the theme of "harmony of the couple" (nn. 17-18) recognize the quality of "charism" in the matrimonial union experienced in reciprocal concord and in the observance of religious norms.

The exercise of prayer, which Origen elsewhere, on the authority of the Pauline dictate, links to agreement of the spouses in the practice of continence[36] and "holy procreation" are indicated as the two complementary factors of a personal relationship which appears dominated by religious experience once the true couple is that constituted from believers. In such a relationship, there is active, as in other authors, the hierarchical man/woman scheme which imposes love on the first and submission on the second, according to the exemplary norms established by the Apostle.

Origen, in conformity with his fundamental postulate which identifies the quality of "image" of God in rational nature in which every creature participates, irrespective of sexual differences, recognizes such a faculty in woman on an equal basis with man, and definitely affirms the equal ethical and religious capacity of the two sexes (no. 16). However, while the sociological parameter remains active of submission of the wife to the husband in the common conduct of life, in Origen a considerable space is occupied by the use of the metaphor, derived from Philo, of woman as "weak," connected with the sphere of the passions, or, frankly, of vice.

Although sometimes there is emphasis on the distinction between the person of the woman, who can be "virile" as far as zeal for virtue is concerned (no. 16), frequently the metaphor is made to reflect all its negative connotations on the female condition to the extent that it therefore becomes considerably devalued with respect to that of the male. So, in text no. 15, with the biblical example of Sarah and Abraham, the theme of subordination of the wife to the husband is reaffirmed, nevertheless religiously defined in the sense that the "following" of the woman should be realized in the context

---

[36] Cf. note 19, p. 68.

of a husband who gives her the lead in the journey to God.

At the same time, in an outline of allegorical exegesis, the identification of the male with intellect and of the female with flesh and its characterization as the reality "wallowing in luxury and pleasures" certainly projects on the status of women an ambiguous qualification and in any case underlines the disparity of values between the two elements chosen to exemplify the teaching of the biblical text.

The same scenario emerges from the exegetical scheme adopted in the *Homilies on Genesis* to explain the "spiritual" significance of the creation of male and female (no. 14).

The motive of harmony between the two is reaffirmed, represented in terms of respect for a hierarchy of grade and function. The positive fruits of the union of the couple, in fact, emerge only in a relationship in which "concord" implies submission of the *anima*/female to the *spiritus*/male, without which the first declines toward the flesh and the related passions, defined as "adulterous."

Naturally in this context the ethico-parenetical finality of the argument of Origen and the power of metaphor prevails. But that does not reduce the significance of an ideological structure modulated on a theme of subordination of the female component of the couple and of the role of guide for the male.

There is, however, a sphere of relationship between the spouses in which Origen, in conformity with the teaching of Paul to which the whole patristic tradition is adapted, does not admit any disparity between the partners. That is the situation related to the nuptial "debt" in which the equal rights of the husband and wife are forcibly affirmed. In front of this yields the same religious imperative to continence, also quite pressing in Origen, even for the protological and eschatological motivations explained above.

In fragment XXXIII of the *Commentary on 1 Corinthians* (no. 19) the author by maintaining on the example of the Apostle a position of equilibrium between the choice of virginity and that of marriage, both open to the Christian, unhesitatingly affirms that at the center of marriage only the voluntary agreement of the two spouses can legitimate the practice of continence which, however meritorious and religiously rich in spiritual benefits, cannot contradict an inalienable right of the marriage partner, by causing spiritual ruin.

The declaration that "it is better that the two be saved by living in matrimony than, because of one, the other should mislay hope in Christ" shows how, in Origen's perspective, whatever about the profound ethico-ascetic tensions and complex intellectual pressures which characterize it, the nuptial reality is represented as one in which the two beings unite in an irrevocable manner their own human and religious destiny by assuming a value and a dignity which no individual unilateral choice, however meritorious be the underlying religious and ethical profile, can contradict.

(IV) LACTANTIUS

In the Latin patristic tradition on the theme under discussion the role of Lactantius remains rather marginal. We present in this anthology just one excerpt which effectively illustrates the common position on the indissolubility of the matrimonial bond and on the equal gravity of adultery, whether committed by the husband or the wife (no. 20).

In the general illustration of the foundations of Christian ethics, the discourse on conjugal chastity — in speaking against a practice and a mentality consolidated in the Greco-Roman tradition, which strongly discriminated against the woman in its judgment on the culpability of adultery — vehemently insisting not only on equal obligation to conjugal fidelity but also on the greater responsibility of the husband whose example of control and of affection should constitute a model and stimulus for the wife, comes like an incision.

The emphasis is placed on sentiments of mutual affection and on the conformity of habits which ought to characterize the couple's lives, on the avoidance of those ethical transgressions which pertain to adultery and on a repudiation of the resulting break-up of the profound unity expressed in terms of the image of "body" which probably suggests also an allusion to the Genesis theme of creation.

(V) AMBROSE

Ambrose's formulations assume a much more profound ideological density and become a more decisive influence on the conduct and spirituality of the Christian community. His role in the diffusion of the ascetic ideal and monastic practice in the West is in no need of detailed illustration here.[37] Equally well known are the influences of Philo and of Origen on the exegetical method of the bishop of Milan,[38] who, without sharing the hypothesis of his Alexandrian master concerning the pre-existence of the soul, shared in the notion of a peculiar contamination inherent in the practice of sex, and in the protological motivation of virginity and continence in the wider picture of ethico-ascetical demands which are the basis of this important dimension of his spirituality.[39]

The explanation in an anthropological key of the first human couple and of their abode in paradise is clearly inspired by the exegetical methods of Philo (no. 21). In the identification, Adam-intellect, Eve-sensibility, and serpent-pleasure, while the Philonian

---

[37] Among numerous studies we might mention L. Castano, 'Sant'Ambrogio apostolo della verginità,' *Salesianum* 2 (1940), 273-288; L. Dossi, 'S. Ambrogio e S. Atanasio nel De virginibus,' *Acme* 4 (1951), 241-262; Y.-M. Duval, 'L'originalité du *De virginibus* dans le mouvement ascétique occidental. Ambroise, Cyprien, Athanase,' in *idem* (ed.), *Ambroise de Milan-XVIe Centenaire de son élection épiscopale*, Paris, 1974, 9-66; V. Grossi, 'La verginità negli scritti dei Padri. La sintesi di S. Ambrogio: gli aspetti cristologici, antropologici, ecclesiali,' in Aa. vv., *Il celibato per il Regno, op. cit.*, 131-164. See, finally, the introduction of F. Gori to the edition, with Italian translation, *Ambrogio, Sulla Verginità e Sulla Vedovanza* in BA 14,1 *Opere morali*, II,I, Rome, 1989, 11-97. [Engl. ed. add: V. Burrus, 'Reading Agnes: the Rhetoric of Gender in Ambrose and Prudentius,' *JECS* 3,1 (1995), 25-41.]

[38] A.R. Sodano, 'Ambrogio e Filone. Leggendo il *De Paradiso*,' *AFLM* 8 (1975), 67-82; E. Lucchesi, *L'usage de Filon dans l'oeuvre exégètique de saint Ambroise. Une "Quellenforschung" relative aux Commentaires d'Ambroise sur la Génèse*, Leiden, 1977; H. Savon, *Saint Ambroise devant l'exégèse de Philon le Juif*, I-II, Paris, 1977. On the exegetical method of Ambrose, cf. L.F. Pizzolato, 'La Sacra Scrittura fondamento del metodo esegetico di sant'Ambrogio,' in G. Lazzati (cur.), *Ambrosius episcopus* (SPM 6), 393-426; *idem*, *La dottrina esegetico di Sant'Ambrogio* (SPM 8), Milan, 1978.

[39] Cf. *Exhortation to virginity* VI, 36: PL 16, col. 346C-D; ed. M. Salvati, *Sant'Ambrogio Scritti sulla verginità* (Corona Patrum Salesiana, Ser. lat. 6), Turin, 1939, 438-439; *Apologia di David* XI, 56, edd. P. Hadot-M. Cordier (SCh 239), Paris, 1977, 150-151; BA, *Opere esegetiche V*, Milan-Rome, 1981, 112-115. Also in the view of Ambrose, as of Tertullian and Origen, temporary abstinence from conjugal relations for more complete dedication to prayer, as seen in 1 Cor 7:5, reveals a substantial incompatibility between the practice of matrimony and divine worship. On this problematic cf. also *Exhortation to virgins* IV,23: PL 16, col. 343A-B; ed. Salvati, 424-425-1 X,26: PL 16, col. 355A-B; ed. Salvati 468-469. See *Enkrateia e antropologia, op. cit.*, 278-290.

model is decisive, there is proposed, as already in Origen, a graduated scheme centered on the couple, which clearly subordinates the
female element, and to it is applied the consolidated metaphor of
"weakness," and proneness to sensuality and pleasure.

The joint action of this exegetical scheme and of the Pauline
formula of Eph 5:32, as well as 1 P 3:16, underlines the subordination of the woman to the man, based on her derivation from him
and on the twofold reference to Genesis c. 3 and 1 Timothy 2:14,
the initiative of Eve is emphasized and as a result her greater responsibility for the sin.[40]

However, Ambrose's vision reveals a profound equilibrium and
a peculiar harmonizing tendency in the value attributed to the female component of the couple and through her typical function of
"helper."[41]

Although the typical motif of female "weakness" intervenes,
together with ethical and intellectual fragility, Ambrose really over-
turns the perspective by saying that notwithstanding her preponderant responsibility in the transgression in the garden, woman is an
element of complementarity and perfection for man himself. Without her, in fact, the creation of Adam had not yet been judged "good"
by God; it was only so pronounced after the woman's body was fashioned from his, and she would become his companion in the procreation of children.

In another passage in On Paradise Ambrose would say that, in
consequence of the sin, God has preferred the salvation of the many
to a humanity fixed in the primordial couple, complete if of course

---

[40] On Paradise 4,24: BA 2/1 66-69=text n. 22. Other loci in Ambrose insist on the motive of the
initiative of the woman in the first sin and consequently on her greater responsibility which
legitimates her subordination to her husband. Apart from the Hexaemeron text (n. 23) see
also On Paradise 6,33-34, pp. 88-91; 13,62, pp. 144-145; 14,70, pp 154-155. However, in
The Education of Virgins a justification for the fault of Eve is indicated in her weakness and
fragility, against which the serpent found victory easy, in that he had an angelic personality,
"the wisest of all." The responsibility of Adam, then, is represented as more serious, who is
left jealous of the woman (III,16-31: PL 16, col. 309C-313A; ed. Salvati, pp. 322-328).

[41] For a careful and articulated analysis of the theme see L.F. Pizzolato, 'La coppia umana in
Sant'Ambrogio,' in R. Cantalamessa (ed.), op. cit., 180-21. On the doctrine of matrimony in
Ambrose, apart from G. Oggioni, art. cit., 286-306, cf. D. Tettamanzi, 'Valori cristiani del
matrimonio nel pensiero di S. Ambrogio,' La Scuola Cattolica 102 (1974), 451-474.

lacking that historical development carried out through generation.[42]

In this way, while, on the one hand, the existential status of the primordial human couple turned out to be prototypical for the definition of the relationships of the actual couple, by implying a subordination of the woman, but also harmony in their respective roles, the text of the *Hexaemeron* (no. 23) develops the theme of love and conjugal fidelity at length along the lines of exegesis already proposed by Basil the Great.[43]

The terrain on which the two partners ought to converge is indicated in the mutual attraction of the sexes, by renouncing attitudes of intolerance or worse, of arrogance, toward husband or wife, whose shortcomings should be tolerated with a view to the realization of a harmonious relationship founded on reciprocal tenderness and understanding.

At the same time the bishop introduces the admonition, directed in the first place at husbands, to avoid adultery, the leading offence against the marriage ideal, yet once more expressed in biblical terms of separation from the original unity of that "body" which the two spouses form on the model of Eve taken from the body of Adam. This theme returns in the passage of the *Commentary on the Gospel of Luke* (no. 24) in relation with the connected problem of divorce, which not only breaks a divine precept but also contradicts the fundamental human sentiments of respect due to the one who has been the companion of one's youth.

It is significant to note that Ambrose's discourse, so exclusively directed toward males, evidently reflects a social situation in which the woman was more frequently exposed not merely to the adultery of her husband but also to abandonment on his part.[44]

---

[42] *On Paradise* 10,47 (cf. text n. 22). Cf. *De educatione virginum* III, 22: PL 16, col. 310D-311A; ed. Salvati, pp. 320-321. On the exegesis of Ambrose and the other Latin Fathers of the account of creation and the fall of the first couple in relation to ascetical appeals, see the observations of E.A. Clark, 'Heresy, Asceticism, Adam and Eve: Interpretation of Genesis 1-3 in the Later Latin Fathers,' in *eadem, Ascetic Piety, op. cit.*, 353-385.

[43] Cf. note *ad locum.*

[44] With regard to the persistence of divorce in the practice of matrimony in the Empire, even after its Christianization, see, J. Gaudemet, 'Les transformations de la vie familiale au Bas Empire et l'influence du Christianisme,' in *Romanitas* 4 (1962), 58-85, in particular 80-81. This study shows, with great balance and critical acumen, all the difficulties that stand in the way of a qualitative analysis of the influence exercised by the new Christian morality in the evolution of the institution of matrimony in juridical terms.

(VI) JEROME

To try to elicit from Jerome an image of the Christian couple might seem at first blush an undertaking of desperation, almost a provocation. We cannot here illustrate in detail the peculiar traits of his complex personality, of a prickly and obscure character, prone to polemic and ferocious satire, who does not concede anything to his adversary, but is also capable of surges of affection for his friends and disciples, especially those women who were guided in the paths of the realization of the ascetic ideal and to whom he dedicated, not just a large part of his correspondence, but also a notable part of his activity in his commentaries on the sacred Scriptures.[45]

Equally well known is the quality of his rigorous ascetic experience, experienced in both the eremitic and cenobitic forms, nourished on knowledge of the scriptures and a profound classical culture, and the decisive role exercised in its diffusion in the West, in particular among the upper-class Roman aristocracy, of the experience and forms of monastic life, male and female, born and solidly installed in the East.[46]

In order to attract the greatest possible number of the faithful to this ideal of virginity and continence, he identified one of the principal elements of the "newness" of the gospel message,[47] and especially its privileged role in its realization. Jerome did not hesitate in the ardor of parenetic or polemical argumentation to use all the

---

[45] On the ascetic and moral doctrine of Jerome it suffices to refer to F. Cavallera, 'Saint Jérôme et la vie parfaite,' *RAM* 2 (1921), 101-127; P. Antin, 'Les idées morales de S. Jérôme,' *MélScRel* 14 (1957), 135-150; *idem*, 'Le Monachisme selon Saint Jérôme,' in *Mélanges bénédictines publiées à l'occasion du XIVe centenaire de la mort de St. Bénoît*, Saint-Wandrille 1947, 71-113; *idem*, 'Saint Jérôme,' in Aa. vv., *Théologie de la vie monastique. Études sur la tradition patristique*, Paris, 1961, pp. 191-199; *idem*, 'Saint Jérôme. Directeur mystique,' *RevHistSpir* 48 (1972), 25-29. Cf. also D. Dumm, *The Theological Basis of Virginity according to St. Jerome*, Latrobe, 1961. [See now: S.D. Driver, 'The Development of Jerome's Views on the Ascetic Life,' *RTAM* 62 (1995), 44-70.]

[46] For more detailed information on the life and work of the personage cf. Introductory Profile in Introduction.

[47] Cf. Letter 22, 21 CSEL 54, 173 where the difference is emphasized between the economy of the Old Testament, in which an abundance of children was cause for happiness, and the New, introduced by the virginal birth of Christ who established virginity. In this way "He established a new household for Himself, so that He who was adored by angels in heaven might have angels also on earth." English trans. C.C. Mierow, ACW 33, 153-155.

instruments of this *vis oratoria*, and of the satiric language which he had acquired at the school of the classical authors by whom he was influenced notwithstanding the well-known frequent affirmations of "repudiation," which he could not, and would not, give up.

The result was that in adhering to notions and formulas by now consolidated and which had come down to him through the extensive literature on the theme, particularly that of Tertullian,[48] in his presentation of the state of virginity and continence, the nature and function of marriage were quite frequently frankly undervalued.

While attentive to confirming forcibly the biblical postulate of the liceity of the practice of marriage, willed by God and aimed at legitimate procreation, and to rejecting the affirmations of those who condemned such activity,[49] Jerome, especially in his polemical tracts, *Against Helvidius* written in defence of the perpetual virginity of Mary, and *Against Jovinianus*, to sustain the superior dignity of the virginal state, but also in a context directed toward instruction on this condition, like the important Letter 22, *To Eustochium*, which constitutes a sort of treatise "on virginity" which he had never written, there is demonstrated, beyond the essential ascetical and eschatological appeals proper to the theme also that whole baggage of ideas which, in the tradition of *enkrateia*, on the axiological plane strongly conditioned the relationship virginity/continence and matrimony.[50]

In the first place, together with the common definition of virginity as the "angelic life,"[51] the protological motivation is imposed as a decisive connotation of the picture, firmly binding the activity

---

[48] Cf. C. Micaelli, 'L'influsso di Tertulliano su Girolamo: le opere sul matrimonio e le seconde nozze,' *AugR* 19 (1979), 415-429. For the reconstruction of the lost treatise of Tertullian, *Ad amicum philosophum*, utilizing its use by Jerome in his *Contra Jovinianum* where there is mention of a work by Seneca cf. P. Frassinetti, 'Gli scritti matrimoniali di Seneca e Tertulliano,' *RIL* 88 (S. III,19) (1958), 151-188.

[49] Among so many places it suffices to cite Ep. 49, addressed to his friend, Pammachius, as a defence against the accusation of condemning marriage, which had been levelled against him after the diffusion of his work, *Against Jovinian*, in which, in fact, there are harsh affirmations on the theme (CSEL 54, 350-387).

[50] For a more ample documentation on this matter cf. *Enkrateia e antropologia...* pp. 290-300. On *Ad Eustochium* cf. P. Cox Millar, 'The Blazing Body: Ascetic Desire in Jerome's *Letter to Eustochium*,' *JECS 1* (1993), 21-45.

[51] See Letter XXII,2: CSEL 54, p. 146; Letter XXII,20: CSEL 54, 171.

of marriage and the sin of our first parents.[52] Virginity therefore so configured, as in all the other authors who participate in this motivation of such a restoration of the integrity of Paradise, while the marriages remain compromised with the regimen of humanity decadent and sinful.

Into this picture reenters the theme, mediated especially through the works of Tertullian, of marriage as a "concession" for the "weakness" of man according to the exegesis of the well-known dictate of Paul in 1 Cor 7:5-6, to which is linked the notion of incompatibility between prayer and religious practice in general and the exercise of the marriage right[53] which brings about "contamination."[54]

Also the theme of *molestiae nuptiarum* which Jerome inherits either from pagan literature, or from Christian, and once again from Tertullian, is unfolded in these writings to accentuate on the very plane of actual life the difference existing between the condition of virginity and continence which ensures a grand spiritual and material liberty, beyond that inequitable advantage of religious perfection, and the condition of marriage, characterized by moral worries and material troubles.[55]

However it is significant to observe how, far from polemical and parenetic exigencies, in an exegetical context like that in the *Commentary on the Epistle to the Ephesians*, occurring at Eph 5:22-23, a text which had exercised a decisive role in the patristic tradi-

---

[52] Recall, above all, the clear declaration to Eustochium: "And, that you may know that virginity is the natural state and that matrimony came after the offence: it is virgin flesh that is born of wedlock, restoring in the fruit what it had lost in the root" (Letter XXII, 19: CSEL 54, p. 169; ACW 33, 151).

[53] *Contra Iovinianum* 1,7: PL 23, col, 220A-C. Cf. also Letter XLIX, 15: CSEL 54, pp. 376-377.

[54] Cf. *Contra Elvidium* 21: PL 23 col. 205B, *Contra Iovinianum*, I 26: PL 23, col. 258 B-C; *ibidem* 1,20: PL 23, col. 249B; *ibidem* 1,37, PL 23, col. 275C; *ibidem* 1,38: PL 23, coll. 276C-277B.

[55] Cf. Letter XXII,22: CSEL 54, 174-175, where Jerome, yet once more on the authority of 1 Cor 7:28, makes reference to his own treatise, *Against Helvidius*: "How many annoyances matrimony involves and by how many anxieties it is entangled, I believe I have briefly set forth in that book I wrote, *Against Helvidius*, on the perpetual virginity of Mary.... But if you want to know from how many vexations a virgin is free, and by how many a wife is bound, read Tertullian's work, *To a Philosopher Friend* (now lost), and his other treatises on virginity." ACW 33 155. [Engl. ed. see now: D.G. Hunter, 'Helvidius, Jovinian and the Virginity of Mary in Late Fourth Century Rome,' *JECS* 1 (1993), 47-71.]

tion on the point at issue, he expresses a very balanced evaluation of man/woman relationship at the heart of marriage and there is a delineation of the image of the human couple that is in substantial conformity with those which have emerged in the patristic writings already analyzed.

For the proper understanding of some of the formulae of Jerome in this context, however, it is necessary to take account of the dependence of Jerome on a Commentary of the same title by Origen. Mentioned in the Prolog, where Jerome mentions the work of Origen, together with those of Didymus and of Apollinaris as sources of his own exegesis,[56] such dependence is however generally passed over in silence in the course of his arguments. It shows up however in a more or less clear way, either in general references to an "interpreter" which occur frequently, or in doctrinal correspondences that show dependency on Origen.[57]

This is not the place to enter into the merits of the complex question of Jerome's debt, in content and in the method of scriptural exegesis, to the great Alexandrian master,[58] of whom he was earlier a fervent admirer only to become later, in the flare-up of the anti-Origenist polemic initiated by Epiphanius,[59] an equally bitter detractor, denouncing the doctrinal "errors" but never denying the merits of a knowledge of scripture unequalled up to that time and which Jerome himself often used as the source of his own teaching.

Let us say merely that, in the harsh polemic which put him at odds with his old friend Rufinus of Aquileia on the orthodoxy of Origen, among the numerous passages which Rufinus adduced to

---

[56] *Commentary on the letter to the Ephesians*, Prolog: PL 26, col. 472.

[57] Cf. F. Deniau, 'Le Commentaire de Jérôme sur Ephésiens nous permet-il de connaître celui d'Origène?,' in H. Crouzel-G. Lomiento-J. Rius-Camps *Origeniana, Premier Colloque international des études origèniennes (Montserrat, 8-21 septembre 1973)*, Bari, 1975 (Quaderni di Vetera Christianorum 12), 163-179 where a comparative examination is conducted of the text of Jerome with that of Origen, which have survived in the fragments in the catenae: J.A.F. Gregg, 'The Commentary of Origen upon the Epistle to the Ephesians,' *JThS* 3, 1901-1902, 233-244; 398-420; 554-576. See also E.A. Clark, 'The Place of Jerome's Commentary on Ephesians in the Origenist Controversy: the Apokatastasis and Ascetic Ideals,' *VigChr* 51 (1987), 154-171.

[58] For a first approach to the question, see P. Courcelle, *Les lettres en Occident. De Macrobe a Cassiodore*, Paris, 1948,[2] 88-102.

[59] For a summary of information on such polemic we refer to the Profiles of Origen and Jerome.

show how in the past the same Jerome had accepted some theories of Origen which at that time had been defined as "heretical," he included one from the *Commentary on the Epistle to the Ephesians* in which the husband/soul // wife/body parallelism is encountered, and the idea of transformation of bodies into souls, and of women into men.[60] Jerome does not deny the paternity in Origen of such an idea, confining himself to saying that he had merely made reference to it without making it his own.[61]

If such justification cannot be accepted, motivated as it is by a desire to distance himself from the accusation of "Origenism" advanced by Rufinus, since the reading of Jerome's text does not in fact show that the author, in composing his *Commentary* had gone the distances of the exegesis of Origen, which appear however perfectly in line with the argument of discourse developed by him on the Pauline text, it remains a significant confirmation of the ample utilization of the interpretive canons of Origen on the part of Jerome in this work. It was in fact composed in the years in which such had appeared as a model for imitation and a precious source to draw from, without of course sharing some of his more daring hypotheses, such as the notion of pre-existence or that of "double creation."

As to the image of the human couple which springs from the exegesis of Eph 5:22-23, it is easy to see the distinctive traits of this scheme of subordination in the interpersonal husband/wife relationship which the same Pauline text proposes and fixes solidly through the exemplary Christ/Church reference.

In Jerome's discourse there intervene two levels of reference, one of which, of obvious lineage from Origen, refers the statement of Paul and the related scheme of subordination to the soul/intellect and body schema, while the other safeguards in concrete reality the man/woman relationship in marriage. Of such relationships Jerome recognizes the physical basis, the total legitimacy of which

---

[60] Rufinus, *Apologia* 1,24: CCL 20, p. 58,14-22. See also, M. Simonetti, in his earlier edition, with Intro. and Italian trans., Alba, 1957.

[61] Jerome, *Contra Rufinum* 1,28 ed. P. Lardet (SC 303), Paris, 1983, 76-77. On the polemical discussion between the two personages with regard to the Commentary of Origen see K. Romaniuk, 'Une controverse entre saint Jérôme et Rufin d'Aquilée à propos de l'épitre de saint Paul aux Ephésiens,' *Aegyptus* 43 (1963), 84-106.

he maintains, and to which are also connected sentiments of mutual affection and dedication on the purely human level.

Scoring the usual polemical points against the "heretics" who condemn marriages, Jerome confirms the natural aspect of the sexual component of marriage, finalized in procreation, while any pleasure ought to be excluded. However, the religious perspective remains prevalent, in the recommendation to give up the exercise of conjugal rights, after the birth of children, or in any case to subordinate it decisively to prayer, because of the well known conflict between this activity and the practice of marriage.

It should further be noted that Jerome, by distinguishing the teaching of St. Paul in 1 Cor 7 as directed toward suckling babes, i.e. to faithful who are imperfect and not yet capable of persisting in total continence, from the teaching enunciated in the Epistle to the Ephesians, which in turn is directed to the perfect,[62] he wants to make it known that the Apostle, in proposing as a model of human marriage the union of Christ and the Church in this second epistle, invites the married couple to perfect continence, i.e. to an imitation of the totally spiritual relationship of that same model.

The exegete takes care to underline how the acceptance of that invitation is left to the discretion of the faithful but the expression with which he concludes his discourse, "Let each one be free to follow the example of the Corinthian or that of the Ephesian, and be saved with the slavery of the first, or the freedom of the second," makes it clear to which of the two alternatives he not merely leans, but rather recognizes as unquestionably superior, obvious from his categorizing the two as "slaves" and "free."

A final, significant fact to emerge from the section in question is Jerome's insistence on the motive of the husband's love for his wife. Apart from references at the level of allegorical exegesis in which it belongs to the soul/body relationship and is finalized in salvation and

---

[62] It should be noted that the distinction, frequently represented as opposition, between the Corinthians and the Ephesians, the latter defined as more advanced in perfection and in knowledge of the profound truth revealed by the Apostle is typical of Origen, from whom evidently Jerome borrowed his own arguments. Cf. F. Deniau, art. cit., p. 164. [See now: J.M. Cambier, 'Doctrine paulinienne du mariage chrétien. Étude critique de 1 Cor 7 et e d'Ép.5:21-33 et essai de leur traduction actuelle,' Église et Théologie 10 (1979), 13-59.]

eschatological transformation of the flesh, such motive is strongly emphasized also in the mutual relationship between the spouses.

Although it emerged in the first place already in the text of Paul which directs the entire discourse, no less notable is the care with which Jerome distinguishes the specificity of this affection from any other type of human love.

Equally worthy of consideration is the interpretation of the motive of "fear," which, according to the Apostle, ought to characterize the behavior of the wife toward the husband. Here Jerome, in fact, in noting the difference between the love assigned to the husband, and the fear to the wife, and as this latter seems to characterize the female condition in a negative sense, he demonstrates a singular sensibility, matured certainly through his contacts with numerous figures of "saintly women" with whom his activity as teacher of the ascetical life had brought him in contact, which unexpectedly overturned the schema of woman/man subordination.

Confronted with the experience of "so many wives much superior to their husbands," those who carry the burden of taking care of the entire domestic life and the education of the children, while the husbands indulge in dissipation, even if only with a diplomatic expression, he sees himself constrained to empty the text of its literal meaning to make way for the allegorical: " Whether women of such stature ought to dominate, or live in fear of, their own husbands, I leave to the judgment of my reader."

In this exclamation of the ascetic at Bethlehem can be perceived, how in the gap separating the ideological model and the concrete experience, in the name of those very religious principles which induce the Fathers to accept and authoritatively sanction the canons of female submission it is possible to turn upside down those very same canons, by recognizing the fundamental and frequently decisive role of the woman in the ambit of the life of marriage.

(VII) AUGUSTINE

The difficulty of presenting in a few pages the doctrine formulated by the bishop of Hippo on matrimony, at the center of which is placed the specific dimension of the man-woman relationship expressed in the structure of a couple, is evident to anyone who knows the centrality of this theme in the entire sweep of the religious and intellectual experience of Augustine and the abundant production of studies on the theme.[63] It will suffice to consider, to establish the notable importance of the problem within the author's horizons, the typical circumstance which directly touches all three of his principal spheres of interest, specifically, that of interpreter of Scripture, of theologian pledged to define the doctrinal teaching of the Church, grounded in the divinely revealed word, often in polemical exchanges with deviant and heretical positions, and finally of a moralist, careful in his role of bishop to provide directives for the behavior of his Christian people.

It is established in fact how the question of marriage, of its beginnings and finality at the center of God's creative project, arises at the time when Augustine began his first efforts at biblical exegesis and accompanies the maturation and sharpening of his interpretive techniques of Scripture and emerges in the first place as soon as the problem in all its urgent seriousness of defining the existential status of man, in his ontological foundations and in his religious calling.

Such a problem is bound up with theodicy itself in virtue of the qualitative gap between the actual condition of suffering and death proper to humanity and an original state of perfection which Sacred Scripture indicates as the prerogative of the first human couple, lost because of a transgression.

What is at stake is to show if and with what motivations it is possible to safeguard the notion of divine justice in face of a situation in which each person born of Adam suffers the consequences of a fault which is not his own and, without any apparent personal responsibility is punished with a series of physical and moral evils, among which death represents the most serious expression and the definitive sanction.

---

[63] We are content here to refer to the ample introduction of A. Trapè to vol. 1 of NBA (*Matrimonio e verginità*, Rome, 1978, IX-CIV), where there is an evaluation of the principal titles of a rich bibliography on the problem.

It is the great theme of original sin which, as is known, Augustine confronts in successive moments of his intellectual parabola, and, in a gradual maturation, stimulated by a hard and painful encounter with the Pelagian positions, ended up in an organic doctrine which substantially imposed itself as the expression of the teaching of the Catholic Church.[64]

In this picture, the question of marriage occupies a central and decisive role. The undertaking in fact was first of all to define the relationship of such a human reality with the original occurrence of the transgression in paradise, once an ample patristic tradition had joined this event, as cause and effect, to the institution of marriage.

In his first attempt at interpretation of the protological scenario delineated in Genesis, Augustine accepted in substance the postulates of this tradition.

In the treatise, *On Genesis, against the Manicheans*, composed in 388/389, a few years after his conversion, with the purpose of confuting the scriptural exegesis of his former correligionists[65] inspired

---

[64] It would be superfluous, not to say impossible, to attempt in this space a history, however brief, of the process of formation of the doctrine of Augustine of the interpretations proposed by modern scholars. See the general sketch of the problematic in the Introduction by A. Trapè in vol. XVII, L of NBA (*Natura e grazia*, I, Rome, 1981) which contains some treatises of Augustine that deal with the theme. See also some useful studies of A. Sage, 'Péché originel. Naissance d'un dogme,' *REAug* 13 (1967), 211-248; *Idem*, 'Le péché originel dans la pensée de Saint Augustin de 412 a 430,' *ibidem* 15 (1969), 75-112; I.G. Bonner, 'Les origines africaines de la doctrine augustinienne sur la chute et le péché originel,' *Augustinus* 12 (1967), 97-116; V. Grossi, *La liturgia battesimale in S. Agostino. Studio sulla catechesi del peccato originale negli anni 393-412* (Studia Ephemeridis Augustinianum 7), Rome, 1970. The importance of the theme of matrimony in the context of anti-Pelagian polemic has been illustrated by M. Meslin, 'Sainteté et mariage au cours de la seconde querelle pélagienne,' in *Mystique et Continence, op. cit.*, 293-307. Cf. also Y. de Montcheuil, 'La polémique de saint Agustin contre Julien d'Eclane d'après l'*Opus imperfectum*,' *RSR* 44 (1956), 142-143. For the rapport between the formulations of Augustine on the theme of sexuality and of marriage, on the one hand, and, on the other, of the necessity of proposing solutions to the theological problems imposed by anti-Pelagian and anti-Manichean polemic, apart from the positions of rigorous asceticism which threatened to discredit marriage and to favor virginity and continence, see the observations of E.A. Clark, '"Adam's Only Companion": Augustinus and the Early Christian Debate on marriage,' *RechAug* 21 (1986), 139-161. [See also P. Brown, *Augustine and Sexuality*, The Center for Hermeneutical Studies, Colloquy 46, Berkeley, CA, 1983; J. Marcilla Catalán, 'El matrimonio en la obra pastoral de san Augustinus,' in *Augustinus* 34 (1989), 31-117.]

[65] On the Manichean experience of Augustine the analysis of P. Alfaric, [cited above in note 16, p. 66] still remains sound. The theme is handled, apart from specialized studies, for example, J.P. De Menasce, 'Augustin manichéen,' in *Freundsgabe für Ernst Robert Curtius zum 14. April 1956*, Bern, 1956, 79-93, in the numerous biographies of Augustine. [On that of Peter Brown, *Augustine of Hippo*, London, 1967, see the observations of A. Trapè, 'Un S.

by a clear-cut dualism and a radical rejection of the Old Testament, Augustine, to overcome the difficulties of a literal interpretation of the biblical text, adopted schemes of allegorical interpretation.

The divine blessing of Gn 1:28 appears to him then to announce a spiritual fecundity of the couple because it is only after the sin that physical union and consequent procreation should occur. In the original condition, in fact, the two were devoted to a chaste union (*casta coniunctio*) having been created in the roles of one as guide and the other as helper in a hierarchical relationship harmoniously finalized toward the generation of "spiritual sons," that is, of intelligible and immortal delights, which would have "filled up" the earth, that is, the material body by living in a manner rendering it exempt from all evil and suffering.[66]

The same perspective, in which it is easy to perceive the sign of Origen's exegesis, is affirmed in a manual for training beginners (*De catechizandis rudibus*) of *circa* 400, where the quality of image of God is understood as a faculty of dominion over earthly creatures in virtue of intelligence, a typically human prerogative. Here it is affirmed that the function of "helper" proper to woman could not have been explained at the physical level in the condition of paradise, the bodies of the protoplasts being exempt from corruption.

To explain such a function Augustine has recourse to the Pauline formula of 1 Cor 11:7 and, in the consolidated hierarchical structure of the man/woman relationship, states that Adam had received "glory" from his companion in virtue of his being her head and guide on the road to God, furnishing an example of sanctity and piety to imitate.[67]

However already in the following year, when he composed the treatise, *On the Dignity of Matrimony* (circa 401), Augustine's posi-

---

Agostino della storia? A proposito di un biografia,' *AugR* 12 (1972), 341-349.] See also A. Trapè, *Agostino. L'uomo, il Pastore, il mistico*, Fossano, 1979, 3 ed., and A. Pincherle, *Vita di Agostino*, Rome-Bari, 1980. For information on Manicheism cf. M. Tardieu, *Il manicheismo. Introduzione, traduzione e aggiornamento bibliografico di G. Sfameni Gasparro*, Cosenza 1988 (orig. ed, Paris, 1981).

[66] *De Genesi contra Manicheos* 1,19,30: NBA X,I, 96-99. [Engl. tr. See now M. Alfeche, 'The transformation from *corpus animale* to *corpus spirituale* according to Augustine,' *Augustiniana* 47 (1992), 239-310.]

[67] *De catech. rudibus* XVIII, 29-30:B Aug 11, Paris, 1949, 94-97.

tion on the theme reveals the first uncertainties and shows him open to new solutions.[68] In this work exegetical considerations yield pride of place to ethical questions confronted by Augustine, well aware of the danger represented by Manichaeism with its dual doctrine on the origin of evil and its radical condemnation of marriage and procreation, arising from its connection with the regimen of corruption and death inherent in matter.

The selection chosen (no. 26) exemplifies in a clear manner a crucial moment in Augustine's evolution on the theme in question. While it shows that he is well aware of the diverse solutions proposed by his predecessors and contemporaries in the patristic tradition on the merits of the question concerning the relationship between the first sin and marriage, it reveals his uncertainty on the protological matter but at the same time his decisive point of view in his value judgment on the actual condition.

His assumption in this treatise in fact is the demonstration that in the situation in which people of today find themselves living, with its alternating birth and death, marriage is a blessing. The relation of male and female at the center of legitimate marriage bond, in its peculiar status of sexual relationship, has as its final end the procreation of children.

Augustine is at pains to make the point that, outside of marriage, it would have been possible "for the two sexes to have a sort of amiable and fraternal union, in which one would act as leader and the other as obeying."

This possibility, which is represented as an alternative with respect to the union of marriage, introduces a discussion of various hypotheses related to the modality of relationship between the sexes without sin.

---

[68] The same position, rather pliable and problematic, is expressed in the first books of *De Genesi ad litteram* whose date of composition as is known is variously placed between 401 and 415. In Book III the exegete poses the question, announced in Gn 1:28 and asks how it could have happened in the integrity of paradise. He shows then the possibility of a union of immortal bodies arrived at by an affection of *pia caritas,* and without the intrusion of the corruption of concupiscence (III, 21, 33: NBA IX, 2, 150-151). On this motive see J. Doignon, 'Une définition oubliée de l'amour conjugal édenique chez Augustin: *piae caritatis adfectus* (*Gen. ad litt.* 3, 21, 33),' *VetChr* 19 (1982), 25-36.

For the relationship between marriage and the first sin cf. D. Covi, 'L'etica sessuale paradisiaca agostiniana,' *Laurentianum* 13 (1972), 340-364.

It is easy to recognize in this the principal solutions proposed in the patristic tradition. In fact, the eventuality of a generation of children without physical copulation is affirmed by an author like Gregory of Nyssa, in a complex picture of an anthropological doctrine according to which sexual differentiations have been conferred on humanity by God in a unique creative act which has placed them in a state of being endowed with a sexual body, but only in prevision of future sin which would have rendered physical procreation necessary and without which humanity could instead have been propagated according to a mysterious modality of angelic type.[69] Such a notion is present also in John Chrysostom, without however the support of an anthropology analogous to that formulated by Gregory of Nyssa.[70]

The alternative solution is that connected to the spiritual exegesis, of an Origenist type, already adopted by Augustine himself, according to which the multiplication foreseen before sin could be understood "in the sense of an increase of soul and of a multiplication of virtue," generation being posterior to, and a consequence of, sin.

In short, Augustine points out an interpretation which, while respecting the literal significance of the text, establishes premises for a successive and definitive position on the problem. He in fact supposes that the body of the protoplasts would have been created "animal" and therefore capable of true marriage and physical generation but would have been preserved from death and corruption, passing to a "spiritual" condition, without trauma, if the disobedience to the divine precept had not occurred.

Although in this context the author states that he does not wish to adhere to any of the solutions proposed, the development of his reflections on the theme, stimulated by the grave problem of nature and the consequences of the first sin, would lead him to adopt the third to which, with partial modifications and reinforcements, the anthropology of Augustine would remain solidly anchored.

---

[69] In this regard see the observations of G. Sfameni Gasparro, *Enkrateia e antropologia, op. cit.*, 235-244 where the relative documentation is provided.

[70] See further note 2, p. 262.

The recognition of the pertinence of carnal union and of procreation to the original creative project of God, rejecting the fundamental postulate of the tradition of *enkrateia* motivated on a protological basis, eliminates from the anthropological perspective the graduated structure deriving from such activity as essential in the actual human condition, to a second and secondary phase with respect to the plan of creation as far as being dependent on the first sin.

At the same time, in the religious evaluation of the existential choice between marriage and virginity/continence such motivations are removed which, by binding marriages in a causal manner to the transgression in paradise and to the beginning of human decadence, would confer on the second option not only a preeminence for ethical-ascetical reasons but would also make them privileged instruments in the regaining of the same original perfection.[71]

The consequences of this change in perspective with respect to the tradition under examination can be seen also with regard to the themes, whose frequency we have already established, of marriage as a "concession" to human weakness and the incompatibility of its practice with prayer and the other religious activities.

In the same treatise, *On the Dignity of Marriage*, Augustine affirms that the words of the Apostle in 1 Cor 7:34 (*the woman who is not married is concerned with things of the Lord in pursuit of holiness in body and spirit*) should not be taken to mean that "a chaste Christian spouse cannot be holy in body." "Then," he concludes on the basis of 1 Cor 6:19, "the bodies of spouses who observe mutual fidelity and regard for the Lord are also holy."[72]

Indeed he strongly denies that the Apostle concedes marriage "as an indulgence" inasmuch as that would imply that marriage itself is a sin. And he continues: "And so it is that sexual intercourse that comes about through incontinence, not for the sake of procreation, that he grants as a concession. Marriage does not force this type of intercourse to come about but only that it be indulged."[73]

---

[71] For a fully nuanced discussion cf. *Enkrateia e antropologia, op. cit.*, 300-322.

[72] *De dignitate matrimonii* 11.13: NBA VII,I, 30-31, FOTC 27,26; Cf. *La dignità dello stato vedovile* 6.8: NBA VII,I, 178-179, FOTC.

[73] *De dignitate matrimonii* 10.11: NBA VII,1,28-29, FOTC 27, 24.

In this way some themes are announced which in a progressive effort of deepening and clarifying the problems would constitute the supporting axes of the teaching of Augustine on marriage and on original sin in what is especially connected to the sphere of sex. We refer to the notion of the intrinsic goodness of marriage and of its primary procreative finality, both prerogatives of human nature which remained substantially complete even after the tragedy of sin.

This, in its consistent motivation of proud rebellion of the creature against the Creator has however introduced into human life the "evil" of concupiscence with its twofold burden of guilt and punishment.[74] This evil inheres in the entire spectrum of human activity but in a specific and radical manner it is concentrated in the sexual sphere.

In Augustine's opinion, in fact, in this sphere is manifested in all its negative efficacy a force, uncontrollable by the human will, of a revolt of the senses against the spirit. Concupiscence introduced by sin is not more to be eliminated by sexual activity, even within the ambit of Christian marriages (cf. no. 28), in which the washing of baptism has cancelled the element of culpability of that same concupiscence which however perdures as a "penalty" for sin and as a vehicle for the transmission of that same sin to one's offspring.

For the bishop of Hippo the hereditary quality of the punishments consequent to the transgression of Adam and Eve could not be just and compatible with the justice and goodness of God if it were not connected with the notion of solidarity in the sin of our first parents on the part of all humanity.

Such solidarity is founded on natural modality of generation which, infected with concupiscence, constitutes at birth every human being as culpable of the same sin of Adam and needing redemption on the part of the divine mercy.

Without being able to illustrate in its delicate articulation the

---

[74] On the complex meanings of Augustine's notion of concupiscence cf. G.I. Bonner, 'Libido and Concupiscentia in St. Augustine,' *Studia Patristica* VI (TU 81) Berlin, 1962, 303-314; F.-J. Thonnard, 'La notion de concupiscence en philosophie augustinienne,' *RechAug* 3 (1965), 95-105; E. Samek Lodovici, 'Sessualità, matrimonio e concupiscenza in sant'Agostino,' in R. Cantalamessa (ed.), *op. cit.*, 212-272.

complex teaching of Augustine on original sin, which is bound up in an inseparable manner with the notion of the necessity and universality of the salvific action of Christ, we will only add that in maintaining a specific connection between the first sin and the sphere of marriage and generation through the channel of concupiscence by now inherent in this sphere, such a doctrine in spite of everything is placed by some in a relationship of continuity with the tradition of *enkrateia* with protological motivations.[75]

Having established these premises, we can understand the reasons why Augustine, despite dedicating ample and elaborate arguments to the theme of matrimony whether in specific treatises, or in conjunction with the exegesis of the opening chapters of Genesis, or finally in the context of anti-Pelagian polemic on the question of original sin, pays little enough attention to the weft of interpersonal relations between the spouses, apart from normative and institutional aspects of the marriage bond. Basically preoccupied with defining these latter, to formulate a clear doctrine on the "dignity" or the "goodness" of matrimony and its constitutive contents, the bishop of Hippo does not devote much space to the illustration of the concrete reality of the couple's relationship.

Having established the three "goods" of marriage in a) the mutual fidelity of the spouses, b) the generation of offspring, and c) the indissolubility of the bond,[76] also indicating in procreation its primary finality, he recognizes the existence of a spiritual bond between

---

[75] See on this G. Sfameni Gasparro, 'Il tema della concupiscentia in Agostino, e la tradizione dell'enkrateia,' *AugR* 25 (1985), 155-183; *eadem*, 'Concupiscenza e generazione: aspetti antropologici della dottrina agostiniana del peccato originale,' in *Congresso internazionale su S. Agostino nel XVI centenario della conversione, Roma 15-20 settembre 1986, Atti II*, Rome, 1987, 225-255. A relationship of filiation between the encratite positions and Augustine's doctrine of original sin is affirmed in P.F. Beatrice *Tradux peccati. Alle fonti della dottrina agostiniana del peccato originale* (SPM X, Milan, 1978) which contains many acute observations and useful suggestions, but we have certain reservations about his conclusions.

[76] Cf. A. Reuter, *Sancti Aurelii Augustini doctrina de bonis matrimonii* (Analecta Gregoriana XXVII), Rome, 1942. The role of the affective and spiritual component in the relationship between husband and wife has been appropriately highlighted in the analysis of E. Schmitt, *Le mariage chrétien dans l'oeuvre de saint Augustin. une théologie baptismale de la vie conjugale*, Paris, 1983, especially 258-295. However this scholar, in evaluating the religious contents of Augustine's teaching on marriage minimizes the theological implications of the profound connection between concupiscence and conjugal relations also present on the author's horizon.

the spouses which transcends the physical one, and becomes all the stronger when the sexual bond is lessened (nn. 26 and 28).

In conformity with the consolidated schemes of a man/woman hierarchy at the center of marriage is the insistence on the function of "helper" of the female component, and the theme of her subordination in obeying her husband, to whom belongs the role of guide and head (nn. 27-28).

We should not however disregard the fact that the exclusively procreative function which the wife should furnish to her spouse in the text *On the Literal Meaning of Genesis* (no. 27) is explained in the light of the assumption that the author wishes here to demonstrate, namely that original pertinence of physical marriage and generation to the ontological status of humanity, for this reason made distinct into male and female, which would contradict those who would make such a reality depend on the sin of our first parents.

The theme of male supremacy at the heart of the couple is moreover qualified in a religious sense and serves the bishop as a weapon in his persistent catecheses on questions of conjugal fidelity.

The excerpts selected from the *Sermons* of Augustine (nn. 29-32) bear witness to a situation which must have been rather widespread in the Christian community, namely the frequency of adultery on the part of men which, according to well-known canons of the common morality of the time were widely tolerated despite a rigid obligation of fidelity imposed on their spouses. Augustine is firmly opposed to such behavior, inviting the wives to stage a rebellion, religiously motivated, but insisting on their obligation to docile submission in all the rest of their conduct.

Finally, the *Epistle to Ecdicia* (no. 33) introduces a particular aspect of a problematic of the couple which will be central in the texts of Paulinus of Nola and of pseudo-Jerome. This refers to a practice of the 4th and the beginning of the 5th century which assumes relatively large proportions in the Christian community, namely, the choice of continence within the marriage relationship undertaken by both spouses for the pursuit of a religious ideal of perfection which the concordant teaching of the Fathers indicate as superior to indulging in conjugal relations and in a manner more or less clear-cut judged incompatible with that same activity. The letter of Augustine sheds light on tensions inherent in such a practice which was already present in ambiences of clearly encratite connotations such as those illustrated in the rich literature of the apocryphal *Acts of the Apostles*,[77] that is, of ascetic and eschatological aspirations just as strong as in the monastic ones.[78]

The bishop administers a rebuke to his correspondent for having unilaterally imposed on her husband her choice of continence which, according to the teaching of Paul, ought to emerge from the voluntary agreement of the two spouses. Besides, after the husband, admittedly with little enthusiasm, had accepted to follow his wife's example, she, by dissipating in excessive almsgiving her own patrimony, had violated another basic canon of correct relationship of the couple, by mortally wounding the authority and prestige of her husband through her personal initiative, independently of his requisite consent.

It is interesting to note how, by repeating the inalienable principle of the reciprocal right of the marriage partners to the marriage "debt," the choice itself of continence, however religiously meritorious, is certainly subordinate to this principle. At the same time the recommendation to safeguard conjugal harmony is founded on the idea of the husband's unquestionable authority which ought to be respected in a pre-eminent way by all who are associated with the practical conduct of the life of the household.

---

[77] It suffices to refer once and for all to the case of the young spouse described in *Acts of Thomas* 10-16, *Apocrypha of the New Testament* where the Savior appears in the guise of the Apostle to exhort him to abstain from conjugal relations (*Acta Thomae* 10-16, Ital. tr. by M. Erbetta, *Gli Apocrifi del Nuovo Testamento, 11, Atti e Leggende*, Turin, 1966, 316-319). For the strong encratite tendency of this literature, apart from *Enkrateia e antropologia, op. cit.*, 87-101, see G. Sfameni Gasparro, 'Gli Atti apocrifi degli Apostoli e la tradizione dell'enkrateia,' *AugR* 23 (1983), 287-307. A different practice, also partially related to matrimonial continence, was that of cohabitation of ascetics, men and women, which formed a sort of "spiritual matrimony." For such practices, which were widely diffused at the beginning of the 3rd century and were strongly criticized and opposed by qualified representatives of the Catholic Church, we refer, apart from the work of E. Testa, 'L'ascetica encratita e i matrimoni putativi come vittoria sul peccato originale,' in *Liber annuus. Studium Biblicum Franciscanum*. 32 (1982), 191-238, to the documentation offered in G. Sfameni Gasparro, 'L'Epistula Titi discipuli Pauli de dispositione sanctimonii e la tradizione dell'enkrateia,' *ANRW* II,25,6, Berlin-New York, 1988, 4551-4664.

[78] See the cases described in the *Historia Lausiaca* of Palladius analyzed by E. Giannarelli, *art. cit.*, 88-94.

(VIII) PSEUDO-JEROME

The theme of the respect owed by a wife to her husband in consideration of his authority in the bosom of the family, such as was sanctioned in the teaching of Paul, operated as one of the hinges in the harmonious relationship of the Christian couple directed to Celantia by an anonymous author whom modern criticism almost unanimously identifies with the person of Pelagius.

Postponing to the Introduction to the text (no. 36) a discussion on the problem of attribution of authorship of the letter, it suffices here to note that its author reveals himself in perfect continuity with the patristic line so far examined in recognizing the full liceity and dignity of the state of matrimony, the preeminence of the religious values of chastity, of modesty in bearing and reserve in the behavior of women.

Without any allusion to the protological theme, while the superior value of continence with respect to the practice of marriage is affirmed, the author with profound equilibrium modulates his entire discourse on the Pauline motive of "mutual consent," repudiating a unilateral choice whose effects prove damaging to one's partner. The reference to personal experience of marriage unions breaking down because of undue desire for continence on the part of one of the married couple confirms the wide diffusion of a practice which, stimulated by ascetic propaganda, to which the Fathers themselves testify, had introduced disequilibrium and dangerous deviations in the Christian community.

The teaching itself of Paul to the faithful of Corinth, moreover, shows how ascetic tensions, very alive in the first Christian generations, could have many dangerous repercussions on the stability of that very marriage bond from which the Apostle, and with him the entire ecclesiastical tradition, is never interested in taking away its intrinsic legitimacy.

(IX) PAULINUS OF NOLA

Without any trauma, but on the contrary in the fullness of its religious contents the ideal of spiritual union between spouses is realized in the experience of this couple which the bishop of Nola re-counts with vivid tones of praise (no. 35).

The figures of Apro and Amanda, in the enthusiastic words of Paulinus, define themselves as an emblematic example of harmoni-ous and total dedication to the religious ideal on the part of two spouses who, abandoning sexual relations, are united by a strong bond in which a complementarity of roles persist, turning upside down the usual patterns.

In fact, the typical domestic "inside" function of the wife, is replaced by the typically masculine role in its "public" dimension of contact with the outside world. What Paulinus underlines is, in fact, Amanda's capacity to address "all the necessities of the age," in this way freeing her spouse from earthly concerns and permitting a com-plete dedication without distraction to his religious mission.

In this way a new model of conjugal relationships is delineated in which the wife appears projected toward a practical dimension certainly different from that sphere of the "political" which was ex-clusive for men in ancient society, but nonetheless jointly involved in the weft of social relationships, while the husband is withdrawn to the internal sphere of religious activity.

About this one can inquire if and to what extent there is at work in this new model the symbolism of Philonian lineage, already invoked in its proper place, of the female, linked to sensibility, and therefore to the physical component, and of the male linked to the rational/spiritual, which frequently in Origen is rendered in the metaphor of woman/body and man/soul-intellect.

In other words, in the structure of the "ideal" couple of the type described by Paulinus there seems to re-emerge the ideological scheme of a female more adapted to a relation with a worldly dimen-sion and of a male turned in a privileged way toward the interior-spiritual one. However, in the portrait sketched by the bishop of Nola who participated himself in an analogous experience of chosen con-tinence within marriage and of the practice of asceticism adopted by the two marriage partners by mutual agreement, it remains note-worthy how this choice is indicated as a perfect adaptation to the Pauline model of the Christ-Church relationship and the consequent sublimation of the same matrimonial ideal.

At the same time it is interesting to perceive the persistence of the theme of "return to unity" realized through abstaining from sexual relations, in which exercise of these relations, while rendering active and operative the male-female distinction, is represented as a sign of "division."

In fact, with a clear reference to the protological scenario of the "construction" of Eve from the rib of Adam, the radical selection of continence is indicated as a means to permit the woman to return to being bone *of the bone* of her husband, that is, to restore the perfect unity of Adam still undivided, that is, the harmonious union of the couple in paradise, still ignorant of physical relations.

Carmen XXV, in its poetic structure of a Christian epithalamium, which, while maintaining the traits of the traditional genre, modifies however the contents and significance[79] in a profound manner, celebrates the marriage between Julian, the future bishop of Eclanum, and Titia. It has been the object of numerous careful analyses.[80]

It is sufficient to note the intervention of some motives already consolidated in the patristic tradition to define the image of the Christian couple and along with it the emphatic reference to chastity which frequently intervenes in the course of the argument to propose to the two young people, at the very moment in which they are contracting marriage, that model of "spiritual union" which we have seen realized in Epistle 44.

This model, entrusted to the free choice of the two spouses, for whom the alternative is to hope for the birth of children who could realize the virginal ideal, is once more based on the mystical relationship, Christ/Church.

Such a relationship, which, in the entire patristic tradition is utilized to exemplify the bond of total dedication and of affection between the spouses beyond the hierarchy of their relationship,

---

[79] Cf. H. Crouzel, 'L'epitalamio di San Paolino: il suo contenuto dottrinale,' in *Atti del Convegno XXXI Cinquantenario della morte di St. Paolino di Nola (431-1981), Nola 20-21 marzo 1982,* Rome, 1984, 143-148. S. Costanza, 'Catechesi e poesia nei Carmi XXII, XXV e XXXI di Paolino di Nola,' in S. Felici, ed., *Crescita dell'uomo nella catechesi dei Padri (Età post-nicena),* Rome, 1988, 237-256.

[80] See the Introductory Profile.

maintaining, however, the necessary distance between the "mystery" of this salvific union, totally spiritual, and the concrete nuptial reality, in the ambit of this type of ascetic spirituality which strongly insists on the practice of continence in marriage become a parameter of specific reference for the couple who assume a pattern of behavior exempt from such physical components.

In the admonition to reject all inappropriate manifestations of pagan type in the celebration of marriage, Paulinus introduces the well-known themes of the first human couple whose modality of creation provide a figure of the indivisible unity of the spouses and of their mutual love, that of the wife as "helper" of the husband, and of him as "head" of her.

In this interweaving of themes from Genesis and Paul, there appears that equally well-known theme, of continence as an instrument for the woman for abolishing the status of submission consequent on sin.

Paulinus's affirmation, according to which "through the merits of such a union Eve ceased to be a slave and Sarah, finally liberated, became the equal of her husband" (vv. 149-150) cannot but invoke the motive, typical of the tradition of *enkrateia*, together with protological motives according to which the practice of marriage, succeeding to and consequent upon, sin, continues to render operative the decree of subordination of the woman to the man which has been determined and from which only the virgin and the widow are on the contrary free.[81]

In the bishop of Nola these motivations do not intervene in an explicit and programmatic manner. They remain however operative at least in a partial and allusive manner even in his argumentation, showing how the ideological directives of such a tradition have worked its way in depth and breadth to the center of Christian spirituality in the early centuries, influencing its language, images and underlying mental structure.

---

[81] The notion that only virginity and continence permit the woman to be free of this condemnation to subjection as a sequel to sin of Eve and expressed in conjugal relations is widely diffused in patristic literature in ascetic discussion, from Cyprian (*De habitu virginum* 22: CSEL 3,I, 203-204) to Origen (Fr. XXXIX Commentary on I Corinthians, ed. C. Jenkins, p. 510, 49-60), Jerome (*Epistola* 22,18) and Ambrose (*De virginibus* I,V1,27: PL 16, col. 196), to mention only some of the more representative authors.

(X) JOHN CHRYSOSTOM

The author who undoubtedly devotes the most space to the problematic of the couple in the vast range of his rich literary production is John, priest of Antioch and later bishop of Constantinople, who earned the appellation of Golden Mouth for the vivacity of his eloquence displayed in the course of his pastoral activity.

Moulard's definition, setting him off as "the defender of marriage and the apostle of virginity"[82] expresses in a satisfactory synthesis the two complementary and converging aspects of his position on the theme and at the same time the two descriptive components of his religious and human experience.

Our author in fact participated at a time of the religious appeal of monastic spirituality which flourished in the 4th century, having also experienced a radical albeit temporary experience of the anchorite variety in his role as deacon and priest at Antioch and then as bishop of Constantinople.

In this peculiar situation of his, in which religious parameters, different but nevertheless necessarily compatible, converge and come in confrontation in the larger picture of the Christian life, one can locate the terrain in which a vision of the man/woman relationship at the heart of matrimony takes root and comes to maturity. This, even if it reflects in large measure the canons already noted, present specific and original connotations by its constant attention to the concrete experience of the couple, and to certain aspects of its effectiveness which in the other Fathers are either passed over in silence or only minimally touched upon.

This clearly emerges in the passages chosen, which are among the most representative in a series of the very rich and articulated contexts in which Chrysostom, in the course of his extensive homiletic, epistolary and literary life in a programmatic, that is to say, occasional manner handles questions pertaining to that reality of

---

[82] A. Moulard, *Saint Jean Chrysostome, le défenseur du mariage et l'apôtre de la virginité*, Paris, 1923. On his ethical and ascetical teaching see L. Meyer, *Saint Jean Chrysostome, maître de perfection chrétienne*, Paris, 1933; J.-M. Leroux, 'Monachisme et communauté chrétienne d'après Saint Jean Chrysostome,' in Aa. vv., *Théologie de la vie monastique, op. cit.*, 143-190.

marriage in which a man and a woman are jointly involved in a varied web of relations which indicate in depth their existential and religious status.

Good syntheses on Chrysostom's teaching on marriage[83] and the detailed analyses of texts furnished by Scaglioni[84] (in Cantalamessa, 1976), besides the recent researches of C. Militello (1986),[85] which are centered on the image of the wife in the ideological horizons of the author, dispense us from an extensive presentation of the theme which in any case is impossible at this juncture.

We will therefore confine ourselves to indicating some essential directives on Chrysostom's positions, such as define in a balanced way the ascetical tensions and the exaltation of continence and virginity, on the one hand, and, on the other, the value attributed to marriage inasmuch as it is the sole legitimate situation in which the relationship of the human couple is realized.

In his treatise, *On Virginity*, which belongs to a literary genre rather widespread in the 4th century, and which reflects the appeals of the ascetic and monastic movement then in full flower, Chrysostom engages, if only in a preliminary way, in polemic against the encratite positions and defends the legitimacy of marriage,[86] not only utilizing all the consolidated rhetorical baggage which illustrate its practical inconveniences, but also revealing a participation in the typical protological motivations of virginity.

This characterized the situation in paradise of Adam and Eve who lived on earth[87] but however "they lived in paradise as in heaven, and they enjoyed God's company. Desire for sexual intercourse, conception, labor, childbirth, and every form of corruption had been

---

[83] D. Gorce, 'Mariage et perfection chrétienne d'après Saint Jean Chrysostome,' *Études Carmelitaines Mystiques et Missionaires* 21,1 (1963), 245-284, G. Oggioni, *art. cit.*, 248-273; K. Tsouros, 'La dottrina del matrimonio in San Giovanni Crisostomo,' *Asprenas* n.s.21 (1974), 5-46; T. Spidlik, 'Il matrimonio, sacramento di unità, nel pensiero di Crisostomo,' *AugR* 17 (1977), 221-226.

[84] C. Scaglioni,' Ideale coniugale e familiare in San Giovanni Crisostomo,' in R. Cantalamessa (ed.), *op. cit.*, 273-422.

[85] C. Militello, *Donna e Chiesa. La testimonianza di Giovanni Crisostomo*, Palermo, 1985, where a large section is devoted to the role of the female in the nuptial relationship.

[86] *De virginitate* 1, I-VI, 2, edd. H. Musurillo/B. Grillet (SC 125) Paris, 1966, 92-111: VIII,I-X,3, 114-125.

[87] On the terrestrial quality of paradise and the literal meaning of the account cf. also *Homily on Genesis* XIII,3: PG 53, 108-109.

banished from their souls. As a limpid river shooting forth from a pure source, so were they in that place, adorned with virginity."[88]

Only the transgression, caused by the envy of the devil, brought about the fall of the pair in corruption inherent in physical reality and in death.[89] "When they shed the princely raiment of virginity," concludes Chrysostom, "they accepted the decay of death, ruin, and a toilsome life. In their wake came marriage: a garment befitting mortals and slaves."[90]

Although elsewhere Chrysostom would recognize in the generation of sons a "consolation" for death, being a gift of God and an image of the resurrection,[91] the causal connection established here between the primal sin and the beginning of a regime of corruption and death, together with the physical form of the union and of procreation,[92] connote in a somewhat ambiguous manner the conjugal reality. This is intimately connected with "concupiscence" (*epithumia*)[93] and teaching that the function of "helper" for which the

---

[88] *De virginitate* XIV, 3, 140-141.

[89] On the post-Fall character of marriage cf. also *Expos. Psalmi CXIII:* PG 55, col 312. Chrysostom says that the invitation to procreation was announced by God after the sin which, by introducing death, made the generation of children necessary. Christ, in teaching that death is like a dream introduced "the beauty of virginity."
In *Homily XVIII,1 on Genesis* PG 53,149-150, FOTC 82, p. 3, he describes the original situation of the firstborn, endowed with a "garment of glory" which did not cover the body, being exempt from the proper need of this. Sin deprived them of such a privilege, and in its place was substituted the "garments of skin," a sign of their condition of mortality, subject to physical needs. The condition in paradise, however, lacked the passions and resembled that of the angels. For the notion of "vestment of glory" of Jewish ancestry, see A. Kowalski, '"Rivestiti di gloria." Adamo ed Eva nel commento di sant'Ephrem a Gn 2:25. Ricerca delle fonti dell'esegesi siriaca,' in *Cristianesimo nella Storia* 3 (1982), 41-60.

[90] *De virginitate* XIV, 5, 140-143. A further emphasis on the "secondary" and downgraded character of the regimen of matrimony is given by its recognition as derived "from disobedience, from malediction, from death." The conclusion is that "where there is death, there is matrimony. Take away one and the other will disappear."
On Virginity, XIV, 6 This harsh statement is parallel to one in Gregory of Nyssa, according to whom virginity is a dike placed against the irresistible cycle of generation-corruption-death (*Grégoire de Nysse De virginitate*, XIV,1, éd. M. Aubineau, SC 119, Paris, 1966, 432-436).

[91] *Homily on Genesis* XVIII,4: PG 53, col. 154. FOTC 82, 12.

[92] In the opinion of Chrysostom, as of Gregory of Nyssa, in the absence of sin, humanity could have equally well multiplied, in a mysterious fashion defined as angelic in type (*De virginitate* XIV,6: PG 53, 142-145; SC 125).

[93] *De virginitate* XI, 1-XXV, SC 125, 126-175 and *passim*. The same relation is repeated in other places, including the text *On the words of the Apostle: "because of fornication,"* 3: PG 51,213. However in marriage is recognized an end which can put a limit and measure to the same concupiscence.

wife has been created was not finalized at the outset in a sexual relationship[94] he states: "it is possible to say with regard to the present life and the procreation of children and physical desires, she displays the help that is her very own."[95]

The woman therefore as such cannot be a "helper" for religious and spiritual activities. Only when she ceases from her procreative activity in marriage can she cooperate in the salvation of her husband.

There intervenes here the typical motif of "transformation of woman into man" as a condition of access to spiritual dignity. Chrysostom will say in fact that he does not wish to subtract from the woman any capacity of collaboration on the religious plane: "I affirm," he says, "not in the exercise of marriage but when, while physically remaining a woman, she overcomes her own nature by elevating herself to the virtue of holy men."[96]

In linking the origin of the practice of marriage to original sin Chrysostom, like other Eastern authors,[97] broadens the perspective in order to include among the consequences of the transgression of Adam, along with the loss of the angelic condition of glory,[98] the creation of an entire picture of practical activity, and of human activities, "cities, crafts, the wearing of clothes, and all our other numerous needs" are in fact a necessity "because of our infirmity."[99]

The date of composition of On Virginity remains uncertain since scholars are undecided whether to attribute it to the period when he was totally involved in the monastic life or to when he exercised his pastoral activity in Antioch.[100]

---

[94] De virginitate XLVI, 1-5, SC 125, 256-263.

[95] Ibidem XLVI, 5, SC 125, 262-263.

[96] Ibidem XLVII, 1, SC 125, 262-263. Also in this context, radical in its exaltation of continence and of virginity, however, Chrysostom reaffirms the notion of Paul, to which all the Fathers remain continuously faithful, the need for "mutual consent" as an indispensable condition for abstinence from conjugal relations (XLVII, 3-XLVIII, 2, SC 125, 266-273).

[97] Cf. M. Harl, 'La prise de conscience de la "nudité" d'Adam. Une interprétation de Genèse 3,7 chez les Pères Grecs,' Stud Pat VII (TU 92), Berlin, 1966, 486-495.

[98] Cf. Homily on Genesis XVI,1: PG 53,126.

[99] De virginitate, XV, 1-2, SC 125, 144-147.

[100] See the introduction of B. Grillet to De virginitate, SC 125, 25, which proposes a date circa 382, while H. Musurillo places the same treatise in the year 392, making it contemporary with the Homilies on 1 Corinthians.

Although this second possibility remains less credible because of the notable differences of tone perceptible on the theme of matrimony between the treatise in question and the other writings of this period, there is need to recognize that the protological motivation of Chrysostom is never denied, who proposes it many times in the *Homilies on Genesis* preached between 386 and 388.[101]

Apart from the purely chronological reference, while important as an indicator of an undeniable process of evolution and maturation in the position of Chrysostom from his first ascetical experiences to his pastoral activity in the period of Antioch and Constantinople, there is need then to evaluate the different purposes of his writings and the quality of the interlocutors addressed by the author.

While the treatise [*On Virginity*] is in fact directed to the defence of the ideal of celibacy and to its propagation, the places in which Chrysostom speaks of the Christian couple are dominated with a preoccupation to furnish to it directives for behavior in specific relation to the status of the spouses in order that the fundamental dictates of Christian ethics may be realized in their peculiar situation.

An articulated and balanced catechesis emerges which, by two-fold references once more constituted from the Genesis account and the teaching of Paul, safeguards sympathetically and with live participation in the nuptial reality, in which two individuals meet, differing by prerogative and function, but really endowed with a dignity substantially equal, albeit on different levels.

Chrysostom, in fact, while he fully accepts, on the authority of St. Paul, the schema of male domination and female subservience, in comparison with that protological parameter found in all the discourses of the Fathers on the couple, he relativizes it historically by attributing its origin to the first sin.[102]

---

[101] Apart from the places here cited, cf. *Hom. on Genesis* XIII, 3-4: PG 53, 108-109 and the entire *Hom. on Genesis* XV which describes in vivid colors the situation in paradise of our first parents in its "angelic" dimension, emphasizing the contrast with that of the actual, especially in its relationship with the sphere of passion and sexual activity before original sin. Cf. FOTC 74, 194-206, esp. 202-203.

[102] Chrysostom himself, however, in other contexts, seems to adopt the position which attributes to sin only the "penal" character of submissiveness which is considered inherent in the cre-

In selection #37, it is said that "submission" on the part of the woman "becomes necessary after the sin," while her original designation as "helper" like to man was an indication of a relationship based on parity between the two.[103]

The all-important responsibility of the woman, according to the well-known interpretation of the dictate in Genesis, justifies all levels of subordination illustrated in the epistles of Paul: obedience to the husband, observing silence in the congregation, the prohibition against teaching. However an exegesis of such a relationship in terms that manage in spite of everything to be positive to the woman is peculiar to Chrysostom. The affirmation of Genesis 3:16 according to which the man will be "master" is understood in the sense that in him his wife will find refuge and protection, while that "desire," which had previously been pointed to in the treatise, *On Virginity*, as a totally negative consequence of the original sin, is here reevaluated. It is in fact the means for inaugurating between the two, the physical bonds which constitute that "indestructible bond" of matrimony which in the present state of affairs makes possible the relationship and the life in common of two different beings in harmonious affection rather than in harsh antagonism (cf. no. 38).

In a similar sense is also interpreted the Pauline theme of "love" on the part of the husband and "fear" on the part of the wife, which intervenes constantly, modulated in all registers, in the Chrysostom account (#41).

---

ative project of God, implying then a constitutive gradation at the interior of the human couple. See for example *Hom. on Genesis, c.1*, VIII,3-4: PG 53, 72-73, where the author in commenting on Gn 1:26 places in intimate connection the faculty of "image" with that of "command" recognizing both as the exclusive prerogative of the male. The woman, also on the authority of Paul who defines her only as the "glory" of the man, is deprived of both these faculties and destined for a subordinate role. Cf. also *Discourse on Genesis* II, 2: PG 54, 589-560; *On the First Epistle to the Corinthians,* Homily XXVI: PG 61, 218. A similar perspective is affirmed in Augustine. Among numerous places cf. *De Gen. et litt.* VIII, XXIII, 44; XI, XXXVII, 50; *De Epistola ad Galatas*, PL 35, 2125.

[103] The quality of parity, however, of such a relationship, results strongly of such a notion, affirmed in other contexts, with a variety of tones of the faculty of "image" of God, connected with that of "dominion." From this latter, in fact, the female is excluded in virtue of her subordinate status which in some passages — as has been said — the author seems to consider as the originator rather than the consequence of sin. [Engl. ed. See V. Karras, 'Male Domination of Woman in the Writings of St. John Chrysostom,' *Greek Orth Theol Rev* 36 (1991), 131-139; W. Vogels, 'The Power Struggle between Man and Woman (Gn 3:16b),' *Biblica* 77,2 (1996), 197-209.]

In fact this is for our author an indication of the reciprocal equilibrium and compenetration of a necessary hierarchical scheme which confers authority and "dominion" on the man and a contextual relationship of parity, founded on the mutual affection of the spouses, in which love and fear find a terrain for encounter and resolution.

In that an analysis in detail of the chosen excerpts is not feasible, we might just add that in them one of the distinctive traits of the image of the couple delineated by Chrysostom consists in the theme of the harmonious union between the two (no. 42). In this, in fact, all the other elements of the picture converge, whether of the one already referred to, the dominion/submission hierarchy, that is to say, the distinct but complementary prerogatives of love and fear, or the numerous practical recommendations directed by the author so that between the spouses there may be reciprocal indulgence and toleration of their respective defects and malevolences in character or habits (nn. 43-44) and there is accomplished that work of "education" of the husband toward the wife, and the wife toward the husband, in virtue of which, in the stated diversity of their respective roles, external and internal, social and domestic, one can discern another particular sign of Chrysostom's ideas on the complementarity of the two members of the couple (nn. 48-49).

In this sphere of parenesis unfolded by Chrysostom, while the first thing to emerge is a series of specific elements revealed to an attentive observer of the multiple aspects of daily reality which enable us to reconstruct a faithful portrait of society and of family behavior in great urban centers like Antioch and Constantinople in the 4th century,[104] one can gather in his concrete experience the whole gamut of human and religious values attributed to the condition of the couple.

---

[104] Cf. J. Dumortier, 'Le mariage dans les milieux d'Antioche et de Byzance d'après Saint Jean Chrysostome,' *Lettres d'Humanité* 6 (1947), 102-166; A.J. Festugière, *Antioche païenne et chrétienne, Libanius, Chrysostome el les Moines de Syrie*, Paris, 1959. For another important aspect of the social life of these large urban centers in which the pastoral activity of Chrysostom took place, such as that of the public spectacles, frequently condemned by the author as a cause of the perversion of morals, see the analysis of O. Pasquato, *Gli spettacoli in S. Giovanni Crisostomo. Paganesimo e cristianesimo ad Antiochia e a Costantinopoli* nel *IV secolo* (Orientalia Christiana Analecta 201), Rome, 1976.

Among them emerges in the first place that of "unity," both physical and spiritual, through the express medium of the twofold images of the creation of Eve from Adam and of the Pauline figure of "head and members" of the body. This unity, if it finds in the generation of children one of its chief expressions according to the formula which makes of the offspring a "bridge" between the two (no. 39) is not exhausted in it; on the contrary, in Chrysostom marriage does not properly have its primary finality in the generative function.

Unlike Augustine, who saw generation, principally, if not exclusively, as the end of marriage, Chrysostom gave precedence to the theme of "desire."

While based on the well-known exegesis of the Pauline statement regarding marriage as a "concession" because of fornication[105] in which background one could single out that protological motivation of a first causal relationship sin/marriage, which, however, does not emerge in any of the contexts considered here, the primary connection of the nuptial relationship with *epithumia* places the interpersonal aspect of the relationship to the forefront, inasmuch as it is based on mutual attraction and destined to give it legitimate exposure.

Naturally one should not neglect how the theme of the "chain of desire," on the one hand, retains some ambiguous meanings through its connection with the sphere of the passionate as a consequence of sin and, on the other hand, has been situated in the broader picture of relations between the spouses, which Chrysostom intends to place under the dominant sign of religious values. In such a portrait the motif of *agape* is fundamental, due particularly by the husband in his dealings with his wife, understood as an expression of his Christian will to pursue the moral perfection of the woman betrothed to him.[106]

We do not intend therefore to exaggerate, in the light of modern ideological schemes, the insistence however strong on the "natu-

---

[105] For an ample treatment of the *loci* in which, on the basis of 1 Cor 7:2, Chrysostom points to marriage as the remedy for concupiscence see C. Scaglione, *art. cit.*, 283-295.

[106] See the appropriate remarks of C. Scaglione, *art. cit.*, 334-343.

ral" attraction between the sexes as a providential instrument, not just physical but also spiritual, of their harmonious composition. However, it remains essential to characterize Chrysostom's vision of the union, and to distinguish in the general patristic panorama that previously noted attention of his to the dimension of mutual attraction bestowed on the dimension of mutual attraction through which, notwithstanding all the historical conditions of that vision, the image of the man/woman relationship emerges from cold institutional schemata to assume the animated and living traits of an existential experience.

BIBLIOGRAPHY

Listed here are those titles only which strictly pertain to the theme and a few works of general character on particular authors.

More detailed documentation will be found in the notes.

Adinolfi, M., ' "Ab initio autem... fuit sic." Osservazioni sulla problematica della coppia in Gn 1-3,' *RivBibl* 18 (1970), 357-378.

———, 'La donna e Il matrimonio nel giudaismo ai tempi di Cristo,' *ibidem* 20 (1972), 369-390.

———, 'Il velo della donna e la rilettura paolina di 1 Cor 11:2-16,' *ibidem* 23 (1975), 147-173.

———, *Il femminismo della Bibbia* (Spicilegium Pontificii Athenaei Antoniani 22), Rome, 1981.

Arrighetti, G., 'Il misoginismo di Esiodo,' in Aa.vv. *Misoginia e maschilismo in Grecia e in Roma*, Genoa, 1981, 27-48.

Arrigoni, G., 'Tra le donne dell'antichità: considerazzoni e ricognizioni,' in R. Uglione (ed.), *Atti del Convegno nazionale di studi su "La donna nel mondo antico," Torino 21-22-23 Aprile 1986*, Turin, 1987, 39-71.

———, (ed.), *Le donne in Grecia*, Bari, 1985.

Aspegren, K., *The Male Woman: a Feminine Ideal in the Early Church*, Stockholm, 1990.

Baer, R.A., *Philo's Use of the Categories Male and Female*, Leiden, 1970.

Balsdon, J.P.V.D., *Roman Women: Their History and Habits*, London, 1962.

Baltensweiler, H., *Il matrimonio nel Nuovo Testamento. Ricerche esegetiche su matrimonio, celibato e divorzio* (Biblioteca di Cultura Religiose 38), Brescia, 1981, orig. ed. Zürich, 1967.

Batey, R., 'The *mia sarx*: Union of Christ and the Church,' *NTS* 13 (1966-67), 270-281.

Bauer, J.B., 'Alle origini dell'ascetismo cristiano' (Studi Biblici 66), Brescia, 1983.

Baur, Ch. *Jean Chrysostome et ses oeuvres dans l'histoire littéraire*, Louvain, 1907.

_____, *John Chrysostom and His Time*, v.1, Antioch; v.2, Constantinople, Westminster, MD, 1959 [German original, Munich, 1929-1930].

Bavel, T.J. van, 'Augustine's View on Women,' *Augustiniana* 39 (1989), 5-53 [='La mujer en san Agustín,' *Estudio Agustiniano* XXIX, I (1994), 3-49].

Beatrice, P.F., *Tradux Peccati. Alle fonti della dottrina agostiniana del peccato originale* (SPM 8), Milan, 1978.

_____, 'Continenza e matrimonio nel cristianesimo primitivo (secc. I-II),' in R. Cantalamessa (ed.), *Etica sessuale e matrimonio nel cristianesimo delle origini* (SPM 5), Milan, 1976, 3-68.

Bianchi, U. (ed.), *Le origini dello gnosticismo. Colloquio di Messina 13-18 Aprile 1966*, Leiden, 1967.

_____, *Prometeo, Orfeo, Adamo. Tematiche religiose sul destino, il male, la salvezza*, Rome, 1976.

_____, *Selected Essays on Gnosticism and Mysteriosophy* (Supplem. to *Numen*, 30), Leiden, 1978.

_____, (ed.), *La "doppia creazione" dell'uomo negli Alessandrini, nel Cappadoci e nella gnosi*, Rome, 1978.

_____, (ed.), *La tradizione dell'enkrateia. Motivazioni, ontologiche e protologiche. Atti del Colloquio internazionale, Milano 20-23 Aprile 1982*, Milan, 1985.

Bianchi, U.-Crouzel, H. (edd.), *Arché e telos. L'antropologia di Origene e di Gregorio di Nissa. Analisi storico-religiosà. Atti del Colloquio internazionale, Milano 17-19 Maggio 1979*, Milan, 1981.

Bianchi, U., Sfameni Gasparro, G., art. 'Protologia,' *DPAC* 11, coll. 2929-2941. [='Protology,' *Encyclopedia of Early Christianity*].

Bird, Phyllis A., '"Male and Female He Created Them" Gn 1:27b in the Context of the Priestly Account of Creation,' *HTR* 74 (1981), 129-159.

Blundell, S., *Women in Ancient Greece*, Cambridge, MA, 1995.

Bolgiani, F., 'La tradizione eresiologica sull'encratismo.' I. 'La notizia di Ireneo,' *AAST* 91 (1956-57), 343-419; II. 'La confutazione di Clemente di Alessandria,' *ibidem* 96 (1961-62), 537-664.

Bonner, G.I., 'Libido and Concupiscentia in St. Augustine,' *Stud Pat* VI (TU 81), Berlin, 1962, 303-314.

Bonora, A., 'La donna eccellente, la sapienza, il sapiente (Pr 31:10-31),' *RivBibl* 36 (1988), 137-163.

Borresen, K.E., *Subordination and Equivalence: the nature and role of woman in Augustine and Thomas Aquinas*, new ed., Kampen 1995 [orig. Oslo-Paris, 1968].

_____, 'Imago Dei, privilège masculin? Interpretation augustinienne et pseudo-augustinienne de Gn 1:27 et 1 Cor 11:7,' *AugR* 25 (1985), 213-234.

_____, 'Patristic "Feminism": The Case of Augustine,' *Augustinian Studies* 25 (1994).

_____, (ed.), *Image of God and Gender Models in Judaeo-Christian Tradition*, Oslo, 1991.

Bouyer, L., *Mariage et virginité dans l'église ancienne*, Paris.

Bradley, K., *Discovering the Roman Family: Studies in Roman Social History*, New York, 1991.

Braun, R., 'Tertullien et l'exégèse de 1 Cor 7,' in J. Fontaine/Ch. Kannengiesser (edd.), *Epektasis. Mélanges patristiques offerts au Cardinal Jean Daniélou*, Paris, 1972, 21-28.

Broudéhoux, J.P., *Mariage et famille chez Clément d'Alexandrie.* (Théologie historique 11), Paris, 1970.

Brown, P., *Augustine of Hippo: A Biography*, London, 1967.

_____, *The Body and Society: Men, Women, and Sexual Renunciation in Early Christianity*, New York, 1988 [See reviews: *RSLR* 28 (1992), 105-125].

_____, *Augustine and Sexuality.* The Center for Hermeneutical Studies in Hellenistic and Modern Culture, 46, Berkeley, CA, 1983.

Buchler, A., 'Ben Sira's Conception of Sin and Atonement,' *JQR* 13 (1922-23), 303-335, 461-502; *ibidem* 14 (1923-24), 53-83.

Buckley, J.J., 'An Interpretation of Logion 114 in the Gospel of Thomas,' *NT* 27, 3 (1985), 245-272.

_____, *Female Fault and Fulfillment in Gnosticism*, Chapel Hill-London, 1986.

Burghardt, W.J., 'The Image of God in Man: Alexandrian Orientations,' in *Proceedings of the Sixteenth Annual Convention*, Ottawa, Ontario, June 19, 20, 21, 22, 1961 (The Catholic Theological Society of America), 147-160.

Burini, C.-Cavalcanti, E., *La spiritualità della vita quotidiana negli scritti dei Padri*, Bologna, 1988.

Calame, C., (ed.), *L'amore in Grecia*, Milan, 1983.

Camelot, P.Th., *Foi et gnose. Introduction a l'étude de la connaissance mystique chez Clement d'Alexandrie*, Paris, 1945.

_____, 'Les traités "De Virginitate" au IV-siècle,' *Mystique, et Continence. Études Carmelitaines* 31 (1952), 273-292.

_____, 'La théologie de l'image de Dieu,' *RScPhT* 40 (1956), 443-471.

_____, s.v. 'ΕΓΚΡΑΤΕΙΑ (Continentia),' *DSp* IV, l, Paris, 1960, coll. 357-370.

Cameron, A./Kuhrt, A. edd., *Images of Women in Antiquity*, London, 1983, 1993².

Cantalamessa, R. (ed.), *Etica sessuale e matrimonio nel cristianesimo delle origini* (SPM 5), Milan, 1976.

Cantarella, E., *L'ambiguo malanno. Condizione e immagine della donna nell'anticità greca e romana*, Rome, 1981.

_____, 'La vita delle donne,' in Aa. vv., *Storia di Roma*, IV (*Caratteri e Morfologia*), E. Gabba-A. Schiavone (edd.), Turin, 1989, 557-608.

Carcopino, J., *La vita quotidiana a Roma all'apogeo dell'Impero*, Bari, 1941, ed. orig. Paris, 1939.

Castano, L., 'Sant'Ambrogio apostolo della verginità,' *Salesianum* 2 (1940), 273-288.

Castiglioni, A., 'La donna nel pensiero dei Padri della Chiesa greca del IV secolo,' *La Scuola Cattolica* 46,2 (1918) 29-51, 131-146, 212-233, 353-365, 439-466; rp. in book form, Monza, 1919.

Cavallera, F., *Saint Jérôme. Sa vie et son oeuvre. Première partie*, T. I-II, Louvain-Paris, 1922.

Chadwick, H., *Augustine*, Oxford-New York, 1986.

Clark, E.A., *Jerome, Chrysostom, and Friends: Essays and Translations* (Studies in Women and Religion 2), New York-Toronto, 1979.

_____, *Women in the Early Church* (Message of the Fathers of the Church 13), Wilmington, DE, 1983.

_____, '"Adam's Only Companion": Augustine and the Early Christian Debate on Marriage,' *RechAug* 21 (1986), 139-161.

_____, *Ascetic Piety and Woman's Faith: Essays on Late Ancient Christianity*, New York-Toronto, 1986.

_____, 'Early Christian Women: Sources and Interpretation,' in *Historical Perspectives on Women in Christianity*, ed. L. Coon, Univ. of Virginia Press, 1990.

_____, (ed.), *Augustine on Marriage and Sexuality*, Washington, DC, 1993.

Clark, G., *Women in Late Antiquity: Pagan and Christian Lifestyles*, Oxford, 1994.

Consolino, F.E., 'Modelli di comportamento e modi di santificazione per l'aristocrazia femminile d'Occidente,' in A. Giardina (ed.), *Società romana e Impero tardoantico 1, Istituzioni, Ceti, Economia*, Bari, 1986, 273-306, 684-699.

_____, 'Figure di donne cristiane: la martire,' in R. Uglione (ed.), *Atti del II Convegno nazionale di studi su "La donna nel mondo antico,"* Torino 18-19-20 Aprile 1988, Turin, 1989, 167-195.

Corsini, E., 'La donna nel Nuovo Testamento,' in Aa.vv., *Sponsa, Mater, Virgo. La donna nel mondo biblico e patristico*, Genoa, 1985, 21-39.

Cortellezzi, G., 'Il concetto della donna nelle opere di Tertulliano,' *Didaskaleion NS 1* (1923) fasc. 1, 5-29; fasc. 2, 57-79; fasc. 3, 43-100.

Costanza, S., 'Catechesi e poesia nei Carmi XXII, XXV e XXXI di Paolino di Nola,' in S. Felici (ed.), *Crescita dell'uomo nella catechesi dei Padri (Età postnicena)*, Rome, 1988, 226-285.

Couliano, I.P., *I miti dei dualismi occidentali. Dai sistemi gnostici al mondo moderno*, Milan, 1989, ed. orig. Paris, 1987.

Covi, D., 'L'etica sessuale paradisiaca agostiniana,' *Laurentianum 13* (1972), 340-364.

Cracco Ruggini, L., 'La donna e il sacro, tra paganesimo e cristianesimo,' in R. Uglione (ed.), *Atti del II Convegno., op. cit.*, 243-275.

Crouzel, H., 'L'anthropologie d'Origène dans la perspective du combat spirituel,' *RAM 31* (1955), 364-385.

_____, *Théologie de l'image de Dieu chez Origène*, Paris, 1956.

_____, *Virginité et mariage selon Origène*, Paris-Bruges, 1963.

_____, *L'Église primitive face au divorce*, Paris, 1971.

_____, *Bibliographie critique d'Origène*, Steenbrugis, Hagae Comitis 1971.

_____, *Bibliographie critique d'Origène. Supplément 1*, 1982.

_____, *Mariage et divorce, célibat et caractère sacerdotaux dans l'Église ancienne*, Turin, 1982.

_____, 'Liturgie du mariage chrétien au V siècle selon l'Epithalame de saint Paulin de Nola,' in *"Mens concordet voci."* *Scritti in onore di Ms. Martimort*, Paris, 1983, 619-626.

_____, 'L'epitalamio di San Paolino: Il suo contenuto dotrinale,' in *Atti del Convegno XXXI Cinquantenario della morte di s. Paolino di Nola (431-1981), Nola, 20-21 Marzo 1982*, Rome, s.d. (1983), 143-148.

_____, *Origen*, Paris, 1985. Engl. tr. A.S. Worrall, San Francisco, 1989.

Daube, D., *La femme dans le droit biblique*, 1962.

Day, P. ed., *Gender and Difference in Ancient Israel*, Minneapolis, 1989.

Delcourt, M., 'Utrumque-Neutrum,' in *Mélanges d'histoire des religions offerts a Henri-Charles Puech*, Paris, 1974, 117-123.

De Lubac, H., *Storia e spirito. La comprensione della Scrittura secondo Origene*, Rome, 1971, ed. orig. Paris, 1950.

Deming, W., *Paul on Marriage and Celibacy: The Hellenistic Background of First Corinthians 7*, Cambridge U. Press, 1995.

Denis, A. M., *Introduction aux pseudépigraphes grecs d'Ancien Testament* (Studia in Veteris Testamenti Pseudepigrapha I), Leiden, 1970.

De Plinval, G., 'Recherches sur l'oeuvre littéraire de Pélage,' *RevPhil S.* 111, 8 (= 60) (1934), 9-42.

_____, 'Vue d'ensemble sur la littérature pélagienne,' *REL* 29 (1951), 284-294.

Dixon, S., *The Roman Family*, Baltimore, 1992.

Doignon, J., 'Une définition oubliée de l'amour conjugal édénique chez Augustin: piae caritatis adfectus (*Gen. ad litt.* 3,21,33),' *VetChr* 19 (1982), 23-36.

Dossi, L., 'S. Ambrogio e S. Atanasio nel *De Virginibus*,' *Acme* 4 (1951), 241-262.

Dover, K.J., *Homosexuality in Ancient Greece*, London, 1978.

Dumm, D., *The Theological Basis of Virginity according to St. Jerome*, Latrobe, 1961.

Dumortier, J., 'Le mariage dans les milieux chrétiens d'Antioche et de Byzance d'après saint Jean Chrysostome,' in *Lettres d'Humanité* 6 (1947), 102-166.

Dupont, J., *Mariage et divorce dans l'Évangile Matthieu 19:3-12 et parallèles*, Bruges, 1959.

Dupuis, J., *"L'Esprit de l'homme."* *Étude sur l'anthropologie religieuse d'Origène* (Museum Lessianum, séction théologique 62), Bruges, 1967.

Duval, Y.-M., 'L'originalité du *De virginibus* dans le mouvement ascétique occidental. Ambroise, Cyprien, Athanase,' in *Idem.* (ed.), *Ambroise de Milan. XVI-Centenaire de son élection épiscopale*, Paris, 1974, 9-66.

Eijk, Ton H.C. van, 'Marriage and Virginity, Death and Immortality,' in Fontaine J.-Kannengiesser Ch. (edd.), *Epektasis. Mélanges patristiques offerts au Cardinal Jean Daniélou*, Paris, 1972, 209-235.

Erbetta, M., *Gli Apocrifi del Nuovo Testamento*, I/1-2, *Vangeli*, Turin, 1975-1981; II, *Atti e Leggende*, Turin, 1966; III, *Lettere e Apocalissi*, Turin, 1969.

Evans, M.J., *Woman in the Bible*, Devon, 1983.

Fabre, P., *S. Paulin de Nole et l'amitié chrétienne* (BEFAR 167), Paris, 1949.

Fantham, E. et al., *Women in the Classical World: Image and Text*, Oxford U. Press, 1994.

Fayer, C., *La famiglia romana. Aspetti giuridici ed antiquari*, 1, Rome, 1994.

Festa, N., *Epitteto. Il "Manuale,"* traduzione di Giacomo Leopardi con saggi delle "Dissertazioni" e coi frammenti di Musonio Rufo, Milan, 1914.

Festugière, A.J., *Antioche païenne et chrétienne. Libanius, Chrysostome et les moines de Syrie*, Paris, 1959.

Feuillet, A., 'L'homme "gloire de Dieu" et la femme "gloire de l'homme" (1 Cor XI, 71),' *RB* 81 (1974), 161-182.

_____, 'La dignité et le rôle de la femme d'après quelques textes pauliniens: comparaison avec l'Ancien Testament,' *NTS* 21 (1975), 157-191.

Filoramo, G., *L'attesa della fine. Storia della gnosi*, Bari, 1983.

Fitzmyer, J.A., 'A Feature of Qumrân Angelology and the Angels of I Cor. XI.10,' *NTS* 4,1 (1957), 48-58, rp. in J. Murphy-O'Connor (ed.), *Paul and Qumran: Studies in New Testament Exegesis*, Chicago, 1968, 31-47.

Flacelière, R., *Amour humain, parole divine. Recueil de textes des Pères de l'Église sur le mariage, avec une introduction*, Paris, 1947.

_____, *L'amour en Grèce*, Paris, 1960.

Forrester Church, F., 'Sex and Salvation in Tertullian,' *HTR* 68 (1975), 83-101.

Frassinetti, P., 'Gli scritti matrimoniali di Seneca e Tertulliano,' *RIL* 88 (S. 111, 19) (1958), 151-188.

Fredouille, J. Cl., *Tertullien et la conversion de la culture antique*, Paris, 1972.

Frey, J.-B., 'L'état originel et la chute de l'homme. D'après les conceptions juives au temps de J.-C.,' *RScPhTh* 5 (1911), 507-545.

⸺, 'Adam (Livres apocryphes sous son nom),' in *DB Suppl.* 1, Paris, 1928, 101-134.

Gallus, T., 'A muliere initium peccati et per illam omnes morimur,' *Verbum Domini* 23 (1943), 272-277.

Gardner, J.F., *Women in Roman Law and Society*, London-Sydney, 1986.

Gaudemet, J., 'L'Église dans l'Empire romain,' in G. Le Bras-J. Gaudemet (édd.), *Histoire du Droit et des Institutions de l'Église en Occident*, t. III, *L'Église dans l'Empire romain (IV-V siècles)*, Paris, 1958, 514-591.

⸺, 'Les transformations de la vie familiale au Bas-Empire et l'influence du christianisme,' *Romanitas* 4 (1962), 58-85.

⸺, s.v. 'Familie 1: Familienrecht,' *RAC* VII, Stuttgart, 1969, coll. 286-358.

⸺, 'Le statut de la femme dans l'Empire romain,' in *Recueils Jean Bodin XI, La Femme*, Iᵉʳᵉ Partie, Brussels, 1959, 192-222.

⸺, *Il matrimonio in Occidente*, Turin, 1989, orig. ed. Paris, 1987.

Gelsomino, R., 'L'Epitalamio di Paolino di Nola per Giuliano e Tizia,' in *Atti del Convegno XXXI Cinquantenario della morte di Paolino di Nola (431-1981)*, op. cit., 213-230.

Giannarelli, E., *La tipologia femminile nella biografia e nella autobiografia cristiana del IV secolo* (Istituto storico italiano per il Medio Evo, Studi storici, fasc. 127), Rome, 1980.

⸺, *S. Gregorio di Nissa, La vita di S. Macrina*, Introduzione, traduzione e note, Milan, 1988.

Giblet, J., 'L'homme image de Dieu dans les Commentaires littéraux de Philon d'Alexandrie,' *Studia hellenistica* 5 (1948), 93-118.

Gilbert, M., 'Ben Sira et la femme,' *RThL* 7 (1976), 426-442.

Goodwater, P., *Women in Antiquity: An Annotated Bibliography*, Metuchen, 1976.

Gorce, D., 'Mariage et perfection chrétienne d'après Saint Jean Chrysostome,' *Études Carmelitaines Mystiques et Missionnaires* 21,1 (1963), 245-284.

Graef, H.C., 'L'image de Dieu et la structure de l'âme d'après les Pères grecs,' *La Vie spirituelle, Suppl.* 22 (1955), 331-339.

Gramaglia, P.A. (ed.), *Tertulliano, De Virginibus Velandis. La condizione femminile nelle prime comunità cristiane*, Rome, 1984.

———, 'Personificazioni e modelli del femminile nella transizione dalla cultura classica a quella cristiana,' in G. Galli (ed.), *Interpretazione e Personificazione. Personificazioni e Modelli del Femminile. Atti del Nono Colloquio sulla Interpretazione (Macerate, 6-8 Aprile 1987)*, Genoa, 1988, 17-164.

———, (ed.), *Tertulliano. Il matrimonio nel cristianesimo preniceno. Ad uxorem — De exhortatione castitatis — De monogamia*, Rome, 1988.

Grant, R.M., *Gnosticism and Early Christianity*, New York, 1959.

Grelot, P. *La coppia umana nella sacra scrittura*, Milan, 1968, orig. ed. Paris, 1964.

Grimal, P. (ed.), *Histoire mondiale de la femme*, I, *Préhistoire et Antiquité*, Paris 1965 II, *L'Occident, des Celtes à la Renaissance*, Paris, 1966; III, *L'Orient, l'Afrique Noire, l'Asie, l'Océanie et l'Amerique précolombienne*, Paris, 1967.

Grossi, V., *La liturgia battesimale in S. Agostino. Studio sulla catechesi del peccato originale negli anni 393-412* (Studia Ephemeridis "Augustinianum" 7), Rome, 1970.

———, 'La verginità negli scritti dei Padri. La sintesi di S. Ambrogio: gli aspetti cristologici, antropologici, ecclestastici,' in Aa. vv., *Il celibato per il Regno*, Milan, 1977, 131-164.

Grubbs, J.E., '"Pagan" and "Christian" Marriage: The State of the Question,' *JECS* 2, 4 (1994), 361-412.

Guilloux, P., 'L'ascétisme de Clément d'Alexandrie,' *RAM* 3 (1922), 282-300.

Guroian, V., 'Family and Christian Virtue in a Post-Christendom World: Reflections on the Ecclesial Vision of John Chrysostom,' *St. Vladimir's Theol. Quart.* 35 (1991), 327-350.

Hagendahl, H., *Latin Christianity and classical culture from Tertullian to Cassiodorus*, Rome, 1988, Göteborg, 1983.

———, *Latin Fathers and the Classics*, Göteborg, 1958.

Harnack, A. von, Marcion. Das Evangelium vom fremden Gott, Leipzig, 1924, 2ed.

Harris, K., Sex, Ideology and Religion: The Representation of Women in the Bible, Brighton-Totowa, 1984.

Harrison, A.R.W., The Law of Athens: the Family and Property, Oxford, 1968.

Hawley, R. and Levick, B., edd., Women in Antiquity: New Assessments, London-New York, 1995.

Hennessey, L.R., 'Sexuality, Family and the Life of Discipleship. Some Early Christian Perspectives,' Chicago Studies 32 (1993), 19-31.

Hinschberger, R., 'Image et ressemblance dans la tradition sacerdotale. Gn 1:26-28; 5:1-3; 9:6b,' RevSR 59 (1985), 185-199.

Hooker, M.D., 'Authority on Her Head: An Examination of 1 Cor 11:10,' NTS 10, 3 (1964), 410-416.

Horowitz, M.C., 'The Image of God in Man. Is Woman Included?', HThR 72 (1979), 175-206.

Hunter, D.G., Marriage in the Early Church (Sources of Early Christian Thought), Minneapolis, 1992.

_____, 'Augustinian Pessimism? A New Look at Augustine's Teaching on Sex, Marriage and Celibacy,' Augustinian Studies 25 (1994), 153-177.

_____, 'The Paradise of Patriarchy. Ambrosiaster on woman as (not) God's image,' JTS 43 (1992), 447-469.

_____, 'Helvidius, Jovinian and the Virginity of Mary in Late Fourth Century Rome,' JECS 1 (1993), 47-71.

Jaubert, A., 'Le voile des femmes (1 Cor 11:2-16),' NTS 18, 4 (1972), 428-430.

Jervell, J., Imago Dei. Gn 1:26f im Spätjudentum, in die Gnosis und in den paulinischen Briefen (Forschungen zur Religion und Literatur des Alten Testament 76, NF 58), Göttingen, 1960.

Jonas, H., Gnosticism, Boston, 1958, 1967.

Jonsson, G.A., The Image of God: Genesis 1:26-28 in a Century of Old Testament Research, Lund, 1988.

Kannnengiesser, Ch., 'Philon et les Pères sur la double création de l'homme,' in Philon d'Alexandrie, Lyon 11-15 Septembre 1966. Colloques Nationaux du Centre National de la Recherche Scientifique, Paris, 1967, 277-296.

Kelly, J.N.D., *Jerome: His Life, Writings and Controversies*, London, 1975.

_____, *Golden Mouth: John Chrysostom and His Time*, Ithaca, NY, 1995.

Kinder, D.M., *The Role of the Christian Woman as Seen by Clement of Alexandria*, The University of Iowa, PhD, 1988.

King, K. ed., *Images of the Feminine in Gnosticism*, Philadelphia, 1988.

Kraemer, R.S., *Her Share of the Blessings*, Oxford University Press, 1992.

Lacey, W.K., *The Family in Classical Greece*, London, 1968.

Lang, B., 'No Sex in Heaven: the Logic of Procreation, Death and Eternal Life in the Judaeo-Christian Tradition,' *Alten Orient und Altes Testament* 215 (1985), 237-253.

Lefkowitz, M.R./Fant, M.B., *Women's Life in Greece and Rome: A Sourcebook in Translation* 2nd ed., London/Baltimore, 1992.

Lilla, S., *Clement of Alexandria: A Study in Christian Platonism and Gnosticism*, Oxford, 1971.

Lodi, E., 'Famiglia-chiesa domestica nella tradizione patristica,' *Rivista di Pastorale liturgica* 18 (1980), 25-30.

Loraux, N., *Children of Athena: Athenian Ideas about Citizenship and the Division Between the Sexes*, Princeton, 1993.

Lutz Cora, E., 'Musonius Rufus "The Roman Socrates",' *YClS* 10 (1947), 3-147.

MacDonald, M.Y., 'The Ideal of the Christian Couple: Ignatius, Polyc. 5, 1-2. Looking Back to Paul,' *NTS* 40 (1994), 105-125.

Malina, B.J., 'Some Observations on the Origin of Sin in Judaism and St. Paul,' *CBQ* 31 (1969), 18-34.

Malingrey, A.-M., "Philosophia." *Étude d'un groupe de mots dans la littérature grecque des Présocratiques au IV siècle après J.-C.*, Paris, 1961.

Manning, C.E., 'Seneca and the Stoics on the Equality of the Sexes,' *Mnemosyne* S. IV, 26 (1973), 170-177.

Mara, M.G., 'I Padri della Chiesa e la donna,' *Parole di vita* 30, 6 (1985), 11-18 (411-418).

Marrou, H.-I., *St. Augustine et la fin de la culture antique*, Paris, 1938, 4 ed., 1958.

_____, *History of Education in Antiquity*, orig. ed. Paris, 1948, 1964[2].

Massingberd Ford, J., 'St. Paul, the Philogamist (1 Cor 7 in Early Patristic Exegesis),' *NTS* 11 (1965), 326-348.

Mattei, P., 'La place du *De monogamia* dans l'évolution théologique et spirituelle de Tertullien,' *Stud Pat* 18,3 (1989), 319-328.

———, 'Du Divorce et de Tertullien,' *REAug* 39 (1993), 23-35.

Mattioli, U., *Astheneia e andreia. Aspetti della femminilità nella letteratura classics, biblica e cristiana*, Rome, 1983.

———, (ed.), *La donna nel pensiero cristiano antico*, Genoa, 1992 [see review by K.E. Borresen, *AugR* 34,2 (1994), 503-511].

———, 'La donna nel pensiero patristico,' in R. Uglione (ed.) *Atti del Convegno nazionale di studi su "La donna nel mondo antico,"* op. cit., 223-242.

Mazzucco, C., *"E fui fatta maschio" La donna nel cristianesimo primitivo*, Florence, 1989.

Mazzucco, C.-Militello, C.-Valerio, A., *E Dio li creò*. Milan, 1990.

McGowen, R.J., 'Augustine's Spiritual Equality: the Allegory of Man and Woman with Regard to *Imago Dei*,' *REAug* 33 (1987), 255-264.

Mees, M., 'Clemens von Alexandrien über Ehe und Familie,' *AugR* 17 (1977), 113-131.

Meslin, M., 'Sainteté et mariage au cours de la seconde querelle pélagienne. Saint Augustin et Julien d'Eclane,' in *Mystique et continence. Études Carmelitaines* 31 (1952), 293-307.

Meyer, A., *Das Bild Gottes im Mensch nach Clemens von Alexandrien*, Rome, 1942.

Meyer, L., *Saint Jean Chrysostome maître de perfection chrétienne*, Paris, 1933.

Meyer, M.W., 'Making Mary Male: the Categories "Male" and "Female" in the Gospel of Thomas,' *NTS* 31 (1985), 554-570.

Micaelli, C., 'L'influsso di Tertulliano su Girolamo: le opere sul matrimonio e le seconde nozze,' *AugR* 1 (1979), 415-429.

———, 'Retorica, filosofia e cristianesimo negli scritti matrimoniali di Tertulliano,' *Annali della Scuola Normale Superiore di Pisa, Cl. lett. e fil-S.III*, 11 (1981), 69-104.

Militello, C., *Donna e Chiesa. La testimonianza di Giovanni Crisostomo*, Palermo, 1986.

Miller, J. M., 'In the "Image" and "Likeness" of God,' *JBL* 91 (1972), 289-304.

Monaci Castagno, A., *Origene predicatore e il suo pubblico*, Turin, 1987.

Mondésert, C., *Clément d'Alexandrie: introduction a l'étude de sa pensée religieuse a partir de l'Écriture*, Paris, 1944.

Moreschini C.-Palla R. (edd.), *San Gerolamo, Lettere*, Milan, 1989.

Moulard, A., *St. Jean Chrysostome. Sa vie. Son oeuvre*, Paris, 1941.

Munier, Ch., *Mariage et Virginité dans l'Église ancienne (Ier-IIIe siècles)*, Bern-Frankfurt-Main-New York-Paris, 1987.

_____, 'Église et cité,' in G. Le Bras-J. Gaudemet (edd.), *Histoire du Droit et des Institutions de l'Église en Occident*, t. II, 3, *L'Église dans l'Empire romain (II-III siècles)*, III partie, Paris, 1979, 3-71.

_____, 'La sollicitude pastorale de l'Église ancienne en matière de divorce et de remariage,' *Laval Théol et Philos.* 44 (1988), 19-30.

Murphy, F.-X., *Rufinus of Aquileia*, Washington, 1945.

Nagel, P., *Die Motivierung der Askese in der alten Kirche und die Ursprung des Mönchtums* (TU 95), Berlin, 1966.

Nautin, P., *Origène. Sa vie et son oeuvre*, Paris, 1977.

Nazzaro, A.V., 'Figure di donne cristiane: la vedova,' in R. Uglione (ed.), *Atti del secondo Convegno nazionale di studi su "La donna nel mondo antico,"* op. cit., 197-219.

Oakley, J.H. and Sinos, R.H., *The Wedding in Ancient Athens*, Madison, WI, 1993.

Oggioni, G., 'Matrimonio e verginità presso i Padri (fino a S. Agostino),' in Aa. vv., *Matrimonio e verginità. Saggi di Teologia*, Venegono Inferiore 1963, 159-405.

Orbe, A., 'El pecado de Eva, signo de división,' *OrChrPer* 29 (1963), 305-330.

_____, 'El pecado original y el matrimonio en la teología del s. II,' *Gregorianum* 45 (1964), 449-500.

_____, *Estudios Valentinianos, I-IV*, Rome, 1955-1966.

Osborn, E., 'La Bible inspiratrice d'une morale chrétienne d'après Clément d'Alexandrie,' in *Le monde grec ancien et la Bible*, sous la direction de C. Mondésert, Paris, 1984, 127-144.

Pagels, E., *Adam, Eve and the Serpent*, New York, 1988.

_____, 'Adam and Eve, Christ and the Church: A Survey of Second Century Controversies Concerning Marriage,' in Logan, A.H.B.-Wedderburn, A.J.M., *The New Testament and Gnosticism: Essays in Honour of R.McL. Wilson*, Edinburgh, 1983, 146-175.

Paoli, U.E., *La donna greca nell'antichità*, Florence, 1955.

Pasquato, O., *Gli spettacoli in S. Giovanni Crisostomo. Paganesimo e Cristianesimo ad Antiochia e Costantinopoli nel IV secolo* (Orientalia Christiana Analecta 201), Rome, 1976.

Pastorino, A., 'La condizione femminile nei Padri della Chiesa,' in *Sponsa, Mater, Virgo...*, *op. cit.*, pp. 109-122.

Penna, R., *Lettera agli Efesini. Introduzzione, versione, commento*, Bologna, 1988.

Peradotto, J. & Sullivan, J.P., *Women in the Ancient World. The Arethusa Papers*, Albany, NY, 1984.

Perrin, M., *L'homme antique et chrétien. L'anthropologie de Lactance (250-325)*, Paris, 1981.

Peterson, E., 'L'origine dell'ascesi cristiana,' in *Euntes Docete* 1, (1948) 195-205 rp. in *Frühkirche, Judentum und Gnosis. Studien und Untersuchungen*, Rome-Freibourg-Vienna, 1959, 209-220.

Pichon, R., *Lactance*, Paris, 1901.

Pietri, Ch., 'IV-V secolo. Il matrimonio cristiano a Roma,' in J. Delumeau (ed.), *Storia vissuta del popolo cristiano*, Turin, 1985, 93-121, ed. orig. Paris, 1979.

Pincherle, A., *La vita di Sant Agostino*, Rome-Bari, 1980.

Pirenne, J., 'Le statut de la femme dans la civilisation hebraïque,' in *Recueils Jean Bodin XI. La Femme*, *op. cit.*, 107-126.

Pisi, P., *Genesis e phthorá. Le motivazioni protologiche della verginita in Gregorio di Nissa e nella tradizione dell'enkrateia*, Rome, 1981.

Pizzolato, L.P., 'La coppia umana in S. Ambrogio,' in R. Cantalamessa (ed.), *Etica sessuale e matrimonio*, *op. cit.*, 180-181.

Plinval, G. de, *Pélage. Sa vie, ses écrits et sa réforme. Étude d'histoire littéraire et religieuse*, Lausanne, 1943.

Pohlenz, M., *L'uomo greco*, Göttingen, 1947.

Pomeroy, S.B., *Women in Athens and Rome*, New York, 1975 [On which, cf. Culham, P. in *Helios* n.s. 13 (1986), 9-30].

Pomeroy, S.B., *Women in Hellenistic Egypt from Alexander to Cleopatra*. Detroit, 1990.

_____, 'Sexuality in the Ancient World,' *Religious Studies Review* 20 (1994), 182-187.

Préaux C., 'Le statut de la femme à l'époque hellenistique, principalement en Egypte,' *Recueils Jean Bodin XI. La Femme*, 127-175.

Prete, S., *Paolino di Nola e l'umanesimo cristiano. Saggio sul suo epistolario* (Studi e ricerche, NS 9), Bologna, 1964.

_____, 'I temi della proprieté e della famiglia negli scritti di Paolino di Nola,' *AugR* 17 (1977), 257-282.

_____, *Matrimonio e continenza nel cristianesimo delle origini. Studio su 1 Cor 7:1-40* (Studi Biblici 49), Brescia, 1979.

Proietti, B., 'La scelta celibataria alla luce della S. Scrittura,' in Aa.vv., *Il celibato per il Regno*, Milan, 1977, 7-75.

Prusak, B.P., 'Woman: Seductive Siren and Source of Sin? Pseudepigraphal Myth and Christian Origin,' in R. Radford Ruether (ed.), *Religion and Sexism*, New York, 1974, 89-116.

Puech, H. Ch., *Sulle tracce della gnosi. I. La gnosi e il tempo. II. Sul Vangelo secondo Tommaso*, Milan, 1985, ed. orig. Paris, 1978.

Quasten, J., *Patrology*, I-II, Turin, 1973-1980, ed. orig. Utrecht, 1950-1953. *Patrologia*, III, A. Di Berardino (ed.), Turin, 1978.

Quére-Jaulmes, F., *La femme. Les grandes textes des Pères de l'Église* (Lettres chrétiennes 12), Paris, 1968.

Quesnell, Q., '"Made Themselves Eunuchs for the Kingdom of Heaven" (Mt 19:12),' *CBQ* 30 (1968), 335-358.

Radice, R., *Platonismo e creazionismo in Filone di Alessandria*, Milan, 1989.

Rambaux, C., *Tertullien face aux morales des trois premiers siècles*, Paris, 1979.

Ramos-Lisson, D., 'Le rôle de la femme dans la théologie de saint Irénée,' *Stud Pat* 21 (1989), 163-174.

Rawson, B. ed., *Marriage, Divorce and Children in Ancient Rome*, Oxford Univ. Press, 1991.

Reale, G.-Radice, R., *Filone di Alessandria. La filosofia mosaica.* Monografia introduttiva, Milan, 1987.

Reuter, A., *Sancti Aurelii Augustini doctrina de bonis matrimonii* (Analecta Gregoriana vol. XXVII, Series Theologica Sectio B n. 12), Rome, 1942.

Reynolds, P.L., *Marriage in the Western Church*, Leiden/New York, 1994.

Rigaux, B., 'Le célibat et le radicalisme évangélique,' *NRTh* 94 (1972), 157-170.

Ritzer, K., *Le mariage dans les Églises chrétiennes du Ier au XIe siècle*, Paris, 1970, ed. orig. Münster, 1962.

Rordorf, W., 'Marriage in the New Testament and in the Early Church,' *JEH* 20 (1969), 193-210.

Sacchi, P. (cur.), *Apocrifi dell'Antico Testamento*, I-II, Turin, 1981-1989.

Sage A., 'Péché originel. Naissance d'un dogme,' *REAug* 13 (1967), 211-248.

_____, 'Le péché originel dans la pensée de saint Augustin, de 412 à 430,' *ibidem* 15 (1969), 75-112.

Sagnard, F., *La gnose valentinienne et le témoignage de Saint Irénée*, Paris, 1947.

Saller, R., 'I rapporti di parentela e l'organizzazione familiare,' in Aa. vv., *Storia di Roma, IV*. Caratteri e Morfologia, a cura di E. Gabba-A. Schiavone, Turin, 1989, 515-555.

_____, 'Familia, Domus and the Roman Conception of Family,' *Phoenix* 38 (1984), 336-355.

_____, 'Roman Dowry and the devolution of property in the Principate,' *ClQ* 34 (1984), 195-205.

_____, 'Men's age at marriage,' *ClPhil* 82 (1987), 21-34.

Samek Lodovici, E., 'Sessualità, matrimonio e concupiscenza in sant'Agostino,' in R. Cantalamessa (ed.), *Etica sessuale e matrimonio, op. cit.*, 212-272.

Savalli, I., *La donna nella società della Grecia antica*, Bologna, 1983.

Savon, H., *Saint Ambroise devant l'exégèse de Philon le Juif*, 1-11 (Études Augustiniennes), Paris, 1977.

Sawyer, J.F.A., 'The Meaning of "In the Image of God" in Genesis 1-11,' *JThS* NS 25 (1974), 418-426.

Scaglioni, C., 'La donna nel pensiero dei Padri greci,' *Vita e Pensiero* 58, 3-4 (1975), 28-50.

_____, 'Ideale coniugale e familiare in san Giovanni Crisostomo,' in R. Cantalamessa (ed.), *Etica sessuale e matrimonio, op. cit.*, 273-422.

Scalco, E., 'Sacramentum conubii et institution nuptiale: une lecture du De bono coniugali et du De sancta virginitate de S. Augustin,' *EThL* 69 (1993), 27-47.

Schmitt, É., *Le mariage chrétien dans l'oeuvre de saint Augustin. Une théologie baptismale de la vie conjugale* (Études Augustiniennes), Paris, 1983.

Schmitt Pantel, P., *Storia delle donne in Occidente*, 1, *L'Antichità*, Bari, 1990.

Scholer, D.M., *Nag Hammadi Bibliography 1948-1969* (*NHS* 1), Leiden, 1971.

_____, 'Bibliographia gnostica.' Supplements, *NT* 13 (1971), annually.

Schwanz, P., *Imago Dei als christologisch-anthropologisches Problem in der Geschichte der alten Kirche von Paulus bis Clemens von Alexandrien*, Göttingen, 1970.

Scuderi, R., 'Mutamenti della condizione femminile a Romà nell'ultima età repubblicana,' *CCC* 3 (1982), 41-84.

Sfameni Gasparro, G., 'Gli Atti apocrifi degli Apostoli e la tradizione dell'enkrateia,' *AugR* 23 (1983), 287-307.

_____, *Origene*. *Studi di antropologia e di storia della tradizione* (Nuovi Saggi 90), Rome, 1984.

_____, *Enkrateia e antropologia*. *Le motivazioni protologiche della continenza e della verginità nel cristianesimo dei primi secoli e nello gnosticismo* (Studia Ephemeridis "Augustinianum" 20), Rome, 1984.

_____, 'Concupiscenza e generazione: aspetti antropologici della dottrina agostiniana del peccato originale,' in *Atti del Congresso internazionale su S. Agostino nel XVI Centenario della conversione* (*Roma 15-20 settembre 1986*), Rome, 1987, II, 225-255.

_____, 'L'Epistula Titi discipuli Pauli de dispositione sanctimonii e la tradizione dell'enkrateia,' *ANRW* 11, 25,6, Berlin-New York, 1988, 4551-4664.

_____, 'La vergogna di Adamo e di Eva nella riflessione dei Padri,' *PSV* 20 (1989/2), 253-270.

Shore, S. Reager, *John Chrysostom On Virginity Against Remarriage*, New York, 1983.

Sierra, S., 'La donna nel mondo ebraico biblico,' in Aa. vv., *Sponsa, mater, virgo*, *op. cit.*, 9-20.

Simonetti, M., *Testi gnostici cristiani*, Bari, 1970.

_____, *Lettera e/o allegoria*. *Un contributo alla storia dell'esegesi patristica*, Rome, 1985.

Sodano, A.R., 'Ambrogio e Filone. Leggendo il De paradiso,' *AFLM* 8 (1975), 67-82.

Solignac, A.-Nuvolone, F.G., 'Pélage et pélagianisme,' *DSp* 12, Paris, 1986, coll. 2889-2942.

Spanneut, M., *Le stoïcisme des Pères de l'Église de Clément de Rome a Clément d'Alexandrie*, Paris, 1957.

_____, *Tertullien et les premiers moralistes africains*, Paris, 1969.

Spidlík, T., 'Il matrimonio sacramento di unità, nel pensiero di Crisostomo,' *AugR* 17 (1977), 221-226.

Strucker, A., *Die Gottenbildlickeit des Menschen in der cristlichen Literatur der ersten zwei Jahrhunderten*, Münster, 1913.

Suso Frank, P., *ΑΓΓΕΛΙΚΟΣ ΒΙΟΣ*, Münster, 1964.

Swidler, L., *Biblical Affirmation of Woman*, Philadelphia, 1979.

Tardieu, M., *Il manicheismo*, Introduzione, traduzione e aggiornamento bibliografico a cura di G. Sfameni Gasparro, Cosenza 1988, ed. orig. Paris, 1981.

Tavard, G., *Women in Christian Tradition*, Univ. of Notre Dame Press, 1973.

Termes Ros, P., 'La formación de Eva en los Padres Griegos hasta san Juan Crisóstomo inclusive,' in *Miscellanea Biblica B. Ubach* (Scripta et Documenta 1), Montserrat, 1953, 5-18.

_____, 'La formación de Eva en los Padres Latinos hasta San Agustin inclusive,' *Estudios Eclesiásticos* 34 (1960), 421-459.

Testa, E., 'L'ascetica encratita e i matrimoni putativi come vittoria sul peccato originale,' in *Liber annuus Studium biblicum franciscanum* (Israel), 32 (1982), 191-238.

Tettamanzi, D., 'Valori cristiani del matrimonio nel pensiero di S. Ambrogio,' *La Scuola Cattolica* 102 (1974), 451-474.

Thonnard, F.J., 'La notion de concupiscence en philosophie augustinienne,' *RechAug* 3 (1965), 59-105.

Thornton, B.S., *Eros: The Myth of Ancient Greek Sexuality*, New York, 1996.

Thraede, K., 'Frau,' in *RAC* VIII, 1970, coll. 239-243.

Tibiletti, C., 'Un opuscolo perduto di Tertulliano: Ad amicum philosophum,' *AAST* 2 Cl, 95 (1960-61), 122-166.

_____, 'Verginità e matrimonio in antichi scrittori cristiani,' *AFLM* 2 (1969), 11-217, rp. Rome, 1983.

_____, 'Motivazioni dell'ascetismo in alcuni autori cristiani,' *AAST* 2 Cl,106 (1972), 489-537.

_____, 'Matrimonio ed escatologia: Tertulliano, Clemente Alessandrino, S. Agostino,' *AugR* 17 (1977), 53-70.

_____, 'La donna in Tertulliano," in *Misoginia e maschilisino*, op. cit., 69-95.

_____, 'Un passo di Clemente Alessandrino su verginità e matrimonio,' *Orpheus* 5 (1984), 437-443.

Tissot, Y., 'Henogamie et remariage chez Clément d'Alexandrie,' *RSLR* 11 (1975), 167-197.

Tosato, A., *Il matrimonio nel giudaismo antico e nel Nuovo Testamento*, Rome, 1976.

_____, *Il matrimonio israelitico*, Rome, 1982.

Trapè, A., Introduzione generale, *Sant'Agostino, Matrimonio e verginità* (NBA Vll,l) Rome, 1978.

_____, S. *Agostino. L'uomo, il pastore, il mistico*, Fossano, 1979.

Tregiarri, S., *Roman Marriage: Iusti conjuges from the time of Cicero to the time of Ulpian*, New York, 1991.

Trenchard, W.C., *Ben Sira's View of Women: A Literary Analysis* (Brown Judaic Studies, ed. J. Neusner et al., No. 38), Chico, 1982.

Trompf, G.W., 'On Attitude Toward Women in Paul and Paulinist Literature: 1 Corinthians 11:3-16 and its Context,' *CBQ* 42 (1980), 196-215.

Tsouros, K., 'La dottrina del matrimonio in San Giovanni Crisostomo,' *Asprenas* N.S. 21 (1974), 5-46.

Turcan, M., 'Saint Jérôme et les femmes,' *Bulletin Ass G. Budé*, 1968, 259-272.

_____, 'Le mariage en question? Ou les avantages du célibat selon Tertullien,' in *Mélanges de philosophie, de littérature et d'histoire ancienne offerts à Pierre Boyancé*, Rome, 1974, 711-720.

Uglione, R., 'Il matrimonio in Tertulliano tra esaltazione e disprezzo,' *Ephemerides Liturgicae* 93 (1979), 479-494.

_____, (ed.), *Atti del Convegno nazionale di studi su "La donna nel mondo antico," Torino 21-22-23 Aprile 1986*, Turin, 1987.

_____, (ed.), *Atti del Il Convegno nazionale di studi su "La donna nel mondo antico," Torino 18-19-20 Aprile 1988*, Turin, 1989.

Vatin, C., *Recherches sur le mariage et la condition de la femme mariée a l'époque hellénistique* (BEFAR 216), Paris, 1970.

Veggeti, M./Lanza, D., *La Donna Antica*, Turin, 1982.

Vérilliac, A.M. éd., *La femme dans le monde méditerranéen*, I. *L'Antiquité*, Lyon, 1985.

Vernant, J.-P., 'Il matrimonio nella Grecia arcaica,' in *Mito e società nell'antica Grecia*, Turin, 1981, 50-75, ed. orig. Paris, 1974.

Veyne, P. ed., *A History of Private Life*, I. *From Pagan Rome to Byzantium*, Cambridge, MA, 1987, esp. cc. 1-3.

———, 'La famille et l'amour sous le Haut-empire romain,' *Annales ESC* 33 (1978), 35-63.

Villers, R., 'Le statut de la femme à Rome jusqu'à la fin de la Republique,' *Recueils Jean Bodin XI, La Femme, op. cit.*, 177-189.

Visonà, G., 'L'uomo a immagine di Dio. L'interpretazione di Genesi 1:26 nel pensiero cristiano dei primi tre secoli,' *Studia Patavina* 27 (1980), 393-430.

Völker, W., *Der wahre Gnostiker nach Clemens Alexandrinus* (TU 57), Berlin-Leipzig, 1952.

Vogt, K., '"Divenire maschio." Aspetti di un'antropologia cristiana primitiva,' *Concilium* 6 (1985), 102-117.

Wilson, R. McL., 'The Early History of the Exegesis of Gn 1:26,' in K. Aland-F.L. Cross (edd.), *Stud Pat* I (TU 63), Berlin, 1957, 420-437.

Winkler, J., *The Constraints of Desire: The Anthropology of Sex and Gender in Ancient Greece*, New York, 1990.

Wolff, H.J., 'Doctrinal Trends in Postclassical Roman Marriage Law,' *Zeitschrift der Savigny-Stiftung für Rechtsgeschichte Romanistische Abteilung*, 67 (1950), 261-319.

———, 'Marriage Law and Family Organization in Ancient Athens,' *Traditio* 2 (1944), 43-95.

Zedda, S., 'Spiritualità cristiana e saggezza pagana nell'etica della famiglia: affinità e differenze tra S. Paolo e i *Coniugalia Praecepta* di Plutarco,' *Lateranum*, NS 48 (1982), 110-124.

———, *Relativo e assoluto nella morale di S. Paolo*, Brescia, 1984.

Ziegler, K., *Plutarco*, Brescia 1965, ed. orig. 1951 (Pauly-Wissowa, *RE* XXI,I, 1951, coll. 636-962).

Zincone, S., *Ricchezza e povertà nelle omelie di Giovanni Crisostomo*, L'Aquila, 1973.

———, 'Il tema dell'uomo/donna immagine di Dio nei Commenti paolini e a Gn di area antiochena (Diodoro, Crisostomo, Teodoro, Teodoreto),' *Annali di Storia dell'Esegesi* 2 (1985), 103-113.

TERTULLIAN

INTRODUCTORY PROFILE

Tertullian occupies a position of absolute preeminence among Christian writers in the Latin language, not only because of the explosive personality which emerges from his writings but also, and especially, because of the newness of his many-faceted literary productions. He was, in fact, the first Latin apologist, the founder of Latin theology, and the creator of a new Christian literature and a new linguistic form.[1]

Notices on Tertullian's life are not very numerous[2] but they allow us to establish some essential data with sufficient certainty. Born at Carthage between 150 and 160 of a pagan family — his father was a centurion of a proconsular cohort — Tertullian acquired a solid philosophical and rhetorical training, in both Latin and Greek. Perhaps prompted by the heroism of the martyrs[3] around 190, Tertullian converted to Christianity, even becoming a presbyter, according to a notice in Jerome, which however has not won the wholesale support of modern scholars.[4] His identification with a jurist of the same name, some citations from whom have been carried

---

[1] H. Hagendahl, *Latin Fathers and the Classics,* Göteborg, 1958.

[2] The biographical notices on Tertullian, apart from those in his own works, are in large part in Jerome; cf. *De Viris Illustribus* 53: BP 12, 150-151 (critical text and translation by A. Ceresa Gastaldo).

[3] The hypothesis has been advanced by some scholars because of the sincere participation with which — in the *Apologeticum* — Tertullian describes the sufferings endured by the first martyrs: cf. C. Moreschini (ed.), *Opere scelte di Quinto Settimio Fiorente Tertulliano,* Turin, 1974, 11.

[4] Cf. the chapter in *De Viris Illustribus* cited above, note 2.

147

down in the *Digest*,[5] is likewise uncertain, although in his writings a profound training in Roman law is obvious.[6]

The complexity of Tertullian's human personality became very clear from his adherence, around the year 207, to the teaching of Montanus[7] in a most extreme current, named Tertullianism, still active in Africa in the time of Augustine.[8] It is impossible to establish with certainty the date of his death, which is placed in any case later than 220.

Tertullian's writing career extended between the end of the second century (his *Apologeticum* was published in 197) and the early decades of the third century, since his last works (*On Chastity*, *On Fasting*, and, perhaps, the enigmatic *On the Pallium*) are considered to be later than 217.[9]

His writings, which come to 31 in number (besides other works, now lost) can be subdivided — simply for practical purposes and with reference to their content — into some definite divisions: *Apologetical works* (*To the Pagans*, the *Apologeticum*) in which he defends Christianity in a vigorous and original manner, and denounces the unjust

---

[5] The term, *Digest* refers to the extensive compilation of juridical writings made in the 6th century at the request of the Emperor Justinian.

[6] On the question of the identification of Tertullian with a jurist of the same name see R. Martini, 'Tertulliano giurista e Tertulliano padre della Chiesa,' *SDHI* 41 (1975), 79-124.

[7] Montanus, of Phrygian origin, devoted his life in the second half of the 2nd century to a religious movement characterized by a strong prophetic stamp and rigid ethical norms .He announced the imminent end of the world and the coming of the new Heavenly Jerusalem in a locality in Phrygia. The movement developed especially in Asia Minor, and sporadically in the West, where it had in Tertullian its most representative follower. For basic information and bibliography on Montanus and the Montanist crisis, cf. B. Aland, 'Montano-Montanismo' in *DPAC*, II, coll. 2299-2301; W.C.H. Frend, 'Montanism: Research and Problems,' *RSLR* 20 (1981), 521-537, [idem, art. s.v., *TRE* 23 (1993) 271-279].

[8] Cf. Augustine, *De haeresibus* 86: CCSL 46, 338-339; *The "De haeresibus" of Saint Augustine*, Patristic Studies, v. 90, tr. L.G. Müller, Catholic University Press, Washington, DC, 1956. On the Tertullianists, cf. in particular, D. Powell, 'Tertullianists and Cataphrygians,' *VigChr* 29 (1975), 33-54.

[9] The chronology of the works of Tertullian is schematized in a useful appendix, in J.C. Fredouille, *Tertullien et la conversion de la culture antique*, Paris, 1972, 487-488. For a fuller examination, cf. R. Braun, *"Deus Christianorum." Recherches sur le vocabulaire doctrinal de Tertullien*, Paris, 1962, 563-577. On the problems of interpretation and of dating present in the work, *De pallio* see S. Costanza, *Tertulliano De pallio*, Naples, 1968. The works of Tertullian are published in PL 1-2; PLS 1,29-32; CSEL 20, 69, 70, 76; CCSL 1-2; in part, French translation and commentary in SC 35, 46 173 216, 217, 273, 280, 281, 310, 316, 332, 343, 319. There are many accessible Italian translations, see selection (up-to-date to 1980) in *DPAC*, II, col. 3423. For a recent, very informative profile of Tertullian, cf. C. Tibiletti, 'Tertulliano' in *Dizionario degli Scrittori Greci e Latini* III, Settimo Milanese 1988, 2225-2242.

persecutions perpetrated against it by the pagans; *Polemical tracts*, against the internal enemies of Christian teaching (*The Prescription of Heretics, Against Hermogenes, Against the Valentinians, Against Marcion, Against Praxeas*); *Writings concerning the customs and morals of Christians*, addressed to directing their behavior, either within the new religion itself or in relations with the outside world, still largely pagan (*On Prayer, On Baptism, On Patience, On Penitence, On Fasting, On Purity, On the Shows, On the Dress of Women, On Virgins Wearing the Veil, On the Crown*).

Among Tertullian's treatises those relating to marriage and chastity occupy an important position: *To His Wife, Exhortation to Chastity, On Marrying Only Once*, to which should probably be added a lost work (*To a Philosopher Friend, concerning the Troubles of Married Life*), in which the African writer, on the basis of wide-ranging and consolidated philosophical theories, warns against the preoccupations inherent in married life, and exalts virginity.[10]

Tertullian's writings on marriage would exert a certain influence on subsequent Christian authors, for example, on Jerome,[11] and manifest, like all the rest of his literary production, not only the writer's rhetorical-stylistic ability, but also his originality, which is characterized in a synthesis, apart from any programmatic rejection,[12] of his pagan cultural patrimony with the biblical-theological dimension of his own thought.[13]

Tertullian's tracts on marriage, though they belong to various

---

[10] Cf. C. Tibiletti, 'Un opuscolo perduto di Tertulliano: Ad amicum philosophum,' *AAT* 95 (1960-1961), 122-166 (now in C. Tibiletti, *Raccolta di studi*, edd. M.G. Bianco, P. Janni, A. Nestori, Rome, 1989, 47-91).

[11] Cf. C. Micaelli, 'L'influsso di Tertulliano su Girolamo: le opere sul matrimonio e le seconde nozze,' *AugR* 19 (1979), 415-429. On the presence of Tertullian in later patristic tradition see *idem.*, 'Ricerche sulla fortuna di Tertulliano,' *Orpheus NS* 6 (1985), 118-135.

[12] Tertullian manifests outright hostility when confronted with pagan literature and philosophy, but the stylistic texture and the ideas expressed in his works amply refute his programmatic intentions. Cf. further the very full and well documented study cited above of Fredouille; H. Hagendahl, *op. cit.*, 38-48; R.D. Sider, *Ancient Rhetoric and the Art of Tertullian*, Oxford, 1971; T.D. Barnes, *Tertullian. A Historical and Literary Study*, Oxford, 1971, new edition, with additions, 1985.

[13] Cf. P. Frassinetti, 'Gli scritti matrimoniali di Seneca e Tertulliano,' *RIL* 88 (1955), 151-188; C. Micaelli, 'Retorica, filosofia e cristianesimo negli scritti matrimoniali di Tertulliano,' *ASNP* 11 (1981), 69-104.

stages of his religious evolution,[14] maintain an undeniable basic homogeneity which substantially reflects the essential presuppositions of his conceptions on marriage. Against the heretic, Marcion, who had shown contempt for the institution of marriage, considering it a perverse instrument of reproduction of wicked materiality, that is to say, the body,[16] Tertullian defends the goodness of marriage, even though in an ideal scale of values he placed it at a lower level and showed a preference for virginity.[17] Matrimony, in fact, typically connected with concupiscence, has been considered a minor evil, on the basis of a reading of Paul, 1 Cor 7:9 (*it is better to marry than to burn*).

In any case, the pessimistic vein present in Tertullian in his handling of matrimony ought not to be absolutized, taking into ac-

---

[14] The treatise, *To His Wife* is, in fact, from 200/206 (his Catholic period); the *Exhortation to Chastity* is from 208/211 (first inclinations toward Montanism); *De monogamia* is from 213/219 (full adherence to Montanism). On the writings on matrimony of Tertullian in relation to the ethics of the time cf. C. Rambaux, *Tertullien face aux morales des trois premiers siècles*, Paris, 1979, 204-262.

[15] On the conceptions of Tertullian with regard to matrimony and virginity cf. C. Tibiletti, *Verginità e Matrimonio in antichi scrittori cristiani*, Rome, 1988, 71-93 (the study had already appeared in *AFLM* 2 (1969) 9-217). See also G. Oggioni, 'Matrimonio e Verginità presso i Padri (fino a S. Augostino),' in Aa. vv., *Matrimonio e Verginità. Saggi di Teologia*, Venegono Inferiore (Varese) 1963, 171-183; P.A Gramaglia (ed), *Tertulliano. Il matrimonio nel cristianesimo preniceno*, Rome, 1988 (with Italian translation of three treatises on matrimony); *Tertullian Treatises on Marriage and Remarriage; To His Wife: An Exhortation to Chastity, On Monogamy* tr. W.P. Le Saint, SJ, ACW 13, 1951.

[16] Marcion, a heretic of the 2nd century, originated in Sinope, in Pontus, was excommunicated — according to some sources — by his father, who was a bishop of that city; going to Rome, Marcion joined a community for a certain period at the end of which in 144, he was alienated from it and founded a church of his own. The Marcionite church spread rapidly and while in the West it died out in the end of the 3rd century, in the east it continued to the end of the second half of the 5th century, especially in the area of Syria. The doctrine of Marcion was founded on a clear-cut dualism relative to the divinity of the God of the Old Testament, just but angry, creator of evil matter, opposed to the Father of the New, who had sent His own Son, Jesus Christ, for the ransom of humanity. From this negative estimate of corporeity derived the firmness with which Marcion propounded a very rigorous asceticism and absolute abstinence from marriage and procreation, considered the vehicle of the creational power of evil. It is important to notice how Marcion utilized his own canon of scripture, based substantially on the Gospel of Luke and on some Letters of Paul, suitably purged. This had accelerated the process of the formation of an orthodox canon on the part of the Great Church. Cf. in this connection, H. von Campenhausen, *Die Entstehung der christlichen Bibel* Tübingen, 1968, especially 174-194.
For a first approach, with bibliography, to the problems connected with the historic-religious evaluation of the positions of Marcion, see the contribution of E. Norelli, 'La funzione di Paolo nel pensiero Marcione,' *RivBib* 34 (1986), 543-597, on the conclusions of which cf. General Introduction to this anthology, note 26, p. 85.

[17] Cf. Tertullian, *Contra Marcionem* I,29, 1-2: CCSL 1, 473-474.

count that he himself was married to a woman described by him as "a most beloved companion in the service of God,"[18] and ought rather to be explained in the light of the strong eschatological tensions which permeate the thought of the African writer. He is so convinced of the proximity of the end of time that he exhorts everybody to await the sound of the angel heralding the Parousia.[19] In a compelling longing he writes even of "desiring" the end of time and fervently calling for it.[20] There are then, those pressing and compelling eschatological necessities to enforce a new pattern of behavior, by relegating marriage itself[21] to the second plane, after virginity, a condition anticipating the future life in heaven.

A most poetical description of "Christian conjugal union" which has rightly been described as "the most beautiful which has survived from the ancient Church"[22] ought to serve as disproof, however, of how such univocal generalizations however misleading could come about proper to Tertullian. This is the conclusion of the treatise, *To His Wife*, a sort of spiritual testament which Tertullian directs to his wife exhorting her not to remarry in the event that she is left a widow, or in case of marriage anew to a Christian.

In the two books into which this work of Tertullian is subdivided, two very sensitive problems in the Church of the early centuries are addressed: the question of second marriage, and that of mixed marriages between Christians and pagans. They were problems which Paul had already addressed in 1 Corinthians (7:8-16).

Tertullian, in accordance with his character, showed himself a real rigorist, whether in his attitude to marriages between Christians and pagans, or to second marriages. In the invitation directed

---

[18] Cf. Tertullian, *Ad uxorem* I, I, I: SC 273, 92.

[19] Cf. Tertullian, *On Prayer* 29, 3: CCSL 1, 274.

[20] Cf. Tertullian, *De Resurrectione mortuorum* 22 2: CCSL 2, 946; *On Prayer* 5,4: CCSL 1, 260.

[21] On the conditions operative in the eschatological conceptions of Tertullian relative to his ideas concerning matrimony and virginity cf. C. Tibiletti, 'Matrimonio ed escatologia: Tertulliano, Clemente Alessandrino, S. Agostino,' *AugR* 17 (1977), 53-70 (now also in C. Tibiletti, *Verginità...*, *op. cit.*, 217-234); 'Motivazioni del'ascetismo in alcuni autori cristiani,' *AAT* 106 (1972), 486-537.

[22] This is the judgment of Ch. Munier, *Tertullien. A son épouse* (SC 273), Paris, 1980, p. 12. In the Introduction to this volume (9-87) an exhaustive analysis of the work is also provided.

to his own wife it is possible to detect an affectionate counsel not to remarry, in the case of widowhood. With the ever more radical adhesion to Montanism on the part of Tertullian, an increasing rigorism, in absolute prohibition of second marriage, is clearly formulated in treatises like *Exhortation to Chastity* and *On Marrying Only Once*.[23]

The intransigence of Tertullian finds a confirmation in some other authors of the Eastern Church, beginning with Athenagoras, a Greek apologist of the 2nd century, for whom second marriage was virtually adultery,[24] while in the West a more moderate line generally prevailed.[25]

With regard to mixed marriages between pagans and Christians, Tertullian shows the same hesitations and the same suspicious distrust as the other Fathers of the first centuries, justified at least in part in the new spirituality which united in an inseparable link faith and daily relationships.[26] Diversity of faiths for a long time was seen on the part of Christianity as an impediment to the realization of a true Christian marriage[27] in which, in fact, man and woman ought to be involved together in a total manner, united in the will to make operative the new ethical precepts of the Gospel in the life of the couple.

The two excerpts from Tertullian presented here, both taken from Book 2 of *To His Wife*, exemplify the difficulties inherent in a mixed marriage, and, by contrast, highlight the goodness of a Chris-

---

[23] Cf. Tertullian *On Monogamy* 1,2 e 4,4-5: CCSL 2, 1229 and 1233. [Add: See now *Tertullien Le Mariage Unique* éd. P. Mattei, SC 343, Paris, 1988; *Tertulliano Le uniche nozze*, ed. R. Uglione, Turin, 1993.]

[24] Cf. Athenagoras, *Supplication for the Christians* 33: SC 3, 19. On the treatises of Tertullian relative to second marriage cf. J.C. Fredouille, *op. cit.*, 89-142 and C. Rambaux, 'La composition et l'exégèse dans les deux lettres *Ad uxorem* e *De Exhortatione Castitatis* et le *De monogamia* ou la construction de la pensée dans les traités de Tertullien sur le remariage,' *REAug* 22 (1976), 201-217; 23 (1977), 18-55.

[25] Cf. in general J. Gaudemet, *Il matrimonio in Occidente*, Turin,1989 [orig. Paris, 1987], 64-66. For further information, on the Latin side, cf. M. Humbert, *Les Remariages à Rome*, Milan, 1972 (for the Christian period, 301-456). On the figure of the widow in early Christianity, cf. A.V. Nazzaro, 'Figure di donne cristiane: la vedova,' in R. Uglione (et al.), *La Donna nel Mondo Antico. Atti del II Convegno Nazionale di Studi*, Turin, 1989, 197-219, with references to earlier literature.

[26] Cf. C. Burini-E. Cavalcanti, *La spiritualità della vita quotidiana*, Bonn, 1988, 97-103.

[27] On mixed marriages in early Christianity see C. Mazzucco, *"E fui fatta maschio." La donna nel cristianesimo primitivo*, Florence, 1989, 36-41.

tian union, for which a shared religion constitutes the foundation of a new life project, chosen and experienced together: to assist the poor, to visit the sick, to sing to the Lord and in this way to attract on oneself the benevolent smile of Christ. Certainly the serene setting, which has been described with such incisiveness by Tertullian, may appear somewhat idealized but does not, because of that, lose its significance.[28] Man and woman, united not only by love, but by the same faith, form a symbiosis which symbolically re-enacts the marriage union of Christ and the Church. There is not between them any discrimination "in the church of God," "brothers of the same Father, servants together of the same Lord": it is a new model which Tertullian intends to present, and at the same time to counterpose to contemporary pagan society, a model of Christian marriage in which the relationship is founded on a freedom that is interior and real at the same time, given by the reciprocal and equal dedication which has, as its essential prerequisite, the consciousness of both being instruments of the will of God.

---

[28] The judgment given on this passage in C. Tibiletti, 'La donna in Tertulliano,' in Aa. vv., *Misoginia e maschilismo in Grecia e Roma,* Genoa, 1981, 91 is very narrow, and not totally justified. What has been written by M. Turcan, 'Le mariage en question? Ou les avantages du célibat selon Tertullien,' in Aa. vv., *Mélanges de philosophie, de littérature et d'histoire ancienne offerts à Pierre Boyancé,* Rome, 1974, 711-720 is much more balanced and acceptable, in our view: "Matrimony which he (i.e. Tertullian) admires — which maybe he had experienced — is completely devoted to the service of God and the neighbor," and exiled from ordinary normal family, but not by this is he impracticable, if the intimate reasons of the couple/God relationship in the actualization of the process of salvation are comprehended. P.T.A. Sabattini, 'La famiglia cristiana nell'Apologetico di Tertulliano,' *RSC* 23 (1975), 51-66, notwithstanding the title, does not offer any appreciable data as his conclusions show too much dependence on an apologetic emphasis which pits Tertullian against the corrupt pagan society of his time, and is limited moreover to a thematic examination without historico-critical study in depth. [Engl. ed. Add: M. Turcan, 'Être femme selon Tertullien,' *Vita Latina* 119 (1990), 15-21.]

OF THE INCONVENIENCES IN A MARRIAGE BETWEEN AN
UNBELIEVING HUSBAND AND A CHRISTIAN WIFE

1

   3,1.   If these things are so, it is certain that believers contracting marriages with pagans are guilty of fornication, and are to be excluded from all community with the brotherhood, in accordance with
the letter of the Apostle, who says that *with persons of that kind there
is to be no taking of food even.*[a] Or shall we *on that day (of judgment)*[b]
produce (our) marriage certificates[1] before the Lord's tribunal[c] and
allege that a marriage such as He Himself has forbidden has been
duly contracted?

   What is prohibited here is not adultery. It is not fornication.
The admission of man (to your couch) less violates the temple of
God,[d] less commingles the members of Christ[e] with the members of
an adulteress. So far as I know, *we are not our own but bought with a
price.*[f] And what kind of price? *The blood of God.*[g] In hurting this flesh
of ours, therefore, we hurt Him directly...

   3,3.   Let us now recount the other dangers or wounds (as I
have said) to faith, foreseen by the Apostle; most grievous not to
the flesh merely, but likewise to the spirit too. For who would doubt
that faith undergoes a daily process of obliteration by unbelieving
intercourse? *Evil communications corrupt good morals;*[h] much more fellowship of life, and indivisible intimacy! Any and every believing
woman must of necessity obey God.

   And how can she serve two lords[i] — the Lord, and her husband — a Gentile at that? For in obeying a Gentile she will carry
out Gentile practices: personal attractiveness, dressing of the head,[2]

---

[a] 1 Cor 5:11   [b] cf. Mt 24:36   [c] cf. Rm 14:10   [d] cf. 1 Cor 3:16-1   [e] cf. 1 Cor 6:15
[f] cf. 1 Cor 6:20   [g] cf. 1 P 1:19   [h] 1 Cor 15:33   [i] cf. Mt 6:24 and Lk 16:13

---

[1]   The contract of matrimony, the so-called "nuptial tablets" (*tabulae nuptiales*) constitutes the
document on the basis of which, in the presence of witnesses, the obligations of the husband and the dowry are recorded. Cf., in general, P. Dacquino, *Storia del matrimonio cristiano
alla luce della Bibbia,* Leumann (To) 1984, 119 and, for a fuller treatment, K. Ritzer, *op. cit.*,
77-79.

[2]   Tertullian had dedicated an apposite work of polemic concerning the habit of women to take
care in a sophisticated manner of exterior aspects, dressing luxuriously and thereby destroying their own interiority. Cf. *Tertulliano, L'Eleganza delle donne,* S. Isetta, ed., BP 6,

worldly elegancies, baser blandishments, the very secrets even of matrimony tainted: not, as among the saints, where the duties of sex are discharged with honor (shown) to the very necessity (which makes them incumbent), with modesty and temperance, as beneath the eyes[3] of God.[j]

4,1. But let her see to (the question) how she discharges her duties to her husband. To the Lord, at all events, she is unable to give satisfaction according to the requirements of discipline; having at her side a servant of the devil, his lord's agent for hindering the pursuits and duties of believers: so that if a station[4] is to be kept, the husband at daybreak makes an appointment with his wife to meet him at the baths;[5] if there are fasts to be observed, the husband that same day holds a convivial banquet; if a charitable expedition has to be made, never is family business more urgent.

4,2. For who would suffer his wife, for the sake of visiting the brethren, to go round from street to street to other men's, and indeed to all the poorer cottages? Who will willingly bear her being taken from his side by nocturnal convocations, if need be?[6] Who, finally, will without anxiety endure her absence all the night long at the paschal solemnities?[7] Who will, without some suspicion of his

---

[j] cf. Pr 15:3

Florence, 1986, where (33-47) the literary precedents of the theme are analyzed, both in classical and in Christian literature, and in later developments, however briefly, in Christian writers subsequent to Tertullian.

[3] The Old Testament motive, especially in the Prophetic and Wisdom scriptures, of God who "sees" human things is present, with different terminology in the works of Tertullian. See the exhaustive treatment by R. Braun, *op. cit.*, 128-132.

[4] By the term *statio* Tertullian refers probably to a liturgy in which a community penitential rite was conducted. Cf. C. Mohrmann, 'Statio,' *VigChr* 7 (1953), 221-245 (republished in *Sur le Latin des Chrétiens, III*, Rome, 1965, 307-330).

[5] As opportunely pointed out by Ch. Munier, *Tertullien A son épouse*, 182, Tertullian refers in a specific manner to "baths" in as much as during the "station" bathing was prohibited as a sign of penitence.

[6] Here Tertullian alludes to the nocturnal reunions without eucharistic celebrations: cf. G. Esser, 'Convocationes nocturnae bei Tertullian, *Ad uxorem*,' in *Der Katholik* 95 (1916), 388-391 and E. Dekkers, *Tertullianus en de geschiedenis der liturgie*, Brussels, 1947, 113. For a different opinion, P.A. Gramaglia, *Tertulliano. Il matrimonio... op. cit.*, 297, note 35, who does not exclude the possibility, however, that there is question of "even special liturgical assemblies."

[7] At the time of Tertullian in Africa the paschal vigil took place from Holy Saturday to Sunday Cf. Ch. Munier, éd., *Tertullien. A son épouse*, 183 and the relevant bibliography cited there.

own, dismiss her to attend that Lord's Supper[k] which they defame?[8] Who will suffer her to creep into prison to kiss a martyr's bonds? nay, truly, to meet any one of the brethren to exchange the kiss? to offer water for the saints' feet?[l] to snatch (somewhat for them) from her food, from her cup? to yearn (after them)? to have (them) in her mind? If a pilgrim brother arrive, what hospitality[m] for him in an alien home? If bounty is to be distributed to any, the granaries, the store-houses, are foreclosed.[9]

To His Wife, II, 3,1-4 and 4,1-3; SC 273, 132-136

---

[k] cf. 1 Cor 11:20   [l] cf. 1 Tm 5:10   [m] cf. 1 Tm 5:10

[8] Obviously there is an allusion to the defamatory accusations which circulated against Christians and their eucharistic assemblies. On the part of the pagans it was in fact believed that during the eucharistic meal Christians abandoned themselves to acts of cannibalism and incestuous couplings. It was the task of apologetic literature to confute these and other similar affirmations. For a good anthology of texts of the first two centuries, with translations in Italian cf. P. Carrara, ed., *I pagani di fronte al Cristianesimo. Testimonianze dei secoli I e II*, BP 2, Florence, 1984.

[9] Tertullian is inspired by the ethical principles of the Gospels as found formulated, for example, in Mt 25:42-43 and which are found, in some cases, particular moments of verification, as visiting the martyrs in prison. Cf. Aristides, *Apologia* 15,6: BP 11, p. 118 and p. 119 (Italian translation). On kissing as a sign of Christian charity, cf. K. Thraede, 'Ursprünge und Formen des heiligens Küsses im frühen Christentum,' *JbAC* 11-12 (1968-1969), 124-180.

SUPERIORITY OF A CHRISTIAN MARRIAGE

2

8,6. Whence are we to find adequate words to describe the happiness of that marriage which the Church cements, and the eucharistic oblation confirms, and the benediction signs and seals;[1] (which) angels carry back the news (to heaven), (which) the Father ratifies? For even on earth in fact children do not rightly and lawfully wed without their fathers' consent.

8,7. What kind of yoke is that of two believers, united in one hope, one desire, one discipline, one and the same servitude? Both (are) brethren, both fellow servants, no difference of spirit or of flesh; no, (they are) truly *two in one flesh*.[a] Where the flesh is one, one only is the spirit too. Together they pray, together prostrate themselves, together perform their fasts; mutually teaching,[b] mutually exhorting, mutually sustaining.

8,8. Equally (are they) both (found) in the Church of God; equally at the banquet of God; equally in straits, in persecutions, in refreshments. Neither has any secrets from the other; neither shuns the other; neither is troublesome to the other. The sick are freely visited, the indigent relieved, alms (are given) without mutual re-

---

[a] Gn 2:24; Mt 19:6 [b] cf. Rm 15:14

---

[1] In the eulogy which Tertullian delivers on Christian matrimony and in the succession of the individual elements (ratification of the Church, celebration of the eucharist, blessing, mediation of angels and final approval of God), J. Moingt, 'Le mariage des chrétiens,' in *Mariage et divorce,* Paris, 1974, has recognized a perfect correspondence with the matrimonial rite in secular society, and to each of its individual phases Tertullian would counterpose significant moments in the Christian liturgy. Also H. Crouzel, 'Deux textes de Tertullien concernant la procédure et les rites du mariage chrétien,' *BLE* 74 (1973), 7-13 republished now in *Mariage et divorce célibat et caractère sacerdotaux dans l'Église ancienne,* Turin, 1982, 119-125, disagrees with the conclusions of K. Ritzer, *Le Mariage dans les Églises chrétiennes du 1er au XI'e siècle,* Paris, 1970, 110-121, who denies to Tertullian's text even the slightest significance in the history of the liturgy of matrimony; Crouzel maintains that even in the antenicene period the Church intervened actively in the celebration of marriage as can be demonstrated on the basis of the text of Tertullian. For a fuller critical discussion and an exhaustive bibliography on the argument cf. P.A. Gramaglia, *Tertulliano. Il matrimonio, op. cit.,* 305-311 (note 73). In any case it is perhaps prudent to attribute to the passage in question a more generic significance, without excluding the possibility that, as Augustine and Possidius attest in Africa, on the basis of a private invitation, a bishop participated in the matrimony ritual and gave his benediction; cf. K. Ritzer, *op. cit.,* 114-115, who cites Sermon 332,4 of Augustine and chapter 27,4-5 of the *Vita* of Augustine written by Possidius.

criminations;[2] sacrifices (attended) without scruple; daily diligence (discharged) without impediment: (there is) no stealthy signing of the cross, no trembling greeting, no mute benediction. Between the two echo psalms and hymns;[c] and they mutually challenge each other which shall better chant to their Lord. Such things when Christ sees and hears, He rejoices, to these He sends His own peace.[d] Where two (are), there withal (is) He Himself.[e] Where He (is), there the Evil One is not.[3]

To His Wife, II,8. 6-8; SC 273, 148-150

---

[c] cf. Col 3:16   [d] cf. Jn 14:27   [e] cf. Mt 18:20

[2] The dispensation of alms not harmoniously agreed to by both spouses could represent one of the most frequent motives of disagreement. Cf. M. Forlin Patrucco, 'Aspetti di vita familiare nel IV secolo negli scritti dei padri cappadoci,' in R. Cantalamessa (ed.), *Etica sessuale e matrimonio cristianesimo delle origini*, Milan, 1976, 158-179.

[3] The interpretation given by P.A. Gramaglia, *Tertulliano. Il matrimonio, op. cit.*, 313-314, of the Christian couple as it emerges in this most poetic page of Tertullian, is, to say the least, arbitrary and prejudicial. For this scholar in fact, there is question "of a couple, without children, totally desexualized, whose conjugal life has been reduced to a species of perennial liturgy." The juxtapositions which are successively instituted with the ethical pagan conceptions on matrimony, especially those of a Stoic matrix, do not contradict or diminish the affirmations of Tertullian, and of Christians in general, if ever they are inserted in an historico-cultural context and can be verified case by case. The excerpt translated previously stands as well as a reminder to demonstrate that Tertullian does not deny the value of sexual relations. The fact that the Christian couple presented in Tertullian lives intensely in a daily mutual affective union the realization of their religious duties certainly does not diminish its credibility. Truth to tell the same Gramaglia in his preceding work (*Tertullian, De virginibus velandis. La condizione femminile nella prima comunità cristiana*, Rome, 1984, 179, note 5) with regard to this same section has affirmed that "the idyllic picture painted at the end of *Ad uxorem* contains without doubt points of real life and makes transparent the religious enthusiasm which must have involved not a few families converted at the beginning of the 3rd century at Carthage."

CLEMENT OF ALEXANDRIA

INTRODUCTORY PROFILE

Clement of Alexandria was born around 150, perhaps in Greece, more specifically in Athens, of a pagan family.[1] According to a testimony of Eusebius he was initiated into the pagan mysteries[2] and later converted to Christianity.[3] One of the most interesting autobiographical points of his works[4] is that which presents him as a spirit anxious to know and restless in his hypothetical dissatisfaction. Clement in fact undertook several trips in search of a teacher who would completely satisfy him. Greece, Western Italy, the East were all stopping points on his itinerary. At last, in Egypt he came in contact with Pantaenus, his last teacher in terms of chronology, but the best of them all in terms of teaching.[5]

---

[1] The uncertainty about Clement's place of birth is already present in the ancient sources. Cf. Epiphanius (*Panarion* 32,6,1: GCS 25, p. 445: Engl. tr., P.R. Amidon, *The Panarion of St. Epiphanius*, New York,1990), "Clement was a deacon, either in Alexandria, or in Athens...." Epiphanius, born in Palestine around 315, after an experience of the monastic life in Egypt, was elected bishop of Salamis in Cyprus in 367. He died an octogenarian in 403. Principally responsible for causing the so-called "Origenist controversy" to flare up — on which see the Introductory Profile on Jerome, pp. 238-240 — he is remembered in patristic literature especially for two works, the *Ancoratus*, expositive syntheses of the principal doctrines of Christianity, and the *Panarion* (a Greek term meaning a medicinal chest), an heresiological work in which 30 heresies are confuted, among which Epiphanius has also included Greek philosophical movements. On the role of Epiphanius in the historico-religious context of his age, cf. C. Riggi, 'La figura di Epifanio nel IV secolo,' in *Stud Pat* 3/2, Berlin, 1966, 86-107.

[2] Cf. Eusebius, *Praeparatio evangelica* 2,2,64: SC 228, pp. 80-81. For some essential details on Eusebius we refer once more to the Introductory Profile on Jerome, note 19, p. 234.

[3] To identify the motives which prompted Clement to conversion is obviously hazardous. For the different hypotheses formulated by scholars cf. M.G. Bianca (ed), *Il Protrettico. Il Pedagogo di Clemente Alessandrino*, Turin, 1971, 14-15.

[4] Cf. *Stromata* I,11,1-2: SC 30.

[5] On Pantaenus practically the only notices available are those in Clement and in the *Historia Ecclesiastica* of Eusebius (V,10-11:SC 41,40-41). From these we gather that he was probably of Sicilian origin, a convert to Christianity after being an adherent of Stoic philosophy, and around 180 he obtained the headship of the school of Alexandria, an office which he held until his death, around 200.

At Alexandria, a flourishing commercial Mediterranean port, a city of imposing architectural splendor and a cultural center of the first importance at the turn of the second century,[6] Clement became a collaborator of Pantaenus and found the optimal conditions to give meaning to his conversion. The genesis and initial development of the so-called catechetical school of Alexandria, which probably only found its official ratification in the teaching of Origen, are sufficiently well known.[7]

Although this fact cannot be documented historically (the succession of Clement to Pantaenus),[8] it is however incontrovertible that his own teaching, even if it took place at a quasi-private level,[9] had a decisive and highly significant role in Clement's own life. It was to the cultivated and wealthy circles of Alexandria that he essentially directed his teaching mission, aimed at defending the Christian message and seeking to give ever more perfection to the figure of the true gnostic, as Clement frequently loved to define the perfect Christian.[10]

Clement's pedagogical activity extended to about 202 when,

[6] On the city of Alexandria, a most important economic and cultural center of the second century, cf. M.G. Bianco (ed.), *Il Protrettico, op. cit.*, 9-14 and J.G. Gussan, *Het leven in Alexandrië volgens de cultuurhistorische gegevens in de Paedagogus (Boek II en III) van Clemens Alexandrinus*, Assen, 1954.

[7] Origen is said by Eusebius (*Hist. Eccles.* VI 3,1-3 and 8; 8,1; 15: SC 41, pp. 86-87; 88-89; 94; Engl. trans. ed. by R.J. Deferarri, *Ecclesiastical History*, New York, 1964), to have been assigned by bishop Demetrius the task of teaching in the School of Alexandria, the well-known Didaskaleion. Some time later Origen left the catechetical teaching to Heraclas, dedicating himself to the administration of higher level students. The necessary starting points for a deeper understanding of the Didaskaleion are the studies of G. Bardy, 'Aux origines de l'école d'Alexandrie,' *RSR* 27 (1937), 65-90, 'Pour l'histoire de l'École d'Alexandrie,' *RB* 50 (1942), 80-109. See also P. Brezzi, *La gnosi cristiana di Alessandria e le antiche scuole cristiane*, Rome, 1950; A. Vaccari, 'Primo abbozzo di università cristiana,' in *Scritti di erudizione e Filologia*, Rome, 1952, 73-96; A. Le Boulluec, 'L'école d'Alexandrie. De quelques aven-tures d'un concept historiographique,' in *Alexandrina. Mélanges offerts à C. Mondésert*, Paris, 1987, 403-417.

[8] Fairly recently an attempt has been made to accredit the succession Pantaenus — Clement — Origen (an immediate disciple of Clement) attested in Eusebius. Cf. F. Pericoli Ridolfini, 'Le origini della scuola di Alessandria,' *Rivista degli Studi Orientali* 37 (1962), 211-230.

[9] Cf. G. Bardy, 'Aux origines,' *op. cit.*, 90. G. Lazzati, in his *Introduzione allo studio di Clemente Alessandrino*, Milan, 1939, has in a certain sense mediated the various hypotheses, by suggesting that some of the works are to be considered the fruit of scholastic notes, others however, destined for publication (pp. 10-24).

[10] Cf W. Völker, *Der Wahre Gnostiker nach Clemens Alexandrinus*, Berlin, 1952; C. Guasco, 'Lo gnostico cristiano in Clemente Alessandrino,' *Sophia* 24 (1956), 264-269.

in consequence of the persecution of Septimius Severus,[11] he was forced to seek refuge with one of his pupils, Alexander, the bishop of Caesarea. Here he spent the last years of his life, and died, probably around 215.[12] The principal works of Clement are the *Protrepticus*, in which he exhorts pagans to conversion, criticizing their traditional religious beliefs; the *Paidagogos*, in three books, which provides converted pagans with the fundamental ethical norms, even down to the most detailed daily particulars (eating, drinking, clothing, conversation, etc.), for the realization of a truly Christian life; the *Stromata*, in eight books, a miscellany in which important doctrinal, ethical and religious problems have been confronted, at times in a provisory and sketchy format meant for later development.

Clement himself explains the interlinking ties between the *Protrepticus* and *Paidagogos* as successive stages in an organic and programmatic plan of treatment and alludes to a pedagogical work on the essential beliefs of Christianity still in the process of being written.[13] It is still a debated question whether the *Stromata* is the conclusion of a trilogy, announced by Clement in a manner created essentially in the scholastic ambit and for predominantly practical reasons related to his teaching activity.[14] In any case, Clement's three

---

[11] Septimius Severus, emperor from 193 to 211, promulgated in 202 an edict against both Christian and Jewish proselytism, to bridle the expansion of the Church. [Engl. tr. The existence of such an edict has been severely doubted; for the *status quaestionis* cf. *Salesianum* 48 (1968) 363-369.] The consequences were negative especially for the School of Alexandria and some catechumens suffered martyrdom. Cf. M. Simon-A. Benoit, *Judaïsme et Cristianisme*, Paris, 1968, p. xx.

[12] The date is arrived at on the basis of a letter of bishop Alexander, directed to Origen and reported in the *Historia Ecclesiastica* (VI,14, 3-9) of Eusebius where he alludes to the unexpected death of Clement.

[13] Cf. *Paidagogos* I,1,3: SC 70, 110; in this volume see also the extensive introduction of H.-I. Marrou, 7-97; also the FOTC translation, vol. 23, Clement, *Christ the Educator.*

[14] It is maintained by some scholars that the *Stromata* constituted a preparatory work amplified in time to the third work planned by Clement. Cf. E. Buonaiuti, 'Clemente Alessandrino e la cultura classica,' *Rivista storicocritica delle Scienze Teologiche* 1 (1905), 393-412; E. De Faye, *Clément d'Alexandrie. Étude sur les rapports du Christianisme et de la philosophie grecque au II siècle*, Paris, 1906.
     The works of Clement of Alexandria are published in PG 8 and 9; and more critically in GCS 12; 15; 17; 39. Good editions, still incomplete, with excellent critical introduction, French translation and commentary in SC 2bis, 23, 30, 38, 70, 108, 158, 278, 279. Finally, we indicate some monographs to complement the studies indicated in the Introduction, note 14, p. 79: A. Méhat, *Étude sur les "Stromates" de Clément d'Alexandrie*, Paris, 1966; O. Prunet, *La morale de Clément d 'Alexandrie et le Nouveau Testament*, Paris, 1966; M. Mees, *Die Zitate aus dem Neuen Testament bei Clemens von Alexandrien*, Bari, 1970; A. Brontesi, *La soteria in Clemente Alessandrino*, Rome, 1972; M. Galloni, *Cultura evangelizzazione e fede nel "Protrettico" di Clemente Alessandrino*, Rome, 1986.

principal works have a cultural significance of undeniable importance inasmuch as they mark the birth of a true and proper Christian "humanism." Clement, in fact, for the intellectual and moral formation of his followers, puts at their disposal almost naturally both his own wide philosophical-literary erudition, the fruit of direct research in the primary sources or in the use of *florilegia*,[15] and his equally extensive knowledge of Sacred Scripture.

From this derives the characteristic sequence in the pages of Clement of biblical citations and classical reminiscences in prose and poetry in a continuous osmosis, which leaves us perplexed and sometimes disoriented[16] but which for Clement must have been the natural method for extending to his hearers the new truths of the faith. With Clement continues, and at the same time becomes clearly defined, that conciliatory attitude in the confrontation with classical culture already operating in some apologists like Athenagoras and Justin, based on the conviction that the knowledge of God was possible by nature to all men and that Greek philosophy had passed on to Sacred Scripture its own theorizings.[17]

The wealthy converts to Christianity in Alexandria must have certainly considered with disturbed perplexity the Gospel invitation to poverty and the manner of reconciling the maintenance of their earthly condition with salvation. That explains why Clement wrote a homily, *What Rich Man can be Saved?* as a commentary on Mark 10:17-31. He assumes a moderate attitude, by not characterizing negatively the person to whom he refers, condemning, not the possession of riches *per se*, but their eventual use of interior virtue. It is

---

[15] There is general agreement that there are citations at first hand of Homer and Plato, while for others it is possible that Clement was served by *florilegia* available in the city of Alexandria. Cf an up-to-date synthesis of the relations of Clement and the classical tradition in M. G. Bianco (ed.), *Il Protrettico, op. cit.*, 24-29.

[16] Cf. G. Pini, *Clemente Alessandrino. Stromati. Note di Vera Filosofia,* Milan, 1985, p. 16. On the joint presence in Clement of classical philosophical motives and Christian elements (confined to the *Paidagogos*), cf. H.-I. Marrou, 'Humanisme et cristianisme chez Clément d'Alexandrie d'après le Pédagogue,' in *Recherches sur la tradition platonicienne (Entretiens sur l'Antiquité classique III)*, Vandoeuvres-Genève, 1956, 183-200.

[17] Cf. M. Simonetti, *Cristianesimo antico e cultura greca*, Rome, 1983, 49-52. On the attitude of Clement toward pagan culture of a philosophical matrix, see the appropriate observations of P.Th. Camelot, 'Les idées d'Alexandrie sur l'utilisation des sciences et de la littérature profanes,' *RSR* 21 (1931), 38-66; 'Clément d'Alexandrie et l'utilisation de la philosophie grecque,' *ibid.*, 541-569.

attachment to riches, not their possession which ought to be avoided.[18]

Other works of Clement are: *Extracts of Theodotus* and *Prophetic Eclogues*. In the first, Clement utilized certain portions of the work of the Valentinian Gnostic, Theodotus, opposing orthodox arguments, the faith of the Great Church. The purpose of the *Prophetic Eclogues* is similar. Here the theological treatment of various themes, such as eschatology, baptism, angelology, and many others, stemming from a reading of the first chapters of Genesis, and from some passages in the Prophets, is developed in polemic with gnostic heterodoxy, in a quasi-esoteric language aimed at a sophisticated reading public and open at the same time to suggestions of gnostic speculations.[19]

Clement of Alexandria is the first Christian author in Greek to treat in a complete and balanced manner the subject of matrimony, its blessings and its dignity.[20] A polemicist in confrontation with encratite radicalism of many sects,[21] he is an outspoken champion of the absolute goodness of the institution of marriage maintaining the constitutive element of the project of creation.[22]

From a strictly institutional point of view Clement considered matrimony as the first form of social association and essentially

---

[18] On the theme of riches in early Christianity see, in general, L. Orabona, *Aspetti e problemi sociali di storia della Chiesa*, Cassino, 1980; M.G. Mara, *Ricchezza e povertà nel cristianesimo primitivo*, Rome, 1980; *Per foramen acus. Il cristianesimo antico di fronte alla pericope evangelica del "giovane ricco,"* Milan, 1986. A good anthology of texts with Italian translations has been published in the Edizioni Paoline, *Retto uso delle ricchezze nella Tradizione Patristica*, ed. M. Todde-A. Pieri, Milan, 1985. See also P. Phan, *Social Thought* (MFC), Wilmington, DE, 1984. On the works of Clement in particular cf. V. Messana, 'L'economia nel *Quis dives salvetur*,' *AugR* 18 (1978), 133-143. An Italian translation has been published by A. Pieri, *Clemente Alessandrino, C'è salvezza per il ricco?*, Ancona, 1965, as well as in the above-cited anthology, *Retto uso*.

[19] On the problems concerning content and form of this work, cf. *Clemente Alessandrino. Estratti profetici*, a cura di C. Nardi (BP 4), Florence, 1985. See also *idem*, *Il battesimo in Clemente Alessandrino. Interpretazione di Eclogae propheticae 1-26*, Rome, 1984.

[20] Cf. the noteworthy synthesis of Ch. Munier, *L'Église dans l'Empire Romain (IIe-IIIe siècles). Église et Cité*, Paris, 1979, 14-16. J.P. Broudéhoux, *Mariage et Famille chez Clément d'Alexandrie*, Paris, 1970; M. Mees, 'Clemens von Alexandrien über Ehe und Familie,' *AugR* 17 (1977), 113-131, are fundamental.

[21] Cf. G. Sfameni Gasparro, *Enkrateia e antropologia... op cit.*, 168. See further F. Bolgiani, 'La tradizione eresiologica sull'encratismo. La confutazione di Clemente,' *AAST* 96 (1961-1962), 537-664.

[22] Cf. what has been said in General Introduction, pp. 78-83.

finalized in the procreation of children. There are traditional concepts of an obvious Stoic matrix,[23] already presented besides in earlier Christian writers like Athenagoras,[24] which are sometimes integrated — with a typical procedure of osmosis already indicated above — with the most genuinely biblical matrixes, like that of Genesis, *Increase and multiply*.[25]

Traditional, already, in the pagan world, are also the other advantages which Clement retraces to the matrimonial union: to fulfill the social obligation to populate the world, to perpetuate one's own stock, to have a companion to give loving care in the case of ill-health or in old age. These analogies, however, should not cause us to lose sight of the quasi-charismatic dimension which matrimony assumes in the estimate of the Alexandrian: it is God himself who with his presence reinforces the nuclear family,[26] and a true "holy" Christian marriage ritualizes this mystical one between Christ and the Church.[27]

To the couple, in particular, Clement dedicated quite a bit of attention for the regulation of day-to-day life. His own preoccupations obviously derive from the contingent situation in Alexandria, an aristocratic city, teeming with luxury, in which the traditional forms of pagan religion flourished, whether local and Egyptian, or

---

[23] Cf. J.P. Broudéhoux, *op. cit.*, 74-79.

[24] Cf. Athenagoras, *Supplicatio* 33: SC 3, p. 19; ed., M. Marcovich, PTuS, 31, New York, 1990, 104-105. The motif is common in the apologists of the second century. Cf. Ch. Munier, *Mariage et virginité dans l'Église ancienne*, Berne-Frankfurt-New York-Paris, 1987, p. XXIX. The passage from Athenagoras, with French translation is at p. 38. See W.R. Schoedel, OECT; Italian translation of the Greek apologists in CTP 59 (ed. C. Burini).

[25] Cf. *Paidagogos* II, X, 83, 2: GCS 12, p. 208: "We have received the command, 'Be fruitful' and we must obey. In this role man becomes like God, because he co-operates, in his human way, in the birth of another human being." FOTC. On biblical influences on Clement cf. the important and suggestive considerations in H.-I. Marrou, 'Morale et spiritualité chrétienne dans le *Pédagogue* de Clément l'Alexandrie,' *Stud. Pat* 2, Berlin, 1957, 538-546. See more recently E. Osborn, 'La Bible inspiratrice d'une morale chrétienne d'après Clément d'Alexandrie,' in C. Mondésert (ed.), *Le monde grec ancien et la Bible,* Paris, 1984, 127-144.

[26] Cf. *Stromata* III, 68, 1-2, where, commenting on Mt 18:20 (*Where two or three are gathered in my name there am I in the midst of them*), Clement sees the three as a typical Christian family: husband, wife and child, which has been formed in the name of Christ, "since the woman is united with her husband by the will of God."

[27] Cf. *Stromata* III, 84,2-3: GCS 50 [15], p. 234: "if the law is holy, matrimony is holy. Accordingly the Apostle points in this mystery in the direction of Christ and the Church," cf. Eph 5:32, tr. J. Ferguson, FOTC 85,30.

Greek and — in the ambit of Christianity itself — manifested various heterodox tendencies. Clement invites husband and wife to regulate their own conduct on the basis of an absolute "temperance" and insists naturally on the necessity of taking care of the internal, rather than the external, aspect of luxurious clothes or precious ornaments, even though, with an observation that is psychologically felicitous, he recognizes the appropriate need for a woman to be concerned about dressing elegantly.[28] The couple will observe a temperate frugality even in meals and nocturnal rest, will avoid for this reason the sumptuousness of pagan banquets for which Clement substitutes the celebrations of the Christian community.

On the purely ethical plane there is absolute parity between man and woman from the moment that both are indoctrinated in the teaching of the divine Logos and both are on a basis of strict equality in the practice of virtue as is demonstrated in a particular way in the ability of each to testify by martyrdom to the strength of their individual faith.[29]

Clement is not slow to point out the part played within marriage by communion of sentiments, by love that is reciprocal, but especially spontaneous, because he affirms in clear terms the freedom of choice that belongs to the woman. Certainly a clear pessimism of Stoic parentage in dealings with the passions and a preoccupation with not lessening too much the ascetical implications of a correct matrimonial relationship, placed considerable limits on references to conjugal love understood as mutual desire, so much so that Clement exhorts the spouses to abstain from open manifestation of their mutual feelings within the house in front of the servants.

To affirm the moral parity of man and woman Clement, by taking account of the physical/biological differences between the sexes and presupposing the greater "weakness" of the female,[30] clearly

---

[28] Cf. *Paidagogos* II, 107, 3 and III, 57, 2 (text n. 10).

[29] Cf. *Stromata* IV,67,4: GCS 50 [15], p. 252: "If it is truly a good thing for a man to die for virtue, for liberty, for his own ideals, so also it is good for a woman to do so. This is not a privilege proper to man, but is a good common to the nature of the good." Cf. J.P. Broudéhoux, *op. cit.*, p. 145.

[30] On the theme of female "weakness" in Clement, cf. J.P. Broudéaux, *op. cit.*, 146-148, with ample references to the works of Clement.

underlines the differentiation of roles at the heart of the union, undoubtedly to the detriment of the feminine contribution. In the domestic sphere, in fact, the wife has to show total submission in her dealings with her husband, responsible for the correct maintenance of the household.[31]

The picture most clearly delineating the female condition is that offered in Book III of the *Paidagogos*, with its stereotypical image of the woman intent on spinning and weaving, on cooking and attending to the needs of her husband's children. It is the typical image of Greco-hellenistic ambience which Clement however seeks to exalt, with recourse to the famous ode to the virtuous woman in Proverbs 31:10-31,[32] and hailing that wife who, by accepting her role, indispensable in the management of the household, and by assimilating it ever more closely to the biblical models of Sarah and Rachel[33] makes on her own the garments necessary for herself and her husband.

The new dimension of the couple emerges for this reason also in Clement in a strictly religious connection, in the celebration of the liturgy, in evening prayer.[34]

And the faith is also the only sphere in which Clement recognizes in the wife the possibility of diminishing the hegemony of the husband; only in the case in which on the plane of religious belief the wife has the obligation transcending the obligation of submission.[35] It is the only form of "liberation" which, apart from any optimistic topicality, a 2nd century Father could concede to the woman.[36]

---

[31] *Loc. cit.*, 182-183.

[32] Cf. text n. 11. On the eulogy on the ideal wife in Proverbs cf. A. Bonora, 'La donna eccellente: la sapienza, il sapiente (Pr 31,10-31),' *RivBibl* 36 (1988), 137-164.

[33] Cf. J. P. Broudéhoux, *op. cit.*, 183.

[34] *Ibidem*, 175-177.

[35] Cf. *Stromata* IV, 67,1: GCS 50 [15] p. 252: "Despite opposition and notwithstanding that some place in their way enormous difficulties, the slave and the woman will have wisdom as their target, even against the threats which the husband or master direct against them." Perhaps it is no accident that Clement joins together two conditions which in ancient society share a strong grade of subordination, which in any case should not condition the quest for virtue, because neither a master of little account nor an evil husband can put limits on this sacrosanct necessity.

[36] Rightly A. Quacquarelli, *Complementi interdisciplinari di Patrologia*, Rome, 1989, 23 has warned against "reading the ancient authors with the eyes and mentality of today, attributing to them principles and ideals which they do not have."

CONVENIENCE AND FINALITY OF THE MATRIMONIAL UNION

3

1. Marriage is a union between a man and a woman; it is the primary union; it is a legal transaction; it exists for the procreation of legitimate children.[1]

2. The comic dramatist Menander says,

> I give you my own daughter
> for the sowing of true children.[2]

3. We ask the question whether it is right to marry. This is one of those questions named after their relation to an end. Who is to marry? In what situation? With what woman? What about her situation? It is not right for everyone to marry; it is not right at all times. There is a time when it is appropriate; there is a person for whom it is appropriate; there is an age up to which it is appropriate.

4. It is not right for every man to marry every woman, on every occasion, in absolutely all circumstances. It depends on the circumstances of the man, the character of the woman, the right time, the prospect of children, the total compatibility of the woman and the absence of any violence or compulsion to drive her to look after the man who loves her.[3]

Stromata II, 137,1-4; GCS 50 [15] 188; FOTC

---

[1] Clement of Alexandria's definition of matrimony recalls a verse in a verbal expression analogous in Stobaeus, II,7: *ed. cit.*, p. 148 where it insists however, on the idea that the union between man and woman finalized in the procreation of children and a life in common constitutes the "first society." On the other hand, as J.P. Broudéhoux, opportunely notes, *op. cit.*, 74-77, the Alexandrian insists more on the character of indissolubility and monogamy innate in Christian matrimony, a peculiarity which has been evoked in the expression "primary union" to be put in relation with another clarifying passage in *Stromata* III, 74, 2: GCS 50 [15], p. 229: "Any of us can marry, according to the law, the woman of our choice — I refer, obviously, to a first marriage." Clement is not absolutely hostile to second marriage after the death of one of the two spouses while he is resolute in prohibiting that following a divorce because of the adultery of the husband: cf. J.P. Broudéhoux, *op. cit.*, pp. 91-98, particularly p. 95.

[2] The citation from the comic poet, Menander (fr. 682 Kock) is the cultivated mode adopted by Clement to reproduce a typically technical formula of the celebration of matrimony current in Athens.

[3] As has already been noted in the Introductory Profile, Clement underlines the potential liberty which the wife has to reject the husband with whom she is no longer in love.

4

1.   So there is every reason to marry — for patriotic reasons, for the succession of children, for the fulfillment of the universe[1] (insofar as that is our business). The poets regret a marriage which is "half-fulfilled" and childless, and bless the marriage which is "abundant in growth."

2.   Physical ailments demonstrate the necessity of marriage particularly well.[2] A wife's care and her patient attention seem to surpass all the earnest devotion of other family and friends;[3] she likes to excel all others in sympathy and present concern; she really and truly is, in the words of Scripture, *a necessary helper*.[a][4]

Stromata II, 140, 1-2; GCS 50 [15] 190; FOTC 85

---

[a] cf. Jn 1:1

---

[1]   The social function of matrimony had already been highlighted before Clement, whether in pagan philosophers like Aristotle or Musonius Rufus, or, in a Jewish ambience by Philo: cf. J.P. Broudéhoux, *op. cit.*, p. 80. At about the same period, but in a situation of a diverse ambience and, especially, in a thematically diverse context, so as to dissuade from second marriage, Tertullian will deny to the procreative act any social function whatsoever in favor of the State with his usual sharp irony: "Through this perhaps one ought to do one's best for the State... for fear the state fails, if no rising generations be trained up, for fear there be no one to raise the cry: 'To the lions, the Christians!'" (*Exhortation to chastity*, 12,4: SC 319, 110-111).

[2]   The unilateral perspective with which Clement guards the advantages inherent in matrimony in the case of illness, which envisages, not a reciprocal assistance but rather the wife helping her husband is not to be taken — according to Broudéhoux, *op. cit.*, 81-82 — as a lack of sensitivity with regard to women, but appears rather conditioned by the passage in Genesis around which the Alexandrian organizes his own discourse. For the wife as "helper" of the husband cf. also *Stromata* III, 82,3: "It is the same man, the same Lord who makes old things new. He introduces monogamy for the production of children and the need to look after the home. Woman was offered as a helpmate in this" (trans. J. Ferguson, FOTC 85).

[3]   The perspective is still "masculine," perhaps justifying the many cases of matrimony in which there was a notable difference between husband and wife.

[4]   In the part omitted, Clement, to censure the celibate, recalls the Spartan legislation (of Lycurgus) and Plato who threatened sanctions on those who did not marry. Celibates in fact, caused destruction in society with demographic decline imputible to them. In the eyes of Clement the only form of celibacy likely to gain approval is that inspired by total love for God, absolute chastity chosen in full awareness and with a view to true "gnosis" because to abstain from marriage without following the principles of sacred knowledge is to fall into hatred of humankind, because to abstain from marrying without a higher motive can lead man "to misanthropy and to the death of sentiments of love" (*Stromata* III, 67,2 = J. Ferguson, tr. FOTC 85, p. 297).

LOVE AND TEMPERANCE

5

1. In general, let our affirmation about marriage, food and the rest proceed: we should never act from desire; our will should be concentrated on necessities. We are children of will,[a] not of desire. 2. If a man marries in order to have children he ought to practice self-control. He ought not to have a sexual desire even for his wife, to whom he has a duty to show Christian love. He ought to produce children[1] by a reverent disciplined act of will.

Stromata III, 58, 1-2; GCS 50 [15] 222; FOTC 85, 292

6

1. For my part, I would advise husbands never to manifest their affection for their wives at home in the presence of slaves. Aristotle[1] does not permit them ever to laugh with slaves, and certainly much less to openly show love for their wives in their presence. It is better to practise reserve at home beginning with the first day of marriage. A chaste union redolent of pure delight is a wonderful thing.

Paidagogos III. XII 84,1; SC 158, 162-163; FOTC 23, 263

---

[a] cf. Jn 1:13

[1] This is a fundamental text to explain Clement's conjugal morality, centered on the necessity of being able to bridle carnal concupiscence and of "loving" one's own spouse in a spirit of Christian "agape," understood as a reciprocal giving. For a full analysis cf. J.P. Broudéhoux, *op. cit.*, 129-131.

[1] Clement refers to Fragment 183 ed. Rose even if it is not possible to be precise about the exact extent of the citation: cf. H.-I. Marrou, *Clément d'Alexandrie. Le Pédagogue* III (SC 158), 163, note 3. Obviously the typically Christian notion of respect for shame intervenes in the recommendation of the Alexandrian. One can compare with this passage an analogous one in the *Conjugal Precepts* of Plutarch (XIII), in which restraint is recommended to spouses, especially in the manifestation of their inner feelings in public.

7

He will therefore prefer neither children, nor marriage, nor parents, to love for God, and righteousness in life. To such an one, his wife, after conception, is as a sister, and is judged as if of the same father; then only recollecting her husband, when she looks on the children as destined to become a sister in reality after putting off the flesh, which separates and limits the knowledge of those who are spiritual,[1] by the peculiar characteristics of the sexes. For souls, themselves by themselves, are equal. Souls are neither male nor female,[a] when they no longer marry nor are given in marriage.[b] And is not woman translated into man, when she is become equally unfeminine, and manly, and perfect?

Stromata VI 100, 3; GCS 50 [15] 482

EQUAL DIGNITY AND CAPACITY FOR VIRTUE

8

(10) 1. Let us welcome more and more gladly this holy subjection, and let us surrender ourselves more and more completely to the Lord, holding to the steadfast cable of his persuasion. Let us recognize too, that both men and women practice the same sort of virtue. Surely, if there is but one food for both, then there is but one Educator[1] for both. One is the Church, one is virtue, one is modesty, a common food, wedlock in common, breath, sight, hearing, knowledge, hope, obedience, love, everything is equal. Those who have

---

[a] cf. Gal 3:28   [b] cf. Mt 22:30; Mk 12:25; Lk 20:35

[1] On the theme of concupiscence as a motive for the breakdown of unity of the human being who has already been overcome in the earthly life after procreation, with separation from sexual activity, and then in eschatological perspective in recuperation of the angelic dimension cf. the extensive treatment in the General Introduction, pp. 80-82.

[1] Clement clearly affirms the moral parity of the sexes, their identical capacity to attain to virtue. It is a motif, as has been already observed, clearly of Stoic origin already encountered in Musonius Rufus or in Seneca, but also in the Greek philosophical ambience of Diogenes Laertius and Antisthenes; Plutarch himself had dedicated a specific treatise (*The Virtue of Woman*) to the demonstration of this assumption. Cf. what has been said in the General Introduction pp. 41-57; J.P. Broudéhoux, *op. cit.*, p. 143.

life in common, have grace in common and also salvation, and their virtue and behavior will also be in common.

3. *In this world*, says Scripture, *they marry and are given in marriage*,[a] then only in this world is the female differentiated from the male. There the reward of a life in matrimony passed in common and sanctified, will not be reserved to male and to female, but to humanity, which is far removed from concupiscence which divides in two.[2]

Paidagogos I. IV 10, 1-3; SC 70, 128; FOTC 23, 11-12

9

59,1. As far as regards human nature, the woman does not possess one nature, and the man another, but rather both have the same.

2. So also with virtue. If, in consequence, self-restraint and righteousness, and whatever qualities are regarded as following them, is the virtue of the male, then it would belong to the male alone to be virtuous, and to the woman to be licentious and unjust. But even to say this is offensive.

3. Accordingly woman is to practice self-restraint and righteousness, and every other virtue, as well as man, both bond and free; since it is a fit consequence that the same nature possesses one and the same virtue.

4. We certainly do not mean to say that woman's nature is the same as man's, as she is a woman For undoubtedly it stands to reason that some difference should exist between each of them, in virtue of which one is male and the other female.

5. Pregnancy and parturition, accordingly we say belong to woman, as she is woman, and not as she is a human being. But if there were no difference both would do and suffer the same.[1]

---

[a] Lk 20:34   [b] Lk 20:35

[2] Cf. what has already been said concerning text n. 7.

[1] After having confirmed the absolute equality of man and woman in the moral sphere, Clement passes on to the differentiation between man and woman from a physical-biological perspective, assigning to the woman her principal special activity: procreation and the care of the household; on this point also cf. General Introduction, pp. 81-83.

60,1. As then there is sameness, as far as respects the soul, she will attain to the same virtue but as there is difference as respects the peculiar anatomy of the body, she is destined for childbearing and housekeeping.

2. *For I would have you know*, says the Apostle, *that the head of every man is Christ; and the head of the woman is the man: for the man is not of the woman but the woman of the man. For neither is the woman without the man, nor the man without the woman, in the Lord.*[a]

3. For as we say that the man ought to be continent, and superior to pleasure, so also we reckon that the woman should be continent and practiced in fighting against pleasures.

4. But I say: *Walk in the Spirit, and you shall not fulfill the lusts, of the flesh*, counsels the apostolic command *for the flesh lusts against the spirit, and the spirit against the flesh. The two are directly opposed*,[b] not as good to evil, but as components which fight with each other advantageously.

61,1. He adds therefore, *So you do not do what you would. Now the works of the flesh are manifest, which are fornication, uncleanness, profligacy, idolatry, witchcrafts, enmities, strifes, jealousies, wrath, contentions, dissensions, heresies, envyings, drunkenness, revellings and such like; of which I tell you as, I have also said before, that they who do such things will not inherit the kingdom of God. But the fruit of the Spirit is love, joy, peace, long-suffering, gentleness, temperance, goodness, faith, meekness.*[d] I believe that he calls sinners, *flesh*, and the righteous, *spirit*.

2. Further, manliness[2] is to be assumed in order to produce confidence and forbearance, so as *to him that strikes on the one cheek, to give to him the other; and to him that takes away the cloak, to yield to him the coat also*[e] strongly restraining our anger. For we do not train our women like Amazons to manliness in war; since we wish the men even to be peaceable.[3]

---

[a] 1 Cor 11:3, 8,11   [b] Gal 5:16-17   [c] Gal 5:17   [d] Gal 5:18-22   [e] cf. Lk 6:29

[2] On the motif of feminine "weakness" in Clement, cf. J.P. Broudéhoux, *op. cit.*, 146-148.

[3] In the part omitted Clement provides some "marvellous" examples of female courage: the Sarmatian women who went to war like men, the women of the Sacae [see Herodotus, IV, 110-117], considered capable archers, etc.; cf. G. Pini, *op. cit.*, p. 468 and note 13.

62,4. Women are therefore to philosophize equally with men though the males are preferable at everything unless they have become effeminate.

63,1. To the whole human race, then, discipline and virtue are a necessity, if they would pursue after happiness.

2. And how recklessly Euripides writes sometimes this and sometimes that! On one occasion: *For every wife is inferior to her husband, though the most excellent one marry her that is of fair fame.*

3. And elsewhere: *For the chaste woman is her husband's slave, while she that is unchaste in her folly despises her consort.*[4]

4. For nothing is in fact better and more excellent than when as husband and wife you both live in a house, harmonious in your sentiments.

Stromata, IV 59,1-63,3; GCS 50 (15) 275-277

THE ROLE OF THE CHRISTIAN WIFE

| 10 |

57,1. The Pedagogue, then, permits women the use of rings made of gold, not as ornaments, but as signet rings to seal their valuables worth guarding at home, in the management of their homes. If all were under the influence of the Educator, nothing would need to be sealed, for both master and servant would be honest. But, since lack of education exposes men to a strong inclination to dishonesty, we always stand in need of these seals.

2. In some circumstances, it is best to relax this stricture. We must be sympathetic with women who sometimes do not succeed in finding restraint in their married lives and who therefore adorn themselves to keep themselves attractive to their husbands. But, let the attempt to win their husband's admiration be their sole motive.

3. For my part, I would not want them to cultivate bodily comeliness but instead, to offer their husbands a self-controlled love, a

---

[4] Clement cites fragments 546 and 545 of the Greek tragedian, Euripides, probably taken from the tragedy, *Oedipus* (Nauck's edition).

remedy that is powerful and honest.[1] However, when they are tempted to be unhappy in mind, let them recall this thought, that, if they wish to continue self-controlled, they will gently appease the unreasonable desires and cravings of their husbands. They must lead them back to simplicity quietly, by accustoming them little by little to what is more restrained.

4. Dignity in dress comes not from adding to what is worn, but from eliminating all that is superfluous.

58,1. It is but right that husbands trust their wives and confide the care of their homes to them. It is for this purpose that wives have been given as helpmates.[a]

Paidagogos, III. XI, 57,1-58,1; SC 158 120-122; FOTC 23, 244-245

11

2. It is absurd for those who have been made *to the image and likeness of God*[a] to adopt some extraneous means of ornamentation, disfiguring the pattern by which they have been created, and preferring the cleverness of men to that of their divine Creator.

3. The Educator bids women approach *in decent dress, adorning themselves with modesty and dignity,*[b] *being subject to their husbands, so that even if any husband does not believe the word, they may without word be won through the behavior of their wives, observing reverently your chaste behavior. Let not theirs be the outward adornment of braiding the hair or of wearing gold, or of putting on robes, but let it be the inner life of the heart, in the imperishableness of a quiet and gentle spirit, which is of great price in the sight of God.*[c] [1]

67,1. It is the work a woman performs with her own hands that creates true beauty. It exercises her body and at the same time adorns her. It is a heart-warming sight to see a woman clothe herself and

---

[a] cf. Gn 2:18   [a] cf. Gn 1:26   [b] 1 Tm 2:9   [c] 1 P 3:1-4   [d] cf. Pr 31:21-22

[1] The role of the woman is still firmly anchored in the domestic domain; however we should certainly note the psychologically felicitous "apertures" of Clement. Women should attend to their exterior looks, albeit in moderation, especially to obviate the risk of her husband being attracted to another woman; besides, the woman is assigned the active role of correcting intemperance on the part of her consort. And if the role of "helper" undoubtedly places the wife on a plane of inferiority with regard to her husband, Clement nevertheless confirms the importance of the female role in the conduct and custody of the house. [Engl. ed. Add: E. Condi Guerri, 'La mujer ideal en el *Pedagogo* de Clemente Alejandrino,' *Helmantica* 37 (1986), 112-114, 337-354.]

her husband with the garments she herself has made; everyone takes pleasure in such a sight: her children, in their mother; the husband, in his wife; herself, in her handiwork; and everyone, in God.[2]

3. In a word, *a treasury of virtue*[3] *is the brave woman, who has not eaten her bread hesitatingly,*[e] *and the laws of mercy are on her tongue,*[f] *who hath opened her mouth wisely and justly, whose children rising up have called her blessed,*[g] as the Holy Spirit says through Solomon, *and her husband has praised her.*[h] *For a pious woman is praised, let her praise the fear of the Lord,*[i] and again *a courageous wife is the crown of her husband.*[j]

Paidagogos, III. XI, 66,2-67,3; SC 158 132-136

12

2. The wise woman, then, will first choose to persuade her husband to be her associate in what is conducive to happiness.

And should that be found impracticable, let her on her own earnestly aim at virtue,[1] gaining her husband's consent in everything, so as never to do anything against his will, with the exception of what is reckoned as contributing to virtue and salvation.

Stromata IV 123,2; GCS 50 [15] 303

---

e cf. Pr 31:27 f Pr 31:26 g Pr 31:26; 31:28 h Pr 31:28 i cf. Pr 31:30; j Pr 12:4

1 Clement insists repeatedly — even in thematically diverse contexts — on the necessity for the woman (but also the man) to avoid splendor of dress and greater preoccupation with the interior: cf., for example, *Paidagogos*, II, X, 114, 1; SC 108, pp. 214-219 and II,X,128,1-2; SC 108, 240-241; FOTC.

2 The eulogy of the self-sufficient woman in the conduct of domestic affairs, extending to the ability to clothe with garments fashioned by her own hands her husband and children, which Clement models on the well-known eulogy of Pr 31:13-28, should be compared with the identical portrait of the perfect Christian "matron" in Tertullian, *Exhortation to chastity*, XII,I; SC 319,108-109, where, however, any reference to the biblical passage in question is missing and is based rather on the traditional — and archaic — figure of the Roman woman who "administers the household, regulates the life of the slaves, guards the cupboards and keys, espouses working in wool, is preoccupied with the provision of food, allocates the various tasks." See also the comment on this passage of Tertullian by C. Moreschini in SC 108,184-185, with just and pertinent observations on the criticisms regarding the conceptions of woman on the part of Christian authors which have been assembled by K.Thraede, art. "Frau" *loc. cit.*, coll. 239-240.

3 The citation is taken from the comic poet Alexander, *Fr. 5: Comicorum Atticorum fragmenta*, ed. Kock, vol. III, p. 373.

1 Clement affirms clearly that because of her spiritual autonomy, the wife has the obligation, even with regard to her husband, to withdraw from his hegemony in case of his unwillingness to follow in the pursuit "of virtue and of salvation." This passage is linked contextually to the succeeding one (n. 13), taken from *Stromata* IV,125,1-127,2. On the spiritual autonomy of the Christian woman cf. C. Mazzucco, "*E fui fatta maschio*"... *op. cit.*, 34-36.

13

125,1. The woman who, with propriety, loves her husband, Euripides describes, while admonishing,

> Then when her husband says aught
> She ought to regard him as speaking well
> if she say nothing;
> and if she will say anything;
> to do her endeavor to gratify her husband.[1]

2. And again he subjoins the like:

> And that the wife should sweetly look sad
> Should aught evil befall him,
> And have in common a share of sorrow and joy.

3. Then, describing her as gentle and kind even in misfortunes, he adds:

> And I, when you are ill, will, sharing your sickness bear it;
> And I will bear my share in your misfortunes.
> And
> nothing is bitter to me,
> For with friends one ought to be happy,
> For what else is friendship but this.[2]

126,1. The marriage, then, that is consummated according to the Word[a] is certainly sanctified, if the union be under subjection to God, and be conducted with a true heart, in full assurance of faith,

---

[1] In Clement's exploitation of citations he draws once more on Euripides (fragment 909, edition, Nauck), to delineate a portrait of the couple in which the woman is partly overshadowed by the preponderant role which the man assumes. The perspective is always "masculine"; however, we should once more underline the complete liberty which the woman recovers in the religious sphere; in the absence of an earthly companion, she should completely entrust herself to God, heavenly "helper and companion" for the present and the future.

[2] These citations of Clement taken from Greek tragic poetry cannot be identified in the testimonies which we possess.

having hearts sprinkled from an evil conscience, and the body washed with pure water, and holding the confession of hope; for He is faithful that promised.[b]

2. And the happiness of marriage ought never to be estimated either in terms of wealth or beauty, but of virtue.

3. The tragic poet says:

> Beauty helps no wife with her husband;
> But virtue has helped many; for every good wife
> who is attached to her husband knows how to practice
> 　　sobriety.

4. Then, as giving admonitions, he says:

> First, then, this is incumbent on her who is
> endowed with mind,
> That even if her husband be ugly, he must appear
> good-looking;
> For it is for the mind, not the eye, to judge.

...127,1. It is evident, then, in my opinion, that she will charge herself with remedying by good sense and persuasion, each of the annoyances that originate with her husband in domestic economy. And if he does not yield, then she will endeavor, as far as possible for human nature, to lead a sinless life; whether it be necessary to die, in accordance with the Logos, or to live; considering that God is her helper and associate in such a course of conduct, her true defender and Savior both for the present and for the future; making Him the leader and guide of all her actions, reckoning sobriety and righteousness her work, and making the favor of God her purpose in life.

Stromata IV 125, 1-127, 2; GCS 50 [15] 303-304

---

[a] cf. 1 Tm 4:5　　[b] cf. Heb 10:22

[3] Ch. Munier, *Mariage et virginité, op. cit.*, 151 cites in a very fitting manner a passage of Tertullian, *The Apparel of Women* II,13,7: [Italian: BP 6, pp. 125-127]; FOTC 40 (1959), 149 in which he exhorts women to "paint your eyes with demureness, your lips with silence; hang on your eyes the words of God, bind on your neck the yoke of Christ; bow your heads to your husbands — and that will be ornament enough for you. Decked out in this manner, you will have God Himself as your lover."

ORIGEN

INTRODUCTORY PROFILE

A substantial biographical notice in Eusebius' *Ecclesiastical History*[1] allows us to reconstruct in its essential outlines and with sufficient wealth of detail the events in the life of a personality who, by the vast sweep of his intellectual interests, the profundity of his spiritual insights and of his secular and scriptural knowledge, emerges with an entirely unique importance in the patristic panorama of the third century.

The *Farewell Address* composed by Gregory, generally identified with Gregory Thaumaturgus (the Wonderworker),[2] a pupil who for years had followed his teaching in Caesarea in Palestine, completes the portrait delineated by Eusebius, illustrating the modality and the effects of Origen's activity as master of sacred and secular doctrine and of mystical spirituality.[3]

---

[1] Book VI of *Hist. Eccles.* is almost entirely dedicated to illustrating the life and literary activity of the Alexandrian master (ed.- G. Bardy, SC 41, Paris, 82-142; FOTC).

[2] The attribution to Thaumaturgus has been put in doubt by P. Nautin, *Origène. Sa vie et son oeuvre*, Paris, 1977, 183-197. This scholar, however, recognizes in the letter an authentic testimony to the pedagogical method of Origen but as the work of another student whose name was Theodore. The arguments of Nautin have been rejected in H. Crouzel, 'Faut-il voir trois personnages en Grégoire Thaumaturge?', *Gregorianum* 60 (1979), 287-320. Crouzel has also given us a critical text, with ample introduction and notes (SC 148, Paris, 1969). See also the Italian translation by E. Marotta, in CTP 40. For the complexity of the problem see M. Simonetti, 'Una nuova ipotesi su Gregorio il Taumaturgo,' *RSLR* 24 (1988),17-41.

[3] Among the copious bibliography on the spirituality of Origen we refer merely to the research of W. Völker, *Das Vollkommenheitsideal des Origenes*, Tübingen 1931 which reevaluates this fundamental aspect of the physiognomy of the Alexandrian author, too often judged in a unilateral manner or predominantly as a "philosopher," of a strong Platonic tendency, and of H. Crouzel, *Origène et la connaissance mystique*, Tournai, 1961.

The *Apology for Origen*,[4] compiled by the martyr Pamphilus of Caesarea in collaboration with Eusebius himself in defence of the Alexandrian, casts light on a complex situation of polemic and of opposing estimates of the person and of the work of Origen which, already represented in tones more or less during the life of the personage, and after his death was further complicated, accentuating the contrasts between the defenders and detractors of his teaching.

This, in fact, radicalized in theological formulas which heightened the typical "gymnastic" character of certain "hypotheses" of Origen on the part of his disciples and admirers, especially numerous in the ambience of Egyptian monasteries,[5] or else submitted to misunderstandings on the part of his adversaries, became the object of lively discussions.[6]

These developed into the first Origenist "crisis" of 393-402, in which the principal protagonists were Epiphanius of Salamis, Theophilus, bishop of Alexandria, and Jerome,[7] who at the outset was a fervent admirer and translator of Origen[8] but later became a bitter and implacable judge of the doctrinal "errors" of the Alexandrian master, and an adversary of Rufinus of Aquileia.[9] The latter remained faithful to his own positions of respect and of a positive evaluation of the author, many of whose works he brought to

---

[4] The work, to which Eusebius refers as consisting of two books (*Hist. Eccles.* VI, XXIII, 4; VI, XXXIII, 4), was actually six (cf. Jerome, *Contra Rufinum* I, 8, ed. P. Lardet, SC 303, Paris, 1983, 24-27). Of these there remains only the first in the Latin translation of Rufinus, composed 397-398 (PG 16, coll. 539-616) and the outline of its contents referred to by the Patriarch Photius (*Biblioteca*, Cod. 118, ed. R. Henry, v. II, Paris, 1960, 90-92).

[5] For the history of Origenism in the Orient see A. Guillaumont, *Les "Kephalaia gnostica" d'Évagre le Pontique et l'histoire de l'origénisme chez les Grecs et les Syriens*, Paris, 1962.

[6] Another apologetical work in defence of the teaching of Origen was known to Patriarch Photius, who furnishes a short synthesis of its contents (*Biblioteca*, Cod. 117, ed. Henry, 88-90).

[7] For the relations of Jerome with Origen and his role in the first Origenist controversy see F. Cavallera, *Saint Jérome. Sa vie et son oeuvre*, I-II, Louvain-Paris, 1922; J.N.D. Kelly, *Jerome: His Life, Writings, and Controversies*, London 1975 and the contributions to *XIV Incontro di studiosi dell'antichità cristiana sul tema: L'Origenismo: apologie e polemiche intorno ad Origene, 9-11 maggio 1985*, in *AugR* 26 (1986).

[8] During his sojourn at Constantinople (379-382) Jerome translated of Origen's works, 14 Homilies *On Jeremiah*, 14 *On Ezekiel* and 9 *On Isaiah*. During his sojourn in Rome, 383-384, he translated 2 Homilies *On the Canticle of Canticles* dedicated to Pope Damasus and finally, between 389 and 392, in polemic with Ambrose, in order to demonstrate the "debt" contracted by the latter vis-a-vis Origen, 39 Homilies *On the Gospel of Luke*.

[9] Cf. F.-X. Murphy, *Rufinus of Aquileia*, Washington, 1945.

the attention of the public in Latin translations of various homilies[10] and of the treatise, On Principles,[11] around which flared up the polemic with regard to Origenist "heterodoxy."[12]

The second Origenistic "crisis" of the 6th century was provoked by extreme positions of Origenists of Evagrian inspiration and in this the emperor Justinian intervened authoritatively, with a first condemnation of Origenism issued in the Letter to Menas, patriarch of Constantinople,[13] in 543, and a second, in 553, in the Council of Constantinople. These official interventions, which were provoked by charges of heterodoxy in trinitarian and christological matters as well as by his anthropological positions characterized by notions about the preexistence of the soul, which traced themselves back to Greek Platonism, ensured the loss of a large part of his rich literary production in the original Greek.

Born in Alexandria in the reign of Commodus, around 185,[14] Origen received a Christian education and was quickly initiated by his father into the study of the sacred and secular disciplines. Ac-

---

[10] In the translation of Rufinus 25 Homilies On Joshua, 9 On Judges, 9 On Psalms 36-38, 16 On Genesis, 13 On Exodus, 16 On Leviticus and 28 On Numbers have survived. To Rufinus also we owe our knowledge of the great Commentary on the Canticle of Canticles, albeit limited to the first part of the work, which extended over 10 books and interpreted the entire biblical text.

[11] The work, edited by P. Koetschau in the GCS series (n. 22), of which ten volumes are dedicated to Origen, without however exhausting his entire production. In Italian the translation and ample commentary by M. Simonetti, Origene. I Principi, Turin, 1968. See also the most recent critical editions of H. Crouzel-M. Simonetti in the SC series (nn. 252-253; 268-269 e 312) and of H. Gorgemanns-H. Karpp (Darmstadt, 1976).

[12] The translation of the treatise, De Principiis, composed by Rufinus in 398, rekindled the polemic with Jerome who, to demonstrate the heterodoxy of Origen, translated "literally" the text which Rufinus, for opposite reasons, had partially rearranged by eliminating or modifying some passages doctrinally ambiguous, retaining interpolations of enemies of Origen. For a first approach to the complex questions related to the two translations of the work of Origen cf. G. Sfameni Gasparro, 'Aspetti della controversia origeniana: le traduzioni latine del Peri Archon,' AugR 26 (1986), 190-205; H. Crouzel, 'Jérôme traducteur du Peri Archon d'Origène,' in Y.-M. Duval (ed.), Jérôme entre l'Occident et l'Orient. Actes du Colloque de Chantilly (septembre 1986), Paris, 1988, 153-161.

[13] Cf. G. Sfameni Gasparro, 'Il problema delle citazioni del Peri Archon nella Lettera a Mena di Giustiniano,' in L. Lies (ed.), Origeniana Quarta. Die Referate des 4. Internationalen Origenes Kongresses (Innsbruck-Wien, 2-6 September 1985), Innsbruck-Wien, 1987, 54-76.

[14] For a reconstruction of the chronology of the life and works of Origen see P. Nautin, op. cit [in note 2], whose findings however have not encountered unanimous acceptance. A more recent presentation of Origen's physiognomy, in a synthesis based on numerous researches on particular themes, is offered in H. Crouzel, Origen, Engl. tr. A.S. Worrall, San Francisco, 1989.

cording to Eusebius (*H.E.* VI,6) he became a disciple of Clement, whom he himself, however, never mentions explicitly.

A decisive event in his earthly experience was the martyrdom of his father Leonidas during the persecution of Septimius Severus (c. 201 A.D.) as a result of which Origen, the eldest of seven brothers, had to undertake, at the age of seventeen, the support of his family, whose property had been confiscated.

This he was able to do by devoting himself to the teaching of grammar. His profound knowledge of this and of the discipline of Greek philosophy, united to that of the Sacred Scriptures, induced the bishop of Alexandria to entrust to him a teaching position in the school of Alexandria which at that time was without teachers because of the persecution.

Attracted by his reputation, numerous scholars flocked to this school, not just Christians but also pagans, interested in the study of grammar and philosophy, so that he entrusted to his student Heraclas the preparatory studies, reserving the higher studies for himself (*H.E.* VI,15). To this period (c. 215) belongs that extreme act which as Eusebius reports (*H.E.* VI, 8, 1-3) Origen had committed in his ascetical fervor, interpreting literally the evangelical counsel to become eunuchs "for the kingdom of heaven" (Mt 19:12).

By such a mutilation he also wished to remove any suspicion concerning his own conduct once the demands of his catechetical responsibilities also put him in frequent contact with women.

Eusebius relates that Origen, to satisfy the intellectual needs of his own hearers, taught not just the sacred but the secular subjects. Origen's method is described in the following terms: "He introduced any pupils in whom he detected natural ability to philosophic studies as well. First he taught them geometry, arithmetic, and the other preparatory subjects; then he led them on to the systems of the philosophers, discussing their published theories and examining and criticizing those of the different schools, with the result that the Greeks themselves acknowledged his greatness as a philosopher."[15]

Notwithstanding the emphasis of the historian, who even

---

[15] *Historia Eccles.*, VI, XVIII, 2-3 ed. G. Bardy, 112-113.

speaks of "thousands" of heretics and of great numbers of pagan philosophers among Origen's audience, his entry can be credited on the
notable success of his work of religious and philosophical teaching.
An effect of this was the conversion to orthodoxy of a Valentinian,
Ambrose, who stimulated Origen's literary activity by furnishing
shorthand writers and copyists for recording and writing down his
teaching and his preaching.[16] Eusebius[17] also reports that the
Alexandrian was for a period a student of the Platonist philosopher,
Ammonius Saccas, who was the teacher of Plotinus, the founder of
Neoplatonism. We possess also the testimony of Porphyry in the lost
polemical work, *Against the Christians*, of which Eusebius himself
makes mention, and in Porphyry's *Life of Plotinus*,[18] of whom he was
a student in Rome. The notices of the Neoplatonic philosopher,
which speak of having known Origen at Caesarea in Palestine, give
rise to serious problems of interpretation because of the difficulty of
reconciling them with the data furnished by Eusebius.[19]

After a first visit to Rome, in the reign of Septimius Severus,
between 222 and 229, as Pierre Nautin maintains, or between 215
and 220,[20] the literary activity of Origen produced a considerable
corpus of work of a predominantly exegetical character, a strong ethical and ascetic tension, and a vigorous intellectual commitment in
showing what sacred revelation teaches about divine, cosmic, and
human reality.

Without ignoring the literal sense, the "body" of Scripture,
Origen strongly insists on the necessity of bringing to light the moral
teaching which constitutes the "soul" of Scripture and in this way
penetrating to the spiritual meaning of the divine word, which un-
veils the multiple "mysteries" of the transcendent reality in which
man has been called to participate.[21]

---

[16] *Ibidem* VI, XVIII, L. 112 and XXIII, 1-2, p. 123.

[17] *Ibidem* VI, XIX, 1-14, pp. 113-117.

[18] Porphyry, *Vita Plotini*, ch. 3, ed. E. Brehier, Paris, 1960, pp. 3-4 and ch. 20, p. 22.

[19] On the question, still open, regarding the identification of a pagan Origen of whom Porphyry
speaks, with our author, who is also known to the Neoplatonic philosopher, see H. Crouzel,
op. cit., 29-32.

[20] Cf. H. Crouzel, *op. cit.*, 33.

[21] On the modality and presuppositions of Origen's exegesis, the analysis of H. de Lubac,
Histoire et Eprit. L'intelligence de l'ecriture d'apres Origène, Paris, 1950, remains still valid.

Origen's exegetical method envisages then three levels of approach to the text, literal, moral, and spiritual or allegorical, the latter being the supreme objective in virtue of which the divine pedagogy, through moral instruction, wishes to conduct the Christian, together with ethico-spiritual perfection, the knowledge of truth revealed with a view to salvation.

This objective, which informs the entire literary production of the Alexandrian, emerges in the first instance particularly in the treatise, On Principles, composed at Alexandria circa 229-230, with the purpose of elaborating a vision of the truth of faith contained in the teaching of Jesus to the Apostles of which the Church becomes the repository and the interpreter.

At the same time the author intended to propose some solutions to those problems which the teaching of the Church had not yet clarified in a definitive manner, such as the origin of the soul and the reasons for the diversity between the conditions of rational creatures, men and angels and demons.

His own solution offered to such a controverted question, with the hypotheses of preexistence and "antecedent fault" of this creature[22] had been, as already noted, the principal cause of the polemic stirred up against the teaching of Origen.

In this teaching and in the related literary activity we can distinguish two main periods corresponding to similar diverse situations of places and persons. Origen's sojourn at Alexandria was punctuated by frequent journeys, among which should be mentioned those to Arabia — to which he was summoned by the local governor who was interested in his teaching — to Palestine — where the bishops permitted him to preach to the people although he was still a layman, in virtue of his exceptional knowledge of Scripture — to Greece and Antioch to meet Julia Mammea, mother of the emperor Alexander Severus. Such a period of intense activity saw the composition of his first exegetical Commentaries On the Psalms, On Lam-

---

For a general picture of exegetical tendencies and techniques in ancient Christianity, in which the role played by Origen is essential, cf. M. Simonetti, *Lettera e/o allegoria. Un contributo alla storia dell'esegesi patristica*, Rome, 1985.

[22] See the General Introduction, 83-92.

entations, On Genesis, and On the Gospel of St. John (the first six books),[23] as well as various works among which was the book, now lost, On the Resurrection.[24]

A decisive turning-point in Origen's life came in 232 when he was ordained a priest at Caesarea in Palestine by the local bishop, Theoctistus, without the permission of the bishop of Alexandria, Demetrius, to whose ecclesiastical jurisdiction Origen belonged. This event provoked a sharp reaction from Demetrius who already had manifested hostility in his relations with his former catechist. He next summoned two episcopal synods at Alexandria, between 232 and 233, to condemn the works of Origen. The latter finally abandoned the city to settle down at Caesarea where he enjoyed the esteem of the local bishops. Here he undertook the teaching of philosophy, directed to a small circle of disciples who constituted a sort of sodality of the ascetic life. At the same time, in his role as priest Origen dedicated himself to the catechesis of the Christian people, of which a record survives in his rich homiletic production.

The Homilies on the Old and New Testament in fact are expressions of this intense pastoral activity; they have survived only minimally in the original Greek[25] but to a greater extent in the Latin translations of Jerome and of Rufinus of Aquileia.

During the same period was completed the extensive *Commentary on Genesis*, begun at Alexandria, of which only a few fragments survive and the *Commentary on the Gospel of John*. The *Commentary on the Gospel of Matthew*, which consisted of 25 books, only eight of which survive in the original Greek, and the Commentaries on the

---

[23] The work consisted in the original of 32 books of which only 9 survive in the original Greek. Apart from the critical edition in GCS (n. 10) and in SC (120, 157, 222 and 290), see Italian translation by E. Corsini, *Commento al Vangelo di Giovanni*, Turin, 1968.

[24] It would be impossible to list here in detail the various editions and translations of Origen's extensive *corpus*. It is enough to say here that Origen's works are published in PG (vol. XI-XVII) and, in the fundamental GCS critical edition (apart from the treatises *De Principiis* and the *Commentary on the Gospel of John*, already recorded, in nn. 2-3, 6, 29-30, 33, 35, 38, 40-41), have been edited almost in their entirety, with French translations and ample commentaries, in the SC series. In the Collana di Testi Patristici, available in Italian translation, are *Commento al Cantico dei Cantici* (n. 1) and numerous Homilies (*On Genesis* n. 14; *On Exodus* n. 27; *On Leviticus* n. 51; *On Ezekiel* n. 67; *On Numbers* n. 76 and *On the Canticle of Canticles*, n. 83).

[25] Namely, 20 Homilies *On Jeremiah* (SC 232 and 238) and the Homily *On the Witch of Endor* (1 Samuel 28:3-25) (SC 328).

Letters of St. Paul, among which was the great *Commentary on the Epistle to the Romans*,[26] which has reached us in the Latin translation of Rufinus which synthesized in 10 books the original Greek consisting of 15 books, and of which fragments are conserved in the *Catenae*.[27]

The *Commentary on the First Epistle to the Corinthians*[28] only survives in fragmentary form, and likewise the *Commentary on the Epistle to the Ephesians*,[29] and other works on the Pauline epistles. Among the numerous works catalogued in the notice of Eusebius and in Letter 33 of Jerome we mention once more the polemical work *Against Celsus*, which we possess in the original Greek.[30] The pagan Celsus had in fact composed, in the time of Marcus Aurelius, a work denigrating Christianity (the *True Discourse*), whose arguments Origen combatted with all the tools of his scriptural and philosophical knowledge.

Among the non-exegetical works we mention among the numerous letters, that to Julius Africanus with regard to the exegesis of the episode of Susanna contained in the Book of Daniel,[31] and that written to a student named Gregory, possibly the Wonderworker,[32] and fragments (cited by Jerome and Rufinus) of a third, addressed *To Friends at Alexandria*, in which he intends to exonerate himself from charges of heresy, among which was that of having affirmed the final salvation of the devil.[33]

We might further mention a treatise, *On Prayer*,[34] another, *On*

---

[26] Cf. F. Cocchini, *Origene. Commento alla lettera ai Romani*, I-II, Casale Inferrato, 1985-1986.

[27] A. Ramsbotham, 'The Commentary of Origen on the Epistle to the Romans,' *JTS* 13 (1911-1912), 209-224; 357-368; 14 (1912-1913), 10-22.

[28] C. Jenkins, 'The Origen Citations in Cramer's Catena on 1 Corinthians,' *JTS* 6 (1904), 113-116; 9 (1907-1908), 231-247; 353-372; 500-514; 10 (1908-1909), 29-51.

[29] J.A.F. Gregg, 'The Commentary of Origen upon the Epistle to the Ephesians,' *JTS* 3 (1902), 233-244; 398-420; 554-576.

[30] See the translation of H. Chadwick, *Origen Contra Celsum*; A. Colonna, *Contro Celso*, Turin, 1971.

[31] Text edited in SC 302.

[32] Text edited in SC 148.

[33] Cf. H. Crouzel, 'A Letter from Origen, To Friends in Alexandria,' in D. Neiman-M. Schatkin (edd.), *Essays in Honor of G.V. Florovsky*, Orientalia Christiana Analecta 195 (1973), 133-150.

[34] See R.J. Daly, *Origen, Treatise on the Passover*, ACW 54, New York, NY, 1992; G. Del Ton, *Origene. La preghiera*, Rome, 1974.

the Passover,[35] the Exhortation to Martyrdom,[36] and the Dialogue with Heraclides,[37] a text discovered among the papyri of Toura in 1941, in which he recounts a debate with a bishop of Arabia on the theme of the corporeity or incorporeity of the soul. Finally we should note his edition of the Hexapla, that is, the recension in parallel columns of the Old Testament in the original Hebrew text together with the Greek versions of the Septuagint, of Aquileia, Symmachus, Theodotion, and of the exegete himself.[38]

In the year 251, during the persecution of Decius, Origen was imprisoned and tortured. He died some time later (c. 253) at Tyre according to a notice in Eusebius, or, according to another tradition, at Caesarea itself.[39]

---

[35] G. Sgherri, Origene. Sulla Pasqua. Il papiro di Tura, LCPM, 6, Milan, 1989.

[36] Ed. P. Koetschau, GCS 2-1; C. Noce, Origene. Esortazione al Martirio, Rome, 1985.

[37] Text edited in SC 67.

[38] Cf. Eusebius, Hist. Eccles. VI, XVI, 1-2, 109-111.

[39] Cf. H. Crouzel, Origène, op. cit., 61-65.

CREATION OF MALE AND FEMALE:
LITERAL AND ALLEGORICAL

14

(14) *Male and female God made them, and He blessed them say-*
ing, "Increase and multiply and fill the earth and subdue it."[a]

It seems to be worth inquiring in this passage according to its
literal sense[1] how, when woman was not yet made, the Scripture says,
Male and female He made them. Perhaps, as I think, it is because of
the blessing with which He blessed them saying, *Increase and multi-*
ply and fill the earth. Anticipating what was to be, the text says, *Male*
and female He made them, since, indeed, man could not otherwise increase and multiply except with the female.[2]

(15) But let us see also how, in an allegorical interpretation,
man, made in the image of God, is male and female.[3] Our inner man[b]
consists of spirit and soul.[4] The spirit is said to be male; the soul can

---

[a] Gn 1:27-28   [b] cf. 2 Cor 4:16

[1] In *Homily* 1, *on Genesis,* Origen proposed to his hearers an exegesis of the biblical account
of the six days of creation. Without neglecting the literal meaning of the sacred text, he however paid special attention to the "spiritual," allegorical sense. In fact his principal interest is
to search for the hidden truths which the sacred word, apart from the literal meaning, wishes
to show to man to allow him to pursue, with the knowledge of his own nature and the whole
of reality, that moral purification which should lead to salvation.

[2] In the remainder of the section which has been omitted, Origen continues to argue on the
literal meaning of the biblical text, by insisting on the theme of the creation of the sexes as a
promise and foundation of a divine benediction. This, relative to the physical multiplication
of humanity, could not have been understood by men, if God had not announced in antici-
pation the future creation of woman. He proposes, then, according to his usual method of
exegesis, an alternative explanation, indicating in the structure of "couple" (heaven/earth;
sun/moon) a characteristic peculiar to creation, expressing harmony and unity which is
manifested also at the human level in the masculine/feminine union.

[3] The central theme of the anthropology of Origen emerges here, that is, the creation "*ad*
imaginem Dei" which defines the intelligent creature in its most intimate essence as the "image" of the Logos, this being the direct image of God. On this theme cf. H. Crouzel, *Théologie*
de l'image de Dieu, Paris 1956, 75-142. This is expressed frequently also in the Pauline formula: "*heavenly*" juxtaposed to "*earthly*" (1 Cor 15:47). On this cf. G. Sfameni Gasparro,
'Restaurazione dell'immagine del Celeste e abbandono dell'immagine del Terrestre nella
prospettiva origeniana della doppia creazione,' in *eadem, Origene,* Rome, 1984, 157-192.

[4] Granted the premise — absolutely essential for Origen — of the totally spiritual quality of
"man in the image," that is, of the rational creature of the "first creation," he is posed with
the problem of interpreting the biblical statement which connects creation *kat eikona* to the
distinction between male and female. Whereas in the *Commentary on the Gospel of Mat-*
thew XIV, 16: GCS 40, pp. 321,23 - 322,22 he will refer this distinction to Christ and the Church,
this understanding, this ensemble of intelligent creatures of the preexistence to which Christ

be called female.[5] If these two elements have concord and agreement among themselves, they increase and multiply by the very accord among themselves and they produce sons, good inclinations and understandings or useful thoughts, by which they fill the earth and have dominion over it. This means they turn the inclination of the flesh, which has been subjected to themselves, to better purposes and have dominion over it, while the flesh, of course, becomes insolent in nothing against the will of the spirit. But now if the soul, which has been united with the spirit and, so to speak, joined in wedlock, turn aside at some time to bodily pleasures and turn back its inclination to the delight of the flesh and at one time indeed appear to obey the salutary warnings of the spirit, but at another time yield to

would be united to procure the redemption after the original fall, and then to an entity entirely spiritual, proposes in this context an interpretation in an antropological key.

According to this interpretation the creation "*ad imaginem*" of Gn 1:27-28 does not refer to the body, whose formation is described in Gn 2:7 and then cannot refer to the sexual distinction. "Male" and "female" are the two components of the "interior man." In fact Origen quite frequently utilizes the thematic of Paul of the "interior man" and "exterior man" (2 Cor 4:16) as an alternative expression of this Genesis account of man "*ad imaginem*" and of man a "*plasmatio*" to indicate the two elements, spiritual-rational and bodily which constitute actual humanity. Cf. G. Sfameni Gasparro, 'La "doppia creazione" di Adamo e il tema paolino dei "due uomini" nell'esegesi di Origene,' in *eadem, Origene, op. cit.*, 139-155.

[5] The Latin translation of Rufinus uses the terms *spiritus* and *anima* to indicate the components of "our interior man." H. Crouzel (*Virginité et mariage selon Origène*, Paris-Bruges, 1963, 136) and with him J. Dupuis ("*L'esprit de l'homme.*" *Étude sur l'anthropologie religieuse d'Origène*, Bruges, 1967, p. 36 n. 26) maintain that the *spiritus* here mentioned corresponds to *pneuma*, that is, to that element of superior origin (Crouzel speaks of "grace," Dupuis connects it with the divine sanctifying spirit) which in such contexts in Origen appears as an "adjunct" to the anthropological structure, whether represented as trichotomous (intellect-soul-body) or dichotomous (rational soul/ body); see *supra*, General Introduction, pp. 87-88. The text in question, according to these scholars, could be the image of a marriage between this "superior" spirit and the soul of man, that is, its rational component endowed with free will, capable then of virtue or of vice. However, in our opinion, this interpretation comes up against the meaning itself of the discourse of Origen elaborated in the Homily in question. In it in fact there is mention of "*interior homo noster*," "our interior man," that is, of rational nature in its constitutive structure of spiritual intelligent being. Therefore, the term "*spiritus*" of the translation of Rufinus in this case corresponds to *nous*, "*intellectus*," representing in our text the trichotomous structure in which the spiritual elements intellect and soul (the latter intend as the product of the "fall" and the former as its superior part, according to the formula of *De Principiis* 11,10,7), constitute a "couple." The relations between members of such a couple remain exemplars with respect to those intercurrents between man and woman in the nuptial dimension. The "harmony" between the components "*homo interior*," implying subjection of the female, "weaker," showing a proclivity to vice, to the "strong" element, the masculine, is the model of behavior for the human couple in which the woman ought to "follow" her husband on the ethical and religious plane, beyond that of practical conduct. The relationship "soul" — "(law of) intellect" in the *Commentary on the Gospel of Matthew* XII, 4: GCS 40, 73-74 is equally presented in the form of a "nuptial" relationship.

carnal vices, such a soul, as if defiled by adultery of the body, is said properly neither *to increase* nor *multiply*, since indeed Scripture designates the sons of adulterers as imperfect.[c] Such a soul, to be sure, which prostrates itself totally to the inclination of the flesh and bodily desires, having forsaken conjunction with the spirit, as if turned away from God will shamelessly hear, *You have the face of a harlot; You have made yourself shameless to all.*[d] She will be punished, therefore, like a harlot and her sons will be ordered to be prepared for slaughter.[e]

Homily I,14-15 On Genesis; GCS 29, pp. 18-19; FOTC, 71, 67-68, tr. R.Heine

15

4. *"Where is your wife Sarah?" they asked Abraham.*[1] *"There in the tent," he replied. One of them said, "I will surely return to you about this time next year, and Sarah will then have a son." Sarah was listening at the entrance of the tent, just behind him.*

Let the wives learn from the examples of the patriarchs, let the wives learn, I say, to follow their husbands. For not without cause is it written that *Sarah was standing behind Abraham*, but that it might be shown that if the husband leads the way to the Lord, the wife ought to follow. I mean that the wife ought to follow if she see her husband standing by God. For the rest, let us ascend to a higher step of understanding and let us say that the man is the rational sense in us and the woman our flesh[2] which, like us, has been united with a

---

[c] cf. Ws 3:16 　[d] Jr 3:6 　[e] cf. Is 14:21

[1] *Homily IV, On Genesis* provides commentary on the episode on the appearance of God to Abraham near the tent by the terebinth of Mamre in the figure of three men. Origen interprets this vision as related to the Lord accompanied by two angels, while other Fathers do not give an exegesis in a trinitarian key. The christological reference is however also present in Origen's discourse in relation to the figure of the "steer" served to his guests by the Patriarch, understood as a figure of *he who humbles himself obediently accepting death on a cross* (Ph 2:8); cf. *Hom. on Gn 4:2* SC 7 bis, 148-149; FOTC, tr. R. Heine, 105.

[2] A different symbolism of the "couple" is here proposed by Origen: the masculine element is the *rationabilis sensus*, the rational sense, while that of the female is the *caro*, the "flesh." This results in a stronger negative connotation in the image of woman, although the discourse moves on a metaphorical plane, as in so many other places in Origen. On the symbolism of the "weakness" of woman, her imperfect nature, tendency to vice, insofar as it betrays a sort of "misogynism" in an author who nevertheless knows and illustrates positive examples of woman in the Sacred Scripture cf. H. Crouzel, *Virginité et mariage, op. cit.*, 134-139.

man. Therefore, let the flesh always follow the rational sense, nor let it ever come into any slothfulness so that the rational sense, reduced in authority, should yield to the flesh wallowing in luxury and pleasures.

Homily 1V,4 On Genesis; GCS 29. 53-54; FOTC, 106-107, 71, tr. R.E. Heine

FEMALE AS METAPHOR AND THE EQUALITY OF THE SEXES

16 For Divine Scripture does not admit a distinction between men and women on the basis of sex. For indeed sex is not a distinction in the presence of God, but a person is designated either a man or woman according to the diversity of spirit. How many of the female sex are counted among the strong men before God, and how many men are reckoned among languid and sluggish women? Or does it not seem to you that a man must be judged among "women" who says: "I am not able to observe those things which are written, I am not able to *sell what I have and give to the poor*[a] I am not able *to present the other cheek to the one who strikes,*[b] I am not able *to bless the person cursing,*[c] I am not able to *pray for the persecutor,*[d] I am not able *to suffer and endure persecution* and other similar things which are commanded." The one who says, "I am not able to accomplish," what else does it seem to you than the one who is not able to be courageous must be counted among women who cannot understand what is virile.[1]

Homily on Joshua IX, 9; GCS 30, 356

---

[a] cf. Mt 19:21   [b] cf. Lk 6:29   [c] cf. Lk 6:28   [d] cf. 1 Cor 4:12

[1] These affirmations of Origen, while continuing to maintain the usual schemata of male-female metaphor as expressions of opposite values and prerogatives of ethical behavior, show at the same time the wish to distinguish on the level of effectual reality the positive capacity of the woman in so far as being endowed with humanity by the same title as the male, of a spiritual rational nature "*homo ad imaginem*" that is, "*homo interior*" of the negative valences of the same metaphor.

HARMONY BETWEEN THE COUPLE

| 17 |

Then, describing what ought to be in the case of those who are joined together by God, so that they may be joined together in a manner worthy of God, the Savior adds, so that they are no longer two; and, wherever there is indeed concord and unison and harmony between husband and wife, when he is as ruler and she is obedient to the word, He shall rule over you, then of such persons we may truly say, "They are no longer two." Then, since it was necessary that for him who was joined to the Lord, "it should be reserved" that he should become one spirit with him, in the case of those who are joined together by God, after the words, *so that they are no more two*, it is added, *but one flesh*. And it is God who has joined together the two in one so that they are no longer two, from the time that the woman is married to the man. And, since God has joined them together, on this account in the case of those who are joined together by God, there is a "gift"; and Paul, knowing this, that marriage based on the commandments of God[1] was a gift, just as holy celibacy was a gift, says, *But I would that all men were like myself; however, each man has his own gift from God, one after this manner, another after that.*[c] And those who are joined together by God both mind and keep the precept, *Husbands love your wives, as Christ also loves the church*[d] then certainly their union represents a charism.[2]

Comm. on Gospel of Matthew, XIV, 16; GCS 40, 323-324

---

[a] Mt 19:6   [b] Gn 3:16   [c] 1 Cor 7:7   [d] Eph 5:25   [e] cf. Eph 5:33

[1] Crouzel moreover properly underlines that for Origen there is question of a "good," which is however considerably inferior to that of virginity and continence, in that it is not accompanied by the presence of the divine spirit because of that "contamination" which, in his view, inheres in the conjugal relationship and renders it incompatible with the exercise of religious practice.

[2] The symbolism Christ-Church as a "figure" of the relationship of spouses correctly viewed of the Christian couple in which the attitude of submission on the part of the wife, and that of "guide" on the part of the husband is essential and is developed in a passage of the *Commentary on the Epistle to the Ephesians* 5:22-23 (fr. XXIX: *JTS* 3, [1901-1902], 566-567). "This discourse wishes to signify that every union between a man and a woman is a symbol of the union between Christ and the Church. The husband if he wishes to care for his marriage as he should, has a model in Christ, spouse of the Church; the wife, if she wishes to live together in the best of modes with her husband imitates, so to speak, the union between Christ and the Church. In fact, the husband is head of the wife in the same way as Christ is

18

34. When the rules are observed marriage is redolent of divine grace which derives from the harmony of the couple. And in truth it is possible to say that, in the case of some, matrimony constitutes for them a divine grace when there is no "instability," when peace[a] reigns supreme, when harmony reigns supreme.

But can it be said, however, that a marriage of a believer to a pagan, or of a pagan to a believer, is a grace coming from God? This I would not say. For in fact, the grace of God cannot be extended to pagans. But if a pagan believes, if a pagan is saved, then he will begin to receive divine grace.[1]

* * *

(Paul) then defines as married that couple in which both partners are believers, both husband and wife. With regard to the others, *those who bear the yoke with unbelievers*[b] he does not include those among the married as is plain from what follows. Are these others then not married? He does not include them among the married. For in the case of these the wife has not been united to her husband by God. But in the case of believers when both participate in prayer, and in holy procreation, and in everything in which it is necessary that Christians be in harmony, then it will be said that the marriage is not alien to God.

Comm. on 1 Cor., fr. 34 and 35: ed. C. Jenkins, *JThS* 9
(1908) pp. 504, 42-505, 49

---

[a] cf. 1 Cor 14:33   [b] 2 Cor 6:14   [c] 1 Cor 7:12

head of the Church. If, then, husband and wife do not live in harmony together in the same way, it cannot be said in their regard that the husband is head of the wife in the same way as Christ is head of the Church. Every husband makes every effort to behave in his dealings with his wife as Christ does in His dealings with the Church and every wife makes every effort in her dealings with her husband as the Church does in dealings with Christ. The husband thinks and does everything in a manner worthy of Christ, and the wife, in a manner worthy of the Church."

[1] For the position of Origen on the theme of unions in which one of the spouses is a non-believer cf. H. Crouzel, *Virginité et mariage, op. cit.*, 145-147. In it the Alexandrian recognizes neither the quality of charism nor the status of true marriage, although both these prerogatives can begin as soon as the non-believing spouse became a Christian.

MARRIAGE AND CONTINENCE: EQUALITY OF RIGHTS AND
"ACCORD" BETWEEN THE SPOUSES

19

Men sin generally in two ways: they transgress the commandments either by insufficient, or by excessive, observance. When, in
fact, in everyday life, we behave ourselves without knowledge, or if
we cheat with no recognition of the norms of justice, and sometimes
go beyond the correct norm, figuring to act for the best, we do not
succeed in the goal which we have set. The living knowledge is then
a "weight," neither "too much" nor "too little," but in due measure.[a]
Are you bound to a wife?[b] "I can observe continence and live in a
more pure manner." But take care that your wife does not go to ruin,
unable to put up with your purity, she for whom Christ has died.[b]

Something like that happened at Corinth. In the houses of the
brothers in that city there was agitation because men and women
wanted to practice continence and rose up against one another. On
this matter the Corinthians then wrote to the Apostle, and the
Apostle responded to their letter with the remarks reported above.
He did not exaggerate his discourse on chastity, he did not condemn
marriages, nor did he, in preferring marriage, condemn virginity, as
a good administrator.[d] In all his discourse you can see his will showing through and how he exhorts them to remain pure. Having admitted the necessity to come to terms with matrimony, he then exhorts them anew to practice chastity. In the exhortation to practice
chastity, he directs his discourse once more to the necessity of making allowance for the weakness of the weaker ones. The Apostle does
not begin with the least important arguments because this was convenient, but from those that were more perfect: *Now for the matters
you wrote about. A man is better off having no relations with a woman.*[e]
In other words, I praise your intention to practice chastity, by abstaining from relations with your wife, but think, not only of your
own interests,[f] but also of your wife's interests. Love is not self-
seeking.[g] But, to avoid immorality, let every man have his own wife
and every woman her own husband.[h]

---

[a] cf. Pr 20:10 [b] 1 Cor 7:2 [c] cf. Rm 14:1 [d] 1 P 4:10 [e] 1 Cor 7:1 [f] Ph 2:4 [g] 1 Cor 13:5
[h] 1 Cor 7:2

It is better, in fact, that the two be saved by living in matrimony than that, because of one of them, the other should lose hope in Christ. How in fact could he be saved who is responsible for the death of his wife? The sanctity of the husband is not perfect when abstinence on the part of both for dedication to prayer is not born of consent freely given by the wife. *The husband should fulfill his conjugal obligations to his wife, the wife hers toward her husband.*[i]

Paul's first concern is to take care of human weakness and to give the proper directives in the most convenient manner. For this reason he said that the husband should fulfill his conjugal obligations to his wife, the wife hers toward her husband. Later, so as not to disturb those who are married, as if one were to become a slave of the other,[1] he says that there is need of reciprocal accord in undertaking the practice of chastity: *a wife's body does not belong to herself, but to her husband, a husband's body does not belong to himself, but to his wife.*[j] The husband, then, has power over the body of his wife, but, though having the power, he may choose not to make use of it.

But we have not wanted to make use of this right, the Apostle says. I believe he says this to throw light on his statement: *Have we not the right to marry a believing woman, like the rest of the apostles and the brothers of the Lord and Cephas?*[k] The wife, then, has power over the body of her husband, and can she not choose not to make use of her power? The expression, "in the same way"[1] is employed twice, to make us realize that in what concerns marriage the man ought not consider himself superior to his wife. Between husband and wife there is likeness and mutual parity.

> *Comm. on 1 Cor., fr. 33:* ed., Jenkins, *JThS* 9 (1908), p. 500, 1- 501, 49

---

[i] 1 Cor 7:3 [j] 1 Cor 7:4 [k] 1 Cor 9:5 [l] cf. 1 Cor 7:3-4

[1] From these statements there emerges the idea already quite developed in Origen, as in a large part of the patristic tradition, according to which only continence and virginity guarantee true spiritual freedom, whereas conjugal relations imply the mutual "slavery" of the married partners. The same Pauline precept of not depriving each other, "unless perhaps by mutual consent for a time, to devote yourselves to prayer" (1 Cor 7:5) is interpreted as an indication of this reciprocal "slavery." Cf. H. Crouzel, *Virginité et mariage, op. cit.,* 160-168. [Engl. ed. See now: D.B. Martin, *The Corinthian Body,* Yale University Press, 1995.]

LACTANTIUS

INTRODUCTORY PROFILE

Undoubtedly it is an arduous if not impossible task to trace a biographical profile of Lactantius. The few uncertain data which are gleaned from reading his works, combined with the notice provided by Jerome,[1] in fact do not permit an outline, in a secure and well articulated sequence, of the events of his life. Only some of them can be retained with certainty and it seems opportune to rely on these.[2]

Lactantius was born in Africa between 250 and 260[3] and, like his teacher, Arnobius,[4] became an outstanding rhetor, so much so that he was summoned by the emperor Diocletian in person to teach

---

[1] Cf. Jerome, *De viris illustribus*, LXXX: BP 12, pp. 186-188. Other notes relating to Lactantius, especially in reference to his literary style and the influence on him of the classical ciceronian tradition are given also by Jerome in his *Letters* LVIII, 10: CSEL 54, p. 539; LXX, 5: CSEL 54, p. 707; LXXXIV 7: CSEL 55, 128. In the last letter, in particular, Jerome uncovers a theological error of Lactantius with regard to the Holy Spirit, but he reiterates the value of the *Divine Institutes*.

[2] On the biography of Lactantius cf. S. Brandt, 'Über das Leben des Lactantius,' in *Sitzungsberichte der Kais. Akademie der Wissenschaften in Wien* 120 (1890), 1-69; R. Pichon, *Lactance. Étude sur le mouvement philosophique religieux sous le règne de Constantin*, Paris, 1901, 1-4 (a study that is now dated, but which is still fundamental for certain aspects); and more recently, J. Stevenson, 'The Life and Literary Activity of Lactantius,' in *Studia Patristica* 4 (1961), 497-503.

[3] Lactantius' date of birth is arrived at by approximation based on the notes of Jerome (*De viris illustribus, op. cit.*) according to which he was "in extreme old age" when he became the tutor of the son of Constantine, around the year 316.

[4] Arnobius is a Latin writer of African origin, who lived between the end of the 3rd and the beginning of the 4th century. He was a teacher of rhetoric at Sicca and after his conversion to Christianity, he wrote a work in 7 books, *Contra paganos*, in which he defended the Christians against the accusation of being responsible for capital crimes against the Empire and at the same time violently assailed the rites and beliefs of the pagan tradition. Critical text: CSEL 4; English translation, G . McCracken, ACW: 7 and 8; R. Laurenti, *Arnobius. I sette libri contro i pagani*, Turin, 1962.

Latin rhetoric at the court in Nicomedia in Bithynia, Asia Minor.

When, in February 303, the emperor Diocletian initiated his cruel repressive measures against the Christians,[5] Lactantius was forced to abandon his teaching career.[6] He had in fact become a convert to Christianity.[7] Later, however, between 316 and 317, he was recalled by the emperor Constantine to Treves in Gaul to be the tutor of his son, Crispus. Notwithstanding various hypotheses formulated by scholars, it is not possible to establish the exact year of his death.[8]

While it is difficult to reconstruct with certainty the individual events in the life of Lactantius, it is much easier to establish the chronological order of the writings which have come down to us.[9] The first of these is undoubtedly *The Workmanship of God*, in which there is allusion to the persecution of Diocletian[10] and which therefore can be dated between 303/304. The work is an anthropological tract in which Lactantius intends above all to show divine provi-

---

[5] The persecution of the emperor Diocletian (284-305) against the Christians began officially in February 303 with the first of four edicts which were issued up until February of 304. The repression was particularly violent and created many victims, even if one must take into account the exaggerations to be found in the Christian sources. The action of Diocletian against the Christians can be framed in the context of his attempts at restoration based also on the strengthening of the religious foundations of political power tied to the divine cult of the Emperor. Cf. the wonderful synthesis of J. Moreau, *La persecuzione del cristianesimo nell'impero romano*, Brescia, 1977 (ed. orig., Paris, 1956), 103-120 and of C. Lepelley, *L'impero romano ed il cristianesimo*, Milan, 1970 (ed. orig., Paris, 1969), 51-55. In the last volume, besides, there are useful documents in Italian (88-111) with a discussion of various problems of historiography (114-129).

[6] Cf. J. Stevenson, *art. cit.*, 662.

[7] It is very probable that Lactantius had been converted to Christianity during his sojourn at Nicomedia and not in Africa. Cf., in this regard, A. Wlosok, *Laktanz und die philosophische Gnosis. Untersuchungen zur Geschichte und die Terminologie der gnostischen Erlösungvorstellung*, Heidelberg, 1960, p. 191, note 28.

[8] Except for S. Brandt, *art. cit.*, who has proposed a later date, around 340, most scholars generally limit themselves to set as a *terminus post quem* the year 325.

[9] Cf. J. Moreau, *Lactance. De la mort des persécuteurs* (SC 39), Paris, 1954, p. 16. Jerome, *De viris illustribus*, tells us of other works of Lactantius which have not come down to us, and precisely three of a profane character (*Symposium*; *A Journey from Africa to Nicomedia*; *A Grammar*) and others following the period of his conversion, *Ad Asclepiade* (in 2 books); 4 books of *Letters to Probus*; 2 books of *Letters to Severius*, 2 books of *Letters to Demetrianus*. Pope Damasus himself, who held them to be wordy and of little use to Christian spirituality on account of their content, did not pass a very benevolent judgment on the letters of Lactantius. Cf. Jerome, *Letter* XXXV, 2: CSEL 54, p. 266.

[10] Cf. *De creatione Dei*, 1, 1: SC 213, p. 107. It is also probable that Lactantius alludes in this initial chapter to his work to his own indigent situation. See the comment of M. Perrin, *Lactance. L'ouvrage du Dieu Créateur* (SC 214), Paris, 1974, 229-230.

dence in the harmonious structural beauty of the human body.[11] At the end of this treatise he alludes in a significant manner to his own intention to write a work of vaster inspiration and greater weight,[12] an idea which saw its realization in the *Divine Institutes* in seven books,[13] written between 305 and 317, compiled in a chronological order which it is difficult to establish except hypothetically.[14] Conceived as an essentially apologetic work for a Christianity unjustly and violently persecuted by the pagans,[15] the *Divine Institutes* constitutes a first attempt to compile in the form of a summa[16] the whole complex of Christian doctrine. The theme of the providence of God, which intervenes negatively to punish wrongdoers, inspired the short treatise, *On the Anger of God*, an amplification of a theme already encountered in the *Divine Institutes*.[17] The same motif of the punitive force of God, projected on the more varied scenario of history,

---

[11] About this work see the heavily documented work of M. Perrin, *L'homme antique et chrétien. L'anthropologie de Lactance 250-325*, Paris, 1981, which constitutes also a useful approach to the bibliography of Lactantius (17-25).

[12] Cf. *De creatione Dei* 20,1: SC 213, p. 214: "These arguments, O Demetrianus, I have set before you for now in a brief and perhaps somewhat obscure manner.... You will have to be satisfied while you await, please God, an opportunity to read them in a fuller and better way. For now I will earnestly urge you in a clearer and more forceful manner to the doctrine of the true philosophy."

[13] The best critical text is still that of S. Brandt, CSEL 10. To date in SC the following have appeared: Bk. I: 326; II: 337; V: 204 and 205. An Italian translation in the whole acceptable but with the omission of several chapters, briefly abridged, is that of U. Boella, *Lattanzio. Divinae Institutiones. De opificio Dei. De ira Dei*, Florence, 1973.

[14] The attempt of J. Stevenson, *art. cit.*, 669, to fix in a well determined order the composition of the various books, placing Books V-VII first and then Books I-IV, was somewhat forced: cf. M. Perrin, *L'ouvrage...*, *op. cit.*, 15-16. Some passages of the work indicate for the most part and in an unequivocal way a succession of interventions and reworking on the part of Lactantius himself, brought to a conclusion, in all likelihood, in the years of his sojourn at Treviri. On the complex question of a double editing of the work, cf. M. Perrin, *L'ouvrage...*, *op. cit.*, 86-94, who accepts the conclusions of the important study of E. Heck, *Die dualistische Zusätze und die Kaiserranreden bei Lactantius*, Heidelberg, 1972, holding, namely, that Lactantius had done a revision of the *Divine Institutes*, marking some additions on his own personal copy which, for that reason had very limited circulation in manuscript form.

[15] Cf. *Divine Institutes* V, 2, 2: CSEL 19, 403-406 and V, 4, 1-7: CSEL 19, 411-413, where Lactantius puts himself in the line of preceding Latin apologetic literature, expressing his opinions of the works of Tertullian, Minucius Felix, and Cyprian. On these aspects of the 5th book of the *Divine Institutes* see P. Monat, *Lactance. Institutions Divines, livre V* (SC 204), Paris, 1973, 45-64.

[16] Cf. M. Perrin, *L'homme...*, *op. cit.*, 30-33.

[17] Cf. *Divine Institutes* II, 17, 4-5: CSEL 19, 172. On the treatise, *De ira Dei*, cf. the excellent introduction of C. Ingremeau, *Lactance, La colère de Dieu* (SC 289), Paris, 1982, 13-56.

shows up again in the work, *On the Death of the Persecutors*, the authenticity of which is no longer in question.[18] Lactantius sees in the wretched end of the emperor, a fierce persecutor of the Christians, the just divine punishment for his misdeeds and offers besides an interesting and useful sidelight for the historic documentation of the events which he himself had experienced at first hand during his sojourn in Bithynia.[19]

Finally, a short work in verse is attributed to Lactantius, *The Myth of the Phoenix*, the bird which rises from its own ashes, as a symbol of the typically Christian motif of resurrection.[20] His literary productions betray a certain weakness on the purely speculative level, not merely because of the archaic nature of some of his theological concepts, conditioned by the Asian ambience in which his conversion came to fruition[21] and which motivated, among other things,

---

[18] On the authenticity of this work cf. J. Moreau, *De la mort...*, *op. cit.*, 22-33, which proposes as the outside limits for the date the years 315-324. For the relationship between *De morte persecutorum* and the Constantinian age, also with respect to the evolution of Lactantius' thought in *Divine Institutes* cf. F. Amarelli, 'Il *"De mortibus persecutorum"* nei suoi rapporti con l'ideologia coeva,' *SDHI* 36 (1970), 207-264. Finally, see the Italian translation of F. Corsaro, Catania, 1970. For the date of the work, which could be calculated to be between the summer of 314 to December 315, cf. I. De Salvo, 'A proposito della datatione del *De mortibus persecutorum*,' *Rivista di Storia della Chiesa in Italia* 31 (1977), 482-484.

[19] Regarding principally the history of *De morte persecutorum* cf. F. Corsaro, 'Le *"mos maiorum"* dans la vision étique et politique du *"De mortibus persecutorum"'* in *Lactance et son temps (Actes du IV Colloque d'Etudes historiques et patristiques, Chantilly 21-23 septembre 1976)*, Paris, 1978, 25-53 and, more recently, A.S. Christiansen, *Lactantius the historian. An Analysis of the "De mortibus persecutorum,"* Copenhagen, 1980. Regarding the links between *De morte persecutorum* and *De ira Dei* cf. U. Pizzani, 'Osservazioni sulla genesi della teologia della storia in Lattanzio,' *Augustinianum* 16 (1976), 53-60.

[20] The little poem, *De ave Phoenice*, insofar as it is attributed to Lactantius has given rise to a long debate among scholars with opposing conclusions depending on whether one accentuates its Christian or its profane elements. An exhaustive and valid panorama of the "state of the question" among the critics is that of S. Isetta, 'Il *"De ave Phoenice"* attribuito a Lattanzio,' *CCC* 1 (1980), 379-409, which holds that the attribution of the poem to Lactantius "is the only acceptable conclusion." Regarding the myth of the Phoenix in classical and Christian tradition cf. R. Van den Broek, *The Myth of the Phoenix according to Classical and Early Christian Traditions*, Leiden, 1972. Among the Italian translations of the poem one can profitably consult that of E. Rapisarda, *Il carme "De ave phoenice" di Lattanzio*, Catania, 1959. Lactantius' own *Epitome*, a reworking of the *Divine Institutions*, whose authenticity has recently been contested by P. Monat in *Lactance et la Bible*, Paris, 1982 (in 2 volumes), has been vigorously defended with strong arguments by M. Perrin, 'L'authenticité lactancienne de l'Epitomé des Institutions Divines: à propos d'un livre réxent,' *RE Aug* 32 (1986), 22-40. Perrin recently published the French language commentary on the *Epitome, Lactance: Epitomé des Institutions Divines* (SC 335), Paris, 1987.

[21] On the archaic foundations of the theology of Lactantius see the indispensable study of V. Loi, *Lattanzio nella storia del linguaggio e del pensiero teologico preniceno*, Zürich, 1970.

his adherence to millenarianism,[22] but especially by his synthesis, not always executed felicitously, between his own traditional philosophical baggage and the newness of the Christian message.[23] Notwithstanding these undeniable shortcomings, which should not be unduly exaggerated, and which are often the result of antenicene theological language[24] as yet technically imprecise in conceptual definitions, Lactantius has given them a fundamental importance on the cultural level.[25] "A Christian Cicero," as he was described by the humanist, Pico della Mirandola,[26] and continues to be so called by modern scholars, Lactantius has also won appreciation for the programmatic choice of a style rhetorically engaged,[27] which takes into account the educated public to which it is directed. It is seen to best effect, and particularly felicitous and acute in confrontation with problems which invest the sphere of human ethics.[28]

It is in this perspective, precisely, that he is concerned with the human couple and with their interpersonal relationship within the bosom of marriage. In his anthropological treatise, *On the Workmanship of God*, the theme of the human couple is encountered, especially from the point of view of physiology in order to differentiate their respective roles on the basis of an etymological interpreta-

---

[22] Millenarianism is a widely diffused belief in the Christianity of the first centuries according to which, prior to the Judgment, there would be a resurrection of the just which would last for a thousand years during which they would enjoy all things together with Christ in the celestial Jerusalem come down from heaven. For the millenarianism of Lactantius cf. V. Loi, *op. cit.*, pp. 250-251.

[23] Cf. S. D'Elia, *Letteratura latina cristiana*, Rome, 1982, 67-68.

[24] Cf. M. Perrin, *L'homme...*, *op. cit.*, 31.

[25] Cf. V. Loi, *op. cit.*, 274-278.

[26] Cf. Pico della Mirandola, *Studio della divina ed umana filosofia*, 1, 7: *Tutte le opere*, Basilea 1573, p. 21. Pico della Mirandola was a Renaissance philosopher who was born in Mirandola (Modena) in 1463 and died in Florence in 1494. In general see E. Garin, *La cultura filosofica del Rinascimento italiano*, Florence, 1961 and the two miscellaneous volumes: *L'opera ed il pensiero di G. Pico della Mirandola nella storia dell'Umanesimo*, Florence, 1965.

[27] Cf. L. Alfonsi, 'Problematica generale dei rapporti tra scrittori cristiani e cultura classica,' *Annali dell'Ist. Sup. di Scienze e Lettere S. Chiara di Napoli*, 1959, 23-34.

[28] For the study of the ethics of Lactantius see especially V. Loi, 'I valori etici e politici della romanità negli scritti di Lattanzio. Opposti atteggiamenti di polemica e adesione,' *Salesianum* 27 (1965), 65-133; 'Il concetto di iustitia e i fattori culturali dell'etica lattanziana,' *Salesianum* 28 (1966), 583-625; 'La giustizia sociale nell'etica lattanziana,' *Augustinianum* 17 (1977), 153-160.

tion present in Varro and widely diffused, relative to the terms *vir/mulier*, man/woman.[29]

Lactantius terms "marvellous" the institution established by God on the basis of which man and woman are mutually attracted to unite and propagate their offspring and he characterizes their rapport with one another in terms of strength and tenderness.[30] The man is strong in order to guide his companion and to help her support with patience the difficulties of married life; the woman, for her part, becomes sublime in the sweetness of her nurturing role as mother.[31]

The distinction strength/patient sweetness, in fact implying adherence to tradition of the time which practically codified the inferiority of the woman, the motive of "the weaker sex,"[32] did not condition Lactantius when he came to define the ethics of a correct relationship between the partners in the bosom of matrimony. On the contrary, reciprocal love, and especially the unconditional respect of conjugal fidelity, are for him the fundamental ethical principles for a balanced matrimonial bond.[33] From this point of view man and woman are on a level of absolute parity; so true is this for him that he condemns both the infidelity of the husband as well as

---

[29] Cf. M. Perrin, *L'homme...*, *op. cit.*, 180-181. On using Varro and other sources in *The Workmanship of God*, cf. in particular L. Rossetti, 'Il *"De opificio Dei"* di Lattanzio e le sue fonti,' *Didaskaleion* 6 (1928), 115-200. M. Terentius Varro, born in 116, can be considered one of the most erudite representatives of ancient Rome on account of his many interests and for his vast literary output, most of which has unfortunately been lost. An erudite student of the antiquities of Rome, its institutions and religious traditions, satiric poet, encyclopedist who would influence with his division of the liberal arts the later medieval traditions of the trivium (grammar, logic and rhetoric) and the quadrivium (geometry, astronomy, arithmetic and music), Varro was also a linguist and his work *Sulla lingua latina* in 25 volumes is fundamental to an etymological interpretation of Lactantius.

[30] Cf. *De opificio Dei* 12, 16-17: CSEL 27, 46 (= SC 213, 182 and, for the relative commentary, SC 214, 264-365).

[31] Cf. *De opificio Dei* 12, 17-18: CSEL 27, 46-47 (= SC 213, 182).

[32] On the subject of "feminine weakness" in Lactantius cf. *Divine Institutes* V, 13: CSEL 19, 439 and 441. Regarding the inclusion of this theme and its cultural development within the patristic tradition cf. the General Introduction to this anthology.

[33] Cf. *Divine Institutes* III, 21: CSEL 19, 249: "What man ever loves his own wife or what wife ever loves her own husband if they have not lived together and for ever, if the devotion of their souls and their reciprocal respected fidelity does not render their love indivisible?"

that of the wife who in such situations resembles a prostitute.[34]

In Book 6 of the *Divine Institutes*, from which the excerpt included here is taken, Lactantius denounces the inequity of the civil laws which, while they find the adultery of the wife blameworthy and prosecute it in a court of law, justify adultery by the husband and leave it unpunished. His arguments, adhering to analogous concepts in pagan moralists like Musonius Rufus, or by recourse to classical authors like Quintilian, are intertwined with typically Christian inspirational motives, such as respect for one's neighbor which is fundamental in the regulation of the life of the couple, and in a reciprocal inclination to align, as far as possible, one's own character and habits with those of one's spouse.

---

[34] Cf. *Divine Institutes* III, 22: CSEL 19, 251: "Nothing else can be said of the men who have many wives than that they are dissolute and prodigal. Likewise, the women who are possessed by many cannot, to be sure, be called adulteresses, since there is no real marriage; they are rather prostitutes and harlots of the most infamous kind." On conjugal parity in primitive Christianity cf. C. Mazzucco, *"E fui fatta maschio,"* *op. cit.*, 28-30.

RECIPROCAL FIDELITY BETWEEN A CHRISTIAN COUPLE

| 20 |

23. I have not yet gone through all the obligations of chastity.[1] God confines them, not only within private walls, but even by the precepts of the marriage bed, so that when anyone has a wife, he may not wish to have besides a slave or free concubine, but must keep faithful to his marriage contract.

24. For such is not the case, as is the interpretation of public law, that she alone is the adulteress who has another man, while the male is free from the charge of adultery, though he have many mistresses.[2]

---

[1] In our excerpt some paragraphs have been omitted at the beginning of ch. 23, inasmuch as we preferred to pause to consider the theme of parity of ethical responsibility of husband and wife vis-a-vis adultery. In the aforementioned paragraphs (1-7), Lactantius exalts the goodness innate in human sexuality including the positive values of desire and pleasure. Already in *The Workmanship of God* 12, 15: SC 213, 182, Lactantius placed in evidence as something truly marvelous the plan of God regarding the mutual attraction of man and woman for the purposes of procreation. The work of the African rhetorician — as has been opportunely noted by M. Perrin, *L'homme...*, *op. cit.*, 180 — dealt a blow to stoic pessimism with regard to the human passions designed by God to exalt the man's virtue. Desire and sexual pleasure for that reason maintain their intrinsic positive value, both because they are a means for propagating the species and because by keeping them under control one acquires merit for the future life. Obviously the libido must be directed towards a just ethical goal, that is it must be channeled to legitimate matrimonial ends and the man who desires another man's wife or frequents houses of ill repute where "unfortunate women" are caught up with him in the whirlwind of perdition becomes a slave of the Evil One. Mention of adulterous relationships will be dealt with further in the paragraphs which follow.

[2] Adultery in Roman law, as also in the Jewish tradition had always been a "feminine" crime. At first relegated to the area of moral reprobation, susceptible however to private vendetta on the part of the father or husband, adultery also carried with it for the woman certain monetary sanctions. It was Augustus who, around the year 18, promulgated a specific law "regarding adultery," which enlarged the sphere of this "crime" to a public penal law. With this law an adulteress caught in the flagrant commission of the crime was subject to the death penalty together with her accomplice at the hands of her father, whereas the husband had the right to kill only the lover. In any case the husband had to immediately repudiate his adulterous wife, otherwise he himself would be charged with the crime of "procuring." The adulterous woman who did not fall under the violent reaction of her father or spouse was forced to lose half of her dowry, while her lover would lose half of his patrimony. About the law of Augustus, its precedents and later changes cf. E. Cantarella, 'Adulterio omicidio legittimo e causa d'onore in Diritto Romano,' in *Studi in onore di Gaetano Scherrillo*, I, Milan, 1972, 243-274.

At the time of Lactantius, adultery remained in the public eye (and in the eyes of the law) a typically feminine crime. Against this state of things, Christian writers strove to propagandize in open denunciation of the discrimination innate in such an attitude. Their efforts, however, were condemned to failure and many conservative approaches — like that of Basil of Caesarea about whom we shall hear more later — perhaps found their explanation in the closed atmosphere of their surroundings. If the Roman legislation had truly incorporated

25. The divine law so joins two with equal right into a marriage, which is *two* in *one flesh*, that whoever breaks apart the joining of the body is regarded as an adulterer....

29. Faith, then, must be kept with the other by each party in a marriage; in fact, the wife is to be taught by the example of continence to act chastely.[3] It is evil to exact that which you yourself are not able to exhibit. This inequity assuredly brought it about that there were adulteries, women bearing it ill that they were remaining faithful to men not exhibiting mutual love.

30. Finally, there is no adulteress of such a lost sense of shame that she does not hold forth this reason for her vices, that by sinning she is not so much doing an injury as repaying one. Quintilian expressed this very well when he said, "A man who does not keep

---

the Christian point of view in matters regarding adultery, it would have held as certain this sublime parity: acute observations in this regard have been made on the part of J. Gaudemet in 'Tendances nouvelles de la legislation familiale au IVe siècle,' *Antiquitas* (Bonn) 29 (1978), 187-206, especially regarding what has been said, 201 (The article has been republished in J. Gaudemet, *Église et société en Occident au Moyen Age*, London 1984 as no. VI; indications of page numbers have remained unaltered). In this matter one can see the Christian influence more keenly felt in the legislation relative to "engagements." A letter of Pope Siricius openly condemns a girl who weds a man other than the one to whom she had been promised (*PL* 13, 1136), the Council of Elvira was intransigent in its expression of condemnation of adultery on the part of both spouses (Canon 69), as well as on the breaking of matrimonial promises (Canon 54). Cf. Ch. Pietri, 'IV-V secolo, Il matrimonio cristiano a Roma,' in J. Delumeau (ed.), *Storia visuta del popolo cristiano*, Italian edition under the care of F. Bolgiani, Turin, 1985, 112-114. On the Christian influence on imperial legislation which provided for monetary sanctions following the breaking of prematrimonial obligations see the still valid book by L. Anné, *Les rites de fiançialles et la donation pour cause de mariage sous le Bas-Empire*, Louvain, 1941. For a contrary opinion see M. Daser, *Das römische Privatrecht*, Munich, 1959, 109-110, who upholds the influence of an Oriental nature. With Gaudemet, *art. cit.*, 195-196, it is perhaps more exact to hold as undeniable the Christian influence on the legislative level that tied to the spirit of the law itself, while the typical sanctions of a mechanism outside the Church are due to Roman law itself.

3 Cf. Musonius Rufus, *Fragment* XII: YCS 10, 1947, 84-89. "Those who are effeminate or perverse, are to consider licit only those venereal pleasures which are had in matrimony and are performed for the procreation of offspring.... Of all other couplings those which are adulterous are more contrary to the law... to alleviate temptation one may not dare to approach either a prostitute or a free woman outside of marriage... whoever believes that it is not dishonorable or untoward for a master to accost his slave and especially if she is a widow, should consider a little how the things might look to him if the mistress of the house might approach her slave! Certainly it would not seem tolerable not only in the case in which, having a legitimate husband, a wife might take to herself a slave, but even if she should do so not having a husband.... The men in fact have to be even more virtuous, since they pretend to have some kind of primacy over the woman...." Cf. the Italian translation of N. Festa, Milan, 1913, 177-179.

away from the marriage of another is not a guardian of his own either."[4]

31. They are connected by nature. For a man concerned about violating the wives of others cannot be free to attend to his own domestic sanctity; and, when a wife falls into such a marriage, aroused by the very example, she thinks that she should either imitate it or get revenge.

32. We must take care, therefore, not to give opportunity for vices by our intemperance, but let the customs of the two get used to each other and bear the yoke with like minds. Let us consider ourselves in the other's place. For the height of justice almost consists in this: that you do not do to another what you yourself would not want to have done to you by another.

33. These are the things which are prescribed by God for continence. But, however, lest anyone think that he is able to circumscribe the divine precepts, there are added these points, that all calumny and chance for fraud be removed; he is an adulterer who takes a wife who has been sent away by her husband; and so is he who has,

---

[4] Quintilian, born in Calahorra in Spain 35 A.D., was a rhetor and famous advocate. The emperor Vespasian nominated him master of eloquence at Rome, a profession which he exercised for nearly twenty years. Having retired from teaching he wrote his most famous work, a treatise on rhetoric and pedagogy combined, in 12 books, on the formation of the perfect orator. He died in 96 after having been the teacher of the grandnephews of the emperor Domitian. Under Quintilian's name have also come down to us a group of *Declamations* (oratorical exercises on fictitious subjects), the so-called *Major*, numbering 19 and *Minor*, 145 (surviving from at least 388). Quintilian's authorship has been the object of controversy on the part of scholars. Cf. in general, R. Tabacco, 'Quintiliano,' in *Dizionario...*, *op. cit.*, III, 1835-1837 (s.v., 'Declamazioni pseudo-Quintilianae'). The citation of Quintilian made by Lactantius is in all probability from one of the declamations that have not survived: cf. R.M. Ogilvie, *The Library of Lactantius*, Oxford, 1978, 49.

aside from the crime of adultery, put a wife away that he may take another.[a] God did not intend for that *one flesh* to be separated and torn apart.[5]

> *Divine Institutes* VI, 23, 23-24 and 29-33: CSEL 19, pp. 564-571; FOTC 49, 460-461

---

[a] cf. Mt 5:32; 19:9

---

[5] This passage of Lactantius, with its veiled but unmistakable reference to Mt 19:9 whose interpretation — as is well known — has represented for the Fathers and presents for the exegetes of the present day a terrain for controversy concerning its evaluation (for the patristic exegesis see: J. Moingt, '"Le divorce" pour motif d'impudicité (Mt 5:32; 19:9),' *RSR* 56 (1968), 337-384 [on Lactantius, 348]; G. Cereti, *Divorzio, Nuove nozze e Penitenza nella Chiesa primitiva*, Bologna, 1977, and (with solutions that differ from Moingt), H. Crouzel, 'Les Pères de l'Église ont-ils permis le remariage après separation?', *BLE* 70 (1968), 3-43; for modern exegesis cf. T. Stramare, *Matteo divorzista?*, Brescia 1986). It has been interpreted by P. Nautin, 'Divorce et remariage dans la tradition de l'Église latine,' *RSR* 62 (1974), 7-54 (on Lactantius, 15) as an example of the antenicene tradition, which gave to the husband the possibility of divorcing an adulterous wife and of remarrying. See also the reply of H. Crouzel, 'Le remariage après sèparation pour adultère selon les Pères latines,' *BLE* 75 [1974], 169-204) which has not won much support. On the other hand, already in *L'Église primitive face au divorce*, Paris, 1971, 111-113, Crouzel had denied that Lactantius in the passage in question implicitly authorized second marriage. The above-mentioned articles of Crouzel have been republished in *Mariage..., op. cit.*, 3-43 and 113-158 respectively. A useful critical clarification of the modern controversy (Moingt/ Nautin/ Crouzel) can be found in E. Bellini, 'Separazione e Nuovo Matrimonio nella Chiesa Antica,' *La Scuola Cattolica* 103 (1975), 376-385. To clarify the ambiguities of this passage in Lactantius it does not help to refer to the parallel passage of *Epitome* 61, 8: SC 335, 238-239, in which the viewpoint is decisively different. Cf. M. Perrin, *Epitomé..., op. cit.*, 274.

AMBROSE

INTRODUCTORY PROFILE

Ambrose was born into a powerful aristocratic family in 339/340 at Trier.[1] After the death of his father, who had been prefect of Gaul, he transferred to Rome where his sister Marcellina had been consecrated a nun by pope Liberius, perhaps at Christmas, 353. In Rome he received an appropriate rhetorical-juridical education. Around 370 he was named governor of the province of Liguria-Emilia with its seat of administration at Milan. He himself, after intervening to settle the disorderly outbursts between Catholics and Arians about the choice of a successor to bishop Auxentius,[2] was himself proclaimed bishop by popular acclaim although he had not yet been baptized.[3] On the 7th December 374,[4] after baptism, he received

---

[1] Ambrose's date of birth is anything but certain. Some scholars, in fact, propose 337 (or even 333/4) on the basis of differing identifications of the "barbaric incursions" to which allusion is made in Letter 59,4 (according to the enumeration of the Maurists=49 CSEL): BA 20, 78-79. For questions of chronology see in general M. G. Mara, 'Ambrogio di Milano, Ambrosiaster e Niceta,' in J. Quasten, *Patrologia* III, 135-169. For further information cf. F.H. Dudden, *The Life and Times of St. Ambrose,* Oxford, 1935 (2 vols.) and A. Paredi, *Ambrogio e la sua età,* Milan, 2ed. 1960, Engl. tr. Univ. of Notre Dame Press, 1964. M. Testard, 'Saint Ambroise de Milan,' *Bull. de l'Assoc Guillaume Budé,* (1992), 367-394. [Add: D.H. Williams, *Ambrose of Milan and the end of the Arian-Nicene Conflicts,* Oxford U.P., 1995.]

[2] Auxentius was a native of Cappadocia and professed ideas of an Arian tendency. In 355 he was named to the see of Milan, from which he could not be dislodged, notwithstanding repeated attempts by Hilary, Eusebius of Vercelli, and Philastrius of Brescia. The emperor Valentinianus in fact took on his defence, supporting him in his episcopal see until his death which took place in 374.

[3] Postponing baptism to adult age was fairly usual at that time.

[4] Other scholars have proposed 1 December, 373 as the date: cf. M.G. Mara, *op. cit.* 136. On the reluctance of Ambrose to accept the election by popular acclaim, and on his attempts at "flight," see the biography of his secretary, Paulinus, written at the suggestion of Augustine, *Life of Ambrose,* 7,1-9,3: Ch. Mohrmann (ed.), *Vite dei Santi III, Vita di Cipriano. Vita di Ambrogio. Vita di Agostino,* Milan, 1981², 60-65. On Paulinus and his biography of Ambrose, apart from the Introduction of Ch. Mohrmann, in the edition cited here, XXVII-XLII, cf. M. Pellegrino, *Paolino di Milano. Vita di S. Ambrogio,* Rome, 1961 and, especially, E. Lamirande, *Paulin de Milan et la 'Vita Ambrosii,'* Paris, 1983.

episcopal consecration. Beginning like this imposed on him a severe obligation to study the sacred disciplines, the need for which he was always conscious of, by reason of the fact that he had a very different type of education, as he himself more than once admitted.[5] His spiritual guide in the early uncertain stages of his episcopacy was the priest Simplicianus, who was both a profound connoisseur of Neoplatonist philosophy and an acute and committed theologian.

The ecclesiastical teaching of Ambrose marked in its varied aspects a fundamental stage in the history of the Western Church and it is certainly not possible in this space to give a comprehensive account of the various phases of its evolution. Accordingly it must suffice here to outline his activity in his own see of Milan to restore unity and to organize the liturgy and, no less significant, his untiring pastoral activity in his dealings with his people for whom he commented on the biblical text with a view to moral admonition, and to whom he addressed fundamental teaching on the Christian sacraments.[6]

On the doctrinal plane Ambrose's struggle was mainly directed against the Arians.[7] Even at the beginning of his episcopacy he showed all his steadfastness, for example, by imposing the election of a Catholic bishop in Sirmium, a city in what is now Serbia, despite the fact that the Arians could count on the support of Justina,

---

[5] Cf., for example, *De Poenitentia* II,8,67: CSEL 73, 190-191.

[6] We refer to works of a catechetical character like *The Explanation of the Creed* directed at the catechumens, and, especially, *De Sacramentis* and *De Mysteriis*, explaining for the neophytes, that is, those who were just baptized, and, in general, in the first week after the Pascha, the mystico-religious significance of Christian initiation (baptism, unction, eucharist). English trans. *St. Ambrose. Theological and Dogmatic Works* tr. R.J. Deferrari, FOTC 44, Washington, DC, 1963. Text and Italian translation of these works in BA 17, ed. G. Banterle.

[7] Cf. M. Simonetti, 'La politica antiariana di Ambrogio,' in G. Lazzati (ed.), *Ambrosius Episcopus. Atti del Congresso Internazionale di studi ambrosiani nel XVI centenario della elevazione di sant'Ambrogio alla cattedra episcopale, Milano 2-7 dicembre 1974*, I, Milan, 1976, 266-285. We remind the reader that of these Acta ten studies are collected in Y. M. Duval, *Ambroise de Milan. XVI centénaire de son election episcopale*, Paris, 1974, representing a fundamental point of departure for a modern, up-to-date study of the historical, literary and dogmatic figure of St. Ambrose. For a bibliographical report relative to the years 1874-1974, cf. Aa. vv., *Cento anni di bibliografia ambrosiana*, Milan, 1981. On Arianism see the important studies of M. Meslin, *Les Ariens d'Occident (335-430)*, Paris, 1967, and M. Simonetti, *La crisi ariana nel IV secolo*, Rome, 1975.

mother of Valentinianus II,[8] who openly sympathized with their ideas.[9] Ambrose's anti-Arian activity culminated in the Council of Aquileia in 381, held at the solicitation of the emperor, Gratian. In a debate that was lively and articulated, as is evident from the Acts of the Council,[10] Ambrose succeeded in having the validity of the Nicene Creed sanctioned, and brought about the deposition of the two indomitable Arian bishops.[11]

The bishop of Milan effectively opposed the coalition of anti-Catholic forces which at a certain moment represented a reactionary threat,[12] in a brilliant dialectical debate with Symmachus, an outstanding representative of pagan conservatism, who, under the auspices of the emperor brought about the restoration of the Altar of Victory in the Senate.[13] In short, he was at the center of the most important events of his time.

---

[8] Ambrose, in fact, succeeded in imposing bishop Anemius, then "his faithful lieutenant in this important episcopal see" (M. Simonetti, 'La politica,' *op.cit.*, 272). Justina, surviving widow of the emperor Valentinianus I (375), notably influenced the politics of her son, Valentinianus II in a pro-Arian direction. She died in 388, after having returned to Italy from Thessalonica where she had sought refuge with her son because of the invasion on the part of the usurper, Maximus.

[9] Justina, widow of the emperor Valentinianus I (375), is universally considered by Christian historiographers the principal source of inspiration for the pro-Arian policy of Valentinianus II, especially after the violent death of the emperor, Gratian, which occurred on August 25, 383.

[10] The Council of Aquileia was held on 3 September 381 and constituted in the West the counterpart of the Council of Constantinople, which for the eastern part of the Empire had been established some months before by Theodosius. The Acts of the Council as an appendix to some scholia are published in SC 267; and, with Italian translation, in BA 21, 338-393. On the historico-doctrinal problems relating to the Council itself cf. *Atti del Colloquio internazionale sul Concilio di Aquileia del 381*, Udine, 1981 (=Antichità Altoadriatiche 21).

[11] There is question of bishops Palladius of Arcer (Bulgaria) and Secondianus of Belgrade.

[12] Cf. L. Cracco Ruggini, 'Ambrogio e le opposizioni anticattoliche fra il 383 ed il 390,' *AugR* 14 (1974), 409-449. Ruggini's *Economia e società nell'Italia Annonaria. Rapporti tra agricoltura e commercio dal IV al VI secolo d. C.*, Milan, 1961 is still fundamental for the historical and economic context in which Ambrose came to work.

[13] The Altar of Victory, on which the senators at the beginning of their new sessions, were accustomed to burn incense as a sign of devotion and propitiation, had been removed from the Curia Iulia, a room where the Senate met, in 357, by order of the emperor Constantius II. Restored to the cult of the senators, in all probability as a result of the attempted restoration of paganism initiated by Julian the Apostate, it had been again removed in 382 by order of Gratian. A delegation of senators, headed by Symmachus, had sought to gain audience at the imperial court, then residing at Milan, but without success. Symmachus, who had been named prefect, repeated his attempt in 384 before Valentinianus II, the successor of Gratian. He, in fact, read in the presence of the court an earnest statement in which he not only called for the restitution of the Altar, but also the withdrawal of those antipagan sanctions which

He was uncompromising also in his dealings with the imperial authorities to the point of excommunicating the usurper, Maximus, guilty of having justified the Spanish heretic, Priscillian,[14] and of binding to a public penance in 390 the emperor Theodosius who was responsible for the so-called massacre of Thessalonica,[15] the same Theodosius who a year earlier had pronounced Christianity the official religion of the Empire.

The undeniable power Ambrose exercised in dealing with various emperors has not failed to arouse reservations and considerable perplexity in many historians. But, with due consideration,

---

had emanated from Gratian, as — for example — the abolition of public subventions in favor of the sacerdotal college, the confiscation of the lands in their possession. To Symmachus's request, Ambrose replied with equally powerful dialectic in Letters 17 and 18, ensuring that no account would be taken of it on the part of the emperor. The pagan party did not give up and turned again in 389 to the emperor Theodosius, but were confronted by an intervention of Ambrose, who once more addressed the question in Letter 57.

Of Symmachus, the principal representative, together with other exponents of the senatorial aristocracy like the family of Nicomachus or Vettius Agorius Pretextatus, of the cultural renewal and of the religious opposition carried forward by paganism in the course of the 4th century there have come down to us, apart from the texts of the *Relationes* pronounced by him, ten books of *Letters*. On the question of the Altar of Victory, cf.; *Simmaco, Ambrogio, L'altare della Vittoria*, F. Canfora, ed., Palermo, 1991; R. Klein, *Der Streit um den Victoriaaltar. Die dritte Relatio des Symmachus und die Briefe 17, 18 und 57 des Mailander Bischof Ambrosius*, Darmstadt, 1972. On the pagan opposition to the Christianity of the 4th century, apart from the by now "classic," but historiographically outdated G. Boissier, *La fin du paganisme*, Paris, 1891, cf. A. Momigliano, ed., *The Conflict Between Paganism and Christianity in the 4th century*, Oxford, 1963; L. Cracco Ruggini, 'Il paganesimo romano tra religione e politica (384-394 A.D.): per una reinterpretazione del *Carmen contra paganos*,' *Atti della Accademia Nazionale dei Lincei* 376 (1979), Memorie Classe di Scienze morali, storici e filologiche, Serie VIII, Volume XXIII, Fascicolo 1; F. Thélamon, *Païens et Chrétiens au IV siècle*, Paris, 1981. Very felicitous points are made in S. Mazzarino, *Antico, tardoantico ed èra costantiniana*, 1, Bari, 1974, particularly 339-461.

[14] Priscillian, a Spanish heretic who professed a rigid asceticism, permeated with encratite motives and supported by an anthropological conception emerging from anti-somatism, was condemned to death by decapitation in 384. On Priscillian, H. Chadwick, *Priscillian of Avila*, Oxford, 1976 is fundamental. Cf. also G. Sfameni Gasparro, 'Priscilliano, asceta carismatico o criptomanicheo? I fondamenti antropologici dell'*enkrateia* priscillianista,' in *Hestiasis. Studi di tarda antichità offerti a Salvatore Calderone*, IV, Messina, 1990.

[15] The citizens of Thessalonica had killed the commandant of the troops in Illyricum, the barbarian Butheric. Theodosius, perhaps not to disturb relations with the barbarians (this is how S. Mazzarino, *Trattato di Storia Romana*, II, Rome 1962, 482 interprets the episode), ordered a bloody reprisal. Repentant, he sought to remedy the situation with a new disposition, but it was already too late. Thousands of people, in fact, attracted to the circus to attend a non-existent horse-race, were mercilessly slaughtered. After his excommunication, Theodosius did public penance at Christmas 390 and was readmitted to the ecclesiastical community. It was on this occasion that Ambrose wrote to the emperor, Letter 51 (=11, Outside the Collection, in CSEL): BA 21, 230-241.

Ambrose's political action developed in an absolute respect for the natural distinction between Church and Empire, even if "the Emperor is within the Church, not above the Church."[16] With the death of Theodosius (395) Ambrose's political influence waned, but this did not cause any slackening in his continuous intense activity in the interests of the organization of the Church. He was instrumental in having Paulinus nominated bishop of Nola,[17] and his intervention brought about the resolution of the problems which afflicted the church of Vercelli.[18] Summoned to Pavia to take part in the installation of the new bishop, Ambrose took seriously ill; he died at Milan, April 4, 397.

Ambrose's literary activity was strictly linked to his pastoral and political activity. The considerable list of his works does not easily admit of a precise chronological arrangement and scholars have assigned widely different dates to them.[19] In that a detailed examination of Ambrose's vast literary output is not possible here, we will limit ourselves to some basic pointers, paying greater attention to the works from which our selected passages are taken.[20]

That Ambrose addressed the theme of virginity in his earliest treatises should not come as a surprise when it is recalled that he had been directly interested in this choice of life in the person of his sister, Marcellina.[21] The anti-Arian speculations are made con-

---

[16] Cf. *Discourse against Auxentius* 36: BA 21, 136. On the political activity of Ambrose, J.R. Palanque, *Saint Ambroise et l'Empire romain*, Paris, 1933 is still fully valid.

[17] On relations between Ambrose and Paulinus of Nola, cf. S. Costanza, 'I rapporti tra Ambrogio e Paulinus of Nola,' in *Ambrosius Episcopus, op. cit.*, II, 220-232.

[18] At the death of bishop Limenius the church of Vercelli had been divided by discords, making the election of a successor impossible. The intervention of Ambrose, documented in the lengthy Epistle 63 (=14, Outside the Collection, CSEL: BA 21, 262-321), was able to reconcile the dissidents with the name of bishop Honoratus.

[19] For the controverted chronology of the works of Ambrose cf. M. G. Mara, 'Ambrogio,' *op.cit.*, in *Patrologia, op. cit.*, III,143-169. A schematic exposition of the chronology of the works of Ambrose is in R. Gryson, *Le prêtre selon saint Ambroise*, Louvain, 1968, 35-42.

[20] The works of Ambrose are edited in CSEL 32; 62; 64; 73; 79; 82; in CCSL 14; in SC 25 bis; 45; 52; 179; 329. And see especially the bilingual edition in Biblioteca Ambrosiana, planned in 26 volumes.

[21] Cf. works like *De virginibus, De Viduis, De virginitate*, composed between 377 and 378 (but *De virginitate*, according to some scholars is later by a decade, to between 387 and 390), following which, between 391 and 394, appeared *De institutione virginis* and *Exhortatio virginitatis*. [English trans. *St. Ambrose Given to Love*, tr. J. Shiel, Chicago/Dublin 1963.] Obviously we use the term "treatise" in the broad sense since even the writings on virginity

crete in some treatises,[22] in which Ambrose depends heavily on eastern Fathers and which, while certainly not shining with speculative profundity, demonstrate an original ability, not so much in formulations of new theological solutions, as in a capacity "to receive and organize the results of the theological works which were available to him."[23]

Exegetical activity occupies considerable space in the works of Ambrose. Above all he comments on episodes and passages in the Old Testament,[24] which gives him the opportunity to develop a type of exegesis essentially allegorical, in the manner of Philo[25] and Origen[26] in which the mystical tension[27] is often very strong, as in the Alexandrian masters, and which also offers occasions to lay bare the excesses of the rich and their failure to give to the poor, and to

---

and widowhood have an essentially homiletic genesis. Apart from the recent Italian translation, Le vergini e Le vedove in Tutti le opere di Sant'Ambrogio, Opere morali, BA 14/I and / 2, 1989, a cura di F. Gori, see the Italian translation of M. Salvati, Sant'Ambrogio, Scritti Sulla verginità (Corona Patrum Salesiana Ser. Lat. VI), Turin, 1955.
For an anthology of the works of Ambrose translated into Italian see also G. Coppa, Opere di Sant'Ambrogio, Turin, 1969. On works of Ambrose that have virginity and widowhood as their theme cf., apart from the studies cited above in the General Introduction, p. 93, note 37, F.E. Consolino, 'Dagli "exempla" ad un esempio di comportamento cristiano: il De exhortatione virginitatis di Ambrogio,' Rivista di Storia Italiana 44 (1982), 455-477; '"Veni huc a Libano": La "sponsa" del Cantico dei Cantici come modello per le vergini negli scritti esortatori di Ambrogio,' Athenaeum 62 (1984), 399-415; A.V. Nazzaro, 'Il De uiduis di Ambrogio,' Vichiana n.s. 13 (1984), 274-298; 'La vedovanza nel cristianesimo antico,' Annali della Facoltà di Lettere e Filosofia Università di Napoli n.s. 14 (1983-84), 103-132.

[22] De fide and De Spiritu Sancto, written at the request of the emperor Gratian, who wished to be instructed on the fundamentals of the faith, are important writings in defence of Nicene orthodoxy against Arianism. Another treatise, De mysterio Incarnationis Domini, treats in particular of the relationship in Christ between the human nature and the divine.

[23] This is the judgment of R. Cantalamessa, in his 'Sant'Ambrogio di fronte ai grandi dibattiti teologici del suo secolo,' in Ambrosius Episcopus, op. cit., I, 483-539 (the citation is from p. 539).

[24] Ambrose's exegetical commentary launches out from episodes or personalities from the Old Testament developing them in accordance with his parenetic intentions. This does not come from an original work but rather in a reworking of diverse homilies.

[25] On the utilization of Philo by Ambrose cf. E. Lucchesi, L'usage de Philon dans l'oeuvre exégètique de Saint Ambroise, Leiden, 1977; H. Savon, Saint Ambroise devant l'exégèse de Philon le Juif, Paris, 1977.

[26] On the influences of Origen on Ambrose cf., for example, R. Palla, 'Temi del Commento origeniana al Cantico dei Cantici nel De Isaac di Ambrogio,' Annali della Scuola Normale Superiori di Pisa 9 (1979), 563-572.

[27] Fundamental for this aspect of the spirituality of Ambrose is E. Dassmann, Die Frömmigkeit des Kirchenväters Ambrosius von Mailand, Münster 1965; Italian translation: La sobria ebbrezza dello spirito. La spiritualità di S. Ambrogio vescovo di Milano, Varese, 1975.

contest their rights of property;[28] it was no accident that one of his first acts after his election as bishop was to donate his own goods, mobile and immobile, to the poor and to the church.[29] Certainly we cannot pass over in silence some of his occasional compositions, like the discourses he pronounced on the deaths of Valentinianus II and of Theodosius,[30] his *Epistles*, an historical resource of the greatest importance, and his *Hymns* which had a determining influence at the birth of Christian hymnology.[31]

Here now are short notations on three works, extracts from which are presented below: *Paradise*, *Hexaemeron*, and the *Exposition of the Gospel of Luke*. *Paradise* is a commentary on the account in Genesis relating the paradise on earth and the original sin. It is a commentary which, while it follows the biblical text in a continuous manner, dwells on some fundamental themes, developed in the

---

[28] The reference is to works like *De Nabuthae historia* and *De Tobia*. On which cf. M.R.P. McGuire, tr. *S. Ambrosii De Nabuthae historia,* Washington, DC, 1927; and *De Tobia,* BA 6, F. Gori, ed., Genoa, 1965.
On the social thought of Ambrose cf. V. R. Vasey, *The Social Ideas in the Works of St. Ambrose. A study on De Nabuthe,* Rome, 1982; M. G. Mara, *Ambrogio. La storia di Naboth,* L'Aquila, 1982; S. Mazzarino, *Storia sociale del vescovo Ambrogio,* Rome, 1989; On Ambrose's concept of private property see, in particular, S. Calafato, *La proprietà privata in Sant'Ambrogio,* Turin, 1958. [See now: S. Mazzarino, *Storia sociali del vescovo Ambrogio,* Rome, 1989.]

[29] Cf. Paulinus, *Vita di Ambrogio, op. cit.,* 38, 4, 102-103.

[30] The funeral oration for Valentinianus was delivered in 392; the one for Theodosius on 25 February, 395 in the presence of his successor Honorius. See T.A. Kelly, *S. Ambrosii liber de consolatione Valentiniani,* Washington, DC, 1940; On the funeral orations of Ambrose cf. F.E. Consolino, 'L'Optimus princeps secondo S. Ambrogio: virtù imperatorie e virtù cristiane nelle orazioni funebri per Valentiniano e Teodosio,' *Rivista Storica Italiana* 46 (1984),1025-1045; M.D. Mannix, *S. Ambrosii Oratio de obitu Theodosii,* Washington, DC, 1925; *Funeral Orations,* FOTC 22, Washington, DC, 1953.

[31] Of the great number of hymns attributed by tradition to Ambrose the four of which St. Augustine speaks: (*Iam surgit hora tertia, Aeterne rerum conditor, Deus creator omnium, Intende qui regis Israel*) and fourteen others are securely held as authentic, with some hesitancy, among various scholars. Text with Italian translation, M. Simonetti (ed.), BP 13, which reproduces with an updated bibliography by S. Zincone, the edition published, Alba, 1956. See also M.-H. Jullien, 'Les sources de la tradition ancienne des quatorze Hymnes attribuées a saint Ambroise,' *RHT* XIX (1989), 57-189. For bibliographical information on Christian hymnology in general and Ambrosian in particular, see M. Simonetti, 'Studi sull'innologia popolare cristiana dei primi secoli,' in *Atti della Accademia Nazionale dei Lincei Roma,* Memorie, Sez. VIII, vol. IV, 1952, 339-485, whose critical conclusions are now in need of integration with the important studies of J. Fontaine, 'L'apport de la tradition poétique romaine a la formation de l'hymnodie latine chrétienne,' *REL* 52 (1974), 318-355; 'Les origines de l'hymnodie chrétienne latine d'Hilaire de Poitiers a Ambroise de Milan,' *Revue de l'Institut catholique de Paris* 14 (1985), 15-51, and especially J. Fontaine, *Saint Ambroise, Hymnes,* Paris, Editions du Cerf, 1993.

characteristic formulation of exegetical literature known as "Questions and Responses."[32] Its date is much controverted, as also the nature of the writing. Certainly going back to the first period of Ambrose's literary activity, it is probably to be placed between 375 and 378.[33] According to some scholars the work shows a homiletic origin, according to others it would have been a treatise destined for reading.[34] A somewhat eclectic position has been recently taken by P. Siniscalco, who maintains that the work basically consists of points and reflections destined for Ambrose himself, in need of clarifying certain fundamental scriptural questions, and perhaps to use them later in his homilies.[35]

The *Hexaemeron* of Ambrose belongs to a very rich and varied exegetic tradition.[36] The work is subdivided into six books and consists of the nine discourses given by Ambrose to the catechumens in Holy Week between 386 and 390. As in the other exegetical works of Ambrose the *Hexaemeron* reflects the literary reworking of a stenographed text. The work strictly depends on one of the same title by Basil of Caesarea but, in spite of the well-known and malevolent affirmations of Jerome,[37] one can recognize in Ambrose the capacity to know how to recreate his own model, at one time for his personal

---

[32] On this particular form of exegetical literature cf. G. Bardy, 'La littérature patristique des "Quaestiones et Responsiones" sur l'Écriture Sainte,' *RB* 41 (1932), 210-236; 341-369; 515-537; 42 (1933), 14-30; 211-229; 328-352. [Add: L. Perrone, '"Quaestiones et Responsiones" in Origene. Prospettive di un analisi formale dell'argomentazione esegetico-teologica,' *Cristianesimo nella Storia* XV,1 (1994), 1-50.]

[33] For the different dates proposed cf. U. Mattioli, *S. Ambrogio, Il Giardino piantato a Oriente*, Rome, 1981, 16; P. Siniscalco, *Sant'Ambrogio, Il Paradiso terrestre. Caino e Abele* (BA 2/I), Milan-Rome, 1984, 10-11.

[34] Cf. P. Siniscalco, *op. cit.*, 19-20. U. Mattioli, *op. cit.*, 20 is convinced that *De paradiso* is certainly derived from his preaching.

[35] *Op. cit*, p. 20.

[36] Cf. F. E. Robbins, *The Hexaemeral Literature. A Study of the Greek and Latin Commentaries*, Chicago, 1912.

[37] Jerome accused Ambrose of plagiarizing the works of others: cf. PL 23, col. 108; PL 25, coll. 229-230. [Engl. ed. see also S.M. Oberhelmans, 'Jerome's earliest attack on Ambrose: *On Ephesians*, Prolog (PL 26.469D-70A),' *TAPA* 121 (1991), 377-401.] The anger which the man from Stridon undoubtedly reveals in his confrontations with the bishop of Milan, according to A. Paredi, *S. Gerolamo e S. Ambrogio*, in *Melanges Tisserant*, V, Città del Vaticano 1964, 198, would have been an indication of a possible involvement of Ambrose in the banishment of Jerome from Rome after the death of Damasus.

parenetic needs,[38] at another resorting to a poetic transfiguration ably orchestrated from the employment of the finest rhetorical devices.[39] The *Exposition on the Gospel of Luke* is the only exegetical work dedicated by Ambrose to the New Testament and it is also his longest. The work is quite heterogeneous in its structure. Derived, in fact, from Sunday homilies delivered at various times, it is also the fruit of notes and in the third book it assumes the appearance of being an autonomous treatise in epistolary format.[40] The assignment of a date to it is somewhat problematic; the only certain date is that the work was already known to Jerome in 389. The actual subdivision into ten books does not seem to reflect Ambrose's original intention; however this division is followed in the best critical editions. The work relies largely on the exegesis of Origen but also depends on the *Commentary on Matthew* of Hilary of Poitiers; it has exercised an undeniable influence on Augustine himself.[41] What was said about the *Hexaemeron* applies equally to this work: Ambrose's cultured personality shows through frequently, in the Marian spirit which animates Book II, in the frequent citations from the classics, even if the composition of the work is not free from certain repetitions and boring redundancies.[42]

---

[38] Cf. G. Coppa, *op. cit.*, 40.

[39] Still fundamental on the "poetic" value of the exegesis of Ambrose is, G. Lazzati, *Il valore letterario della esegesi ambrosiana*, Milan, 1960. On the utilization of Basil, especially in the selections in this anthology cf. A. V. Nazzaro, *Simbologia e poesia dell'acqua e del mare in Ambrogio di Milano*, Naples, 1977, 118-120.

[40] Cf. G. Coppa, *Sant'Ambrogio. Esposizione del Vangelo secondo Luca* (BA 11), Milan-Rome, 1978, 18-25. [Engl. ed. see now: C. Corsato, *La expositio evangelii secundum Lucam di sant'Ambrogio. Ermeneutica, simbologia, fonti,* Rome, Augustinianum,1993.]

[41] Cf. P. Rollero, *La expositio evangelii secundum Lucam come fonte della esegesi agostiniana,* Turin, 1958.

[42] Cf. G. Coppa, *op. cit.*, 58.

THE COUPLE IN PARADISE: ALLEGORICAL EXEGESIS

21

(11) Many people nevertheless are of the opinion that the Devil was not present in Paradise, although we read that he stood with the angels in heaven.[a] These persons interpret the statement of Scripture according to their own fancy. In this way they put aside any objection which they may have to the words of Scripture. We stand by the conviction held by one who preceded us that sin was committed by man because of the pleasure of sense. We maintain that the figure of the serpent stands for enjoyment and the figure of the woman for the emotions of the mind and heart. The latter is called by the Greeks *aisthesis*. When, according to this theory, the senses are deceived, the mind, which the Greeks call *nous*, falls into error. Hence, not without reason the author to whom I refer accepts the Greek word *nous* as a figure of a man and *aisthesis*, as that of a woman.[1] Hence, some have interpreted Adam to mean an earthly *nous*.[2]

In the Gospel the Lord sets forth the parable of the virgins[b] who awaited the coming of the bridegroom with either lighted or extinguished lamps. Thus He exemplifies either the pure emotions of the wise or the impure senses of the unwise. If Eve, that is, the emotions of the first woman, had kept her lamp lighted, she would not have enfolded us in the meshes of her sin. She would not have fallen from the height of immortality which is established as the reward of virtue.

(12) Paradise is, therefore, a land of fertility — that is to say, a soul which is fertile — planted in Eden, that is, in a certain delight-

---

[a] cf. Zc 3:1   [b] cf. Mt 25:1-13

[1] Cf. Philo, *De Creatione Mundi secundum Mose*, 165: "Pleasure does not venture to bring her wiles and deceptions to bear on the man, but on the woman, and by means of her on him... for in us 'mind' corresponds to man, and the 'senses' to woman." *Philo*, Loeb Classical Library, v.1, 131. The references to Philo are very numerous and can be verified in the edition of *De Paradiso*, CSEL 32/1. For an excellent analysis of this passage of Ambrose see F. Pizzolato, 'La coppia umana in Sant'Ambrogio,' in R. Cantalamessa, *Etica sessuale*, *op. cit.*, 182-185.

[2] Cf. Philo, *Alleg. Leg.* I, 90: "...when you hear the word 'Adam,' understand by it the terrestrial and perishable mind." LCL, 207.

ful or well-tilled land in which the soul finds pleasure. Adam exists there as *nous* [mind] and Eve as "sense."

On Paradise, 2,11-3,12: BA 2/I, pp. 50-52; FOTC 42, 293-294

THE RELATIONSHIP BETWEEN ADAM AND EVE;
THE FOUNDATION AND PROTOTYPE OF ACTUALITY

22

4,24. *The Lord God then took man whom He had created and settles him in the garden to cultivate and care for it.*[a] Note the fact that man was created outside Paradise, whereas woman was made within it. This teaches us that each person acquires grace by reason of virtue, not because of locality, or of race. Hence, although created outside Paradise, that is, in an inferior place,[1] man is found to be superior, whereas woman, created in a better place, that is to say, in Paradise, is found to be inferior.[2] She was first to be deceived and was responsible for deceiving the man. Wherefore the Apostle Peter has related that holy women have in olden times been subject to the stronger and recommends them to obey their husbands as their masters.[b] And Paul says: *Adam was not deceived, but the woman was deceived and was in sin.*[c] This is a warning that no one ought to rely on himself, for she who was made for assistance needs the protection of a man.[d] The head of the woman is man,[e] who, while he believed that he would have the assistance of his wife, fell because of her. Wherefore, no one ought to entrust himself lightly to another unless he has first put that person's virtue to the test. Neither should he claim for himself in the role of protector one whom he believes is subservient to him. Rather, a person should share his grace with another. Especially is this true of one who is in the position of greater strength and one who plays the part of protector. We have advice of the Apostle Pe-

---

[a] Gn 2:15   [b] cf. 1 P 3:16   [c] 1 Tm 2:14   [d] cf. Gn 2:18   [e] cf. 1 Cor 11:3

[1] That Ambrose adheres to the doctrine of "double creation" — on which cf. U. Bianchi, *La doppia creazione dell'uomo negli Alessandrini, nei Cappadoci e nella gnosi*, Rome, 1978 — seems extremely improbable: see however, P. Siniscalco, *Il Paradiso..., op. cit.*, p. 67, note 3.

ter, in which he recommends that husbands pay honor to their wives: *Husbands, in like manner, dwell with your wives considerately, paying honor to the woman as to the weaker vessel and as co-heir of the grace of life that your prayers be not hindered.*[f]

(25) So then man was placed in Paradise, while the woman was created in Paradise. The woman, even before she was deceived by the serpent, shared grace with a man, since she was taken from a man. Yet, as the Apostle said, *this is a great mystery.*[g] Wherefore He traced the source of life from it.

On Paradise, 4, 24-25, BA 2/1, 66-68; FOTC 42, 301-302

22a

10,46. Still another question[1] arises, that concerning the saying of the Lord: *It is not good for man to be alone.*[a] Recognize the fact, first of all, that, when God created man from the slime of the earth, He did not add: *God saw that it was good,*[b] as He did in the rest of His works. If He had said at that time that the creation of man was good, then the other statement that "it is not good" would be a contradiction in terms, although He had said that the creation of what preceded the formation of man was good.

That was the situation at the time of the creation of Adam alone.[c] But, when He perceived that man and woman were joined together[d] in creation, He did not treat each even then in a special manner, for He soon after states: *God saw that all He had ever made was very good.*[e] The meaning is clear. The creation of both man and woman is considered to be good.

10,47. From this question another problem arises. How did it

---

[f] 1 P 3:7 [g] cf. Eph 5:32 [a] cf. Gn 2:18 [b] Gn 1:4; 1:10; 1:12; 1:18; 1:21; 1:27 [c] cf. Gn 2:7
[d] cf. Gn 1:27 [e] Gn 1:31

[2] The motif of female inferiority is encountered rather frequently in the writings of Ambrose. See by way of example *Letter* 69, 4 (Maurists = 15 CSEL): BA 19, pp. 156-157: FOTC 26, 436, tr. "...but why should men want to assume the appearance of the inferior sex?"

[1] Ambrose in his exposition proceeds in the exegetical technique of Questions and Responses; cf. *supra*, 216, n. 32.

happen that, when Adam alone was created, it was not said that it was good, but when a woman also was made, then are we to understand that everything was good?[f] Whereas God in one case commended the whole of creation, as well as every creature in it (including man who is held to be a part of nature), a special reference to man did not then seem necessary. Wherefore, when Adam alone was created, an assertion that this work was good was not thought to be by any means a fitting climax to a satisfactory achievement. It was said, moreover, that it was not good for man to be alone. Yet we know that Adam did not commit sin before woman was created. However, after creation, she was the first to disobey the divine command and even instigated her husband to sin.

If, therefore, the woman is responsible for the man's sin, how then can her accession be considered a good? But, if you consider that the universe is in the care of God, then you will discover this fact, namely, that the Lord must have gained more pleasure for Himself in being responsible for all creation than in the condemnation of that which would have been the initial cause of sin. Accordingly, the Lord declared that it was not good for man to be alone, because the human race could not have been propagated from man alone. God preferred the existence of more than one whom He would be able to save by forgiving their sin, than to have to confine this possibility to Adam alone who was free from fault.

Inasmuch as He is the Author of both man and woman, He came into this world to save sinners.[g] Finally, He did not permit Cain, a man accused of fratricide, to perish before he generated sons.[h] For the sake, therefore, of the successive generations of men it followed that woman had to be joined to man. Thus we must interpret the very words of God when He said that it was not good for man to be alone. If the woman was to be the first one to sin, the fact that she was the one destined to bring forth redemption must not be excluded from the operations of Divine Providence. Although Adam was not deceived, the woman was deceived and was in sin. Yet woman, Scrip-

---

f cf. Gn 1:31   g 1 Tm 1:15   h cf. Gn 4:15-17

ture tells us, *will be saved by childbearing*,[i] which childbearing generated Christ.[2]

10,48. Not without significance, too, is the fact that woman
was made out of the rib of Adam. She was not made of the same earth
with which he was formed, in order that we might realize that the
physical nature of both man and woman is identical and that there
was one source for the propagation of the human race.

For that reason, neither was a man created together with a
woman, nor were two men and two women created at the beginning,
but first a man and after that a woman. God willed it that human
nature be established as one. Thus, from the very inception of the
human stock He eliminated the possibility that many disparate natures should arise. He said: *Let us make him a helper like himself*.[j] We
understand that to mean a helper in the generation of the human
family — a really good helper.[3] If we take the word "helper" in a good
sense, then the woman's co-operation turns out to be something of
major importance in the process of generation, just as the earth by
receiving, retaining, and fostering the seed causes it to grow and produce fruit in time. In that respect, therefore, woman is a good helper
even though in an inferior position. We find examples of this in our
own experience. We see how men in high and important offices often enlist the help of men who are below them in rank and esteem.

11,49. Besides this, there is a reason why every species of animal was brought to Adam.[k] In this way he would be able to see that
nature in every aspect is constituted of two sexes: male and female.
Following these observations, he would become aware that association with a woman was a necessity of his lot.

---

[i] 1 Tm 2:14-15   [j] Gn 2:18   [k] cf. Gn 2:19

---

[2] Ambrose surpasses — as L.F. Pizzolato acutely observes, *art. cit.*, 193-195 — the perspective of Philo in which the woman is in a definitely subordinate position, in a new theological
dimension of the female which, even if it has been caused by the fall, is nevertheless "a
promoter of salvation" (cf. D. Ramos-Lissón, 'Aspectos teológicos de la feminidad en S.
Ambrosio y S. Agustín,' in Aa. vv., *Masculinidad y feminidad en la patrística*, Pamplona, 1989,
125-167).

[3] The best comment on the statement that the woman is the best "helper" for man, and not
just in the matter of procreation, is given in a passage in his *On Duties*, 1, 134, BA 13, pp.
104-105: "Amongst all the living creatures therefore, there was none meet for him, or to put
it plainly none to be his helper. Hence a woman was looked for as a helper for him," NPNF
ser. 2, v. X, 23.

11,50. *And God cast Adam into a deep sleep and he slept.*[1] What does the phrase "deep sleep" signify? Does it not mean that when we contemplate a conjugal union we seem to be turning our eyes gradually in the direction of God's kingdom? Do we not seem, as we enter into a vision of this world, to partake a little of things divine, while we find our repose in the midst of what is secular and mundane? Hence, after the statement, *He cast Adam into a deep sleep and he slept*, there follows: *The rib which God took from Adam He built into a woman.*[m] The word "built" is well chosen in speaking of the creation of a woman, because a household, comprising man and wife, seems to point toward a state of full perfection. One who is without a wife is regarded as being without a home. As man is considered to be more skilful in public duties, so woman is esteemed to be more adaptable to domestic ministrations. Reflect on the fact that He did not take a part from Adam's soul, but a rib from his body, that is to say, not soul from a soul, but *bone of my bone and flesh of my flesh* will this woman be called.[n]

On Paradise, 10,46-48; 11,49-50, BA 2/1, pp. 112-118; FOTC 42, 327-329

LOVE AND THE RESOLUTION OF CONTRASTS

23

18. Since the example of the astute serpent[1] has been offered, let us be astute also, in regard to entrance into the state of matrimony and to remaining therein. Let us love this mutual association which has become our lot. If those who have at the time of their births lived in entirely different regions yet agree to live together, if it happens that the husband should undertake a trip to a foreign land, no distance or abstinence should diminish the cherished love of the pair. The same law binds the present and the absent; the same bond of nature cements together the rights of conjugal love between the

---

[1] Gn 2:21   [m] Gn 2:22   [n] Gn 2:23

[1] Ambrose immediately before, at the end of paragraph 17, had cited Mt 10:16: *Be ye wise as serpents.*

absent as well as between the present. The necks of both parties are linked together in the same beneficent yoke, even if one of them should find himself in regions entirely remote, because both parties share in the yoke of grace which is one of the spirit,[2] not of the body.

When the viper, the deadliest kind of animal and the most cunning of the whole species of serpents, evinces a desire for copulation, he searches for a sea-lamprey already known to him, or he seeks for a new mate.[3] Proceeding toward the shore, he makes his presence known by a hissing sound, whereby he invites conjugal embrace. The sea-lamprey does not repulse the appeal and yields to the poisonous serpent the desired enjoyment of their conjugal bond.

What is the purpose of such a discussion as this, if it does not mean that we should put up with our married partner and, if he is away from home, that we should await his return to his family? Although he may be cruel, deceitful, uncouth, wayward, and drunken, can this be more intolerable than the poison which is no obstacle to the sea-lamprey in dealing with her mate? When invited, she does not fail to respond and embraces the slimy serpent with great affection.

Your husband endures your defects and your feminine levities.

---

[2] On Ambrose's concept of the nuptial bond, D. Tettamanzi, 'Valori cristiani del matrimonio nel pensiero di S. Ambrogio,' La Scuola Cattolica 102 (1974), 451-474, is fundamental and also useful for further bibliography.

[3] The coupling between the viper and the sea lamprey is a widespread notion in antiquity, mentioned, for example, by Pliny the Elder, Natural History 32,14. Ambrose's source, however, is Basil of Caesarea, On the Hexaemeron, Homily 7,5: SC 26 bis, 418-419 (see p. 418, note 2, for other sources on the legend of the coupling of the viper and the sea lamprey). Even though the source in Basil is evident, at times expressed with precise correspondences, however the freedom with which Ambrose enlarges on his model can also be recognized, for the original parenetic intentions of his preaching. On the originality of Ambrose in the opening and closing of the Hexaemeron in relation to his model cf. A.V. Nazzaro, 'Esordio e chiusa delle omelie esameronali di Ambrogio,' AugR 14 (1974), 559-590. However it seems indispensable to point out the enormous differences that intervene between Basil's estimates with regard to women and those of Ambrose. It suffices to read the famous Epistle 188, Ad Amphilochium (On the Canons) particularly canon 9 (Saint Basil, Lettres, vol. II, Y. Courtonne, ed., Paris, 1961, p. 128), to get an idea of how the Bishop of Caesarea strongly discriminated against women on this point as well as on that of adultery for which the patristic tradition is almost unanimous in holding the parity of both spouses. Is it the fault of his surroundings? Possibly, although to lend credence to Basil: "But the custom [regarding adultery on the part of men and women] is different, and with regard to women we find a higher precision of norms." The Western counterpart of Basil could be the Anonymous Author, now generally identified as Ambrosiaster. On Basil's viewpoint in the matter of adultery, with regard especially to canon 9, cf. H. Crouzel, 'Séparation ou remariage selon les Pères anciens,' in Gregorianum 47 (1966), 472-494, especially 480-483; the article also appears in La Civiltà Cattolica 16 (1966), 137-157.

Can you not bear with your husband? Adam was deceived by Eve,
not Eve by Adam.[a] It is right that he whom the woman enticed to
do wrong should assume the office of guide, lest he fall once more
because of feminine instability.

But he is repugnant and uncouth! Yes, but he pleased you at
one time. Do you think that a husband should be chosen more than
once? The ox and the horse look for and cherish their mates, and, if
a substitution takes place, they are unable to carry the yoke together.
They feel that they do not form an integral part of the team. You
repudiate your yoke-mate and think that a frequent change should
be made. If one day he fails you, you bring in a rival and straight-
way, without knowing why, yet knowingly, you do violence to your
sense of modesty.

The viper searches for his absent mate, calls to her with a hiss
of invitation. When he feels his mate approaching, he spits forth the
poison with due regard for his consort and the nuptial rite. Why do
you repel your husband coming back from a far country? The viper
gazes upon the sea in an endeavor to find his consort. You put ob-
stacles in the path of your husband. You stir up the poison of litiga-
tion. You reject him and in the conjugal embrace emit dread poison, scorning your husband and putting to shame your nuptial bond.

19. As for the man — for we can apply this example to him,
also — lay aside the inordinate emotions of your heart and the rudeness of your manners when you meet your patient wife. Get rid of
your obstinacy when your gentle consort offers you her love. You are
not a master, but a husband. What you have acquired is not a
handmaid, but a wife. God designed you to be a guide to the weaker
sex, not a dictator.[4] Be a sharer in her activities. Be a sharer in her
love. The viper pours forth his poison; can you not get rid of your
hardness of heart? Although you have by nature a severity of character, you ought to temper it in consideration of your married state

---

[a] cf. 1 Tm 2:14

[4] The comment of *Letter* 63 seems significant to this statement of Ambrose (Maurist ed. = 14,
Outside the Collection CSEL), 107: 21, pp. 318-319: See now: CSEL 82, pt. 3 (1982), 268-
295; FOTC: "The wife respects her husband, she is not his slave; she allows herself to be
guided, not constrained. The husband is not worth much who merits a law-suit. Even the
husband leads his wife like a steersman, he honors her as the companion of his life, and
shares with her — as a co-heir — in the reputation he enjoys."

and control your tendency to rudeness by holding in respect your conjugal relationship.

There are occasions for sin. Do not seek the bed that belongs to another. Do not by guile enter into another's union. Adultery is a grievous offense. It does violence to nature. At the beginning God formed two creatures. Adam and Eve; that is, man and wife. He formed woman from the man; this is, from the rib of Adam. He bade them both to live in one body and in one spirit.[b] Why, then, do you cleave one body apart? Why do you divide one spirit? That is an adulterous offense against nature. It is a lesson which is taught us by the willing union of sea-lamprey and viper, a union grounded not on similarity of species, but on ardent desire.

Give ear, men! He who desires association with such a serpent may be likened to one who seeks occasion to have adulterous relations with another man's wife. It can be said that he has the very traits of a serpent. He hastens to the viper who embraces him in the devious ways of lubricity, not in the righteous ways of love. He hastens to one who takes up again his poison like the viper and who is said to consume again the poison, once the act of copulation has been completed. The adulterer is like a viper. Hence Solomon says that when a man is intoxicated his passions are aroused. His body is swollen as if bitten by a snake and his poison is spread abroad like a basilisk's.[c] That you may realize that he has spoken of an adulterer, he added these words: Thine eyes shall behold strange women and thy mouth shall utter perverse things.

20. And do not imagine that our argument is self-contradictory in that we have made use of the example of a viper in order to point both a good and a bad moral. It serves the purposes of instruction to bring forward a twofold consideration.[5] On the one hand, we are like the serpent in being ashamed to be loyal to our beloved. Again, by severing the bonds of holy matrimony we prefer the harmful and the lubricious, as in the case of union with a serpent, to what is really and truly salutary.

Hexaemeron, V, VII, 7,18-20: BA 1, pp. 258-264; FOTC 42, 172-176

---

[b] cf. Gn 2:21-22   [c] cf. Pr 23:31-33

---

[5] It is a peculiarity of exegetes of the allegorical type to give more significance to the same biblical passage or the same episode for the purposes of moral exhortation.

DIVORCE BREAKS THE LAW OF GOD

24

3.[1] The law and the prophets were in force until John, not because the law failed, but because the preaching of the gospel commenced. *Everyone who divorces his wife and marries another commits adultery. The man who marries a wife divorced from her husband likewise commits adultery.*[a] This is what Solomon says: *Home and possessions are an inheritance from parents but a prudent wife is from the Lord.*[b]

Read in Greek one finds no contradiction. Because the Greek rightly says: *harmozetai* there is harmony when there is an assembly, a union which brings together when the pipes of an instrument arranged in order maintain the agreement of a legitimate melody when the assemblage of strings remain in tune.

Therefore there is no harmony in a marriage when a pagan woman is joined illegitimately to a Christian husband. Accordingly where there is a marriage there is harmony; where there is harmony it is God who joins; where there is not harmony there is quarrelling and dissension which does not come from God because *God is love.*[c]

4. Take care, then, not to divorce your wife, lest you deny that God is the author of your union. Moreover, if you have an obligation to put up with and try to emend the morals of others, how much more so are you obliged to do so in the case of your wife? Listen to what the Lord has said: *Everyone who divorces his wife forces her to commit adultery,*[d] since the lust of sinning can creep in on a wife who is not allowed to change her marriage during the lifetime of her husband. Therefore the one who is responsible for the error is also guilty of the fault, because the childbearing mother is divorced together with her little children, because she who is ageing with wavering

---

[a] Lk 16:18   [b] Pr 19:14   [c] 1 Jn 4:8   [d] Mt 5:32

[1] Ambrose's treatment relating to matrimony and to divorce starts out from an explanation of Lk 16:18: *"Everyone who divorces his wife and marries another commits adultery and the man who marries a woman divorced from her husband likewise commits adultery."* In the portion of text omitted here Ambrose discusses the so-called Pauline privilege of 1 Cor 7:15 upholding the right of a Christian wife to leave an unbelieving husband since a marriage of that nature is not based on divine law. And immediately after he clinches his argument, from another angle, saying that there is no harmony in the union between a "Gentile" and a Christian, because it has not been legitimatized.

footsteps is pushed out. It is cruel, if you send away the wife, but keep custody of the children, adding to the outrage to her love the wounding of her maternal feelings; it is crueler still, if you send away the children too on account of their mother, since children ought to redeem from the father the fault of the mother. What a risk it is to expose the tender age of an adolescent to sin! How cruel it is to leave her now that she is old, after you have cultivated the flower of her youth![3] How impious if you make the old age destitute of the person whose youth you have deflowered. By that logic an emperor can dismiss a veteran without remunerating his services, without military honors, and a farmer can drive from his farm the laborer worn out from his labors. Or is what is unlawful in the case of subjects permitted in the case of an equal?[4]

5. Do you divorce, then, your wife as if within your rights and without feeling guilty, and think that this is lawful for you, because the civil law does not prohibit it?[5] But the divine law forbids it. You who obey men should fear God. Listen to the law of the Lord which even legislators obey: *What God has joined let man not separate.*[e] But it is not just a command of God but a part of God's handiwork that is destroyed here. Would you allow your children, I ask you, to live with a step-father during your own lifetime, or to live with a step-mother while their real mother is in good health? Suppose that the

---

[e] Mt 19:6; Mk 10:9

[2] Ambrose — it is hardly necessary to say — is revealed as skilled in his choice of observations of a psychological character and behaves in a way that is striking to his audience.

[3] It seems to echo Mal 2:14-16: "Because the Lord is witness between you and the wife of your youth with whom you have broken faith, though she is your companion, your betrothed." On this passage of Scripture cf. M. Adinolfi, *Il femminismo della Bibbia*, Rome, 1981, 61-71.

[4] Note, also, because of what has been said earlier regarding Basil of Caesarea, the absolute parity which Ambrose initiated between husbands and wives (*comparem*).

[5] Roman law made a distinction between *repudium* and *divortium*, at least according to the opinion of some scholars. In the legislation of the Late Empire, in any case, *repudium* indicates the dissolution of matrimony through the initiation of only one spouse — in practice almost always the husband, while *divortium* involves the consent of both spouses. Constantine had established the limits of *ripudio* — possible only for three just reasons (murder of the husband, violation of the grave, poisoning; adulterous wife, poisoner, prostitute) — whereas he left free for all practical purposes bilateral divorce. Cf. B. Rawson, ed., *Marriage, Divorce and Children in Ancient Rome*, Oxford, 1991.

divorced wife does not marry: should she be displeasing to you, her husband, she who remains faithful to you, an adulterer? Suppose that she is married. Her financial plight is your fault and what you think is a marriage is adultery.[f] What difference does it make if you commit adultery openly confessing your crime or under the guise of being married, except that it is more serious to legalize a crime than to do it in secret.

Exposition on the Gospel of Luke, VIII, 3-6: SC 52, 101-103

---

[f] cf. 1 Cor 7:39; Rm 7:2

JEROME

INTRODUCTORY PROFILE

Whether on account of the qualities of his intellectual endowments or the defects in his none too tolerant character, Jerome emerges as one of the more outstanding figures of the Christian West in the 4th century. Born in Stridon, in Dalmatia, in 331, if credence can be given to the ancient sources, or between 340 and 347 in the view of the majority of modern scholars,[1] Jerome transferred to Rome while still a youth to complete his own studies at the school of the celebrated grammarian, Aelius Donatus.[2] His contact with the classics, which for Christians also constituted the foundation of school training,[3] engendered in him a profound interest in pagan culture[4] which

---

[1] J.N.D. Kelly, *Jerome: His Life, Writings, and Controversies*, London, 1975, 337-339 has proposed the date of 331, from an indication furnished by Prosper of Aquitaine, a Christian chronicler between the end of the IVth and the first half of the Vth century. Apart from Kelly's well-argued monograph, we might indicate some other studies of a general character, fundamental for a balanced view of the personality of Jerome: F. Cavallera, *Saint Jérôme. Sa vie et son oeuvre*, Paris-Louvain, 1922; C. Favez, *Saint Jérôme peint par lui-meme*, Brussels, 1958; A. Penna, *San Gerolamo*, Rome, 1949; J. Steinmann,*Saint Jérôme*, Paris, 1958; P. Antin, *Recueil sur Saint Jérôme*, Brussels, 1968; M. Testard, *Saint Jérôme l'apôtre savant du patriarciat romain*, Paris, 1969. An agile but suggestive and personal profile of Jerome has recently been furnished by S. Pricoco, in *Dizionario degli Scrittori Greci e Latini*, II, Settimo Milanese, 1988, 1049-1060; see also J. Duff, *The Letters of St. Jerome: A Selection*, Dublin, 1942.

[2] For the relations between Jerome and Donatus cf, G. Brugnoli, 'Donato e Girolamo,' *Vet Chr* 2 (1965), 139-149. Aelius Donatus, commentator on Terence, was the outstanding *grammaticus* of the IVth century. His manual on grammar, *Ars grammatica*, subdivided in two parts, respectively for lower and upper schools, had a formative influence on the medieval scholastic tradition.

[3] Cf. in general, P. Monceaux, *St. Jerome: The Early Years*, tr. F.J. Sheed, London, 1933; M. Simonetti, *Cristianesimo antico, op. cit.*, 76-78.

[4] On the influence of the classics on Jerome see H. Hagendahl, *Latin Fathers and the Classics*, Göteborg 1958; H. Hagendahl, 'Jerome and the Latin Classics,' *VigChr* 28 (1974),215-227; W.C. McDermott, 'Saint Jerome and Pagan Greek Literature,' *VigChr* 36 (1982), 372-382. For more general information cf. H. Hagendahl, *Cristianesimo e cultura classica,* Rome, 1988, 165-171.

involved him in a maelstrom of emotional conflict ending only with his death.[5] It was a love/hate relationship with the culture which was basically an acute psychological schizophrenia, issuing in the famous "dream" which he had in the desert of Chalcis or at Antioch,[6] recounted some time later in a letter to the virgin Eustochium.[7] In it, as in a nightmare, the Supreme Judge appeared to Jerome accusing him of being a "Ciceronian," not a "Christian," and punished him severely, making him promise that henceforth he would not read "profane texts."

At Rome, even though totally given over to a life rich in juvenile escapades which he later recorded with frustrating remorse and burning nostalgic desire for a time,[8] Jerome made important friendships like that with Rufinus of Aquileia;[9] he deepened his readings, even of Christian authors, he was involved in an attentive and moving visit to the catacombs;[10] at Rome, finally he received baptism. From Rome he went to Trier, an ideal city for a young man who was ambitious and perhaps desirous of entering upon a career in administration, for this was still the location of the preferred residence of the imperial court.[11]

---

[5] Cf. J. Steinmann, *op. cit.*, 23.

[6] On the place where the dream of Jerome occurred cf.C. A. Rapisarda, 'Ciceronianus es non Christianus. Dove e quando avvenne il sogno di S. Gerolamo?', *Miscellanea di Studi di Letteratura Cristiana Antica* 4 (1954),1-18; P. Antin, 'Autour du songe de Saint Jérôme,' in *idem, Recueil sur Saint Jérôme*, 71-100.

[7] Cf. the famous *Letter 22 Ad Eustochium*, 30: CSEL 54,189-191. For English translation: C.C. Mierow, *The Letters of St. Jerome, vol. i, Letters 1-22*, ACW 33, Westminster, MD, 1963,134-179; Italian translation cf. *San Gerolamo. Lettere*, int. by C. Moreschini, trans. by R. Palla, Milan, 1989, 163-167.

[8] *Letter 22 Ad Eustochium, 7:* CSEL 54,152-154 (ACW 33, 139-140, trans., C.C. Mierow).

[9] Rufinus was born at Concordia, near Aquileia, around 345. After his sojourn for studies at Rome and a brief ascetical experience in the community at Aquileia he departed for the Orient, settling in Jerusalem in the monastery on Mount Olivet. On his return to the West he was involved in Origenist polemics which also caused the rupture in his friendship with the young Jerome. Following the invasion of the Goths he fled to Sicily, where he died in 410. The literary activity of Rufinus is represented by numerous translations of Greek works (apart from *De Principiis* and numerous Homilies of Origen, the *Ecclesiastical History* of Eusebius), and their merit, more than on the aesthetic speculative plane, should be sought in their undoubtedly mediating role between East and West. For further information, J. Gribomont, 'Le traduzioni. Girolamo e Rufino,' in J. Quasten, *Patrologia* III, Casale Monferrato, 1973, 234-240.

[10] Jerome records with emotion the sentiments he experienced in his visit to the catacombs in his *Commentary on Ezekiel*, written at the age of over 75. Cf. C. Moreschini, *San Gerolamo, op. cit.*, 73.

[11] On motives for the sojourn at Trier, cf. J.N.D. Kelly, *op. cit.*, 25-30.

Here in all likelihood Jerome began to be attracted to that ideal of ascetical monasticism which was circulating in the West,[12] so much so that, after an interlude of a brief sojourn in a small ascetic community formed at Aquileia under the influence of bishop Valerian,[13] who had come from the East, he stopped first at Antioch because of an illness, and then retired to the solitude of the desert of Chalcis, in northern Syria. In Jerome's intentions the eremitical life was not merely the occasion for the spiritual development of his own desire to renounce "the world," but also the ideal setting in which to devote himself to the study of Sacred Scripture. It was in the desert, in fact, that Jerome reached the decision to undertake the study of Hebrew, not without toil and difficulty,[14] and in the East also he perfected his knowledge of Greek, becoming an example, not merely rare but unique, of "trilingualism" in the late Antique world.

After a period of about two years, disappointed and disturbed by theological controversies of the so-called Antioch schism[15] from which not even the tranquil life of the monks in the desert could distract him, Jerome betook himself to Chalcis to return once more to Antioch in 379 where he was ordained a priest by bishop Paulinus, without however, having to assume the related obligations and to renounce the ascetic ideal. At Antioch he had contacts with Apollinaris of Laodicea, a famous exegete of that time,[16] and he dedi-

---

[12] On Western monasticism cf. S. Pricoco, 'Aspetti culturali del primo monachesimo d'Occidente,' in *Tradizione dei Classici. Trasformazioni della Cultura* (Società Romana e Impero Tardoantico, IV), a cura di A. Giardina, Bari, 1986, 189-204 and 274-282 (notes).

[13] Cf. Kelly, *op. cit.*, 30-35.

[14] On Jerome as *vir trilinguis* see A. Kamesar, *Jerome, Greek Scholarship, and the Hebrew Bible*, Oxford University Press, 1993. Letter 125,12: CSEL 56,131.

[15] By the term "Schism of Antioch" is designated that series of complicated events by which, between 327 and circa 482 there were counterposed, often with exasperated fanaticism, Arians, Orthodox of the faith of Nicaea, and Orthodox who had not completely broken with the less extreme Arians. At the time of Jerome's sojourn in the desert, the struggle flared up between bishop Meletius, somewhat open to the Arian moderates, and bishop Paulinus, the defender of the creed of Nicaea. On the experience in the desert of Calchis cf. in particular, P. Monceaux, 'St. Jérôme au désert de Syrie,' *Revue des Deux Mondes* 58 (1930), 136-157 and 377-394.

[16] On the exegetical activity of Apollinaris of Laodicea see M. Simonetti, *Lettera e/o allegoria*, Rome, 1985, 130-132. In particular, on his relations with Jerome, cf. P. Jay, 'Jérôme auditeur d'Apollinaire de Laodicée à Antioche,' *REAug* 20 (1974), 36-41.

cated himself to drafting some works.[17] Between 379 and 380 he transferred to Constantinople where he knew Gregory of Nazianzus,[18] deriving profit from his teaching, while at the same time beginning his own activity of translating by composing a Latin version of the *Chronicle* of Eusebius of Caesarea.[19]

In 382 Jerome availed himself of an opportunity to return to Rome in the retinue of Paulinus and Epiphanius of Salamis to par-

---

[17] The composition of the *Life of Paul*, an early hermit, predecessor of Antony, goes back to this period. Let us recall in this connection that Jerome also wrote the *Life of Hilarion* and the *Life of Malchus*, other eremitical figures. It is less certain whether in this same period Jerome had composed his first polemical work: *Dialogue between a Luciferian and an Orthodox*, in which he attacked the extremist positions of Lucifer of Cagliari, an inveterate upholder of the Nicene creed who remained hostile to the least opening to the heretics whom he judged by the same standards as pagans.

[18] Gregory of Nazianzus (329-390), with Basil of Caesarea and Gregory of Nyssa is considered one of the great Fathers of the Greek Church. A profound theologian, author of the famous Five Theological Orations against the Arians, preached at Constantinople, Gregory of Nazianzus is also the greatest Christian poet in the Greek language. Among his *carmina*, on biblical or moral themes, an autobiographical poem *De vita sua* is prominent; also noteworthy is an anthology of passages from Origen, edited with Basil of Caesarea for purposes of mystical edification, the *Philocalia*. On relations between Jerome and Gregory Nazianzus cf. C. Moreschini, 'Praeceptor meus. Tracce dell'insegnamento di Gregorio Nazianzeno in Gerolamo,' in *Jérôme entre l'Occident et l'Orient. Actes du Colloque de Chantilly (septembre 1986)* publiés par Y.M. Duval, Paris, 1988, 129-138. [See now: P.M. Beagan, 'The Cappadocian Fathers, Women and Ecclesiastical Politics,' *VigChr* 49 (1995), 165-179.]

[19] Eusebius of Caesarea can be considered "together with Origen the greatest philologist in the early Church" (M. Simonetti, *La Letteratura Cristiana Antica Greca e Latina*, Florence-Milan, 1969, 211). Born around 265 his teacher was Pamphilus, with whom he collaborated on a systematization of the library of Origen. During the persecution of Diocletian he fled to Egypt, but could not evade arrest or avoid prison, where he spent time until the edict of religious tolerance, in 311. Elected bishop of Caesarea in 313, he was involved in the Arian controversy sympathizing at first with the heretics. In 325 he was actually excommunicated by a synod of Antioch, but participated in the Council of Nicaea and by subscribing to the condemnation of Arius won his rehabilitation. After the Council he continued however to support the Arian faction by deposing bishops of the Nicene faith. Closely connected to the emperor Constantine in writing his *Life*, he exalted politics in favor of the Church. He died around 339. Among his works we should mention: Apologetical: *Praeparatio evangelica*, *Demonstratio evangelica*; erudite Scripture commentaries: *Evangelical Canons*, *Onomasticon*, a biblical gazeteer; *Gospel Questions and Answers*; Commentary on the *Psalms*; Historical works: *Chronicon* (surviving in the translation of Jerome and continued down to 378, with additional notes on Roman history and literature); the *Ecclesiastical History*, in 10 books, relating Church events from its beginnings down to 324, the year of the definitive declaration of Constantine following the defeat of Licinius. Cf. C.Curti, 'Eusebio,' in DPAC, 1, coll. 1285-1293.On the political theology of Eusebius see R. Farina, *L'impero e l'imperatore cristiano di Eusebio di Cesarea*, Zürich, 1966 and more recently S. Calderone, 'Eusebio e l'ideologia imperiale,' in M. Mazza/C. Giuffrida (edd.), *Le trasformazioni della cultura nella Tarda Antichità, 1*, Rome, 1985, 1-26.

ticipate in a synod convened by pope Damasus.[20] At Rome Jerome won the confidence and esteem of the pope, becoming his personal secretary and expert on biblical matters. This second stay in Rome was undoubtedly the happiest and most gratifying period in Jerome's life but also the most turbulent because of the endless frictions between himself and the envious clerical ambience frequently hostile in dealings with the new papal secretariat.

Notwithstanding the misunderstandings which greatly intensified after the death of pope Damasus, at Rome Jerome could assiduously pursue those ideals which were always to the forefront in his aspirations: asceticism and the study of Sacred Scripture. Jerome's ascetic propaganda found a response in fact among a group of noble women who were in the habit of assembling in a "domestic church" organized by the widow Marcella in her stately residence on the Aventine.[21] Outstanding among the group were other women, who belonged to the Roman aristocracy, like Paula and her two daughters, Eustochium and Blesilla, the widow Lea, and the virgin Asella. To all of them Jerome sent important letters which reveal their writer as a master of exegesis and asceticism but also as a sincere friend, a trusted spiritual and cultural guide, a studious person delighted to

---

[20] Damasus (304-384) was a deacon under pope Liberius. His episcopal succession underwent no few contests, in that his opponents supported the deacon Ursinus, and tumults and violent encounters ensued between the two factions. It climaxed between 366 and 368 and the emperor himself, Valentinianus, was constrained to intervene. The tensions never ceased at all since even from exile Ursinus continued his intrigues and a penal process was directed against the pontiff by one Isaac, a Jewish convert of the capital. On all aspects of the pontificate of Damasus cf. the basic work, in two volumes of Ch. Pietri, *Roma Christiana. Recherches sur l'Eglise de Rome, (311-440)*, Rome, 1976, particularly chapters VI-X of volume I. For Damasus's cultural interests, testified to by the Epigrams in verse, see A. Ferrua, *Epigrammata Damasiana*, Città del Vaticano, 1942 (also a critical re-evaluation of them, on the esthetic-cultural plane in J. Fontaine, 'Damase poète théodosien,' in Aa. vv., *Saeculiaria Damasiana*, Città del Vaticano, 1986, 113-145).

[21] On what can be rightly called "the Hieronyman group on the Aventine" cf. G.D. Gordini, 'Origine e sviluppo del monachesimo a Roma,' *Gregorianum* 37 (1956), 220-260; S. Jannaccone, 'Roma 384. (Struttura sociale e spirituale del gruppo geronimiano),' in *Giornale italiano di Filologia* 19 (1966), 32-48; V A. Sirago, *Cicadae noctium. Quando le donne furono monache e pellegrine*, Soveria Mannelli (CZ) 1986, 93-110; F.E. Consolino, 'Modelli di comportamento e modi di santificazione per l'aristocrazia femminile d'Occidente,' in A. Giardina (ed.), *Società Romana e Impero Tardoantico, 1, Istituzioni Ceti Economie*, Bari, 1986, 273-306 and 684-699 (notes).

find among these women keen intellectual endowments.[22] After the death of Damasus, which occurred in 384, his enemies rekindled calumnies in their dealings with Jerome, accusing him of remaining close to a number of women with intentions less elevated and spiritual than were appropriate.[23] In 385 he was forced to depart for Palestine whither he was shortly followed by Paula, one of his most devoted friends during his sojourn at Rome, together with her daughter, Eustochium. The visit to the holy places preceded a definitive stay in Bethlehem where in 386 Jerome and Paula dedicated their lives to monastic communities, one for men and three for women. Here Jerome remained permanently until his death, September 30, 420, dedicated, on the one hand, in tranquillity to his beloved studies, to his writing activities, and, on the other, to resisting the numerous threatening attacks on the part of bands of heretics, barbarians and brigands.

It is not possible to give an exhaustive account here of his multiform literary productions; it must suffice to give an outline of the various typologies of his numerous works and to enter into some detail on a few of them.

The divisions of Jerome's scholarly activities are basically three: (i) translations; (ii) polemical doctrinal works; and (iii) biblical commentaries. Among the translations, apart from the *Chronicle* of Eusebius of Caesarea which has been mentioned already, should be mentioned those of some works of Origen (*Homilies on Jeremiah*, *Homilies on Ezekiel*, *Homilies on the Canticle of Canticles*, *Homilies on Luke*, *On First Principles*) as well as the treatise of Didymus the Blind, *On the Holy Spirit*. Among the polemical treatises (*Against Helvidius*, *Against Jovinian*, *Against Vigilantius*, *Against John of Jerusalem*, *Against Rufinus*, and *Dialogue against the Pelagians*) Jerome gives more frequent displays of his verbal violence, pungent satire which annihilated his

---

[22] On these aspects of the relationship which bound Jerome to the group of aristocratic Roman women even though on occasion suffering from observations of questionable acceptability, M. Turcan, 'Saint Jérôme et les femmes,' *Bulletin de l'Association G. Budé*, 63 (1968), 259-272.

[23] On the malicious calumnies directed against him Jerome himself writes in epistle 45 *ad Asellam*, CSEL 54,243-257.

adversary without leaving any possibility of replying,[24] than of his acuteness and theological preparation.

Of particular importance, in that they offer a systematic defence of the ascetic ideals, are his *Against Helvidius* and *Against Jovinian*. Helvidius, a Roman layman, possibly a disciple of the Arian bishop, Auxentius,[25] had published a work in which he denied the perpetual virginity of Mary, maintaining that after the birth of Jesus she had other children by Joseph. Helvidius' work clearly conflicted with the defence of the practice of virginity by asserting the absolute parity of virginity and marriage as a result of the non-perpetual virginity of Mary. Jerome's reaction to Helvidius' thesis naturally aimed at correcting, on the one hand, his adversary's scriptural interpretations, and reestablishing Mary's perpetual virginity, and, on the other, reaffirming the superiority of virginity over the married state. Jerome's *Against Helvidius* is distinguished not so much for the profundity of its theological arguments as for the caustic tones in which the Dalmatian unmasked the hypocrisy of the "false virgins," the violence with which he condemned the worldliness of so many monks, and the pungent satire with which he depicted matrimony in a bad light, considering it at a lower level than virginity.[26]

Similar tones characterize the *Contra Jovinianum*, even if the artistic result is undoubtedly superior. The person against whom Jerome wrote is scarcely known in that his writings are completely lost. He was a monk who propagated a certain type of monasticism, less extreme than that of Jerome who described him in polemical terms as "an Epicurean with rounded belly," a man dedicated to, and

---

[24] See P. Jay, 'Combien Jérôme a-t-il traduit d'homélies d'Origène?', *Stud Pat* 23, 133-137. The studies of D. S. Wiesen, *St. Jerome as a Satirist. A Study in Christian Thought and Letters*, Ithaca-New York, 1964; I. Opelt, *Hieronymus' Streitschriften*, Heidelberg, 1973 are fundamental.

[25] Auxentius, Arian bishop of Durostorum, was forced to leave his own see following the regulations of Theodosius against ecclesiastics in sympathy with Arius. In 382 he sought refuge in Milan, where he was nominated bishop of the Arian community, entering into conflict with Ambrose on the question of the restoration of the basilica to the Arians.

[26] On *Contra Elvidium* cf. A. Casamassa, 'L'Adversus Helvidium di S. Girolamo,' *La Scuola Cattolica* 48 (1920), 225-235 and 326-340 (republished in A. Casamassa, *Scritti Patristici*, 1, Rome, 1955, 67-88). Italian translation: E. Camisani (ed.), *Opere scelte di San Girolamo*, 1, *Uomini Illustri, Vita di S. Paolo eremita, Contro Elvidio, Lettere e omilie*, Turin, 1971, also see now M.I. Danieli, *La perenne Verginità di Maria*, in CTP n. 70.

for this reason proving to be very acceptable to, the most corrupt circles in Rome.[27] Jovinian in reality emphasized the salvific power of baptism, discredited the more extreme forms of asceticism and fasting, and placed virgins, widows, and married women, provided that their conduct was honorable, on the same level. Jovinian's message made quite a lot of inroads in Roman circles, even on some consecrated virgins;[28] it is understandable, then, how immediate the response of the champions of extreme asceticism had to be. Jovinian and eight of his followers were condemned by a synod of Rome convoked by pope Siricius, and also later by the church of Milan, as a letter of St. Ambrose attests.[29]

Two other polemical works of Jerome — his *Against John of Jerusalem* (in 396) and the *Apology against Rufinus* (401/402) — were issued at the height of the so-called Origenist controversy, which broke out in the East at the end of the 4th century. In 393, in fact, Epiphanius, the bishop of Salamis in Cyprus, who called for the condemnation of Origen and of his ideas regarded as heretical, found himself in opposition to a defender of Origen's views. Jerome, who up to that time was a convinced Origenist, lined up with the side of Epiphanius, while the friend of his youth, Rufinus of Aquileia, was unwilling to subscribe to the act of faith against Origen which a certain Atarbius had directed to him in his monastery in Palestine.[30] The following year, his brother, Paulinianus, was ordained a priest by an act which was within the competence of the bishop of Jerusalem for jurisdiction; the latter, in resentment, called for the expulsion from Bethlehem of the monastic community to which Jerome belonged. The measure was not enforced but John of Jerusalem, in

---

[27] The text of *Contra Jovinianum* is published in PL 25 211-338. On the personality and ideas of Jovinian cf. F. Valli, 'Un eretico del secolo IV, Gioviniano,' *Didaskaleion* 2 (1924), 1-66 and idem, *Gioviniano. Esame delle fonti e dei frammenti*, Urbino 1954. [Engl. ed. See now: B. Clausi, 'La Parola stravolta. Polemica ed esegesi biblica nell' "Adversus Iovinianum" di Gerolamo,' *Vetera Christianorum* 32 (1995), 21-60.]

[28] Cf. e.g. what Augustine says in *Retractationes* II, 22: BAug 12, 488-489.

[29] Cf. Ambrose, Letter 42 (according to the numeration of the Maurists = 15, Outside the Collection), in CSEL 14: BA 21, 332-333.

[30] On the question of Origenism, apart from H. Crouzel, art. 'Origenismo,' DPAC, II, 2533-2538 (with the basic bibliographical references) cf. also *Atti del XIV Incontro di Studiosi dell'Antichità Cristiana su L'Origenismo: Apologie e Polemiche intorno ad Origene*, AugR 26 (1986), fascicles 1 and 2.

no way resigned, turned to Theophilus, bishop of Alexandria, sending him a letter in which he accused both Jerome and Epiphanius of schism, and defended the orthodoxy of Origen. It was in response to this accusation that Jerome wrote his *Against John of Jerusalem,* in which he defended the activity of Epiphanius, refuted the theses of Origen injurious to orthodoxy, and turned the charge of schism against the bishop of Jerusalem himself. In 397 a truce seemed to put an end to this odious and far from edifying event: John, Jerome and Rufinus were publicly reconciled, but it was a fire of straw destined to blaze again a short time later.[31] Rufinus had returned to Rome and had translated the *De Principiis* of Origen, seeking to purge the more incriminating passages and invoking especially, in defence of the orthodoxy of the Alexandrian, the authority of Jerome himself. Jerome produced another more literal translation — unfortunately lost — and wrote a resentful letter to Rufinus in which he urged him not to defend his own opinions in the guise of others'.[32] Meanwhile in 400 pope Anastasius I, in a synod at Rome, condemned the teachings of Origen, presumed heretical, ratifying the condemnation which had already been sanctioned by bishop Theophilus of Alexandria in the East. Rufinus then tried to reply, writing an *Apology against Jerome.* The latter very quickly reduced to silence one who had been a sincere friend in his first sojourn at Rome.

The name of Jerome is commonly linked, less to his fiery polemical disputes, than to that immense task of the revision of the biblical text, and the related translation into Latin which constitutes the well-known *Vulgate.* The activity of the biblical scholar was initiated in Rome, perhaps as an assignment from pope Damasus himself, and was continued in the busy tranquillity of the monastery at Bethlehem. At Rome he reviewed the old Latin translations of the Gospels, comparing them with the Greek text, making some corrections, and selecting the textual readings which he considered supe-

---

[31] Cf. F. Cavallera, *op. cit.,* I, 227

[32] Cf. Letter 81,1-2: CSEL 55, 106-107. An Italian translation of this and all the letters of Jerome: S. Cola, *San Girolamo Le Lettere,* Rome, 1961-1963 in 4 volumes. On the polemic between Rufinus and Jerome with regaard to the Latin version of the *De Principiis* of Origen cf. G. Sfameni Gasparro, 'Aspetti della controversia origeniana: le traduzioni latine del *Peri Archon,*' *AugR* 26 (1986), 191-205.

rior; he also reviewed the text of the Psalms producing that version called the "Roman Psalter" in use in the Basilica of St. Peter.[33]

Jerome, having returned to the East after the events narrated above, had occasion to consult the most famous work of biblical philology in Christian antiquity, the *Hexapla* of Origen. This convinced him that it was impossible in the case of the Old Testament to confine himself to a synopsis of the Greek text, but that it would be indispensable to refer to the Hebrew text, which he loved to define as the *veritas hebraica*. Jerome's translation of the Old Testament, conducted on the basis of the Hebrew canon, had not an immediate success, also by the resistance which was offered by eminent exponents of culture, as, for example, Augustine,[34] but gradually it succeeded in gaining entrance to liturgical usage.

Closely connected with his work of translating was that of his commenting on the biblical texts. Jerome's most important exegetical work is the *Commentary on the Prophets*, both the major and the minor ones. Worthy of mention also are the commentaries *On Ecclesiastes, On the Psalms,* and *On Matthew,* as well as those on certain epistles of Paul (*On Philemon, On Galatians, On Titus*). In particular the three books, *Commentary on the Epistle to the Ephesians,* were composed between 387 and 388 to respond to requests, including those from Paula and Eustochium, and the noble Marcella.[35] In his scripture interpretation, in this and in his other commentaries on Paul, Jerome was strongly influenced by the exegesis of Origen,[36]

---

[33] Cf. J. Gribomont, 'Le Traduzioni,' *op.cit.*, 212-213. This chapter has an exhaustive treatment of all the works of Jerome (203-233).

[34] Augustine was convinced that he should continue to favor the Septuagint version considered in tradition as inspired, and to abandon which could upset the faithful. There developed a lively exchange of letters between Augustine and Jerome on the question.

[35] Cf. *Commentarius ad Ephesianos* prologus: PL 26, col. 439. For more detailed notices on the exegetical commentaries on the Epistles of St. Paul, cf. J.N.D. Kelly, *op. cit.*, 144-149.

[36] On the criteria of exegesis in Jerome see especially: A. Penna, *Principi e caratteri dell'esegesi di S. Gerolamo,* Rome, 1950; M. Simonetti, *Lettera e/o allegoria, op. cit.,* 321-337 (in particular on the influence of Origen on the commentaries of Paul, p. 322); P. Jay, 'Saint Jérôme et le triple sens de l'Écriture,' *REAug* 26 (1980), 214-227; P. Jay, 'Jérôme et la pratique de l'exégèse,' in J. Fontaine and Ch. Pietri (edd.), *Le monde latin antique et la Bible,* Paris, 1985, 523-541.

which is easily demonstrable, among other reasons by the other exegetical writings; it suffices here to mention that *On Ecclesiastes*.[37] It is moreover true that the influence of the allegorical exegesis of Origen became slack with the passage of time, in Jerome, not so much, or certainly not only, through adhering to the condemnation of the Alexandrian, as through an ever stronger emergence of philological-grammatical and geographical-antiquarian[38] interests which directed him naturally to a type of exegesis more attentive to the "literal" meaning of the sacred text. A value judgment on the work of Jerome as translator and exegete is not called for here, even though much has been written and sometimes rightly on the hurried nature, the lack of organization, and the unequal quality of his various compositions. But despite the areas of light and of darkness in his character, which we have tried to highlight in this brief profile, despite the limited, but coherent insistence on themes connected with virginity, to renunciation of temporal goods, to asceticism, Jerome has undoubtedly merited to have given flesh to a new figure of the monk, culturally *engagé*, contributing in this way "more than anyone else to modelling Western monasticism and because of that to the history of late antique and medieval Europe."[39]

A feminist, in the undoubtedly exaggerated judgment of Marie Turcan,[40] a misogynist in the judgment of the greater part of scholars too attentive, perhaps, to the literal sense of his statements uttered in a polemical or parenetic context, Jerome offers in the pages which are presented here a timid but clear signal of an opening toward Christian conjugal union. The denunciation, albeit tepid, was

---

[37] Cf. S. Leanza, *L'Esegesi di Origene al Libro dell'Ecclesiaste*, Reggio Calabria, 1975, 56-68 and more recently, S. Leanza, 'Sulle fonti del *Commentario all'Ecclesiaste* di Girolamo,' *Annali di Storia dell'Esegesi* 3 (1986), 173-199.

[38] Cf. C. Moreschini, *San Gerolamo, Lettere, op. cit.*, 70-71.

[39] Cf. S. Pricoco, *art. cit.* p.1058. The works of Jerome are published in PL 22-30. Some of the exegetical and polemical works have appeared in CCL 72-79; important editions of the Epistles in CSEL 54-56; *Commentary on Matthew* in SC 242, 259; *Comm. on Jonah*, SC 323, *Apology against Rufinus*, SC 303.

[40] See M. Turcan, "St. Jérôme et les femmes,' *art. cit.*, esp. 272; G.J. Campbell, 'St. Jerome's Attitude toward Marriage and Women,' *American Ecclesiastical Review* 143 (1960), 310-320, 384-394. [Engl. ed. Add: J. Oppel, 'Saint Jerome and the History of Sex,' *Viator* 24 (1993), 1-22.]

certainly outside the ordinary, which he made of the unjust submission to which the woman was submitted in her dealings with the man to whom on the ethical level she was far superior. Society, be it pagan or Christian, remained radically tied to male prejudices: Jerome could only inoculate his own doubts, immediately shaded in the symbolism of allegorical exegesis.

LOVE AND FEAR IN THE CHRISTIAN COUPLE

25

(vv. 22,23) *Let wives be submissive to their husbands as to the Lord: the husband is the head of his wife as Christ is head of the Church.*

The expression which has been added in the Latin text — *let them be submissive* — is not found in the Greek codices, seeing that it refers to what is immediately preceding, and is overheard: *and be subject in turn out of reverence for Christ,*[a] so that the term *be submissive* is understood by zeugma[1] we have the reading: *and wives to their husbands as to the Lord.* But this is more clearly understood in the Greek than in the Latin *As the Church,* then, *is submissive to Christ, so the wife should be submissive to her husband.* Husband and wife should be bound to the same relationship as that of Christ as head and the Church as subject.

It should be seen that in the same way as a holy union is formed between Christ and the Church a similar bond can be formed between husband and wife.

But just as every congregation of heretics cannot be called the church of Christ, nor is Christ their head, so not every marriage, in that the wife is not united to her husband according to the precepts of Christ, can be defined as matrimony in the full sense, but rather as adultery.

Besides, the wife is subjected to her husband as to her lord, since *your desire shall be for your husband, and he shall rule over you.*[b] And Sarah also called Abraham her *lord,*[c] but this spontaneous service, insofar as it is undertaken voluntarily, tends to make itself into equality: no, more, by virtue of her services, she makes her ruler into her servant.

---

[a] Eph 5:21   [b] cf. Gn 3:16   [c] cf. Gn 18:12; 1 P 3:6

[1] The observations of a "philological" character on the text and of a rhetorico-grammatical character (for the figure of zeugma — which consists in referring to two elements a term that grammatically refers to one of them only — cf. H. Lausberg, *Elementi di retorica*, Bologna, 1969, 172-176) are a clear indication of how Jerome did not totally neglect exegesis of the type known as "literal," even in a text where the influence of the allegorism of Origen strongly prevailed.

Some interpret this citation in an allegorical sense, in which the wife is meant to be a symbol of the body, and the husband a symbol of the soul. And just as the Church is submissive to Christ, so bodies ought to be submissive to intellect and be reduced to one only spirit: *whoever is joined to the Lord becomes one spirit with him*.[d]...

> v. 24 *As the Church submits to Christ, so wives should submit to their husbands in everything.*

...If, in fact the wife ought to be submissive to the husband as the church to Christ, between husband and wife there ought to be a holy union and they will not be slaves of passion.

If someone objects then that the Epistle to the Corinthians says that the husband should fulfill his conjugal obligations to his wife, and the wife hers toward her husband,[e] it should be borne in mind that there is a great difference between the Epistle to the Corinthians and the Epistle to the Ephesians. To the former he writes as if to children[2] or rather infants at the breast[f] among whom there were quarrels[g] and divisions, and people guilty of fornication worse, even, than that among the gentiles. For this reason it was granted to them to return to one another, after a time for prayer, lest they be tempted by Satan[h] but immediately after this in the same epistle it is made clear that this is not a command which was directed at them but a concession.[i]

The Ephesians, however, among whom he spent a period of three years and to whom he revealed all the mysteries of Christ, have been instructed differently, and let each person have his own freedom of choice, whether to follow the example of the Corinthians or the Ephesians, whether to be saved in the servitude of the Corinthians or in the liberty of the Ephesians. *Woe*, says the Savior, *to the*

---

[d] 1 Cor 6:17   [e] cf. 1 Cor 7:3   [f] cf. 1 Cor 3:1   [g] cf. 1 Cor 3:3   [h] cf. 1 Cor 7:5   [i] cf. 1 Cor 7:6

[2] The anthropological division into "perfect" and "more simple" Christians which is replicated on the exegetical level into the two senses of scripture — the literal and the spiritual — is a motive which, beginning with Origen, has widely permeated patristic exegesis. Also the sucklings/ mature men image finds a very characteristc confirmation in the exegetic tradition; cf. C. Magazzù, *Tecnica esegetica nei "Commentarii super Cantica Ecclesiastica" di Verecondo di Junca*, Messina, 1983, 33.

women who are pregnant or nursing at the breast in those days,[j] referring to the day of judgment and in particular to those situations
proper to marriage.

There is need then to strive to imitate the Ephesians rather
than the Corinthians. Let us take care not to be surprised, as at the
time of the flood, in the course of buying and selling, marrying and
being given in marriage,[k] but let us hold the lights burning in our
hands and have our waists belted around.[l]

> v. 25 And you, *husbands, love your wives as Christ loved the
> Church. He gave himself up for her to make her holy, purifying
> her in the bath of water by the power of the word, to present to
> himself a glorious Church without stain or wrinkle or anything of
> that sort, but holy and immaculate.*

Although a husband and wife are bound in mutual love (we
recall the example of the wife of Hasdrubal who, after the capture of
her husband, cast herself into the flames of the city together with all
the other women who did not want to survive the death of their
husbands),[3] however a wise man will never compare such an affection to that which binds Christ and the Church. Certainly he ought
to hold her in veneration with a love like that of Isaac for his wife
Rebekah, which is interpreted Patience. From Mesopotamia,[4] which

---

[j] Lk 21:23   [k] cf. Mt 24:38   [l] cf. Lk 12:35

[3] Jerome uses as an example of "reciprocal affection" an episode from the Third Punic War
related to the destruction of Carthage. Hasdrubal had organized extraordinary resistance
against the Roman troops under Scipio Emilianus and, effectively, Carthage fought at length
with the strength that comes from desperation. In the Spring of 146 B.C., the Romans pen-
etrated the besieged city and fought for six days in the streets, shedding an enormous amount
of blood. When the situation was already beyond saving, Hasdrubal fled to surrender himself to the victors in order to save his life, at least according to the account of the affair in the
historical records of those most hostile to him (especially the historian Polybius, *Hist.* 38, 1-
2). Indignant over the cowardice of her husband, his wife let herself be killed along with the
last defenders of the city in the flames of the temple of Eshmun, the last defensive bulwark
of the, by now, dying city of Carthage. As we see, Jerome provides us with a positive version which, if well adapted to the wives of other defenders, is not so certainly applicable —
if one takes into account the ancient sources — to the wife of Hasdrubal. For the essential
facts cf. *Oxford Classical Dictionary* s.v. 'Hasdrubal' [4].

[4] The symbolism of Mesopotamia as the kingdom of evil is from the matrix of Origen, parallel
to that of Babylon interpreted as "confusion" (cf. *Homilies on Ezekiel* I, 3) or, on the other
hand — much more frequently — of Egypt, a figure of the terrestrial world as a place of the
manifestation of demoniac power and at the same time as body *qua* prey of the passions.
See, among many instances, the developments on the theme in *Homilies on Genesis* XV-
XVI.

is girded on all sides by the floods of this world, he introduced her to the Promised Land to console himself for the death of his mother.[m] Similarly the Church consoles Christ for the death of the Synagogue.

With these assertions we give an opportunity to those heretics who maintain that marriages should be completely repudiated and use as a proof especially those words of Paul. To these we must briefly respond that the Apostle here prohibits between husband and wife passions, indecency and luxury, but not legitimate embraces. Otherwise, if he had prohibited the marriage embrace altogether, what need would there be to say: *Your wives*, when he could have said, Men, love women, or wives? For *your* is properly applicable to marriage. And again in the words that follow: *and men ought to love their own wives as their own bodies:*[n] and further on, even more pointedly, *he who loves his own wife loves himself. For no one ever hates his own flesh but nourishes and cherishes it,*[o] because according to what the law of old has inaugurated and the Gospel has ratified, husband and wife become one flesh.

In marriage, then, as we have said, sexual activity that is directed toward the procreation of children is admissible. In the case of a wife, however, the pleasures which are received from the embraces of prostitutes are condemned. Reading this, let every husband and every wife understand that after conception there is need to dedicate themselves more to prayer than to conjugal relations. And what in the case of animals and beasts is prescribed by the law of nature itself, that there be no sexual advances to the pregnant, let them know that in the case of humans they are left with freedom of choice so that they may gain merit from abstaining from pleasures. Because according to the allegorical interpretation we have said that men are souls and wives bodies, so let the soul love the flesh (or body), as Christ the Church, that she may lay down her life for his salvation, and he sanctify her by the word of teaching, so that she may present her to himself not having any stain or wrinkle of age: especially let him know that she must be saved on the day of resurrection and shall see the salvation of God.[p]

---

[m] cf. Gn 24:67   [n] Eph 5:28   [o] Eph 5:29   [p] cf. Lk 3:6

Such a husband has Christ for his head and when, humbling himself for the salvation of the flesh, he will have been made with his wife one flesh, he leads her back to the spirit and, united to the Lord, she ceases to be flesh.[5]

Because he was speaking of matrimony, the Apostle has adapted in an opportune manner to the aspect of the Church, the motive of stains and wrinkles, elements that are typically female. For just as women are always concerned to clean off from their bodies what might seem to deface, and to display beauty of countenance to their husbands: so also souls must be purged of all the uncleanliness of sins, so that the wrinkles of the old man may be rejuvenated and renewed into the new man from day to day.[q]

v. 28 *Even so husbands should love their wives as their own bodies.*

And in Genesis, in the person of Adam speaking to his wife, it is written: *This at last is bone of my bones and flesh of my flesh.*[r] And, similarly, in the gospel, it is confirmed by the Lord himself speaking: *He who made them from the beginning, made them male and female, and He said: on account of this a man shall leave his father and mother and be joined to his wife, and they shall be two in one flesh.*[s] Since, therefore, husbands and wives may be taken to be one flesh, so we should make provision for our wives as for our own bodies. No one, however, loves his own body in a foul way or loves himself in a coital manner, but, as if it were the vessel of his soul, he cares for his body and nourishes it lest, if the vase be broken, the soul which it contains flow forth and be spilled.

Furthermore, however: according to the literal interpretation, for as long as the wife is in the service of childbirth and of caring for children, she is as different from her husband as the body is from the soul. If, however, she prefers to become a servant of Christ than of

---

[q] cf. 2 Cor 4:6   [r] Gn 2:23   [s] Mt 19:4-5

---

[5] On this theme, yet once more of Origenian imprint, cf. the General Introduction, pp. 86-88.

the secular sphere, she ceases to be a woman (*mulier*) and is called a man (*vir*), since we all aspire to the condition of perfect manhood.[t]

If we further interpret it also in an allegorical manner we will love our body and the senses, regarding them however at a lower value than the spirit, but however as a path by which the practice of good deeds and of virtue arrive at the soul.

> v. 29 *He who loves his wife loves himself. Observe that no one ever hates his own flesh, no, he nourishes it and takes care of it as Christ did the Church.*

As to the simplest meaning, that is, the literal, what the Apostle says refers to the proper bond of love between husband and wife; the husband is bound to nourish and care for his spouse, making provision for what she eats and wears and all her necessities.

If it can be objected that the Apostle does not tell the truth when he says *no one ever hates his own flesh*, since those who are afflicted with leprosy, or, cancer, or running sores, would prefer death and actually hate their own body. But let us refer rather to the allegorical meaning and say that the soul rather loves that flesh which would see the salvation of God, nourishing it, seeing to its education, feeding it on the bread of heaven, bathing it in the blood of Christ, so that it can run freely behind its spouse, pure and reassured, and not be burdened by any infirmity.

In the same way in which Christ nourishes and cares for the Church and, turning to Jerusalem, says: *How often have I yearned to gather your children as a mother bird gathers her young under her wings but you would not.*[u] Let souls therefore cherish their bodies as this corruptibility cherishes incorruptibility and, suspended on the levity of wings, may it be hoisted aloft more easily to the heavens.

Let us husbands therefore care for our wives as our souls care for our bodies, so that women may be transformed into men and bodies into souls. Let there be diversity in no way between the sexes, but as near us the angels do not exist in terms of man and wife, so

---

[t] cf. Eph 4:13   [u] Mt 23:37

we also who are like unto the angels,[v] may commence to be what has been promised that we will become in the life to come.

Then, to exhort husband and wife to reciprocal affection, he treats of the example of Adam and Eve. Just as a rib was taken from the side of Adam and he became recreated in his spouse, and she became reconstructed in one flesh with her husband, because he who loves his wife loves himself, so also let us love our own wives. This statement can refer allegorically to Christ and his Church, who were prefigured in Adam and Eve. The final Adam in fact became a soul endowed with life.[w]

> v. 33 *Let each one of you then love your own wife as you love yourself.*

For it is written in fact, *love your neighbor as yourself,*[x] and here it says, *Let each one of you then love your own wife as you love yourself.* Therefore loving your neighbor and loving your wife would be the same thing.

If, according to what the Savior says, each man constitutes for another man his neighbor, there will be no difference between the sentiment of love which is experienced between man and wife and between one man and another. But to say this is an absurdity. With regard to the neighbor, in fact, the assimilation in fact consists in the fact that you love him as yourself and desire that he be saved. But insofar as it concerns the husband the adverb "as" does not signify likeness, but rather consent and acceptance.[6]...

There is need to pay attention because to the husband it is ordered to love his wife, but the wife is ordered to fear her husband. To the husband in fact love is entrusted, but to the wife, fear, as Paul a little later says: *Slaves, obey your human masters with fear and trembling.*[y]

The woman, however, fears her husband. If fear of God, because

---

[v] cf. Mt 22:30   [w] cf. 1 Cor 15:45   [x] Lv 19:18   [y] Eph 6:5

[6] Conjugal affection certainly implies a relationship of mutual understanding which differentiates it from the generic sentiment of "charity" which ought in any case distinguish the Christian in his relations with his neighbor.

of fear of punishment, disqualifies the one who fears from being perfect, how much more imperfect will be the wife who fears, not only God, but also her husband? Because of this it should be asked whether "wife" and the "fear of a wife" should be understood in a literal sense since frequently wives are found to be much superior to husbands at ordering them, and running the house, and educating the children, and maintaining family discipline: while the husbands live in luxury and pursue mistress after mistress. Whether wives of such caliber should rule, or fear, their husbands, I leave to the reader's judgment.

But if, however, "wife," as we said above, is to be understood allegorically in terms of "body," and "husband" in terms of "soul," then there is nothing incongruous in a wife fearing a husband just like a slave, constituted as she then is of a substance of inferior worth and less importance.

Commentary on the Epistle to the Ephesians, III, 5, PL 26, 530-537

AUGUSTINE

INTRODUCTORY PROFILE

In that it is impossible in a few pages to offer a complete portrait of the human, spiritual and literary events in the life of Augustine, who has been rightly described as "the greatest of the Fathers and one of the outstanding geniuses of the human race,"[1] we invite the reader to be content with a few basic notes, which are intended merely to orient, and not to inform in a comprehensive manner.

Augustine was born at Thagaste, located in present-day Algeria, in 354. His father was Patricius, a landlord of modest means, and his mother, Monica, a fervent Christian, later a saint of the Church. The mother gave him an adequate religious education but not sufficient to prevent the young Augustine from entering a profound inner crisis leading to his adherence to Manicheism of which he was an auditor for nine years.[2] At the age of twenty Augustine began his

---

[1] So Trapè, in 'Agostino' in J. Quasten, *Patrologia, op.cit.*, 325. Among the different biographical profiles of Augustine see, if only for their diverse methodological approaches, P. Brown, *Augustine of Hippo*, London, 1967; A. Trapè, *S. Agostino. L'uomo, il pastore, il mistico*, Fossano, 1976; A. Pincherl, *Vita di Sant'Agostino*, Bari, 1980. For a recent profile of the various stages in the intellectual conversion of Augustine: H. Chadwick, *Augustine*, 1989. A good biographical introduction is that of V. Paronetto, *Agostino. Messaggio di una vita*, Rome, 1981. Because a complete bibliography of Augustine is out of the question,let us indicate a few general studies. See especially *Atti* of recent Conventions, e.g. Aa. vv., *Congresso Internazionale su St. Agostino nel XVI centenario della conversione (Roma 15-20 settembre 1986)*, Rome, 1987, 3 vols.; Aa. vv., *L'umanesimo di Sant'Agostino*, Bari, 1988; Also H.-I. Marrou, *Saint Augustin et la fin de cultura antique*, Paris, 1949²; A. Mandouze, *St. Augustin, L'aventure de la raison et de la grâce*, Paris, 1963; F. van der Meer, *Augustine Pastor of Souls*, ed. orig. Colmar-Paris, 1955; O. Perler, *Les voyages de Saint Augustin*, Paris, 1969. For an excellent synthesis, with bibliography cf. art. 'Agostino,' by M. Marin, DPAC 1, 29-46.

[2] On the hierarchical organization of the Manichean church cf. M. Tardieu, *Il Manicheismo*. Introduzione, traduzione: aggiornamento bibliografico di G. Sfameni Gasparro, Cosenza 1988, 140-145. [Add: S.N.C. Lieu, *Manicheanism in the Later Roman Empire and Medieval China*, Tübingen, 1992.]

teaching career, first as a teacher of grammar at Thagaste (374), then of rhetoric at Carthage (375-383), and finally, after a preliminary period in Rome which he quit after a short period, disillusioned because of his students' failure to pay tuition punctually,[3] he obtained a chair at the governor's court in Milan (384-386). In the years of his early education at Carthage he had a woman friend with whom he lived, unmarried, for fourteen years and by whom he had a son, named Adeodatus.

Whether on the religious or the philosophical plane his sojourn at Milan represented for Augustine a decisive experience and a fundamental prelude to his conversion. Listening to the inspired preaching of Ambrose, inspired in turn by the allegorical exegesis of Origen, opened for him, in fact, the mystic meanings hidden in the Old Testament, a text which initially seemed to him, educated as he was on the limpid prose of Cicero,[4] uncouth on the linguistic-expressive level and unacceptable in its contents.

No less significant was the encounter with the Neoplatonic circle in Milan, since the philosophy of Porphyry and Plotinus represented before all else a stimulus to reflect on himself and on his own soul and enabled him also to overcome the Manichean notions of evil, as ontologically opposed to good, retaining instead a deprivation of good (*privatio boni*).

Also profitable in this period was the knowledge of the monastic literature of ascetic edification and the letters of St. Paul, especially the Epistle to the Romans, centered on the motif of grace. This was the crucial moment of conversion. After a withdrawal to Cassiciacum, the modern Cassaco Brianza,[5] in which he began to write his first philosophical works,[6] Augustine returned to Milan and

---

[3] Cf. *Confessions* V,12,22-13,23: *BAug* 13, 504-507; FOTC 21, 123-125, tr. V.J. Bourke.

[4] On the classical culture of Augustine see M. Testard, *Saint Augustin et Cicéron*, Paris, 1958, 2 vols.; H. Hagendahl, *Augustine and the Latin Classics*, Göteborg, 1967, 2 vols.; J. Pepin, *Ex Platonicorum persona. Études sur les lectures philosophiques de Saint Augustin*, Amsterdam, 1977.

[5] Cf. on the controverted identification of Rus Cassiciacum, S. Colombo, 'Ancora sul Rus Cassiciacum di Agostino,' in Aa.vv., *Agostino e la conversione cristiana*, Palermo, 1987, 85-92.

[6] The early philosophical works: *Against the Academics*, ACW 12 (1950), tr. J.J. O'Meara; *On the Happy Life, On Order, Soliloquies*, FOTC 5 (1948) tr. Schopp, Kavanagh, Russell, Gilligan [see NBA III,1]. On the activity of Augustine at Cassiciacum before his return to Milan and subsequently, cf. Aa. vv., *L'opera letteraria di Agostino tra Cassiciacum e Milano*, Palermo, 1987.

under the guidance of the catecheses of Ambrose prepared himself for baptism which he received from the bishop of Milan himself on the night between 24 and 25 April, 387. By a sudden decision he prepared to return to Africa.

During the return journey, his mother Monica died at Ostia and Augustine then settled for a time in Rome. After about a year he settled down at Thagaste where, together with a group of friends, he dedicated his life in a coenobitic community. In 391, recalled to Hippo to establish a new monastery, he was ordained a priest by popular acclaim by bishop Valerius, whom he succeeded as bishop in 396.[7] This began another radical change:[8] from coenobitic asceticism he took on his indefatigable pastoral activity in the instruction of the faithful and his resolute defence of orthodoxy, menaced by the Manicheans, Pelagians, or irreconcilable schismatics like the Donatists.[9] He also made frequent journeyings to resolve the problems of the Church.[10]

In 410 Rome was sacked and burned by the barbarian troops of Alaric: a dramatically traumatic event for the ancient world which inspired *The City of God*, one of his major works. In 430 it was Hippo's turn to be besieged by barbarians: in the midst of this siege by the Vandals its bishop expired.

Few writers can match the prolific output of Augustine. His literary production is truly imposing and embraces philosophical works, theological treatises, works of exegesis, of moral theology, antiheretical polemic and a great number of sermons and of letters. In that it is impossible to mention them all here even summarily,[11] we

---

[7] Cf. *Confessions* X, 43,70: BAug 14, 226-269, FOTC 21,325. See also Possidius, *Vita Augustini* 7, 1-8, 6: *Vite dei Santi* III, *op. cit.*, 146-151.

[8] On the pastoral teaching of Augustine cf. M. Pellegrino, *Verus Sacerdos*, Cuneo, 1965.

[9] For a complete list of the writings against the Manicheans (for example, the 33 books *Against Faustus the Manichean*), against the Pelagians (*De meritis et remissione peccatorum*, in 3 books; *On Nature and Grace*), against the Donatists (3 books, *Against the letter of Parmenianus*) cf. A. Trapè, 'Agostino,' *op.cit.*, 360-371.

[10] On the journeys of Augustine, cf. O. Perler, *op.cit.* at note 1.

[11] We refer once more, to A. Trapè, 'Agostino,' *op.cit.*, 337-382. The works of Augustine are accessible in PL 32-47, in CSEL and in CCSL, but limited to some of them. See also important editions, with commentary and French translation in the series Bibliothèque Augustinienne [BA] and the Italian series Nuova Biblioteca Agostiniana [=NBA] editions with translation, useful introductions and notes on all the works of Saint Augustine. [See T. Halton,

will limit ourselves, apart from the works from which selections have been made for this anthology, to mentioning four works, important for a variety of reasons: *The Confessions, On The Trinity, On Christian Doctrine,* and *The City of God.*

The Confessions, in 13 books, composed between 397 and 400, constitutes one of the chief works, not just of Latin literature, but of the literature of all time. Inspired, as far as immediate motivations are concerned, by accusations about his Manichean past, the work transcends the occasion of the moment to become the stimulus for a total autobiographical memoir of what had happened through diverse, painful religious and human tensions. The characteristic feature of the *Confessions,* which broke the traditional canons of classical literature, used only to recounting from memory enterprises and heroic virtue, is evident in the structure; the "autobiographical" account relating to the past occupies the first nine books, while the tenth book relates the author's present experience and the last three added on are a commentary on the Genesis account of creation, in which anthropological and soteriological preoccupations occupy the entire attention of the bishop of Hippo. From this we understand why Augustine develops only certain particulars and remains silent on episodes and personages to which we moderns might wish that he would have devoted more space. We understand too the entirely personal tone of the work, an intimate outpouring in the form of a confession to God himself, praised almost psalm-like for his merciful love.[12]

On the Trinity in 15 books, was written in various stages between 399 and 420. It is a mature treatment of the complex problem of the relations between the three divine persons, a debated

---

'Augustine in Translation: Achievements and Further Goals,' in *Augustine From Rhetor to Theologian,* ed. J. McWilliam, Waterloo, Ont., 1992, 207-229 for details.] The recent discovery of 30 letters: edited with commentary and translation, in BAug 46B; a critical text by J. Divjak, the one who discovered the letters, in CSEL 88. For an in-depth critique of the contents of the discovery cf.AA.-vv., *Les lettres de saint Augustin découvertes par J. Divjak,* Paris, 1983.

[12] Fundamental for the *Confessions* are the studies of P. Courcelle, *Recherches sur Les Confessions de Saint Augustin,* Paris, 1968, 2ed.; *Les Confessions de Saint Augustin, dans la tradition littéraire Antécédents et postérité,* Paris, 1963; but no less valid in its basic thesis: L.F. Pizzolato, *Le Confessioni di S. Agostino. Da biografia a "confessio,"* Milan, 1968; also *idem, Le fondazioni dello'stile delle "Confessioni" di Sant'Agostino,* Milan, 1972.

subject which had passionately and profoundly torn Christianity during the 4th century.

The claim of newness and originality is secure especially by the analogical relationship which Augustine instituted between creation, and particularly the human soul, and the Trinity. The relationship between the three persons is, in fact, similar to that which is found in the human soul between the three fundamental faculties of memory, intellect and will,[13] but also to love which becomes the most complete way to perceive the Trinity.[14]

Equally important is the treatise of biblical hermeneutic and Christian rhetoric, *On Christian Doctrine*,[15] a key text of medieval culture,[16] having fixed, in a manner more radical than in the past, the exemplary principle of subordinating all the knowledge derived from the profane sciences to the needs of the study of sacred Scripture. This work of Augustine is also the first point of awareness of the superiority of Christian to pagan culture.

If the historical profile of Christian writers traced by Jerome, originating for the most part from the work done by Eusebius of Caesarea[17] caused an awareness of a new culture, this work of Augustine is now a mature attempt to the possibility of finding in their own literary texts, be they the writings of the Old Testament, the letters of Paul, the works of Cyprian, or those of Ambrose, the basis for a useful rhetorical education.[18]

---

[13] *De Trinitate* X, 11, 17-18: BAug 16, 152-157; FOTC 45, 310-311, tr. S. McKenna.

[14] Cf. S. Nicolosi, 'La filosofia dell'amore in Sant'Agostino. Dalla comununicazione alla comunità,' *Orpheus* n.s. 4 (1983), 42-66, esp. 47-55.

[15] For a bibliographico-critical study relative to this work of Augustine see the recent, very full treatment of L. Alici, *S. Agostino d'Ippona. La Dottrina Cristiana*, Milan, 1989, 9-83. On the exegetical theory of Augustine cf. C. Basevi, *San Agustin. La interpretacíon del Nuevo Testamento. Criterios exegéticos propuestos por S. Agustin en el "De Doctrina Christiana,"* en el *"Contra Faustum"* y en el *"De Consensu Evangelistarum,"* Pamplona, 1988; G. Ripanti, *Agostino teorico dell'interpretazione*, Brescia, 1980; M. Simonetti, Lettera. *op. cit.*, 338-354; B. De Margerie, *Introduzione alla storia dell'esegesi, III, S. Agostino*, Rome, 1986.

[16] Cf. F. Simone, 'La reductio artium ad Sacram Scripturam quale espressione dell'umanesimo medioevale fino al sec.XII,' *Convivium* n.s.4 (1949), 887-927.

[17] On the historico-literary significance of the *De viris illustribus* of Jerome see I. Opelt, 'Hieronymus Leistung als Literarhistorischer in der Schrift *De viris illustribus*,' in *Orpheus* n.s. 1 (1980), 52-75; S. Pricoco, *Storia letteraria e storia ecclesiastica dal De viris illustribus di Girolamo a Gennadio*, Catania, 1979 and finally, from various viewpoints, Aa. vv., *Gerolamo e la biografia letteraria*, Genoa, 1989.

[18] Cf. *De Doctrina Christiana* IV, 7, 11-25; IV, 17, 34-21, 50: BAug 11, 438-467; 480-533.

The sack of Rome in 410 had rekindled pagan accusations against the Christians, seeing in the new religion, which had even become the official religion of the Empire, the principal cause of the loss of the gods' protection.

The City of God, in 22 books, published in various stages, which occupied Augustine from 413 to 426, was intended to be a work of apologetic in reply to this accusation. In reality, Augustine's original plan was expanded and assumed a complexity of much greater importance, the more the historico-theological thought of the African bishop put its seal on the work.

After the indictment against pagan religion and a careful examination of the global failure of all of paganism and of the Roman Empire, founded on the overwhelming defeat of its adversaries, Augustine produced a universal history in the second part of the work beginning with creation, in the perspective of Christian teaching, juxtaposing the two cities, that of the "earthly" and that of the "heavenly," the one an expression of evil and destined to perdition, the other, projected toward the transcendent and for that reason having nothing to do with politico-earthly compromise of any kind. The optimism toward the polity of the Christian emperors of Eusebius of Caesarea and of Ambrose himself has by now yielded ground to a certain pessimism in the face of human actions and a decisive orientation toward the transcendent "city of God."[19]

In all of patristic literature, the treatise, *On the Good of Marriage*, is the only synthesis expressly dedicated to the topic of marriage which makes it impossible to realize its importance. It was composed around 401 as a further response to the debate which Jovinian's polemic had stirred up at Rome. At first sight the revival of a debate which had already been concluded for some years[20] might seem unreal, but it is Augustine himself who clarifies in his *Retractations*, the

---

[19] Cf. S. D'Elia, 'Storia e Teologia della Storia nel *De Civitate Dei*,' in Aa.vv., *La storiografia Ecclesiastica nella Tarda Antichità*, Messina, 1980, 391-481. In the great proliferation of studies on the *City of God* we limit our references to P. Brezzi, *Analisi e interpretazione del De civitate Dei di S. Agostino*, Tolentino, 1960; and, more recently, G. Lettieri, *Il senso della storia in Agostino. Il "saeculum" e la gloria nel "De Civitate Dei,"* Rome, 1988.

[20] On Jovinian cf. *supra*, Introductory Profile on Jerome, pp. 237-238.

totally new perspective in which he re-examines the question: for him, the purpose is not to denigrate matrimony at the expense of virginity — which Jerome had already done — but rather to exalt its intrinsic positive side, while not losing sight of the validity of the ascetic alternative.[21] Augustine insists through this motive on the social value of the union of husband and wife and synthesizes in the three "goods" of offspring, mutual fidelity, and indissolubility, the three essential values of matrimony, confuting point by point the affirmations of Jovinian which had upset the spirits of many Christians.

As has been said, Augustine dedicated the last three books of the *Confessions* to Genesis, but he also devoted other exegetical writings to it. Genesis, in fact, and particularly its first three chapters, had been utilized by various gnostic currents, and by Manicheans in particular, to give a scriptural foundation to their own dualistic conceptions. Augustine therefore applied himself with notable attention to the commentary of this part of the Old Testament interpreted both allegorically[22] and literally, especially to propose to adversaries objective arguments drawn from an exegesis with a purely historical basis.

To this latter aim the work, *On the Literal Meaning of Genesis*, in 12 books, composed between 401 and 415 is the precise mode of response. It is a systematic, verse by verse commentary (which stops however at Genesis 3:24) which, with a certain prolixity, sets out to

---

[21] Cf. *Retractations* 2, 22: BAug 12, 488-49 1. For *On the Good of Marriage* in general cf. M. Palmieri, in NBA VII/I, 3-7. The other work which we have excerpted, *De Nuptiis et Concupiscentia*, in 2 books, was composed by Augustine at the end of 418 or in the early months of the following year. The first book was written to respond to the accusations of the Pelagians and of Julian of Eclanum in particular who saw in the teaching of Augustine on original sin and on concupiscence an implicit negation of the goodness of matrimony. Julian replied immediately with a work in 4 books, forcing Augustine to write circa 420, the second book of *De Nuptiis et Concupiscentia*. On the complex problem of the relation in Augustine between matrimonial ethics and concupiscence cf. E. Samek Lodovici, 'Sessualità, matrimonio e concupiscenza in sant'Agostino,' in Aa.vv., *Etica sessuale e matrimonio nel cristianesimo delle origini*, Milan, 1976, 212-272; G. Sfameni Gasparro, 'Concupiscenza e generazione: aspetti antropologici della dottrina agostiniana del peccato originale,' in Aa. vv., *Congresso Internazionale*, *op. cit.*, 225-255.

[22] Augustine commented on Genesis with ample concessions to allegorical interpretation in the 2 books of *De Genesi contra Manichaeos*, written at Thagaste around 389: NBA IX/I.

resolve in a logical-literal key the complex anthropological problems which the text presents.[23]

Apart from the sermons which gave a commentary in continuous form on the Psalms, the Gospel of John, and his First Epistle[24] Augustine's indefatigable activity is testified to by a great number of other sermons, about a tenth of which were actually delivered by him.[25] In 1683 the Maurists, Benedictine monks of the Congregation of St. Maur in France, published 398 sermons of Augustine, subdivided into four categories: 1) scriptural; 2) liturgical; 3) on the saints; 4) on various subjects. Later discoveries or attributions proposed by scholars have further increased that number, to the point that today the sermons of Augustine, retained on good grounds as authentic exceed 500 in number.[26]

To justify such a numerical output one should take into account that the bishop of Hippo considered it a duty toward the faithful that they have the assurance that they would not lack the comfort and instruction of his words.[27] His biographer, Possidius, testifies that he continued to preach with fervent zeal right up to his death, even though old and in failing health.[28] He was capable of speaking on the same day in different sanctuaries and never missing a liturgical occasion, and during the Pasch he preached every day for the entire

---

[23] On *De Genesi ad Litteram* see the observations of A. Di Giovanni-A.Penna in the Introduction to NBA IX/1, VII-CII. On the presence of the various books of the Bible in Augustine's works the researches of A.-M. La Bonnardière, *Biblia Augustiniana*, Paris, 1960-1975 are noteworthy (already published for the Old Testament: Deuteronomy, Historical Books, Minor Prophets, Sapiential Proverbs, Jeremiah; for the New Testament, the Epistles to the Thessalonians, to Titus, to Philemon). [Engl. ed.: See updates in *REAug*.]

[24] On the nature of these writings and on their genesis, the fruit in part of discourses delivered to the people and in part dictated, cf. A. Trapè, 'Agostino,' *op. cit.*, 374-377.See also Introduction by M. Pellegrino to *The Works of St. Augustine: A Translation for the 21st Century, Sermons, I*, Brooklyn, NY, 1990, 13-137. [Engl. ed.: See now FOTC 78, 79, 88, 90, 92 (1989-1995), tr. J. Rettig.]

[25] Cf. M. Marin, 'Agostino,' *op. cit.*, 43.

[26] On the complex problems relative to the authenticity of the sermons of Augustine cf. P.P. Verbraken, *Études critiques sur les Sermons authentiques de St. Augustin*, Steenbrugge, 1976 and *Supplément*.

[27] Augustine considers the faithful the true and proper exactors of the debt of his preaching: cf. M. Pellegrino, *Verus, op. cit.*, 93-100. [Engl. ed.: This is reproduced in English translation in the new Villanova project.]

[28] Cf. Possidius, *Vita Augustini* 31,4: *Vite dei Santi, op. cit.*, 236-237.

week and on Sunday he actually preached two sermons; normally he preached twice a week and sometimes twice on the same day.[29]

Augustine was a shrewd preacher who adapted his words most effectively to the public whom he addressed, made up of both the educated and the unsophisticated, the intelligent and those slow to grasp the meaning of his arguments. Even the rhetorical structure of phrase is obviously carefully crafted and serves to reach his hearers with the greatest effectiveness, to arrest their attention, to render more acceptable the parenetic exhortations,[30] in a word, to bend the will of his audience. At the center of his sermons, even in those which cannot be classified as scriptural, there is obviously a meditation on Scripture. In his preachings Augustine abounds in allegorical interpretations superimposing the diverse meanings which with inexhaustible riches he knew how to draw out from the biblical text,[31] because naturally some of them were more adapted to his intention to draw the faithful to a more integrally Christian ethical behavior. This paraenetic intent explains the insistence with which Augustine addresses the theme of conjugal fidelity in his sermons.

Mutual fidelity is a fundamental theme of Augustine's matrimonial ethic and certainly it is no accident that it is one of the three "goods" of the matrimonial union. Hippo would certainly offer a fairly representative case history of this point of view in all of Christian antiquity: men who retained their own right to have frequent extramarital unions, women who supinely accepted this state of affairs, convinced that the only weapon in their possession was endurance.[32] On the other hand, Augustine had seen at first hand in his own house a similar situation between his father, Patricius and his mother, Monica:

---

[29] On the place and time of delivery of the sermons of Augustine, cf. M. Pellegrino, *Sant'Agostino. Discorsi* I, NBA XXIX, Rome, 1979, pp. XIV-XVI.

[30] Cf. J. Oroz Reta, *La retórica en los Sermones de San Agustín*, Madrid, 1963; Chr. Mohrmann, 'Saint Augustin prédicateur,' in *Études sur le latin des Chrétiens*, Rome, 1961, 391-402. On the symbolism of the images employed by Augustine in his preaching cf. S. Poque, *Le langage symbolique dans la prédication de Saint Augustin*, Paris, 1984.

[31] Cf. M. Pontet, *L'exégèse de saint Augustin prédicateur*, Paris, 1944, and, more recently, M. Simonetti, 'Sulla tecnica esegetica di Agostino in alcuni Sermones veterotestamentari,' *AugR* 25 (1985), 185-203.

[32] Cf. A.G. Hamman, *La vie quotidienne dans Africa de Saint Augustin*, Paris, 1985, 79-82.

> My mother ... put up with wrongs of infidelity, never per-
> mitting any dissension with her husband. She looked forward
> to Your mercy upon him, that he might become chaste as a
> believer in You.[33]

Augustine shows himself resolute in confronting male infidelity even though he incurred the maledictions, more or less concealed,
of the married. Masters with impunity exploited the sex of their
employees, who were slaves in every sense of the word, and gave their
masters the excuse of not going in search of the love of prostitutes;
that was an alibi of conscience that the bishop was obviously not
willing to tolerate.[34] Even though occasionally, Augustine indulges
in irony about those unfaithful husbands "at the mercy of their lovers,"[35] he more than once stigmatizes their behavior which offends
not only their wives but also Christ of whose body they are mysti-
cally a part. From the frequency with which the theme recurs in his
sermons it can be seen that adultery, together with the physical abuse
to which the husband frequently had recourse,[36] constituted the most
serious problem for the Christian couple insofar as it infringed on
the unity of their union, bringing into disgrace the sacramental significance of the sign of the mystic marriage between Christ and the
Church.

---

[33] *Confessions* IX, 9, 19: NBA 1, p. 277; FOTC 21, 247-248, tr. V.J. Bourke. On Augustine's conception of the family: cf. B.D. Shaw, 'The Family in Late Antiquity: the Experience of Augustine,' *Past & Present* 115 (1987), 3-51, especially, for relations of spouses, 23-39.

[34] Cf. Sermon 224, 3: NBA XXXII/I, 372-375.

[35] Cf. Sermon 161, 10: PL 38, col. 883.

[36] Cf. E. Schmitt, *Le Mariage chrétien dans l'oeuvre de Saint Augustin,* Paris, 1983, 259-295; [Add: D. Hunter, 'Augustinian Pessimism? A New Look at Augustine's Teaching on Sex, Marriage and Celibacy,' *Augustinian Studies* 25 (1994), 153-177.] For a collection of passages from Augustine on women cf. K. Thraede, 'Augustin. Texte aus dem Themenkreis "Frau," "Gesellschaft" und "Gleischeit"' 1, *Jahrbuch für Antike und Christentum* 22 (1979), 70-97.

MARRIAGES IN PARADISE AND THE ACTUAL STATUS OF THE SPOUSES; HYPOTHESIS AND REALITY

26

1,1. Forasmuch as each man is a part of the human race, and human nature is a social reality, and has, for a great and natural good, the power of friendship, on this account God willed to create all men out of one, in order that they might be held in their society, not only by likeness of kind, but also by bond of kindred.[1]

Therefore, the first natural bond in human society is man and wife. Nor did God create these each by himself, and join them together as alien by birth; but He created the one out of the other, setting a sign also of the power of the union in the side, whence she was drawn, was formed.[a]

For they are joined one to another side by side, who walk together, and look together to where they are walking. The connection of fellowship in children then follows, which is the one only worthy fruit, not of the union of male and female, but of the sexual intercourse. For it were possible that there should exist in either sex, even without such intercourse a certain friendly and true union of the one ruling and the other obeying.

2,2. Nor is it now necessary that we enquire, and put forth a definite opinion on that question whence could originate the progeny of the first men whom God had blessed, saying, *Increase and multiply, and fill the earth,*[b] if they had not sinned; whereas their bodies by sinning deserved the condition of death and there can be no sexual intercourse except between mortal bodies.

For there have been expressed several different opinions on this question, and if we must examine which of them is most conformable with the truth of divine Scriptures there will be too long a discussion. Therefore, without intercourse in some other way, had they

---

[a] cf. Gn 2:21:22   [b] Gn 1:28

[1] The assimilation of conjugal bonds to those operating in society was a datum already present in the juridical writings of the classical era. Cf. Modestinus in *Digest*, 23, 2, I. Obviously in the Christian perspective the force of the social relationships joined to the matrimonial union acquired a religious value unknown to the juridical classical tradition, especially in the light of the account of Genesis on the creation of woman.

not sinned, they would have had sons from the gift of the Almighty Creator, Who was able to create themselves also without parents, Who was able to form the Flesh of Christ in a virgin womb and (to speak even to unbelievers themselves) Who was able to bestow on bees a progeny without sexual intercourse.[2]

Or perhaps many things in the account were spoken by way of mystery and allegory, and we are to understand in another sense what is written, *Fill the earth, and rule over it*; that is, that it should come to pass by fullness and perfection of life and power, so that the very increase and multiplication, whereby it is said, *Increase, and be multiplied*, be understood to be by increase of understanding, and abundance of virtue, as it is set forth in the Psalm, *You shall multiply me in my soul by virtue;*[c] and that succession of progeny was not given unto man, except after that, by reason of sin, there was to be hereafter departure in death; or perhaps the body was not made spiritual in the case of these men, but at the first was made animal, in order that by merit of obedience it might afterwards become spiritual, to lay hold of immortality,[4] not after death, which by the malice of the devil entered into the world, and was made the punishment of sin; but after that change, which the Apostle signifies, when he says, *Then we living, who remain, together with them, shall be caught up in the clouds, to meet the Lord in the air.*[e]

In this way we may understand both that those bodies of the first pair were mortal, in their first forming, and yet that they would not have died, had they not sinned, as God had threatened: even as

---

[c] Ps 137:3   [d] Ws 2:24   [e] 1 Th 4:17

---

[2] Augustine addresses the problem, much debated and resolved in a greatly controverted manner, relative to generation before original sin. The first solution which made its appearance was one of a procreation entrusted to channels different with respect to physical union: this is a solution in line with that of Gregory of Nyssa and of John Chrysostom: cf. G. Sfameni Gasparro, *Enkrateia, op. cit.*, 305. [Engl. ed. For a new look at *On the Good of Marriage* cf. R. Markus, in *Agostino d'Hippona "Quaestiones Disputatae" (Palermo 3-4 dicembre 1987)*, Palermo, 1990, 913-925.]

[3] The second solution is that connected with the spiritual exegesis bearing the stamp of Origen, which gives to "increase and multiply" a symbolic significance linked to the moral sphere of virtue.

[4] The third possibility in exegesis, is that of attributing to our first parents, not a spiritual, but an animal body, and it is this which permits the continuing evolution of Augustine's thought, quick to admit "the possibility of true marriage in paradise and without sin" (G. Sfameni Gasparro, *op. cit.*, 307).

if He should threaten a wound, in that the body was capable of wounds; which yet would not have happened, unless that which He had forbidden were done. Thus, therefore, even through sexual intercourse there might take place generations of such bodies, as up to a certain point should have increased, and yet should not pass into old age; or even into old age and yet not unto death; until the earth were filled with that multiplication of the divine blessing.

For if to the garments of the Israelites[f] God granted their proper state without any wearing away during forty years, how much more would He grant unto the bodies of such as obeyed His command a certain most happy temperament of sure state, until they should be changed for the better, not by death of the man, whereby the body is abandoned by the soul, but by a blessed change from mortality to immortality, from an animal to a spiritual quality.

3,3. This we now say, that, according to this condition of being born and dying, which we know, and in which we have been credited, the marriage of male and female is some good; the compact whereof divine Scripture so commends, as that neither is it allowed one put away by her husband to marry, so long as her husband lives: nor is it allowed one put away by his wife to marry another, unless she who has separated from him be dead.

Therefore, concerning the good of marriage, which the Lord also confirmed in the Gospel, not only in that He forbade to put away a wife, except in the case of fornication,[g] but also in that He came by invitation to a marriage,[h] there is good ground to inquire for what reason it be a good.

And this seems to me not to be merely on account of the begetting of children, but also on account of the natural society itself in a difference of sex. Otherwise it would not any longer be called marriage in the case of old persons, especially if either they had lost sons, or given birth to none.

But now in a good marriage, although the spouses are advanced in age, although there has withered away the passion of youthful ardor between male and female, yet there lives in full vigor the order of

---

f cf. Dt 29:5   g cf. Mt 19:9   h cf. Jn 2:1-2

love between husband and wife: because, the better they are, the earlier they have began by mutual consent to abstain from sexual intercourse with each other: not that it should be matter of necessity afterwards not to have power to do what they would, but that it should be matter of praise to have been unwilling at the first, to do what they had power to do. If therefore there be kept good faith of honor, and of services mutually due from either sex, although the members of either be languishing and almost corpselike, yet of souls duly joined together, the chastity continues, the purer by how much it is the more proved, the safer, by how much it is the calmer.

Marriage has this good also, that carnal or youthful incontinence, although it be faulty, is turned to the honorable task of begetting children in order that out of the evil of lust the marriage union may bring some good to pass. Finally, the concupiscence of the flesh, being tempered by parental affection, is repressed and becomes aroused more modestly. For there is interposed a certain gravity of glowing pleasure, when in that when the husband and wife unite in the marriage act, they think of themselves as father and mother.

On the Good of Marriage 1, 1-3, 3; NBA VII, I, 10-14; FOTC 27, 9-13

FINAL END OF THE COUPLE IN THE PROJECT OF CREATION:
MARRIAGE AND PROCREATION

27

3,5. If one should ask why it was necessary that a helper be made for man, the answer that seems most probable is that it was for the procreation of children,[1] just as the earth is a helper for the seed in the production of a plant from the union of the two. This purpose was declared in the original creation of the world: *Male and female He made them. And God blessed them and said, "Increase and multiply and fill the earth and subdue it."*[a] This reason for creation and union of male and female, as well as this blessing, was not abrogated after the sin and punishment of man. It is by virtue of this blessing that the earth is now filled with human beings who dominate it.[2]

5,9. Now, if the woman was not made for the man to be his helper in begetting children, in what other way was she to help him? She was not to till the earth with him, for there was not yet any toil to make help necessary. If there were any such need, a male helper would be better, and the same could be said of the comfort of another's presence if Adam were perhaps weary of solitude. How much more agreeably could two male friends, rather than a man and woman, enjoy companionship and conversation in a life shared together. And if they had to make an arrangement in their common life for one to command and the other to obey in order to make sure that opposing wills would not disrupt the peace of the household,

---

[a] Gn 1:27-28

---

[1] If, in the preceding excerpt, Augustine attributed a not exclusive significance to procreation within the ambit of matrimony, here is now delineated an anthropological conception which will follow in all his subsequent works, even in the tormented period of his polemic against Pelagius. The woman has essentially a function of "helper" in the act of procreation; any other explanation whatsoever is irreconcilable with the account in Genesis. It is true moreover that some paragraphs later (7,12: NBA IX/2, p. 465) Augustine will state more precisely the significance of matrimony, not only in terms of procreation but also of "fidelity" and of "sacrament," that is to say, indissolubility.

[2] In the part omitted, Augustine affirms that for the protoplasts there would not have been any impediment in paradise to "an honorable matrimonial union and a bed undefiled" prior to the sin. If they had not transgressed, in fact, God would have allowed them to have children "without the disordered ardor of concupiscence, without the difficulty and the pains of childbirth" and the generations would have come to an end with the completion of a determined number, when all the material bodies would have been transformed into spiritual ones.

there would have been proper rank to assure this, since one would be created first and the other second, and this would be further reinforced if the second were made from the first, as was the case with the woman. Surely no one will say that God was able to make from the rib of the man only a woman and not also a man if He had wished to do so. Consequently, I do not see in what sense the woman was made as a helper for the man if not for the sake of bearing children.

On the Literal Meaning of Genesis, IX, 3,5-5,9;
ACW 42,73, tr. J.H. Taylor (1982)

THE THREE "GOODS" OF MARRIAGE; CONDITIONS
FOR A CHASTE RELATIONSHIP OF THE SPOUSES

28

8,9. The married believer, therefore, must not only not use another man's vessel, which is what they do who lust after others' wives but he must know that even his own vessel is not to be possessed in the disease of carnal concupiscence. And this counsel is not to be understood as if the Apostle prohibited conjugal — that is to say, lawful and honorable — cohabitation; but so as that cohabitation (which would have no adjunct of unwholesome lust, were it not that man's perfect freedom of choice had become by preceding sin so disabled that it has this fatal adjunct) should not be a matter of will, but of necessity, without which, nevertheless, it would be impossible to attain to the fruition of the will itself in the procreation of children.

And this will is not in the marriages of believers determined by the purpose of having such children born as shall pass through life in this present world, but such as shall be born again in Christ, and remain in Him for evermore. Now if this result should come about, the reward of a full felicity will spring from marriage; but if such result is not realized, there will yet ensue to the married pair the peace of a good conscience.

9,10. Nor can it be doubted, that it is more consonant with the order of nature that men should bear rule over women, than women over men. It is with this principle in view that the Apostle says, *The head of the woman*[a] *is the man* and, *Wives, submit yourselves unto your own husbands.*[b]

10,10.   So also the Apostle Peter writes, *Even as Sarah obeyed Abraham, calling him lord.*[c] Now, although the fact of the matter is, that while nature loves singleness in her dominations, but we may see plurality existing more readily in the subordinate portion of our race; yet for all that, it was at no time lawful for one man to have a plurality of wives, except for the purpose of a greater number of children springing from him. Therefore, if one woman cohabits with several men, inasmuch as no increase of offspring accrues to her therefrom, but only a more frequent gratification of lust, she cannot possibly be a wife, but only a harlot.

To Christian believers who are in wedlock, it is certainly not fecundity only, the fruit of which consists of offspring, nor chastity only, whose bond is fidelity, but also a certain sacramental bond in marriage which is recommended. Accordingly it is enjoined by the Apostle: *Husbands, love your wives, as Christ also loved the Church.*[d] Of this sacramental bond the substance undoubtedly is this, that the man and the woman who are joined together in matrimony should remain inseparable[2] as long as they live; and that it should be unlawful for one consort to be parted from the other, except for the cause of fornication.[e] For this is preserved in the case of Christ and the Church; so that as a living one with a living one, there is no divorce, no separation, for eternity. And so complete is the observance of this bond in the city of our God, in His holy mountain[f] — that is to say, in the Church of Christ — by all married believers, who are undoubtedly members of Christ, that although women marry, and men take wives, for the purpose of procreating children,

---

[a] 1 Cor 11:3   [b] Col 3:18   [c] 1 P 3:6   [d] Eph 5:25   [e] cf. Mt 5:32   [f] Ps 47:2

[1]   There are three "goods" of matrimony (*proles, fidelitas, sacramentum*), which will constitute a point of reference even for the Magisterium of the Church. The Encyclical *Casti connubii* issued by Pope Pius XI, 31 December, 1930 refers to them explicitly; no less operative is their influence on Vatican Council II, or on the pastoral activities of John Paul II. Cf. R. Garcia de Haro, *Matrimonio e Famiglia nei Documenti del Magistero*, Milan, 1989, 63-92; 172-175; 227-274.

[2]   On Augustine's position in regard to divorce cf. H. Crouzel, *L'Église primitive, op. cit.*, 317-358; G. Cereti, *Divorzio, op. cit.*, 252-264.

it is never permitted one to put away even a barren wife for the sake of having another to bear children, and whosoever does this is held to be guilty of adultery by the law of the gospel; though not by this world's rule, which allows a divorce between the parties, without even the allegation of guilt, and the contraction of other nuptial engagements — a concession which, the Lord tells us, even the holy Moses extended to the people of Israel, because of the hardness of their hearts.[g] The same condemnation applies to the woman, if she is married to another man.

But God forbid that the marriage bond should be regarded as broken between those who have by mutual consent agreed to observe a perpetual abstinence from the use of carnal concupiscence. Nay, it will be only a firmer one, whereby they have exchanged pledges together, which will have to be kept by an especial endearment and concord — not by the voluptuous ties of bodies, but by the voluntary affections of souls.

On Marriage and Concupiscence, Bk. 1, 8,9-11,12; NBA VII,I, 410-414;
NPNF ser. 2, vol. 5, 267-268.

DIFFERENT ROLES AND EQUAL ZEAL IN CONJUGAL CHASTITY

29

3.[1] You are told, *You shall not commit adultery*[a] that is, do not go after any other woman except your wife. But what you do is demand this duty from your wife, while declining to repay this duty to your wife. And while you ought to lead your wife in virtue (chastity is a

---

[g] cf. Mt 19:8; Mk 10:5   [a] Ex 20:14

[1] This sermon was delivered by Augustine at Carthage or, according to some scholars, at Chiusa, a place probably not too far from Hippo. Cf. C. Lambot, 'Le sermon 9 de saint Augustin,' *Revue Benedectine* 79 (1969), 129-133. The passages from Scripture commented on are chapter 20 of Exodus and Psalm 143. The initial exhortation is directed to an audience, and in regard to the commandments of God, it moves early on to the theme of adultery. Augustine addresses it decisively: "I will speak out!", he exclaims very firmly toward those who were married and who would prefer his silence. He wants wives to be conscious of how wrong they are in being excessively passive, persuaded that putting up with the transgressions of their husbands is a normal thing. Male and female adultery was a sin judged in an extremely discriminatory manner, even if in the eyes of divine law it was equally applicable.

virtue, you know), you collapse under one assault of lust. You want
your wife to conquer; you yourself lie there, conquered.

And while you are the head of your wife, she precedes you on
the path to God, she whose head you are. Do you want your household to hang upside down? *The husband is the head of the wife.*[b] But
where the wife lives better than the husband, the household hangs
its head downward. If the husband is the head, the husband ought
to live better and outdistance his wife in all good deeds, so that she
may imitate her husband and follow the lead of her head. Just as
Christ is head of the Church,[c] and the Church is ordered to follow
its head and, as it were, walk in the footsteps of its head,[d] so everyone's
household has as its head the man, and as its body the woman. Where
the head leads, there the body ought to follow. So why does the head
want to go where it doesn't want the body to follow? Why does the
husband want to go where he doesn't want his wife to follow? In
making this command the word of God becomes the adversary, since
men don't want to do what the word of God prescribes. And what
am I saying? Because the word of God is your adversary in giving such
commands.

I am afraid that I too may become some people's adversary
because I am speaking like this. Well, why should that upset me? May
he who terrifies me into speaking make me brave enough not to fear
the complaints of men. Those who don't want to be faithful in chastity to their wives — and there are innumerable men like that —
don't want me to say these things. But want me to or not, I'm going
to say them.

For if I don't urge you to come to an agreement with the adversary, I myself will remain at odds with him. The one who tells
you to behave is the same as the one who prompts me to speak. If
you are his adversaries by not doing what he tells you to do, I shall
remain his adversary by not saying what he tells me to say to you...

4. What has proved more time-consuming is that evil which
is so widespread, which our adversary finds all the more annoying,
who makes such a clamor merely because he wants to be seen one of

---

[b] Eph 5:23   [c] cf. Eph 5:23   [d] cf. 1 P 2:21

these days as a friend. There are daily complaints about this, even though wives themselves do not yet dare to come out and blame their husbands. This habit has become so pervasive that it has become mistaken for a law, so much so that wives seem convinced that adultery is lawful for men, but not for women. It is commonly heard that wives are brought to court because they have been caught with their men servants. But nobody has ever heard of a husband being taken to court who has been caught with his housemaid, with sinful intent. Though their sin is the same, what makes the wife seem guilty and the man more innocent is not God, but human perversity.[2]

And presuming that today someone has to put up with more complaints and grumbling from his wife because she has heard in church that it is not all right for her husband to do what she used to think was all right, so her husband has to listen to her complaining: "What you are doing is not lawful. We both heard him saying: You are Christians. Treat me the same as you expect to be treated by me. I owe you fidelity; you owe me fidelity. Both of us owe fidelity to Christ. Even if you succeed in cheating on me, you cannot cheat on him to whom we belong, you cannot cheat on the one who ransomed us."

When he hears words like these to which he is unaccustomed, if he is not ready to assume responsibility he becomes self-defensive. He becomes angry and abusive. He might even curse me and say: "Who sent him here?" Or: "Why did my wife go to church today?" I certainly think that he will keep these remarks to himself, that he would never have the courage to say them out loud, not even in his wife's presence in private. Because, if he did come out and say it, the wife might respond: "Why are you now bad-mouthing the man that at first you were applauding? Are we not man and wife? If you cannot live with your own words how can you live in harmony with me?"

---

[2] Cf. a very significant passage in *On Adulterous Marriages* 11,8,7: NBA VII/I, 286- 289: "Yet they become indignant if they should hear that men guilty of adultery should pay the same penalty as adulterous women. However there are some who are not pleased at the fact that, in the matter of chastity, there is a single norm for both husband and wife. They would prefer to be subject to the law of the world than the law of Christ because civil law does not seem to restrict men with the same bonds of chastity as it does women." Engl. tr. FOTC 27, 109.

If a doctor listened to the words of his patients he would never cure them. Don't do what you should not do, what God forbids. Certainly it would have been better for those who want to be their own physicians if I had never come here, or expressed sentiments like this, or better that I never said anything like this, now that I have come.

Sermon 9, 3-4; NBA XXIX, pp. 154-158; tr. Hill, 261-263

30

2.[1] You who are husbands, stay faithful to your wives. Give back to them what you expect from them. Man, you expect your wife to be chaste; show her by example how to be so, not just by words. You are the head; watch your step. You should be going, after all, where it won't be dangerous for her to follow you; you yourself should travel the road on which you want her to follow. You are demanding self-discipline from the weaker sex; both of you have the urgings of the flesh to deal with; let the stronger one be the first to overcome them. And yet the sad fact is that many husbands are surpassed in this matter by their wives. Wives preserve their chastity; husbands are not prepared to do so; and, in the very fact of not doing so, they like to have the reputation of being real men; as though what makes it the stronger sex is that it is more easily overcome by the Wicked One. This is a struggle, it is a battle, it is a fight of body with body.

The man is stronger than the woman; the man is the head of the woman;[a] the woman fights and wins; do you just surrender to the enemy? Does the head topple over? Those of you who are not yet married and yet are in the habit of approaching the Lord's table and eating and drinking the body of Christ, if you intend to take a wife, remain chaste for your wives. As you would like them to come to you that is exactly how they should find you. What young man would not want to marry a wife who is chaste? And if he is engaged to a young woman can you imagine him not wanting her to be undefiled?

ª Eph 5:23

[1] This sermon provides commentary on Jn 6:56-57 and was preached during Lent but there is no certainty about the year or place of delivery.

If you are looking for a wife who is undefiled, do not be impure your-self. It is just not possible that she can be pure but that you can not. Either both of you can, or neither. But now that she can, let her teach you how it can be done. God is her guide in her effort to maintain her purity. But if you do the same you will have greater glory. Why greater glory?

Because she is under the pressure of parental vigilance; she is reined in by the modesty of the weaker sex. And last of all she has laws to fear that you do not. That is why you will have greater glory. Because if you remain pure it will be because you fear God.[2]

A young woman has many things to fear as well as God. But you have only God to fear. But the One you fear is greater than ev-erything else. You should fear him in public; you should fear him in private. You go out; He is watching you. You come in; He is watch-ing you. The lamp is lit; He is watching you. The lamp is extin-guished; He is watching you. You enter your bedroom; He is watch-ing you. You stand by yourself; He is watching you. Fear him whose one concern is watching you. And if only out of fear, be pure. Or if you want to sin, find a moment in which He is not watching you and then do as you please.

Sermon 132, 2; PL 38, 735-736; tr. Hill, 326-327

31

This is the city which has come down from heaven.[1] Make sure that we are worthy to enter into it. You have learned, I am sure, what kind of people can enter, and what sort cannot. Don't follow the example of those who are refused entrance, especially fornicators. When the Scripture reading listed murderers among those who do not enter, that provoked no reaction from you. But when fornica-

---

[2] That the bridle placed on inhibiting his own carnal tensions is a source of greater recogni-tion in the man rather than the woman, is a theme present also in Tertullian, who asserts that man being "more avid for sex and more drawn toward woman" acquired greater merit for holding concupiscence in check (cf. *On wearing the veil* 10,2).

[1] This sermon of Augustine was delivered in an unknown location on the occasion of the Feast of Martyrs between 410 and 412. The allusion to the heavenly Jerusalem has its origin in the preceding citation of Jn 3:27 (*No one can lay hold on anything unless it is given him from heaven*).

tors were mentioned[a] I heard you beating your breasts. I heard; I saw. What I did not see in your bedroom I saw in your gestures; I saw in your breasts when you beat them.

Cast out sin because beating your breasts and going on repeating the same sins is no different than solidifying your state of sin. My sons, my brothers, be chaste, embrace chastity, show a preference for purity, because God who promotes chastity *in his temple, which is what you are* requires it.[b] He drives far away from his temple those who are impure. Be satisfied with your wives, because you would like your wives to be satisfied with you. You would not want her to do anything with anyone apart from you. So don't you do anything apart from her. You are the master; she, the servant.[2] God made both of you. Sarah was obedient to Abraham calling him "Lord."[c]

It is true. The bishop has signed those marriage certificates. Your wives are to be subservient to you. You are the lords and masters of your wives. But when it comes down to the business which differentiates the sexes, and the sexes copulate, *the wife does not have authority over her own body, but the husband does.*[d] That is what appeals to you; that is what you find so gratifying. That is what you applaud. The Apostle, the chosen vessel, has said it well: *the wife does not have authority over her own body, but the husband does.* Because I am the lord and master. You applaud. But listen to the next sentence, the one you do not like, the one I ask you to like. What is that? Listen: *Likewise also the husband* — the lord and master he has just mentioned — *Likewise also the husband does not have authority over his own body, but the wife does.*[e]

Be equally glad to hear this also. It is vice, it is not authority that is being taken away from you. It is adultery that is being forbidden to you; it is not that your wife is being made your equal. You are the man. Prove it. The word "man" is derived from "manliness"; in Latin *vir*[3] derives from *virtus*, or *virtus*, from *vir*. So where is your

---

[a] cf. Gal 5:19   [b] cf. 1 Cor 3:16-17   [c] 1 P 3:6   [d] 1 Cor 7:4   [e] 1 Cor 7:4

[2] Notwithstanding the terminology employed Augustine does not deny the equal dignity of husband and wife in the marriage relationship. Cf. E. Schmitt, *Le mariage, op. cit.*, 287-292.

[3] This is a well-known etymology of Varro, already encountered in Lactantius; cf. *supra,* p. 202.

"manliness," where is your "virtue"? Conquer lust. *The head of the woman*, Scripture says, *is the man*.[f] If you are the head, give the lead and let her follow. But see to where you are leading her. You are the head, give the lead. Don't give the lead to where you would not like her to follow. Lest you tumble over the precipice, be careful to walk along the straight path.

In that way prepare to go to that newly wed bride, to that beautiful bride adorned for her husband, adorned, not with jewels but with virtues. If you go to her, you see, as men who are chaste and holy and good, you too will be members of this same newly wed bride, of the blessed and glorious heavenly Jerusalem.

Sermon 332, 4-5; PL 39, 1711-1712

32

4. Finally, my dear brethren,[1] you, men, listen to me, women listen to me, why are you angry at me? Would that you would do what the Scripture says: *Be angry and sin not*.[a] Should I fear to meet the same fate as the Apostle Paul in the words just read, which you heard if you were listening carefully? *Have I then, become your enemy because I tell you the truth?*[b] Well, so be it, if that is the situation. If I must, I prefer being your enemy to being an enemy of justice.

I recommend that you be solicitous in protecting your wives. They are my daughters just as you are my sons. Let them listen to me; let them be zealous for their husbands; let them not preserve vainglory for themselves for which women are wont to be praised by immoral husbands because they put up with their husbands' infidelity with equanimity. I do not want Christian wives to have similar patience. Accordingly, let them be zealous for their own husbands,

---

[f] 1 Cor 11:3 [a] Ps 4:5 [b] Gal 4:16

[1] This sermon of Augustine was delivered during Lent in an unknown location on an unknown date. It seeems to be composed of two distinct parts, both authentic. Paragraph 1 constitutes an autonomous sermon (162B), and the other 5 paragraphs make up sermon 392. In PL 39 coll. 1709-1713 it bears the title, *To the married*. In the part of the sermon which we have omitted Augustine violently attacks concubinage and confirms the prohibition on second marriage even in the case of repudiation "for fornication."

not on account of their own body but on account of their husband's souls.

I absolutely counsel it; I order it, I command it; the bishop orders it; Christ in me orders it. He knows in whose sight my heart burns. I order it, I repeat. Do not permit your husbands to fornicate. Invoke the church against them. I do not mean for you to have recourse to the State judiciary. I do not mean the proconsul. I do not mean the vicariate. I do not mean a staff member of the governor; I do not mean the Emperor; I mean Christ.

In everything else be the handmaids of your husband; be subject out of deference. Let there be no impudence in you, no haughtiness, no stiff-necked stubbornness, no other manifestation of disobedience. Be completely docile, just like the servants.

But when it comes to that business where the Apostle has placed you both, saying: *Let the husband render the debt to the wife; likewise, the wife to the husband.* He appends the remark, the *wife does not have power over her own body: her husband does.* Why do you elevate yourself? Hear what follows: *Likewise the husband also does not have power over his body, the wife does.*[c]

Whenever it comes to conjugal obligations, demand your rights. The husband sells your gold for his own needs. Put up with it, wife; put up with it, servant. Do not be contentious. Do not talk back. You owe contempt to your gold. You owe love to your husband. Even if he sells your house for his own requirements, even that which belongs to you (for it cannot be his what is not yours, if there is that charity in you which ought to be in a wife) bear it with patience; and if he hesitates, offer it yourself. Make light of all things for the love of your husband. But long for him to be chaste; litigate for chastity. Patiently allow your villa to perish, but do not be patient if his soul is in danger of perishing.

5. I do not say to husbands that in this case they should be zealous for their wives. I know that they are. I know it. Who would put up with an adulterous wife? And he orders his wife to put up with an adulterous husband. What a travesty! Why, I ask you? Why? Be-

---

[c] 1 Cor 7:3-4

cause I am a man, you say. You are a man? Overcome lust. How are you a man if your wife is stronger than you? You, man, are head of your wife,[d] it is true. If he is head, let the man lead, let the wife follow. Where the household is right, the man is head of the woman. If you are head, give the lead. Let her follow the one who is her head. But watch where you go. Do not go where you do not wish her to follow. Do not go where you fear lest you rush at the same time into the pit of adultery, lest in doing it you teach what you yourself are doing. Your soul will regret it if you both rush together into the pit of adultery. Let you regret it also if you rush in alone. You are concerned; you do not wish that she rush in; be afraid lest you rush into it on your own.

However, most chaste wives, do not you imitate your unchaste husbands. Far from it. Either let them live with you, or let them perish on their own.[2] A woman does not owe her chastity to an unchaste man, but she owes it to God, she owes it to Christ. Let her not do it for the one who does not deserve it. Let her do it for Christ. Let her await Christ's reward. Let her read her marriage contracts. Finally, let her experience what is pleasing. because the Scripture says: *Rebuke a wise man and he will love you, rebuke a foolish man and he will go on hating you.* It did not say: "he will begin," but "he will go on" because he hated you already. Therefore I know that wise men love me for this.

Let those who know that I know their sins abstain from communion lest they be turned back from the altar rails. Those whose sins I am unaware of, I summon them to the presence of God. Let them also do penance and in future let them abstain from the uncleanliness of their fornications.

Sermon 392, 4-5; PL 39, 1711-1712

---

[d] cf. Eph 5:23

[2] This is a theme already encountered in Clement of Alexandria: the spiritual autonomy of the wife in dealing with a sinful husband.

MODERATION AND MUTUAL CONSENT IN RELIGIOUS CHOICES

33

1. After reading your Reverence's letter and questioning the letter carrier on the points that remained to be asked, I felt a very deep regret that you had chosen to act toward your husband[1] in a manner that the edifice of continence which he had begun to build should have collapsed into the melancholy downfall of adultery by his failure to persevere.

This great evil arose from your not treating him in his state of mind with the moderation you should have shown, because, although you were refraining by mutual consent from sexual intercourse, as his wife you should have been subject to your husband in other things according to the marriage bond, especially as you are both members of the Body of Christ.[a]

And, indeed, if you, a believer, had an unbelieving husband, you ought to have conducted yourself with a submissive demeanor that you might *win him for the Lord*,[b] as the Apostles advise.

2. I say nothing of the fact that I know you undertook this state of continence contrary to sound doctrine, before he gave consent. He should not have been defrauded of the debt of your body you owed him before his will joined yours in seeking that good which surpasses conjugal chastity.[2]

---

[a] Eph 5:30   [b] cf. 1 Cor 7:13; 1 P 3:1-2

[1] The Letter to Ecdicia (ep. 262) was written circa 395 and is another significant example indicating how the Fathers came to stigmatize certain religious excesses that lacked the most elementary good sense. Ecdicia had made donations to the poor without consulting her husband, had broken that indispensable community of intent which ought to regulate the life of the couple, and had thereby achieved the opposite end from that intended: she had caused her husband to fall into the sin of adultery; she is prohibited to embrace chastity without mutual consent.

[2] Augustine, in his *On the Sermon on the Mount* 1,15,42, defined the brother-sister relationship established between two spouses as the most elevated form of Christian matrimony. Some scholars have wanted to see in the exaltation which Augustine grants to chastity a residue of old Manichean ideas, a conditioning, perhaps even unconscious, of the teaching to which he had as a young man adhered. On the widespread nature of models of continent couples among Christians at the time, cf. Sermon 51,13,21 and epistles 127,9 and 242,4. The Epistles of Augustine, numbering 279 letters, is without doubt one of the most important collections from Christian antiquity. It offers not only a cross-section of social life, whether pagan or Christian, but represents at the same time an important testimony on the doctrinal or moral questions which Augustine had confronted.

According to these words of the Apostle, if he had wished to practice continence and you had not, he would have been obliged to render you the debt. God would have given him credit for continence if he had not refused you marital intercourse, out of consideration for your weakness, not his own, in order to prevent you from falling into the damnable sin of adultery. How much more fitting would it have been for you, to whom subjection was more appropriate, to yield to his will in rendering him the debt in this way, since God would have taken account of your intention to observe continence which you gave up to save your husband from destruction!

3. But, I pass over this, as I said, since, after you had refused to agree to render him the conjugal debt, he agreed to this same bond of continence and lived in perfect continence with you for a long time. By his consent he absolved you from your sin of refusing him the debt of your body.

For, if you had never obtained his consent, no lapse of years would have excused you, but, if you had consulted me however long afterwards, I should have made you no other answer than what the Apostle said: *The wife has not power over her own body, but the husband.*[c] By this power he had already given you permission to practise continence and, for himself, undertook to practice it with you.

4. But there is a point which, I am sorry to say, you did not observe, because you should have given way to him all the more humbly and submissively in your domestic relationship since he had so devotedly yielded to you in such an important matter, even to the point of imitating you. For he did not cease to be your husband because you both were refraining from carnal intercourse; on the contrary, you continued to be husband and wife in a holier manner because you were carrying out a holier resolution, with mutual accord.

Therefore, you had no right to dispose of your wardrobe, or of gold, or silver, or any money, or of any of your earthly property without his consent, lest you scandalize a man who joined you in vowing higher things to God, and had continently abstained from what he could demand of your body in virtue of his lawful power.

---

[c] cf. 1 Cor 7:4

7. However, when I say this, I do not mean that if our good works prove a stumbling-block to anyone we should think of leaving them off. The case of strangers is different from the case of persons bound to us by any tie; the case of believers is not the same as that of unbelievers; the case of parents toward children differs from that of children toward parents; and, finally, the case of husband and wife (which is the one given special consideration in the present circumstances) differs from the others, and the married woman has no right to say: "I do what I please with my own property," since she does not belong to herself, but to her head, that is, her husband.[d] For *after this manner*, as the Apostle Peter says, *certain holy women who trusted in God adorned themselves, being subject to their own husbands; as Sarah obeyed Abraham, calling him her lord, whose daughters* he says *you all are*,[e] and he was speaking to Christian, not to Jewish, women.

8. Therefore you should have taken counsel together about everything; together you should have regulated what treasure is to be laid up in heaven and what is to be left as a means of support for yourselves, your dependents and your son, so that other men be not eased and you burdened. In making and carrying out these arrangements, should any better plan have occurred to you, you should have suggested it respectfully to your husband and bowed obediently to his authority as that of your head. In this way all who prize common sense, whom the news of this good way of life could reach, would rejoice at the fruitfulness and the peace of your household, and your enemy would be turned back, having nothing evil to say of you.

9. Moreover, if in the matter of almsgiving and bestowing your property on the poor, a good and great work about which we have precise commandments from the Lord, you ought to have taken counsel with your husband, a believer, and one who was observing with you the holy vow of continence, and not to have scorned his will, how much more necessary was it for you not to change or adopt anything in your costume and garb against his will. Even if it had been a nun's habit that attracted you could you not have assumed it

---

d Eph 5:23   e 1 P 3:5-6

with greater grace if you had submitted to your husband and received his permission, rather than presuming to put on widow's garb without consulting or deferring to him? And if he absolutely refused his permission, how would your purpose have suffered? Perish the thought that God would have been displeased at you wearing in your husband's lifetime the dress, not of Anna[f] but of Susanna.[g]

11. I have written this, not with the intention of breaking down your virtuous resolution by my words but because I am grieved at your husband's conduct which is the result of your reckless and ill-considered misconduct.

You must now give serious thought to reclaiming him, if you truly want to belong to Christ. Clothe yourself with lowliness of mind and, that God may keep you in constancy, do not scorn your husband for his fall. Pour out devout and continuous prayers for him, offer a sacrifice of tears as if it were the blood of a pierced heart, write him your apology begging pardon for the sin you committed against him by disposing of his property according to your own wishes for its disposition, without asking his advice and consent.

Epistle 262 to Ecdicia; NBA XXIII, 906-919; FOTC

---

[f] cf. Lk 2:36-38   [g] cf. Dn 13:1-64

PAULINUS OF NOLA

INTRODUCTORY PROFILE

Paulinus, future bishop of Nola, was born between 353 and 355 in Bordeaux into a wealthy family which belonged in the senatorial aristocracy.[1] He acquired a rhetorical education suited to his status under the affectionate tutelage of Ausonius, one of the most famous poets and illustrious teachers of his time.[2] The literary success of the

---

[1] On the various hypotheses formulated by scholars on the year of Paulinus's birth cf. *Meropio Ponzio Paolino. Antologia di Carmi*, S. Costanza, ed., 1, Messina, 1971, 46 note 3. The recent hypothesis of A.D. Booth, 'Sur la date de la naissance de Saint Paulin de Nole,' *Classical Views* 1 (1982), 57-64 of downdating to 348 the birthdate of Paulinus does not seem to be supported by sufficiently cogent arguments. For a well delineated biographical profile of Paulinus we cite two recent contributions: *Paolino di Nola, Epistole ad Agostino*, ed. T. Piscitelli Carpino, Naples-Rome, 1989, 11-24 (where all the earlier literature is indicated exhaustively) and J.L. Charlet, 'Saint Paulin de Nole, le converti,' *La Vie Spirituelle* 143 (1989), 341-354. For an updated bibliographical and critical approach to the figure of Paulinus see: *Atti del Convegno XXXI Cinquantenario della morte di S.Paolino di Nola (431-1981)*, Rome, 1983. For a critical assessment of studies on Paulinus in the decade 1977-1987 cf. C. Magazzù, 'Dieci anni di studi di Nola (1977-1987),' *Bollettino di Studi Latini* 18 (1988), 84-103, where moreover at p. 84, note 1-5, important earlier studies are also indicated.

[2] Ausonius was born in Bordeaux around 310. He taught grammar and rhetoric for about 30 years, acquiring such a reputation that he was summoned by the emperor Valentinian I to the role of tutor of his son Gratian. After having been prefect of Gaul, he became a senator in 379. He died around 395. Author of numerous poetical compositions among which it suffices to mention here the poem, *Mosella*, a description of the rustic beauty of the river of that name, he also left behind a corpus of epistles including his correspondence with Paulinus. His adherence to Christianity seems to have been at best perfunctory and has left no trace on his literary production. On this debated question cf. C. Riggi, 'Il cristianesimo di Ausonio,' in *Salesianum* 30 (1968), 642-695 (reprinted in *idem*, *Epistrophe-Tensioni verso la divina armonia. Scritti di filologia patristica*, Rome, 1985, 59-112). For detailed information on the poet from Bordeaux cf. R.P.H. Green, ed., *The Works of Ausonius*, Oxford, 1991; A. Pastorino, *Opere di Decimo Magno Ausonio*, Turin, 1971, 11-121, as well as the epistolary verses sent by Paulinus to Ausonius, in an appendix.

young Paulinus,[3] proceeded apace with his political acumen, culminating around 380 in his being named governor of Campania where we get the first indications of his subsequent spiritual growth. In fact, while celebrating at Nola the feast of St. Felix, the patron of the city, Paulinus manifested a certain awakening of his own faith. He decided to have a hospital for the poor erected and consecrated to the saint.[4] After his return to Bordeaux he undertook a voyage to Spain where he married his wife, Therasia, a wealthy heiress, whose solid faith was no small influence on the ever burgeoning conversion of Paulinus, who, around 389, received baptism from Delphinus, bishop of Bordeaux.

The couple set out once again for Spain where they were smitten by a most tragic happening: the death only eight days after birth of their son, Celsus, who had been so desired and longed for. Paulinus and Therasia at once decided by mutual agreement to enter upon a program of absolute asceticism: they devoted the proceeds of the sale of their property to the poor, and lived for the future in a sort of spiritual marriage. In the case of the two there was realized in practice an ideal of the life of the couple which precisely in the 4th century found its most decisive affirmation,[5] even if examples of sexual abstinence among couples were not lacking for better dedication to religious practice in earlier centuries.[6]

The action of Paulinus made a notable impression on Christian circles,[7] and grieved Ausonius who had tried in vain to dissuade him from his adoption of the ascetic life.[8] On Christmas day, 393,

---

[3] Cf. Ausonius, Letter 20, vv. 2-5, A. Pastorino, *op. cit.*, 734-735, where the poet from Bordeaux records how Paulinus had then obtained the laurel of the poetical triumph. Of the 25 letters of Ausonius, only one (no. 17) is entirely in prose; the others are in verse or a mixture of prose and verse.

[4] Of these residences Paulinus informs us himself in *Carmen* 21: CSEL 30, 158-186. For an analysis of the autobiographical elements of the components cf. A. Ruggiero, *Nola crocevia dello spirito*, Nola, 1982, 142-143 (reprinted in *Atti del Convegno, op. cit.*, 203).

[5] Cf. E. Giannarelli, *La tipologia femminile nella biografia e nell'autobiografia cristiana del IV secolo*, Rome, 1980, 88-94.

[6] Cf. C. Mazzucco, *"E fui fatta maschio,"* *op. cit.*, 29-30.

[7] Cf. *Meropio Ponzio Paolino. Antologia, op. cit.*, 54 and notes 35-36

[8] Between 390 and the Spring of 393 Ausonius wrote at least 4 letters to Paulinus hoping to dissuade him from his proposal. In the summer of 393 Paulinus responded, *Carmen* 10, to which Ausonius replied in 394 with a fifth letter followed by the definitive reply of Paulinus,

Paulinus was ordained priest at Barcelona, but his intentions already were to leave Spain and withdraw to Nola near the tomb of St. Felix who continued to be the inspiration and support of his choice of life. Together with Therasia, he departed in 394 and stopped off for a time at Rome where he was the object of a very tepid reception on the part of an ambience, which, in the person of Pope Siricius himself, regarded with suspicion the growing phenomenon of monasticism.[9] Arrived at Nola, Paulinus founded a small monastic community, occupying with his brother monks the upper floor of the hospital which he himself was responsible for constructing when he was governor of Campania. Life was lived in complete frugality and in prayer, not forgetting manual labor, which consisted essentially in the care of a small garden.[10] Paulinus gave himself also to an intense practical activity, having always a particular interest in the cult of Felix. He had a new basilica erected, decorated with wall paintings depicting scenes from the Old Testament; the old basilica was enlarged and decorated with scenes from the New Testament. In this way he pursued a precise aesthetic-parenetic plan, in which a practical interest in giving joy to his people corresponded to caring for the external beauty of the monument, offering to pilgrims, especially uneducated ones, the immediacy of images to stimulate their personal and intimate understanding of Scripture.[11]

Following the death of Therasia (which occurred around 408), and his being named bishop of Nola in 409,[12] dependable references

---

Carmen 11. This is the chronological reconstruction arrived at by P. Fabre, *Essai sur la chronologie de l'oeuvre de saint Paulin de Nole,* Paris, 1948, 106, which enjoys the most credibility among scholars (cf. A. Pastorino, *op. cit.,* 101-104) even if it has not been demonstrated incontrovertibly. [See P.G. Walsh, ACW 40, 1975, 20-24.] The most recent contribution to the chronology of the life and works of Paulinus of Nola is J. Desmulliez, 'Paulin de Nole,' *RechAug* 20 (1985), 35-64.

[9] J.T. Lienhardt, *Paulinus of Nola and Early Western Monasticism,* Cologne-Bonn, 119-127.

[10] *Ibidem,* 70-81.

[11] Cf. H. Junod-Ammerbauer, 'Les constructions de Nole et l'esthétique de Saint Paulin,' *REAug* 24 (1978), 22-57, treats of this hostility and suspicion.

[12] The election to the episcopacy of Paulinus cannot be dated with certainty. In the *City of God* (Book I, 10,2. NBA V/1, p. 38), Augustine speaks of Paulinus as "bishop of Nola" which indicates that in 413, the probable date of composition of Book I of the *City of God,* Paulinus was already a bishop, but does not demonstrate that it was in 410, or that the acts of plunder completed by the barbarians to which Augustine refers correspond to those at Nola: cf. the considerations of T. Piscitelli Carpino, *op. cit.,* 52-53.

to him become scarcer. One of the few well-attested events was his invitation, received from the imperial court itself, to preside over a synod of Italian bishops which would decide the outcome of a controversy sprung up between Boniface and Eulalius over who would succeed to the dead pope Zosimus.[13] It is a further proof of the esteem which surrounded Paulinus that he had truly made of Nola a crossroads of the spirit,[14] and was regarded with profound respect by Augustine himself,[15] and illustrious personages like Melania the Younger,[16] or bishop Nicetas of Remesiana[17] flocked there because of the attraction which the purity of the asceticism of Paulinus exercised. The monastic life did not in fact signify total isolation from the external world, but rather a way of bringing to realization at the heart of the Christian community the gospel teaching in its most complete fashion. Paulinus returned annually to Rome on the occa-

---

[13] At the death of pope Zosimus (418), who after much uncertainty had acceded to the request of the African bishop for the condemnation of Pelagius and Celestius, an unpleasant struggle arose concerning the succession between Boniface and Eulalius. In a letter written to Paulinus by the same Galla Placidia (cf. S. Cristo, 'Some Notes on the Bonifacian-Eulalian Schism,' *Aevum* 51 (1977), 163-167) it is noted that, after the pope, the bishop of Nola was recognized as the most authoritative spokesman of the Italian episcopate: cf. T. Piscitelli Carpino, *op. cit.*, 22-23.

[14] This is the felicitous definition of A. Ruggiero, *op. cit.*, 125; cf. also Y.M. Duval, 'Les premiers rapports de Paulin de Nole avec Jérôme: moine et philosophe? Poète ou exégète?', in *Polyanthema.Studi di letteratura cristiana antica offerti a Salvatore Costanza*, I, Messina, 1989, p. 216 where a relationship between Nola and Bethlehem is established, another crossroads of "spiritual and intellectual relations of Christianity."

[15] Cf. for example *Letter* 26: NBA XXI, p. 158, in which the bishop of Hippo advises the young Licentius to have recourse to Campania, near Paulinus, in whom he will find a peerless guide.

[16] Paulinus himself speaks in *Carmen* 21 about the visit made to Nola by Melania the Younger, along with her husband Pinianus. Melania the Younger, born in 383, had donated a large part of her possessions to the poor, giving herself to a life conducted according to the most profound principles of Christian spirituality. Founder of monasteries in Palestine, she passed away in Jerusalem in 439. On Melania the Younger cf. A. Giardina, 'Carità eversiva: le donazioni di Melania la giovane e gli equilibri della società tardo-antica,' in Aa. vv., *Héstiasis*, II, Messina, 1986, 77-102.

[17] Nicetas sojourned twice at Nola; the first time in 399/400; the second in 402. Bishop of Remesiana, modern Bela Palamka in Serbia, he exercised his own mission of evangelization also among the barbarians of Dacia. To him Paulinus dedicated *Carmen* 17, in which he has described in a wishful manner the voyage which the bishop is preparing to face to reach Dacia. The presence of Nicetas on the occasion of the feast in honor of Felix in 402 is however confirmed by *Carmen* 27. Of the works attributed to Nicetas, apart from the most famous and most widely diffused in the entire Latin West, the *Te Deum*, we should mention a work on the usefulness of the ecclesiastical chant (*On the Good of the Psalmody*) and an incomplete work on catechesis (*Instructio ad Competentes*).

sion of the Feast of Saints Peter and Paul;[18] he welcomed pilgrims, especially maintaining close contacts by letters, from a spontaneous need to offer in charity his own friendship, of giving to others with a sincere affection, inspired by the most intimate foundations of Christian spirituality: the Christian meaning of friendship is one of the most characteristic traits of his personality.[19]

The last years of Paulinus's life are, as has been said already, the most obscure and are partly shrouded in an aura of legend;[20] the date of his death, however, is certain: June 22, 431.[21]

If, on the human and religious level, Paulinus is one of the personages most representative of the latter part of the 4th century, no less important, especially in the field of poetry, is the significance of his literary activity. Of considerable importance is his Letters,[22] whether as indirect witness to contemporary events, or as a mirror of the human relations which Paulinus managed to create around himself with the notable personages of his time, like Jerome, Sulpicius Severus, and Augustine. These are 51 in number in which the bishop of Nola, even if he does not shine too much by his theological acumen,[23] nonetheless shows himself an able exegete in the utilization of different sources, bent to the dictates of his parenetic needs,[24] and

---

[18] Cf. *Epistulae* 18,1; 20,2; 47,1: CSEL 29.

[19] Emblematic in this sense is the title of one of the most important monographs dedicated to Paulinus: P. Fabre, *Saint Paulin de Nole et l'amitié chrétienne*, Paris, 1949.

[20] We allude to an episode narrated by Gregory the Great, *Dialogues* III,1-8: SC 260, 256-265, on the basis of which Paulinus would have been offered as a hostage to the Vandals and carried off to Africa. An examination of this hagiographic tradition with the evident goal of reevaluation has been conducted by G. Santaniello, 'La prigioni di Paolino: tradizione e storia,' in A. Ruggiero-H.Crouzel-G.Santaniello, *Paolino di Nola, momenta della sua vita e delle sue opere*, Nola, 1983, 223-249.

[21] Cf. Uranius, *De morte Paulini*, 12: PL 53, col. 866. Uranius, a disciple of Paulinus, wrote a letter on the death of the bishop of Nola, to honor the request of Pacatus: cf. A. Pastorino, 'Il De obitu sancti Paulini di Uranio,' *AugR* 24 (1984),115-141. There is an Italian translation of the text of Uranius in CTP 42.

[22] On the letters of Paulinus cf. S. Prete, *Paolino di Nola e l'umanesimo cristiano. Saggio sopra il suo epistolario*, Bologna, 1964; P.G. Walsh, *The Letters of St. Paulinus of Nola*, ACW 35-36, 1963,1966. [A new edition of the Letters: G. Santaniello, *Paolino di Nola Le lettere*, 2 v., Naples, 1992.]

[23] On the theological thought of Paulinus cf. J. T. Lienhard, *op.cit.*, 141-144; in particular on his christology see G. Morelli, *De S. Paulini Nolani doctrina christologica*, Naples, 1945.

[24] Fundamental on the exegetical aspects of the epistles of Paulinus — with references also to the *Poems* — S. Leanza, 'Aspetti esegetica dell'opera di Paolino di Nola,' in *Atti del Convegno*, *op. cit.*, 67-91.

a most felicitous artist in adapting the images and language of the
Bible to the fabric of discourse and to the rhetorical construction of
the letter, as is manifest, for example, in epistle XI.[25]

To Paulinus, however, acknowledgments of greater merit came
in the field of poetry. For long underestimated by modern scholars,
if only because of his being systematically compared with his contemporary, the Spanish poet, Prudentius, unanimously recognized as
the most effective exponent of Christian Latin poetry,[26] in recent
decades the judgments have become more balanced. In fact, the
contributions of Paulinus to the formulation of a Christian poetic[27]
have been better defined, and the innovative nature of his verses has
gained recognition, albeit within the continuity of the formal tradition of genres of classical Latin poetry.[28] He has been rediscovered
in short as a figure who, even if he has not the speculative acumen
of Augustine, or the biblical training of Jerome, or the historico-
political importance of Ambrose,[29] cannot be considered "on the
outside of history" but capable of affecting it "in depth and for ever."[30]

The poetic output of Paulinus consists of 33 poems, four of
which, however, are doubtfully ascribed to him.[31] Some of these
belong to the period of his youth;[32] others consist of poetic para-

---

[25] Cf. A. Salvatore, 'Immagini bibliche e strutture discorsive — La lettera II di Paolino,' in *Atti del Convegno, op. cit.,* 253-280.

[26] Prudentius, a Spaniard from Calahorra, lived between 348 and the beginning of the 5th century. Notices on his life are scarce, while his literary production is copious. It consists of
poems political (*Contra Symmachum*), lyrical (Book of Daily Songs; *Peristephanōn*), didac-
tic (as, for example *De origine peccati*). In general cf. S. Costanza, 'Prudenzio,' in DPAC,
op. cit., 11, 1811-1825. On the methodological inopportuneness of an aesthetic Paulinus/
Prudentius confrontation cf. K. Kohlwes, *Christliche Dichtung und stilistische Form bei
Paulinus von Nola,* Bonn, 1979, 1-13.

[27] Cf. S. Costanza, 'La poetica di Paolino,' in Aa. vv., *Studi in onore di Q. Cataudella,* III, Catania,
1972, 593-613; H. Junod-Ammerbauer, 'Le poète chrétien selon Paulin de Nole,' *REAug* 21
(1975), 13-52.

[28] Cf. S. Costanza, 'I generi letterari nell'opera poetica di Paolino di Nola,' *Augustinianum* 14
(1974), 637-650.

[29] Cf. J.L. Charlet, *art. cit.,* 353.

[30] Cf. S. D'Elia, 'Sullo sfondo storico-culturale dell'opera di S. Paolino di Nola,' *Impegno e
Dialogo* 4 (1986-87), Nola, 1988,17-32.

[31] The reference is to *Carmina* 4, 5, 32 and 33: cf. *Meropio Ponzio Paolino. Antologia, op. cit.,*
68-71, notes 70-73.

[32] These are *Carmina* 1, 2 and 3, on which cf. L. Carrese, 'I carmi profane di Paolino di Nola,'
Annali della Facoltà di Lettere e Filos. Univ. Napoli, n.s. 16 (1985-1986), 5-14.

phrases of Psalms 1, 2 and 136, outlining, along with *Carmen* VI, dedicated to John the Baptist, a first project in Christian poetry, more theologically oriented and far from the secular contents of his early juvenile compositions.[33] Still others are occasional compositions.[34] Finally, the greater part are birthday poems, written for the annual celebration of the feast of St. Felix.[35]

To the group of occasional compositions belongs Poem 25, an epithalamium[36] composed in honor of the marriage of Titia to Julian, future bishop of Eclanum, and a polemical adversary of Augustine. Composed in conscious imitation of an epithalamium which the pagan poet, Claudian, had written for the marriage of Honorius and Maria,[37] the poem of Paulinus, while preserving many traditional rhetorical canons of the classical epithalamium,[38] constitutes a Christianization and, at the same time, a radical transformation of the epithalamium genre itself.[39]

It is Christ, in fact, who by substituting for the pagan divinities as protectors of marriage, guides the new spouses and, in the

---

[33] Cf. A.V. Nazzaro, 'La parafrasi salmica di Paolino di Nola,' in *Atti del Convegno, op. cit.*, 93-119, which examines *Carmina* 7, 8, 9. On *Carmen* 6 see S. Prete, 'Paolino di Nola: la prafrasi biblica della "laus Iohannis" (*Carmen* 6),' *AugR* 14 (1974), 625-635; R. Herzog, *Die Bibelepik der lateinischen Spätantike*, I, Munich, 1975, 212-223.

[34] Such are *Carmina* 17, 25, 31, on which see *Meropio Ponzio Paolino, Antologia, op. cit.*, 152-156; 182-191; 210-219.

[35] These are the *carmina natalicia* written annually on the occasion of the feast of Felix, the 14th January. Paulinus began composing them in 395 and finished 14 by 408. [See chart in ACW 40, pp. 6-7.]

[36] The epithalamium was a poetic genre largely diffused both in Greek and in Latin poetry.

[37] Cf. R. Gelsomino, 'L'Epitalamio di Paolino di Nola per Giuliano e Titia (*Carmen* 25),' in *Atti del Convegno, op. cit.*, 213-230. Claudian, perhaps a native of Alexandria, can be considered the greatest and most representative pagan poet of his time. Born around 370, he came to Rome in 394, transferring next to Milan in the retinue of the great general Stilicho. In this way he became the official cantor at the imperial court, celebrating personages and directing invectives against the enemies of Honorius and Stilicho (*Contra Rufinum, Contra Eutropium*). To Claudian are also attributed Christian *carmina*, like the one written to exalt the Savior, more a concession perhaps to the Christian court than to a religious conscience. He died in 405.

[38] Cf. A. Sbrancia, 'L'epitalamio di S. Paolino di Nola,' *AFLM* 11 (1978), 84-129, which sets out to demonstrate the adhesion of Paulinus to traditional rhetorical "topoi," which have been renewed by new Christian content.

[39] Cf. R.Herzog, 'Probleme der heidnisch-christlichen Gattungskontinuität am Beispiel des Paulinus von Nola,' in Aa. vv., *Christianisme et Formes littéraires de l'Antiquité tardive en Occident*, Vandoeuvres-Geneva, 1977, 373-411.

person of the officiating bishop, joins their right hands. Instead of the deities typical of paganism (Juno, Cupid, Venus), the Christian virtues enter, namely, Peace, Modesty, and Piety. To the pomp of pagan marriage, moreover, the poet opposes the decorum of the Christian rite, which has been instituted by God and which has been sanctified by Christ by his presence at the wedding feast of Cana.

This last gospel reference opens the properly doctrinal part of the poem (vv. 153-190), a sort of theology of Christian marriage, seen as an actualization of the union between Christ and the Church and in which the spouses, now brothers through being sons of Mary, are united to the mystical body of which Christ is the head. In the preceding verses Paulinus had directed moral injunctions both to Titia and to Julian not to be too preoccupied with the external physical beauty of the body but rather with interior virtue; in the sequel, almost in a paradoxical fashion, after having described the ceremony in its liturgical aspects,[40] he exhorts the spouses to live their union in absolute chastity[41] but at the same time in the case of not renouncing the physical relationship, to hope that they might give life to offspring destined for the priesthood.

The doctrinal part of the poem, in this way, judged negatively on the aesthetic level by the majority of critics,[42] fulfills an important catechetical function for the spouses (and the readers), by balancing the ring composition of the poem,[43] which in fact is transformed, adjusting the classical canons of the genre of epithalamium in a celebration of chastity albeit in subdued tones, without radical extremes, but in recognition that continence realizes the type of

---

[40] On liturgical aspects present in the epithalamium of Paulinus cf. H. Crouzel, 'Liturgie du mariage chrétien au V siècle selon l'Epithalame de S. Paulin de Nole,' in Aa. vv., *Mélanges Martimort*, Paris, 1983, 619-626.

[41] Cf. C. Tibiletti, 'Nota teologica a Paolino di Nola (*carmen* 25,199),' *AugR* 18 (1978), 389-395 according to which the apparent *aporia* of exhortation to live in chastity finds its justification in the eschatological context of the passage.

[42] Cf., for example, the limited judgment of S. Prete, 'I temi della proprietà e della famiglia negli scritti di Paolino di Nola,' *AugR* 17 (1977), 272-273.

[43] On the structure of *Carmen* 25 cf. the felicitous notations of S. Costanza, 'Catechesi e poesia nei carmi XXII, XXV e XXXI di Paolino di Nola,' in S. Felici (ed.), *Crescita dell'uomo nella catechesi dei Padri* (Età Postnicena), Rome, 1988, 237-256.

union proper to the condition of angels in the union in paradise and anticipates the eschatological condition of those who will be saved.

Paulinus had no immediate successors in the evolution of Christian literature. There will be, in fact, medieval writers to restore all the novelty of his mode of treating the epithalamium genre.[44]

---

[44] Cf. R. Herzog, *Problème, op. cit.*, 415. The works of Paulinus are published in CSEL 29 (Letters), 30 (*Carmina*). A new Italian translation of the *Carmina* in CTP n. 88 (A. Ruggiero, ed.); *Letters of St. Paulinus of Nola,* tr. P.G. Walsh, ACW 35, 36, New York, 1966, 1967. Partial translation of the Epistles, *Epistolaria*, A. Esposito, ed., Naples-Rome, 1976.

A POETIC CELEBRATION OF A SPIRITUAL COUPLE

34

Souls harmonious are being joined in chaste love, a boy who is Christ's virgin and a girl who is God's. Christ God, draw these matching doves towards Your reins, and govern their necks thrust beneath Your light yoke,[1] *for Your yoke*, Christ, *is indeed light*[a] when assumed by an eager will and borne with the ready complaisance of love. This holy burden of the law of chastity is oppressive for the reluctant, but for persons of devotion it is a pleasant imposition to keep in subjection the role of the flesh. This marriage must see nothing of the wanton conduct of the mindless mob; Juno, Cupid, Venus, those symbols of lust, must keep their distance. The chaste, dear offspring of a bishop is being joined in sacred alliance, so Peace, Modesty, and Holiness must assemble as attendants. For a harmonious marriage-alliance is at once a holy love, an honorable love, and peace with God. God with His own lips consecrated the course of this alliance, and with His own hand established the coupling of human persons. He made two abide in one flesh, so that He might confer a love more indivisible. While Adam[2] slept he was deprived of the rib which was removed from him, and then he obtained a partner formed of his own bone. He felt no loss in his side, for his flesh[b] was extended to replace it; he acknowledged the accession of a twin. Once he beheld this other self sprung from himself in the flesh they shared, he then became the prophet of his own situation, speaking with tongue renewed. *This flesh*, he said, *is the flesh of my flesh. I recognize the bone of my bones. She is the rib from my side.*[c] So, since this pair are the ancient type of the holy alliance now being sealed between the dear children of Aaron,[3] our joy must be re-

---

[a] cf. Mt 11:30   [b] cf. Gn 2:21   [c] cf. Gn 2:23

---

[1] The coach of Venus, drawn by doves in pagan literature and iconography, is here juxtaposed with, and augmented by, Christian symbolism; cf. S. Costanza, *op. cit.*, 240, n. 42.

[2] The biblical account emphasizes the character of indissolubility which distinguishes Christian marriage, but is also introduced to replace the mythological apparatus of pagan poetry.

[3] Aaron had been destined for the priesthood to perpetuate a priestly family (cf. Ex 28:1; Lv 8:1-36). The poet's allusion is to be explained by the fact that Julian, son of Memor, a bishop (of Capua?) was a lector and destined for priesthood.

strained and our prayers unimpassioned. Christ's name must resound everywhere on the lips of his devoted people. There must be no mob dancing in decorated streets. None must strew the ground with leaves, or the threshold with foliage. There must be no crazed procession through a city where Christ dwells. I would have no secular display befoul devoted Christians. No wind must waft the scent of foreign ritual, for our entire proceedings must be redolent of the elegance of chastity. Saintly people recognize as their sole perfume that sprinkled by Christ's name, which breathes forth the chaste fragrance of God. There must be no trays lavishly laden with superfluous gifts, for real worth is adorned by character and not by wealth. The holy wife of a bishop's son, the spouse of a boy already consecrated, must receive as dowry the light of life. She must reject garments decked with gold or purple, for the shining grace of God is her golden garment.

She must spurn also necklaces adorned with motley jewels, so that she herself may be a notable jewel for the Lord God, for no weight of loathsome avarice must oppress a neck dedicated to bearing the yoke of Christ the Lord. Rather, her adornment designed to please must depend on an inward grooming, and her mind must be decked with the dowry that brings salvation.[d] She must not long to squander her income vainly on costly jewels or silken wraps; instead, her soul must be adorned with the virtues of chastity so that she may be a precious asset and not a liability to her husband. When a person seeks to attain a name by bodily display, such a fault cheapens and devalues. The mind is sorely blinded by lust a fault for this debased aim, the body's gleaming spoils begrime the mind. The shameless individual fails to realize the foulness of the adornment thus put on, which makes the wearer delighting in such garments cheaper than the clothing itself. God forbid that one who has become a daughter in the house of an apostolic family should appear as the daughter of the temple where idols are worshipped. Her skin should not be foully disguised with rouge, her eyes with mascara, her hair with yellow tint. The girl who spurns the chaste beauty of nature is

---

[d] cf. 1 P 3:3-4

guilty of the sin of pride, for she condemns God's creation of her. A woman adorning herself with such a range of disguises will gain no credence when she claims she is chaste. Avoid the adornment of such endowments, new bride of a saintly husband for these are the delights of a vacant mind. Do not wander abroad with perfumed clothes and hair, seeking recognition from men's nostrils wherever you pass; do not sit with your hair structured and castellated, with layers and ropes of interwoven in a cause of unhappy locks. Do not through your lustre be vexatious to many, nor an evil cause of baneful attraction. You must not seek with foul purpose to delight even your own husband by thus adding inches to your person.

You, too, saintly boy, so dedicated to the consecrated books, must show a love which spurns all eagerness for a handsome appearance.[4] Christ has compensated you by generously adorning your handsome soul with perennial riches, and He has enriched both of you with holy chaste wedding gifts — hope, devotion, fidelity, peace, chastity.

A cleric must love a wife who glories in Christ as her hair, whose beauty lies in her heart's radiance. A lector must learn from the divine history that she was made as man's helpmate[e] by God's dispensation. In her turn the woman must strive to attain equality with her consecrated husband by welcoming Christ's presence in her spouse with humility of heart. Thus she can grow into his holy body and be interwoven with his frame, so that her husband may be her head as Christ is his.[f] In such a marriage as this Eve's subservience came to an end, and Sarah became the free equal of her holy husband. When Jesus' friends were married with such a compact as this, He attended as a groomsman, and changed water into wine[g] like nectar. A bridal couple like this will fittingly be visited by Mary, mother of the Lord, who gave birth to God without loss of her virginity. In this consecrated virgin God built Himself a pleasing temple with a hidden roof aperture. Silently He glided down like the rain that falls

---

e cf. Gn 2:18   f cf. Eph 5:23   g cf. Jn 2:1-11

4   On this part of the poem, in which, according to a topic, by now well codified in Christian literature, the luxury and vanity of woman is being rebuked, cf. S. Costanza, *op. cit.*, 345-347.

as noiseless dew from a high cloud upon a fleece. None was ever privy to this secret visitation by which God took the form of man from His virgin mother.

How remarkable was the design of the Lord which sought the salvation of men! Without intercourse, a woman's womb conceived new life. This bride did not submit to a mere human husband. She was a mother and bore a child without the woman's role in intercourse. The compact made her a spouse, but she was no wife in body. She became the mother of a Boy though she was untainted by a husband.

What a great mystery was this, by which the Church became wedded to Christ and became at once the Lord's bride and His sister! The bride with the status of spouse is a sister because she is not subject.

So she continues as mother through the seed of the eternal Word alike conceiving and bringing forth nations. She is sister and spouse because her intercourse is not physical but mental, and her Husband is not man but God.

The children of this mother comprise equally old and infants; this offspring has no age or sex. For this is the blessed progeny of God which springs from no human seed but from a heavenly race. This is why the teacher Paul says that *in Christ there is no male or female,*[h] *but one body and one faith, for all of us who acknowledge Christ as Head of our body are one body,*[i] *and are all Christ's limbs.* Because we have now put on Christ and stripped off Adam, we are at once advancing towards the shape of angels.[5] Hence for all born in baptism there is the one task; both sexes must incorporate the perfect man, and Christ as all in all must be our common Head, our King who hands over His limbs to the Father in the Kingdom. Once all are endowed with immortal bodies, the frail condition of human lives forgoes marriage between men and women.

So remember me, and live in chaste partnership forever. Your

---

h cf. Gal 3:28   i cf. 1 Cor 12:27

5 On the profound doctrinal significance of this extensive and articulated part of the epithalamium, cf. what was said in the General Introduction, pp. 113-116, and, further, H. Crouzel, 'L'epitalamio di San Paolino: il suo contenuto dottrinale,' in *Atti del Convegno, op. cit.*, 143-148.

yoke must be the revered cross. As children of that mother who is both spouse and sister, you must train your hearts to be worthy of the holy names you bear. As brother and sister hasten together to meet Christ the Bridegroom, so that you may be one flesh in the eternal body. You must be enmeshed with that love by which the Church holds fast to Christ, and by which Christ in turn hugs her close. Christ, instruct the newly married pair through your holy bishop. Aid the pure hearts through his chaste hands,[6] so that they may both agree on a compact of virginity, or be the source of consecrated virgins. Of these prayers, the first condition is preferable, that they keep their bodies innocent of the flesh. But if they consummate physical union may the chaste offspring to come be a priestly race. May the whole house of Memor be a house of Aaron. May this house of Memor be a house of anointed ones. Preserve the memory of Paulinus and Therasia, and Christ will preserve the memory of Memor[7] forever.

Carmen XXV; CSEL 30 pp. 238-245; ACW, tr. P.G. Walsh

AN EXAMPLE OF SPIRITUAL MARRIAGE: APRO AND AMANDA

35

3.[1] In your letter, too, your wife, who does not lead her husband to effeminacy or greed but brings you back to self-discipline and courage to become the bones of her husband is worthy of admiration because of her great emulation of God's marriage with the Church. She is restored and reinstated into unity with you, for Christ's love joins you with spiritual bonds which are all the stronger for being more chaste. You have passed from your own bodies into Christ's.

---

[6] Following the ms. reading, *iuva*, not *iuga*.

[7] In late Latin poetry, even Christian, formal jokes were frequent: the poet exploits the name of the bishop, father of the bridegroom, to do a play on words (Lat. *memor, Memor*).

[1] Apro was a magistrate of Aquitaine, who, with his wife, Amanda, after exercising consecrated priesthood, dedicated his life to one of the not so rare examples of spiritual matrimony in the 4th century. The correspondence between Apro and Paulinus also includes Epistles 38 and 39.

4. The Lord has blessed you, for He who alone does wonderful things has made both one,[a] establishing the two in Himself. He transforms not only souls but also feelings, changing the transient into the eternal. See how you remain the married couple you were, yet not coupled as you were. You are yourselves, yet not yourselves. Now you know each other, as you know Christ, apart from the flesh.[b] *This is the change of the right hand of the Most High*[c] which contains itself yet makes all things new, which *turns the sea into dry land*[d] reducing the stream of vices to the solid land of self-control. Blessed is Amanda amongst women,[e] faithful and most acceptable to the Lord by reason of that further dedication[2] with which on your behalf she has confronted worldly needs as a tower founded on unbudging rock confronts storms. Established on that rock, on which a house once built shall not fall,[f] with the steady immobility of her unremitting mind, she has *become your tower of strength against the face of the enemy;*[g] she breaks the force of the worldly waves and whirlpools by interposing her holy slavery, so that you may be shielded from the sea and preserve your mind unshaken like a ship safe in the harbor of the Church, plying the oars of salvation which are persistent meditation on studies and works of godliness. This godliness made you submit to Christ, for you preferred *even to lie abject in the house of the Lord rather than be prominent in the tabernacles of sinners*[h] and bound your fellow servant Amanda to physical labors on behalf of your soul out of spiritual love for you, so that she might make her service the price of your freedom. In the transactions of the world she serves, not the world but Christ, for whose sake she endures the world that you may avoid enduring it.

Truly she has become the help to you that God's work and word[i] prescribes. To you she turns, hanging on your nod, standing where you stand, walking in your footsteps, enlivened by your spirit.[j] She suffers need on behalf of your life, that she may be refashioned by it. She takes charge of secular business so that you may forget it; she

---

[a] cf. Gn 2:23   [b] cf. 2 Cor 5:16   [c] Ps 77:10   [d] Ps 66:6   [e] cf. Lk 1:29   [f] cf. Mt 7:24   [g] Ps 61:3   [h] Ps 84:10   [i] cf. Gn 2:18   [j] cf. Gn 3:16

[2] E. Giannarelli, *La tipologia, op. cit.*, 92, points out more or less veiled Mariological references in the figure of Amanda.

handles it so that you may handle God's. She gives the appearance of having possessions so that you may be possessed, not by the world but by Christ. No discordant will severs her from your committed life; more remarkable, harmonious faith keeps her apart from your work but joins her to you in will.

Being such a wife, *her husband entrusts his heart to her*[k] — as it is written — because she brings him good, and not evil all the days of his life[l]; and that you might not be overly concerned about what takes place in your earthly home, you can freely and with dedication concern yourself with that of your heavenly home.... You are, in Christ,[m] the head and she is for you the foundation, by whose sake you are able to follow the way of the Lord.... Therefore, to you will be given the fruit of your hands, and your husband will be praised at the gates of Zion[n] in the Lord who prepares a common table for you, fruit of the seed of the works which, with various degrees of fatigue but with an equal amount of love, you have sown, that on that day you will come rejoicing, carrying your sheaves,[o] your wife, helpmate in the sowing, and you, sower in virtue of your office....

Epistle XLIV to Apro and Amanda; CSEL 29, 372-375; ACW, tr. P.G. Walsh.

---

[k] cf. Pr 31:11   [l] cf. Pr 31:12   [m] cf. 1 Cor 11:3   [n] cf. Pr 31:31   [o] Ps 126:6

PSEUDO-JEROME

INTRODUCTORY PROFILE

The *Letter to Celantia* is attributed in the text tradition in some manuscripts to Jerome, in others to Paulinus of Nola. As a result it sometimes is published in the Letters of Jerome, sometimes in the Letters of Paulinus.[1]

In 1934 G. De Plinval, in publishing the results of his research on the literary activity of Pelagius,[2] presented evidence of thematic connections between the famous *Letter to Demetriades*, written by

---

[1] Cf. Jerome, Letter 148, CSEL 56 329-356. Earlier, however, J. Labourt did not include this letter in his edition of the letters of Jerome, *Les Belles Lettres,* Paris, 1949. G. Hartel, editor of Paulinus, has published the *Letter to Celantia* in an appendix to the text of the other letters: CSEL 29, 436-459. It should be noted that the authenticity of Paulinus was contested by L. Muratori, 'Dissertazioni sui poemi di San Paolino,' reproduced in PL 61, coll. 779-836 (on this letter in particular coll. 791-792).

[2] Cf. G. De Plinval, 'Recherches sur l'oeuvre littéraire de Pelage,' *Revue de Philologie* 8 (1934), 9-42. Pelagius, born in Britain around 354, originated the movement called Pelagianism, condemned as heretical by the Church. As A. Solignac, from whom we have a recent excellent synthesis on the movement and its most representative exponents (cf. art. 'Pelage et Pelagianisme,' in *DSp* 12, coll. 2889-2936 [bibliography by F.G. Nuvolone, coll. 2936-2942]), has justly observed, it is hazardous to unite under the one rubric heterogeneous events and personages and it is especially dangerous to consider Pelagianism as a sort of monolith, torn from its socio-theological context. The discussions which occupied on the one hand Pelagius and, on the other, his adversaries among them Augustine especially, turned on the evaluation of the relations between grace, sin and free will. Pope Zosimus, who at first had absolved Pelagius, had to yield to the imperial authority which in 418 had condemned as a "superstition," the Pelagian doctrine, and in July of this year he invited the Churches of the East and West to subscribe to the condemnation. The Council of Ephesus in 431 definitively sanctioned the condemnation of Pelagius, his doctrines, and his followers. It is a merit of recent historiography to have presented in a more objective form the figure of Pelagius and the sociological context of his teachings, which remain incontrovertibly unacceptable on the theological level: cf. V. Grossi, 'Avversari e amici di Agostino,' in J. Quasten, *Patrologia* III, 437-465; A.Trapè, 'Verso una riabilitazione del Pelagianesimo?' *AugR* 3 (1963), 482-516.

Pelagius around 413,[3] and the *Letter to Celantia*. The latter in fact traces the rules which ought to guide the conduct of a married woman just as the one to Demetriades defined that of a virgin consecrated to the Lord.[4]

As well as some thematic similarities, as, for instance, the image of Scripture as having to be "the mirror" of our actions (*Letter to Demetriades*, 23 = *Letter to Celantia*, 15) De Plinval has particularly underlined the identical tone which permeates the two letters, the similar method of citing some scriptural passages, and the literary and moral development of Pelagius' own discourses.

The attribution to Pelagius of the *Letter to Celantia* has been reiterated by De Plinval in subsequent studies[5] and, more recently, another scholar, R.F. Evans, has inserted it in a group of letters that are securely assigned to the British writer.[6] It is well to emphasize that, despite the thematic and stylistic agreements, there is always a margin of hypothesis which another chance discovery could undermine completely, but it can be presumed with a good measure of likelihood that the *Letter to Celantia* belongs to Pelagius.

---

[3] Demetriades, belonging to the Anici family, one of the most powerful of the Roman aristocracy, converted to Christianity, decided to consecrate himself as a virgin to God and received the bishopric of Carthage, to which he moved after the sack of Rome in 410.

[4] Cf. G. De Plinval, *art. cit.*, 14-15.

[5] Cf. G. De Plinval, *Pélage. Ses écrits, sa vie et sa réforme. Étude d'histoire littéraire et religieuse*, Lausanne, 1943; *idem, Essai sur le style et la langue de Pélage*, Fribourg, 1947; *idem*, 'Vue d'ensemble sur la littérature pélagienne,' *REL* 29 (1951), 284-294.

[6] Cf. R.F. Evans, *Pelagius. Inquiries and Reappraisals*, London, 1968; and especially *Four Letters of Pelagius*, London, 1968, 21-22. [Engl. tr. See most recently B.R. Rees, *The Letters of Pelagius, and His Followers*, The Boydell Press.]

TO CELANTIA:
CHASTITY OUGHT TO BE FREELY CHOSEN BY BOTH PARTNERS

36

24. Let your home be the object of your concern in such a way that you can still set aside a period of respite for your spiritual life.[1] Choose a convenient place, a little removed from the noise of the household, to which you can betake yourself as to a harbor out of a great storm of cares and there, in the peace of inner seclusion, calm the turbulent waves of thoughts outside. There let your study of divine readings be so constant, your alternations in prayers so frequent, your meditation on the future world so steadfast and deliberate, that you have no trouble in making up for all the employments of your remaining time by this spell of freedom from them. Nor do we say this with the purpose of detaching you from your family; rather our intention is that in that place you may learn and meditate as to what kind of person you ought to show yourself to your own kin.

25. Control and cherish your household in such a way that you wish to be seen to be a mother of your family rather than a mistress and win their respect by kindness[2] rather than strictness. Obedience is always more dependable and more acceptable when it is received from love than from fear. But, above all else, let the arrangement prescribed by apostolic rule be observed in a marriage that is respected and without stain.

26. First and foremost, see that your husband's authority is upheld and that the entire household learns from your example the

---

[1] Celantia, a person not otherwise known, had written to Pelagius (?) to outline a model of the Christian life which could be conformable to the situation of a married person and the principles of Scripture. Our author in his reply first of all prescribed respect for the neigbor and the commandments of God; imposed on Celantia the expulsion of "evil, hatred, and envy"; to avoid malicious gossip, lies, pride; and recalled that abstinence and fasting which she had undertaken represented a principle of "sanctity" and had no value if not accompanied also by "a soul devoid of vices." At this point begins the section of the letter dedicated to advice on marital life, the point where our translation selection begins.

[2] Christianity — as is known — was unable to abolish the problem of a social structure firmly rooted in the Greco-Roman world like slavery. Within the ambit of new ethical principles of the message of the Gospel Christian writers sought to promote the religious ransom of slaves, exhorting their masters also to a more humane behavior. See, for example — John Chrysostom *On the Epistle to the Ephesians*, 22, 2; PG 62, col. 157. In general, on the problem of Christian slavery cf. Ch. Munier, *L'Église, op. cit.*, 73-81; J. Gaudemet, *L'Église, op. cit.*, 564-567.

degree of respect due to him. Show by your obedience that he is the master and indicate his importance by your humility, since the more abundantly you honor him the more you will be honored yourself. For, as the Apostle says, *the husband is the head of the wife*,[a] nor does the rest of the body derive its honor from any other source than the dignity of its head.[3] Hence the same Apostle says elsewhere: *Wives, be subject to your husbands, as is fitting in the Lord*;[b] and the blessed Apostle Peter also says: *Likewise you wives, be submissive to your husbands, so that any of them who do not believe in the word of the gospel may be won over, apart from preaching, through their wives' conduct.*[c] If, then, on the basis of matrimonial law, respect is due to pagan husbands, how much more is owed to those who are Christian?

27. And, to indicate what ornaments are appropriate for a married woman, he adds: *Your adornment should not be on the outside: adorning with braiding of hair, decoration of gold or wearing of robes, but let it be the hidden person of the heart with the imperishable jewel of a gentle and quiet spirit, which is in God's sight very precious.*[d] For once, in fact, the holy women, who hoped in God also used to adorn themselves and were submissive to their husbands, as Sarah obeyed Abraham, calling him lord. But in giving these instructions he is not ordering them to wear filthy clothes and to be covered with rough patches of cloth; rather he is forbidding extravagant apparel and sophisticated ornament and is commending simple adornment and dress. And on this subject the vessel of election [St. Paul] says also that *women should adorn themselves modestly and sensibly in seemly apparel, not with braided hair or gold or pearls or costly attire but by good deeds as befits women who profess chastity.*[e]

28. I have discovered that several years ago now, fired by a remarkable fervor caused by faith, you resolved upon celibacy and dedicated the remainder of your life to chastity. It is the mark of a great soul and an indication of perfect virtue suddenly to renounce a pleas-

---

[a] 1 Cor 11:3   [b] Col 3:18   [c] 1 P 3:1   [d] 1 P 3:3   [e] 1 Tm 3:9

[3] An old anthropological conception, already in Plato; and in the very etymology of the word "head" in Varro, the head assumed a preeminent and guiding role in the rest of the body (cf. M. Perrin, *L'homme, op. cit.*, 88-92).

ure already experienced, to shun the well-known allurements of the flesh and to quench with fervor the flames of a time of life still hot with passion. But I also learned at the same time something which causes me no slight anxiety and disquiet, namely, that you clearly began to observe this so great and good practice without the consent and agreement of your husband,[4] although apostolic authority altogether forbids this, an authority which in such a case has not only subjected wife to husband but also husband to the power of the wife, *For the wife*, it says, *does not rule over her own body, but the husband does; likewise the husband does not rule over his own body, but the wife does.*[f] But you, as if forgetful of your marriage contract and of this agreement and law, vowed your chastity to the Lord without consulting your husband. And a promise is hazardous, if it is still within the power of another to veto it, nor do I know how much pleasure is derived from a gift, if one is offering an object which belongs to two people.

We have already both heard of and seen many marriages broken through ignorance of this kind; and, as I am grieved to recall, adultery committed on the pretext of chastity; for while one party abstains even from acts which are permitted, the other lapses into acts which are not permitted at all. And in such a case I do not know who is to be accused more and who blamed more, whether it be the man who commits fornication after being repulsed by his wife or the woman who, by repulsing her husband, has in a manner exposed him to fornication. And, so that you may know what the truth is, I must set down a few points on the matter of divine authority.

The rule of apostolic doctrine neither makes works of continence equal to those of marriage with Jovinian, nor does it condemn marriage with Mani.[5] So the vessel of election and teacher of the

---

[f] 1 Cor 7:4

[4] This is the kernel of the letter: abstinence from sexual relations ought to come about from the mutual agreement of the spouses based also on the precept of 1 Cor 7:5. For an attentive reading of this Pauline text cf. M. Pesce, 'Stare in Cristo, ma continuare ad essere una carne sola: la coppia coniugale in I Cor 7,' *PSV* 13 (1986), 119-134.

[5] On Mani, born in 216, died between 274 and 277, founder of Manicheism, cf. M. Tardieu, *Il Manicheismo, op. cit.*

gentiles [St. Paul] follows a moderate, middle path between either extreme, in this way conceding a remedy for incontinence and at the same time encouraging continence to seek its reward. The whole sense of his ruling in this matter is that either chastity be proposed only as the result of the decision of both parties or, at least, the obligation common to both be discharged by both.

29. But now, let us set down the Apostle's very own words and reconsider this whole subject from its beginning. He says to the Corinthians: *And now concerning the matters about which you wrote: It is well for a man not to touch a woman.*[g] And though he has praised chastity here, he yet adds, in order that he may not seem to be trying to prevent marriage: *But because of the temptation to immorality, each man should have his own wife and each woman her own husband. The husband should give to his wife her conjugal rights, and likewise the wife to her husband. For the wife does not rule over her own body, but the husband does; and the husband does not rule over his own body, but the wife does.*[h] Do not refuse one another. And again, lest he might seem to be excluding the possibility of chastity by saying so much from the standpoint of marriage, he follows it up with: *Except perhaps by agreement for a season to devote yourselves to prayer.*[i] And, immediately after, he almost protests against what he has just said, that is, *for a season*, lest he seem to be teaching not so much perpetual as temporary and brief continence. For he says: *Through lack of self-control. But I say this by way of concession, not of command.*[j] Hence this phrase of his, "*for a season*," teaches that there ought to be rehearsal of chastity, so that, when they have, as it were, explored the strength of their self-control for fixed intervals of time, both parties may safely give promise to each other of what both ought to be maintaining always. He states his full meaning quite clearly: *But I wish that all were as I myself am.*[k] That is, in continuous and perpetual chastity.

30. Do you see how carefully, how prudently the master has declared his judgment on chastity without providing any occasion for sin? And, not wishing so great a good to become insecure through

---

[g] 1 Cor 7:1 [h] 1 Cor 7:2-4 [i] 1 Cor 7:5 [j] 1 Cor 7:6 [k] 1 Cor 7:7

the rashness of one of the two parties, when it should be confirmed and strengthened by the agreement of both?

And what, in all truth, is stronger and safer than that chastity which, having begun with the agreement of the two, is maintained by both for their common benefit, so that the one party may not set itself to persevere in virtue for both when, in fact, it is only concerned for itself. For this good, like others too, is to be praised in a person not only for having been begun but for having been completed. As you realize for some time now, our discourse has been engaged in traversing a rocky and difficult place nor does it dare to turn to one side or the other, fearing both equally as it does, but you should recognize your own peril from our difficulty, for we have preferred to depress you perhaps by speaking the truth than to deceive you with false adulation.

The evil, as you see, is twofold, a danger which is equally critical on both sides, and you are hemmed in by constraints on either side. To shun and despise your husband altogether is clearly contrary to the Apostle's judgment; but to betray a chastity of such duration and not to render to God what you promised him is something to be feared and dreaded. As the common saying has it, you can easily turn a friend into an enemy, if you do not fulfil your promises to him. For this is what the Scripture says: *But when you make a vow to the Lord your God, you shall not be tardy in it; for the Lord God will surely require it of you, and it would be a sin in you.*[l] That is why Paul tells you to render your husband the honor owed to him,[m] so that both of you may be able to repay to the Lord the debt which you have vowed on both sides.

In respect of his (i.e. your husband's) conscience we do not lack confidence, if you had expected us to have only a little; nor is it that we are trying to hold you back from the good of chastity but, rather, that we are urging his spirit with all our strength towards the mercy-seat of chastity, so that he may offer a voluntary sacrifice to God, as a fragrant offering,[n] that his mind may be divested of all worldly bonds and bodily pleasures, and that thus you may both be able to adhere

---

[l] Dt 23:21   [m] cf. 1 Cor 7:3-4   [n] cf. Eph 5:22

more completely to the Lord's commands. But — lest you should think that there is anything which we have said without due care — we have given you this instruction on the testimony of divine Scripture, as the Apostle also says: *And two shall be one flesh; but now no longer one flesh, but one spirit.*[o]

---

[o] 1 Cor 6:16-17

JOHN CHRYSOSTOM

INTRODUCTORY PROFILE

John Chrysostom was born in Antioch of a distinguished Christian family at a date which cannot be determined with certainty,[1] but which historians place between 344 and 354.[2] His father, Secundus, was a civil functionary in the administration of the military governor of Syria; his mother, Anthusa, having survived his death, remained a widow for twenty years and imparted his primary education to her son,[3] who frequented the school of the philosopher, Andragathius, and was probably a student of the rhetor, Libanius.[4]

---

[1] The ancient sources at our disposal are not much use: a *Dialogue* (PG 47, coll. 5-82) by Palladius; critical ed., A.-M. Malingrey-P. Leclercq, *Palladios, Dialogue sur la vie de Jean Chrysostome*, t. I, SC 341, Paris, 1988; A.-M. Malingrey, t. II, SC 342, Paris, 1988 [English trans. R.T. Meyer, *Palladius, Dialogue on the Life of St. John Chrysostom*, ACW 45 New York, 1985. Also Engl. tr. R.T. Meyer, *Palladius, The Lausiac History*, ACW 34, 1965; Ital. tr. *Storia Lausiaca di Palladio* (ed. G.J.M. Bartelink, Milan, 1974)]; *Historia Ecclesiastica* of Socrates (PG 67, coll. 29-736); *Historia Ecclesiastica* of Sozomenus (PG 67, coll. 843-1630); *Historia Ecclesiastica* of Theodoret of Cyrus (PG 82, coll. 879-1280).

[2] For the biographical data and the cultural ambience, the work of Ch. Baur, *John Chrysostom and His Time*, v.I, *Antioch*; v.2, *Constantinople*, Westminster, MD, remains fundamental; *idem*, *Jean Chrysostome et ses ceuvres dans l'histoire littéraire*, Louvain,1907. Cf. also A. Moulard, *St. Jean Chrysostome. Sa vie. Son oeuvre*, Paris, 1941; B. Altaner, *Patrology*, Turin, 1977 (rp.1981), 332-343 (orig. ed. Freibourg-Basel-Vienna, 1938) and J. Quasten, *Patrology*, III (1960), 424-482, with relevant bibliography. The articles devoted to Chrysostom by A. Wenger in *DSp* VIII, 1974, coll. 331-355 and by A.-M. Malingrey in *DPAC* II, 1983, coll. 1551-1558 are also useful.

[3] These notices are contained in the treatise *De sacerdotio* (PG 48, coll. 623-692); critical ed., A.-M. Malingrey, *Jean Chrysostome, Sur le sacerdoce* (SC 272, Paris, 1980); Engl. trans: G. Neville, *St. John Chrysostom. Six Books on the Priesthood*, London, 1964, rp. Crestwood, NY, 1984; Italian: A. Quacquarelli, *Giovanni Crisostomo, sul sacerdozio* (CTP 24, Rome, 1980).

[4] He was a pagan, a celebrated teacher of rhetoric, who taught at Constantinople, Nicomedia and Antioch, where he numbered Chrysostom among his pupils (cf. Sozomen, *Historia Ecclesiastica* VIII,2).

After being baptized, John attended the exegetical school of Diodorus, later bishop of Tarsus,[5] and fervently dedicated himself to the ascetical life. In 371 he was named a lector within the circle of Meletius, bishop of Antioch. His yearning for perfection caused him to remove himself from the world and, after spending the next four years in the mountains in the company of an old monk, he retired to a solitary cave to lead a life of austerity and study of the Scriptures.

Weakened in physique because of his deprivations and the cold climate, he was forced to return to Antioch where, in 381, he was ordained deacon by Meletius and in 386 priest by Meletius's successor, Flavian, who entrusted to him the task of preaching in the metropolitan church. John acquitted himself of this duty brilliantly, succeeding in winning over the masses by his eloquence, whence he got the name "Golden Mouth" with which he was designated from the sixth century.

Soon the situation changed when, upon the death of Nectarius in 397, John was called to succeed him as bishop of Constantinople. Conducted by deception and violence to the capital by order of the emperor, he was consecrated bishop on February 26, 398 by Theophilus, patriarch of Alexandria. This episode marked the beginning of a tormented period of his life in which, once joined to the capital and taking account of the atmosphere which prevailed there, John proposed a program of reform and of rehabilitation of the city and of its clergy from the corruption into which it had fallen in his predecessor's time. Although he gave a personal example of simplicity by assigning his considerable revenues to the construction of hospitals and the upkeep of the poor, he encountered the hostility of some, and when, in a synod at Ephesus (401), he deposed some bishops, found guilty of simony, the tension mounted.

Besides, his relations with the imperial court deteriorated as soon as authority passed into the hands of the empress, Eudoxia, who,

---

[5] He is one of the better representantives of that group of theologians and exegetes known collectively as the School of Antioch, characterized by an exegetical direction particularly consistent in the literal interpretation of Scripture. For basic information on the exponents and the hermeneutical criteria of this school see M. Simonetti in *DPAC* I, 1983, coll. 241-243 and *idem, Lettera e/o allegoria* (1985), 156-201.

while remaining the object of the bishop's invective against luxury and the evil customs governing the city, showed herself badly disposed toward John.

In the so-called Synod of the Oaks, named from the locality in which it was held, some bishops and monks prevailed on Theophilus to depose Chrysostom and he was condemned to exile by the emperor (August 403). A short time later the bishop was recalled and a brief period of peace ensued.

In fact the very next year John was again condemned to exile, at first to Cucusa in Lower Armenia (9 June 404) where he remained three years, and then to Pityus, in Colchis on the east coast of the Black Sea. Exhausted by the tedious pace of the journey, he died on the way at Comana, a province of Pontus, on September 14, 407.

The emperor Theodosius II, son of Eudoxia who had already died in 404, had Chrysostom's mortal remains brought back to Constantinople to the Church of the Apostles on January 27, 438. He himself went to meet the funeral cortege and, as described by Theodoret,[6] asked pardon for his parents, who had been guilty of persecuting the bishop. Chrysostom's remains were transported to Rome in 1204 where they now repose in St. Peter's Basilica.

John Chrysostom's abundant literary production, only equalled in the West by that of Augustine, can be divided into two main sections: homilies and treatises. The homilies, into which Chrysostom poured his vast learning and the resources of his eloquence, are divided on the basis of content into: exegetical homilies on the Old[7] and New Testament,[8] almost all going back to his Antiochene pe-

---

[6] *Hist. eccl.* V. 36.

[7] 67 *Homilies on Genesis* (PG 53, coll. 21-384 and PG 54, coll. 385-580); [Engl. tr. *St. John Chrysostom. Homilies on Genesis,* R.C. Hill, FOTC v. 74 (Homs. 1-17), v. 82 (Homs. 18-45), v. 87 (Homs. 46-67), Washington, DC 19, 1990, also PG 54]; 8 *Homilies on the Book of Kings* (PG 54, coll. 631-708); 58 *Homilies on Psalms* (PG 55, coll. 35-528) transmitted under the rubric, Commentaries, not Homilies, 6 *Homilies on Isaiah* (PG 56, coll. 97-142; critical edition J. Dumortier, *Jean Chrysostome, Commentaire sur Isaïe,* SC 304, Paris, 1983).

[8] There are 90 *Homilies on the Gospel of Matthew* (PG 57-58) [Engl. tr. NPNF]; 88 *Homilies on the Gospel of John* (PG 59); [Engl. tr.: Sr. T.A. Goggin, FOTC v. 33, Homs. 1-47, 1957; v. 41, Homs. 48-88, 1960]; 63 *Homilies on the Acts of the Apostles* (PG 60, coll. 13-384). A conspicuous part is represented by 200 *Homilies on the Letters of St. Paul* of which there are 32 *Homilies on the Epistle to the Romans* (PG 60, coll. 583-682), 44 *Homilies on the First Epistle to the Corinthians* and 30 *Homilies on the Second Epistle to the Corinthians* (PG 61, coll. 9-610); [Ital. tr. D.C. Tirone, *San Giovanni Crisostomo. Commento alle lettere di S.*

riod (386 to 397); dogmatic and polemical homilies;[9] homilies on liturgical feasts;[10] homilies of an ascetic-moral character,[11] and occasional homilies.[12]

Besides, John pronounced a great number of panegyrics[13] in honor of personages of the Old Testament and of martyrs and bishops of the church of Antioch, and a group of homilies in honor of

---

Paolo ai Corinthi, I-II, Siena, 1962]; the *Commentary on the Epistle to the Galatians* (PG 61, coll. 611-682; Ital. tr., S. Zincone, *Giovanni Crisostomo. Commento alla lettera ai Galati*, CTP 35, Rome, 1982); 24 *Homilies on the Epistle to the Ephesians* (PG 62, coll. 9-176); 15 *Homilies on the Epistle to the Philippians* (PG 62, coll. 177-298); 12 *Homilies on the Epistle to the Colossians* (PG 62, coll. 299-392; Ital. tr., C. Piazzino, *S. Giovanni Crisostomo, Omelie sulla lettera di S. Paolo ai Colossi*, Corona Patrum Salesiana, ser. graeca 6, Turin, 1939); 16 *Homilies on the two Epistles to the Thessalonians* (PG 62, coll. 391-500); 18 *Homilies on the First, and 10 on the Second, Epistle to Timothy;* 6 *Homilies on the Epistle to Titus* and 3 *Homilies on the Epistle to Philemon* (PG 62, coll. 501-719); 34 *Homilies on the Epistle to the Hebrews* (PG 63, coll. 9-236). In all these works it is possible to grasp the exegetical method followed by Chrysostom, trying to give an accurate literal interpretation of the text, according to the tradition of the school of Antioch, of which he was one of the greatest exponents. Cf. M. Simonetti, *Lettera e/o allegoria* (1985), 180-188.

9   To this group belong in two series the 12 *Homilies on the Incomprehensible Nature of God* (PG 48, coll. 701-812; critical ed. J. Daniélou-A.M.Malingrey-R.Flaceliere, *Jean Chrysostome. Sur l'incomprehensibilite de Dieu*, SC 28 bis, Paris, 1970, Engl. tr. P.W. Harkins), composed to refute the texts of the Anomeans, the extreme Arian party, who denied equality of nature between God the Father and the Son; 8 *Homilies Against the Jews* [Engl. tr. *St. John Chrysostom. Discourses against Judaizing Christians*, tr. P.W. Harkins, FOTC 68, Washington, DC, 1979] given at Antioch in 386 and 387, in which he admonishes the faithful to discontinue celebrating certain Jewish feasts, for example, the New Year, the Fasts, or not to celebrate the Pasch along with the Hebrews (PG 48, coll. 843-942), and finally the *Baptismal Catecheses*, recently discovered, very important for the knowledge of the liturgy of baptism at the end of the 4th century (PG 49, coll. 223-240; critical ed. by A. Wenger, *Jean Chrysostome, Huît Catéchèses baptismales inédites*, SC 50, Paris, 1985; Engl. tr. P.W. Harkins, *St. John Chrysostom. Baptismal Instructions*, ACW 31,1963; Ital. tr., A. Ceresa Gastaldo, *Giovanni Crisostomo, Le Catechesi Battesimali*, CTP 31, Rome, 1982).

10 From among those we mention, *On the Nativity* (PG 49, coll. 351-362), *On Epiphany* (PG 49, coll. 363-372), *On the Pasch* (PG 50, coll. 433-442 and PG 52, coll. 765-772), and *On the Ascension* (PG 50, coll. 441-452 and PG 52, coll. 792).

11 Apart from the famous *Contra circum et theatrum* (PG 56, coll. 263-270), pronounced on the 3rd July, 399 when a great part of the community of Constantinople had deserted the church to go to the games, we have the 3 *Homilies on the Devil* (PG 49, coll. 243-276); 9 *Homilies on Penance* (PG 49, coll. 277-350) [Engl. tr. G.G. Christo, FOTC, forthcoming]; and those *On Almsgiving* (PG 51, coll. 261-272).

12 The most celebrated are the 21 *Homilies on the Statues* (PG 49, coll. 15-222), considered among the most outstanding for eloquence, pronounced at the end of a revolt in Antioch against the Emperor Theodosius in 387. [Engl. tr. See now F. Van de Paverd, *St. John Chrysostom. The Homilies On the Statues. An Introduction*, Rome, 1991.] We also possess the first sermon given by John on the occasion of his elevation to the priesthood (PG 48, coll. 693-700; ed. crit., A.-M. Malingrey, *Jean Chrysostome sur le sacerdoce, op. cit.*); the two discourses *On the vanity and transitoriness of this earth* which he gave after the fall of the minister Eutropius, and those pronounced after his return from exile in 403 (PG 52, coll. 427-448; ed. crit. A.-M. Malingrey, *Jean Chrysostome, Lettres d'exil*, SC 103, Paris, 1964).

13 The *Panegyrics on the Saints* are all found in PG 50.

St. Paul.[14] As well, 236 letters have survived, going back to the time of his second exile, addressed to more than a hundred recipients, including pope Innocent I,[15] and his most faithful disciple at Constantinople, the widow and deaconness, Olympias,[16] who was his active collaborator in organizing and carrying out works of charity.

Among his treatises should be mentioned that *On the Priesthood*,[17] in six books, written around 386 in the form of an imaginary dialogue between the author and his friend, Basil, on the duties and privileges of the priestly state. Various tracts were devoted to the exaltation of the monastic life[18] and the ascetic ideal. To this last group belong *On Virginity*,[19] *To A Young Widow*,[20] and *On Not Remarrying*,[21] in which, following a well-established tradition, he af-

---

[14] PG 50, coll. 473-514; ed. crit. A. Piédagnel, *Jean Chrysostome, Panégyriques de St. Paul* (SC 300), Paris, 1982; Engl. tr. T. Halton, *St. John Chrysostom. In Praise of St. Paul* (Boston, 1963); Ital. tr., S. Zincone, *Giovanni Crisostomo, Panegirici su San Paolo* (CTP 69), Rome, 1988.

[15] PG 52, coll. 529-536.

[16] PG 52, coll. 549-623; ed. crit., A.-M. Malingrey, *Jean Chrysostome. Lettres à Olympias* (SC 13 bis), Paris 1968. For the relations between Chrysostom and Olympias cf. C. Militello, *Donna e chiesa. La testimonianza di Giovanni Crisostomo*, Palermo, 1985, 21-66.

[17] See note 3, p. 305.

[18] We refer to the three small treatises *Contra adversarios vitae monasticae* (PG 47, 319-386), which confute the accusations of the enemies of monasticism and persuade Christian fathers to entrust to the monks the education and formation of their sons [Engl. tr. D.G.Hunter, *A Comparison between a King and a Monk/Against the Opponents of the Monastic Life. Two Treatises by John Chrysostom*, Lewiston, 1988]; the three exhortations, *Ad Stagirium* (PG 47, coll. 423-494), a friend monk who, following a nervous breakdown, had doubts about his own vocation; the two exhortations *To Theodore* (PG 47, 277-316; ed. crit. J. Dumortier, *Jean Chrysostome À Théodore*, SC 117, Paris, 1966), to the future bishop of Mopsuestia who, fascinated by a woman's charms, had abandoned the monastic life.

[19] PG 48, coll. 533-596; ed. crit., H. Musurillo-B. Grillet, *Jean Crysostome, La Virginité* (SC 125), Paris 1966; Engl. tr. Sally Rieger Shore, *John Chrysostom On Virginity; Against Remarriage* New York, 1983; Ital. tr., S. Lilla, *Gregorio di Nissa. Giovanni Crisostomo, La verginità* (CTP 29), Rome, 1976, 121-280.

[20] In this treatise, composed probably around 380, Chrysostom is preoccupied with consoling a young wife on the loss of her spouse with the purpose of inducing her to persevere with resignation and dignity in her state of widowhood (PG 48, coll. 599-610; ed. crit., B. Grillet-G. H. Ettlinger, *Jean Chrysostome, A une jeune veuve. Sur le mariage unique*, SC 138, Paris, 1968, 112-159; Engl. tr. Sally Rieger Shore, *John Chrysostom On Virginity; Against Remarriage*, New York, 1983, Ital. trans. G. Di Nola, *Giovanni Crisostomo, L 'unita delle nozze*, CTP 45, Rome, 1984, 49-83).

[21] With this treatise John poses the problem of second marriage which he recognized as licit but an indication of "a weak spirit inclined to the pleasures of the flesh" (*ibid* 2). Therefore, while not condemning second marriage, he counselled perseverance in widowhood to respect the dignity of the husband (PG 48, coll. 610-620; ed. crit.: B. Grillet-G.H. Ettlinger, *op. cit.*, 161-201; Ital. tr., G. Di Nola, *op. cit.*, 21-47).

firmed the superiority of the state of virginity over that of marriage.[22]

The homilies give a sufficiently clear and articulated picture not merely of the ecclesiastical but also of the social and political situation of the city in which his apostolate unfolded.[23] John, in fact, can be considered more as a pastor than a theologian and as such placed his considerable knowledge of the sacred texts and his rhetorical ability at the service of the faithful. For them, now that the dogmas were sufficiently clear and Christian doctrine established, the need was to preach and explain the Gospel to bring about the emergence of the moral teaching contained in it. If in his youth he desired for himself and preached about detachment from the world, later on, continual contact with his own faithful confronted him with the concrete social reality in which Christians are called to live in the world and induced him to occupy himself with the form of life most common among them, matrimony.[24] This theme is encountered in some of the Discourses *On Genesis*,[25] in the 20 *Homilies on the Epistle to the Ephesians*[26] in the 12 *Homilies on the Epistle to the Colossians*,[27] and in the so-called three homilies, *On Matrimony*.[28]

Making the divine Scripture his starting-point, he elaborated

---

[22] For Chrysostom's position in the broad and articulated panorama of opinions on this theme cf. G. Oggioni, 'Matrimonio e verginità presso i Padri,' in Aa. vv., *Matrimonio e verginità, Saggi di Teologia*, Venegono Inferiore, 1963, 248-273.

[23] For information on the situation in Antioch in the time of Chrysostom, A.J. Festugière, *Antioche paienne et chrétienne. Libanius, Chrysostome et les moines de Syrie*, Paris, 1959 remains useful; also the articles of H. Leclercq, in *DACL* I, 2, 1924, coll. 2359-2439 and, by various authors, articles in *DPAC* I, 1983, coll. 228-246. For notices relating to the other city in which Chrysostom operated see the articles of H. Leclercq (s.v. 'Byzance'), in *DACL* II, 1, 1925, coll. 1363-1454 and *DPAC* I, 1983, 806-823 (s.v. 'Costantinopoli') by various contributors.

[24] Cf. J. Dumortier, 'Le mariage dans les milieux chrétiens d'Antioche et de Byzance d'après Saint Jean Chrysostome,' in *Lettres d'Humanité* 6 (1947), 102-166 and K. Tsouros, 'La dottrina sul matrimonio in S. Giovanni Crisostomo,' in *Asprenas* n.s. 21 (1974), 5-46. V. Guraion, 'Family and Christian Virtue in a Post-Christendom World: Reflections on the Ecclesial Vision of St. John Chrysostom,' *St. Vladimir's Theological Quarterly* 35 (1991), 327-350.

[25] There exist two series of *Homilies on Genesis*. The first, delivered during 386, consists of 9 Homilies, of which 8 refer to the first three chapters. The second series, probably composed in 388, are concerned with the whole book of Genesis.

[26] The homilies on the Epistles of St. Paul almost certainly go back to the Antiochene period.

[27] The 12 *Homilies on the Epistle to the Colossians* were delivered at Constantinople.

[28] This name designates the three homilies, delivered probably at Constantinople, better known as: *Because of fornication Let the wife have a bill of divorce* and the *Eulogy of Maximus* (*Quales uxores* in PG 51, coll. 207-242). For the *Eulogy of Maximus* we have an English translation: C.P. Roth, *St. John Chrysostom On Marriage*, Crestwood, NY, 1986, and an Italian one, ed. G. Di Nola, *Giovanni Crisostomo, L'unita delle nozze, op. cit.*, 85-128.

his own concepts on the theme of the family, and furnishes the modern reader with an insight into the reality and the family customs of Christians in Antioch and Constantinople, presented with vivid realism and historical concreteness.[29] At the same time, it helps to dispel the pedagogical intent which animates the words of Chrysostom to offer to his own people faithful models and Christian values which were imprinted on family life.[30]

In conformity with the traditions of a society which placed woman in a role subordinate to men,[31] John found in the theology of St. Paul the key for a harmonious relationship of the couple. After having made basic reference to the protological foundation of the actual condition,[32] Chrysostom, on the exemplary plan of Christ and His Church, defined the role of submission of the woman and of the dominion of the man in terms of "body" and "head."[33] Husband and wife are like complementary elements of a single reality where, as in the body it is difficult to distinguish the point of separation since the neck, placed midway between the head and the body has the function of a link to join rather than to divide them (no. 39).

Moreover, the biblical saying, *they will be two in one flesh*[34] explicitly recognizes in the conjugal union an extraordinary force and potency, establishing between the partners a bond, a relationship of such profundity and intensity that it can be expressed in terms of

[29] Cf. E. Cavalcanti, 'La spiritualità del popolo cristiano nei secoli IV e V,' in C. Burini-E. Cavalcanti, *La spiritualità della vita quotidiana negli scritti dei Padri*, Bologna, 1988, 155-217.

[30] Through matrimony it is in fact possible to reach perfection. For this, Chrysostom has been called "the first master of conjugal spirituality"; cf. G. Oggioni, *op. cit.*, 258.

[31] For a review of the positions of Christian authors on this theme, apart from A. Castiglioni, 'La donna nel pensiero dei Padri della chiesa greca del IV secolo,' in *La Scuola Cattolica* 46 (=S.V. 15) (1918), 29-51; 131-146; 212-233; 353-365; 439-466 (rp. in book form, Monza, 1919), see the more recent studies of C. Scaglioni, 'La donna nel pensiero dei Padri,' in *Vita e Pensiero* N.S. 58 (1975), 28-50 and U. Mattioli, 'La donna nel pensiero patristico,' in R. Uglione (ed.), *Atti del Convegno Nazionale di Studi su "La donna nel mondo antico," Torino 21-22-23 Aprile 1986*, Turin, 1987, 223-242.

[32] On the theme see General Introduction 5-27; 59-65. Cf. nn. 37 and 38.

[33] On this image amply utilized by Chrysostom see the arguments developed by C. Scaglioni, 'Ideale coniugale e familiare in San Giovanni Crisostomo,' in R. Cantalamessa (ed.), *Etica sessuale e matrimonio nel cristianesimo delle origini* (SPM 5), Milan, 1976, 315-345 and by C. Militello, *op. cit.* 177-194.

[34] Ample considerations are provided in C. Scaglioni, *op. cit.*, 295-315 and C. Militello, *op. cit.*, 156-176.

the relationship between the head and the body. To seal the unity and the intimate fusion joining the two partners a baby is born to them which is like a bridge, a point of conjunction between them.[35]

Chrysostom, affirming the supremacy of the husband over the wife, emphasizes that he has authority primarily for the purpose of teaching love to one who, as "body" is his necessary member. From the husband, furthermore, is demanded the function of head and guide of the wife, who is weak and fragile,[36] but at the same time he is bound to exercise this authority with love, affection and benevolence. The wife is recommended to have an attachment inspired by fear so that in their respective roles peace and concord may reign in the family.[37]

In fact, Chrysostom's thought oscillates between the customary notion of the woman's submission and the wish to safeguard the dignity of one who, in spite of everything, is "the second authority" in all matters pertaining to the family (nos. 41; 47). Chrysostom recognizes in the wife a role different from, but essentially equal to, that of her husband. If the sphere of public activity belongs to the latter, the wife's competence is the procreation of children, collaboration in their education[38] and the management of the household. Further-

---

[35] Even if procreation is among the motives which legitimate matrimony, it does not represent its primary end. For Chrysostom, in fact, the preeminent aim of marriage is continence, on which is based the honor of marriage. Cf. *Propter fornicationem,* 3: PG 51, 213; *Elogium Maximi* 5, PG 51. 232; Ital. tr., G. Di Nola, *op. cit.,* 107-108; *On the Epistle to the Hebrews,* Hom. 33, 3: PG 63, 228, and further *On Virginity* 15-16: crit. ed., H. Musurillo-B. Grillet, *op. cit.,* 144-149; Engl. tr. S. Rieger Shore, *op. cit.;* Ital. tr. S. Lilla, *op. cit.,* 159-161, where the theme is amply and explicitly treated.

[36] Chrysostom speaks often of the "weakness" of the female sex, an obvious instance of the influence exercised by the well-known affirmation of 1 P 3:1-7 which is the basis of this theme. Cf. nn. 42 and 44.

[37] For the theme of conjugal harmony in its diverse aspects of "concord," "friendship," etc., cf. C. Scaglioni, *op. cit.,* 303-307.

[38] The pedagogic problem represents a constant preoccupation for our author. With the aim of furnishing parents with the instruments for a good education, inspired by Christian principles, John composed the treatise, *On Vainglory and the Education of Children* which poses not a few problems concerning dating and attribution. On these see the ample introduction and critical edition by A.-M. Malingrey, *Jean Chrysostome Sur la vaine gloire et l'éducation des enfants* (SC 188), Paris, 1972; Engl. tr. M.W.L. Laistner, *Christianity and Pagan Culture in the Later Roman Empire,* Ithaca, N.Y. 1951, 85-122; Ital. tr: A. Ceresa Gastaldo, *Giovanni Crisostomo Vanità. Educazione dei figli. Matrimonio* (CTP 7), Rome, 1977, 23-74; L. Gallinari, *Cristianesimo Primitivo ed Educazione II* Peri kenodoxias kai hopōs dei tous goneas anatrephein ta tekna, *di S. Giovanni Crisostomo,* Cassini, 1970. In relation to this theme as perceived in Chrysostom, see the studies of J. Dumortier, 'L'éducation des enfants

more, if the wife is rich in virtue, she becomes a secure haven where the husband can seek refuge from the adversities of daily life (no. 42).

Chrysostom exhorts the husband to be understanding and patient with his wife, and admonishes him especially not to have recourse to violence (no. 43). No fault can be so grave that it spurs a husband to strike his own wife; on the contrary, even when his wife is full of defects, the husband ought to treat her with sagacity and solicitude, protecting her, and seeking to make her better (no. 44).

To illustrate in the most efficacious manner the right behavior that should characterize a Christian wife, Chrysostom resorts to the examples of the wives of ancient patriarchs, and in particular, to Sarah who distinguished herself by the many trials that her obedience and her deep love for Abraham had enabled her to overcome. In the same way the wife is well disposed toward her own husband, even though he is arrogant, knowing that this ensures for her a heavenly recompense.

But she could do much more; spending all her time at home, she could dedicate herself to prayer, to reading, and to "philosophy," in all the vast array of meanings which that term assumed in the works of our author.[39] In such a way, by giving proof of modesty, temperance, wisdom, availability, benevolence, the notions acquired, the wife can become a wise and competent teacher for her children, her husband and her slaves (no. 49).

In The Praise of Maximus, really a "theoretical-practical manual of pedagogy and psychology of behavior"[40] our author has given con-

---

au IVᵉ siècle. Le témoinage de Saint Jean Chrysostome,' Revue des Sciences Humaines 15 (1947), 222-238; T. Halton, 'St. John Chrysostom On Education,' Catholic Educational Review 61 (1963), 163-175 and Santiago Abengoehea, 'Ideas pedagogicas de S. Juan Crisostomo,' Helmantica 12 (1961), 343-360. In a recent work O. Pasquato, 'Rapporto tra genitori e figli. Eredità giudaica in Giovanni Crisostomo,' AugR 28 (1988), 391-404 stresses the influence of Jewish pedagogic tradition in concepts of Chrysostom on the relations between parents and children.

[39] On the meaning of this term in Chrysostom see A.-M. Malingrey, "Philosophia" Étude d'un groupe de mots dans la littérature grecque des Présocratiques au IVᵉ siècle d'après J.-C., Paris, 1961, 263-288.

[40] Cf. G. Di Nola, op. cit., 11.

crete directives for the criteria to follow in the selection of a marriage partner.

In denouncing the widespread practice in his milieu of regarding matrimony as a commercial affair, John castigates the superficial way in which marriage is entered upon and the unseemly way in which it is celebrated. Marriage, being in fact a "mystery," an extraordinary reality modelled on the example of the union of Christ and His Church, the wedding feast should not be a pompous occasion, or be transformed into a theatrical show,[41] but should opportunely mark the beginning of that life, inspired by criteria of decorum, wisdom and temperance, which the couple will lead in the future.

To men on the threshold of entering marriage (and also to women) John recommends not seeking after riches,[42] a frequent source of disputes and quarrels, nor physical beauty,[43] destined to vanish, but rather virtue, fear of God and all the other and positive qualities which endure for ever.

In a passage, certainly among the most suggestive in his whole output, "for the imprint it bears of delicacy and interiority of affective relationship,"[44] Chrysostom suggests what the spouse should say when for the first time he addresses his wife. In this moment, so delicate, but also so decisive for the new life which the two, up to now strangers, are about to undertake together, the husband confesses all his own love and the special position his wife enjoys in his life, and with sweet and appropriate words he establishes the rules to attain harmony and concord.

---

[41] The polemic against the theatre is a favorite theme of our author who sees in spectacles in general a grave temptation for weaker souls. O. Pasquato, *Gli spettacoli in S. Giovanni Crisostomo. Paganesimo e Cristianesimo ad Antiochia e Costantinopoli nel IV secolo*, Orientalia Christiana Analecta 201, Rome, 1976, has singled out the importance which the problem of the spectacles assumed in Chrysostom not only in the profile of moralist but also as a moment culminating in the conflict between paganism and Christianity in the society of the 4th century.

[42] Cf. n. 45.

[43] Cf. n. 46.

[44] These are the words of C. Scaglioni, *op. cit.*, 311, note 92.

[45] Cf. D. Gorce, 'Mariage et perfection chrétienne d'après Saint Jean Chrysostome,' *Études Carmélitaines Mystiques et Missionaires* 21,1 (1963), 245-284.

These, in fact, are his own values which Chrysostom points out to the faithful who live in matrimony.[45] This is a sharing of life, in which the distinction between "mine" and "yours" no longer exists when there comes into operation a fusion of persons and of belongings; it is a living together in which the children constitute an ulterior element of cohesion and each of the spouses has a well-defined role. Love and reciprocal attachment produce the concord which is the "salvation" of marriage.[46]

When concord rules in every segment of married life and the married couple uphold the same ethical and religious values, then, says Chrysostom, "if any marry thus, with these views, he will be but little inferior to monks; the married but little below the unmarried" (no. 48).

---

[46] Such is the definition of C. Scaglioni, *op. cit.*, 306.

PROTOLOGICAL FOUNDATIONS OF THE COUPLE'S
RELATIONSHIP: "SUBMISSION" AND "DOMINION"

| 37 |

1. Therefore, this is the first type of submission in virtue of
which men have dominion over their wives. For this indeed became
necessary after the original sin. In fact, before the act of disobedience in paradise, woman had equal honor[1] with man; in fact when
God was creating Eve He used for her creation the same words which
He had used in the creation of Adam. However, just as for man He
said, *Let us make man in our image and likeness*,[a] and not: "let us make
man," similarly, in her case He did not say: "let us make woman,"
but, also in her case: *let us make for him a helpmate*, and not simply "a
helpmate," but *a helpmate like to him*,[b] a further demonstration of their
equality in dignity.

From the moment when the animals furnished much help in
the needs of our lives He introduced a sharing in helping. *And He
brought the animals to the man but none proved to be the suitable helper
for the man.*[c] And what, then? Was not the horse a help, which enters battle along with him? Was not the ox a help, which draws the
plough and works along with him at the season of sowing? Was not
the donkey and mule a help, which collaborate with us in transport-
ing our belongings? But, so as to prevent you from saying this, he
introduces an opportune distinction. He does not say simply "there
was not found a help for him," but *none proved to be the helper suitable for the man.*[d]

So also in this case he did not simply say: Let us make a helper,
but *let us make for him a helpmate, like to him.*[e] This however refers to
the period before the original sin; however, after the sin: *your urge
shall be for your husband and he shall be your master.*[f] He says: "I have
created you equal to man with regard to honor: you have not made
a right use of the faculty of command, pass now to a condition of

---

[a] Gn 1:26   [b] Gn 2:18   [c] Gn 2:19-20   [d] Gn 2:20   [e] Gn 2:18   [f] Gn 3:16

[1] This notion of the original *homotimia* (equality of honor) implying a relationship of parity be-
tween man and woman also turns up in other contexts. Cf. *On the First Epistle to Timothy,
Homily* IX,1: PG 62, 543; *On Genesis, Homily* XIV, 4: PG 53, 115; XV, 3: PG 53, col. 121;
XVII, 8: PG 53, col. 144.

subordination; you have not known how to maintain liberty; be submissive now to servitude. You have not known how to command and have not given proof with your operation. You will be one of the subjects and will recognize man as your master." *Your urge shall be for your husband and he shall be your master.*[g]

But observe the divine benevolence on this point. In fact, while stating: *he shall be your master,*[h] imposing the grave restriction of the man's power over her, he directs attention to the first point, saying: *your urge shall be for your husband,*[i] that is, he will be your refuge, your port, your security in all adversities that present themselves. And not only this but also the physical bonds of nature that unite them like an indestructible chain, the chain of desire.[2]

Do you see how sin introduced submission and how God, in His ability and wisdom, turned this reality to our advantage?

Hear also how Paul expresses himself with regard to this subjection so that you may perceive also the harmony between the Old and New Testament. He says: *A woman must listen in silence and in complete submission.*[j]

You have seen then how he subordinates the woman to the man? But look and hear the cause. Why does he say: *a woman must be completely submissive?*[k] He says in fact: *it is not permitted a woman to act as teacher.*[l] For what reason? Because once, in fact, she taught Adam badly. He does not permit a woman *to have authority over a man.*[m] But why? Because once she exercised this power badly. *A woman must listen in silence.*[n] And he also gives the reason. In fact he says: *it was not Adam who was deceived, but the woman. It was she who was led astray and fell into sin.*[o]

It was for this reason that he removed her from the teacher's chair. He says, in fact, let her learn who does not know how to teach. For if you want to teach and are unwilling to learn you will destroy both yourself and your pupils. Which is what happened then in the case of the woman. But that she was made subject to her husband

---

g Gn 3:16   h Gn 3:16   i Gn 3:16   j 1 Tm 2:11   k 1 Tm 2:11   l 1 Tm 2:12   m 1 Tm 2:12
n 1 Tm 2:12   o 1 Tm 2:14

2 Cf. General Introduction, 124-125.

and made submissive to him because of sin is clear from the saying: *your urge shall be for your husband and he will be your master*.[p]

2. I would like to know in what way Paul speaks of this solicitude and joins together supremacy with affection. Where is this encountered? Writing to the Corinthians he said: *Husbands, love your wives*.[q] Note this expression: *your urge shall be for your husband;*[r] *the wife for her part showing respect for her husband*.[s] And notice: *and he shall be your master*.[t]

See how the supremacy is not burdensome, when the master's supremacy is joined to warm affection, when the wife's fear is mingled with love. In this way, then, is eliminated all trouble deriving from submission.

It was disobedience, then, that introduced one sole authority.

On Genesis, Disc. IV. 1-2; PG 53 593-595

38

Wives, be subject to your own husbands, as to the Lord. For the husband is the head of the wife, as Christ also is the head of the Church: being Himself the Savior of the body. But as the Church is subject to Christ, so let the wives also be subject to their husbands in everything.[a]

A certain wise man,[1] setting down a number of things in the rank of blessings, set down this also in the rank of a blessing, *A wife agreeing with her husband*.[b] And elsewhere again he sets it down among blessings, that a woman should dwell in harmony with her husband.[c] And indeed from the beginning, God appears to have made special provision for this union; and discoursing of the two as one, He said thus, *Male and female He created them;*[d] and again, *There is neither male nor female*.[e] For there is no relationship between man and man so close as that between man and wife, if they be joined together as they should be. And therefore a certain blessed man too, when he would express surpassing love, and was mourning for one that was dear to him, and of one soul with him, did not mention father, nor

---

[p] Gn 3:16 [q] Eph 5:25 [r] Gn 3:16 [s] Eph 5:33 [t] Gn 3:16 [a] Eph 5:22-23 [b] Si 25:1 [c] cf. Si 25:1, 40:23 [d] Gn 1:27 [e] Gal 3:28

---

[1] The homily, delivered at Antioch around 390-391, comments on Ephesians 5:22-24.

mother, nor child, nor brother, nor friend, but what? *Your love to me was wonderful*, said he, *surpassing the love of women*.[f] For indeed, in very deed, this love is more despotic than any despotism: for others indeed may be strong, but this passion is not only strong, but unfading. For there is a certain love deeply seated in our nature, which imperceptibly to ourselves knits together these bodies of ours. Thus even from the very beginning woman sprang from man, and afterwards from man and woman sprang both man and woman. Do you perceive the close bond and connection? And how that God suffered not a different kind of nature to enter in from without? And mark, how many providential arrangements He made. He permitted the man to marry his own sister; or rather not his sister, but his daughter; no, not quite his daughter, but something more than his daughter, even his own flesh.[2] Hence Christ said, *He who made them from the beginning, made them male and female*.[g] For great evils are hence produced, and great benefits, both to families and to states. For there is nothing which so welds our life together as the love of man and wife. For this many will lay aside even their arms, for this they will give up life itself.

And Paul would never without a reason and without an object have spent so much pains on this subject, as when he says here, *Wives, be subject to your own husbands, as to the Lord*.[h] And why so? Because when they are in harmony, the children are well brought up, and the servants are in good order, and neighbors, and friends, and relations enjoy the fragrance. But if it be otherwise, all is turned upside down, and thrown into confusion, and just as when the generals of an army are at peace one with another, all things are in due subordination, whereas, on the other hand, if they are at variance, everything is turned upside down; so, I say, is it also here. Where-

---

[f] 2 S 1:26   [g] Cf. Mt 19:4   [h] cf. Eph 5:22; Col 3:18

[2] A section is omitted here in which the author, wishing to repeat the idea that with the intervention of matrimony a profound unity between the spouses is realized, records the circumstances relative to the formation of Eve. In fact, at the beginning God took her from Adam and later intimately joined her to him by means of the marriage bond, which was based on reciprocal love. Therefore, the unity realized in matrimony can mean not only concord and harmony, fundamental presuppositions for a correct relationship between a couple, but also a reconstitution of the division in operation at the outset. For this aspect see T. Spidlík, 'Il matrimonio, sacramento di unità, nel pensiero di Crisostomo,' *AugR* 17,1 (1977), 221-226.

fore, said he, *Wives, be subject to your own husbands, as to the Lord.*[i] Yet how strange! for how then is it, that it is said elsewhere, *If one bid not farewell both to wife and to husband, he cannot follow me*[j]? For if it is their duty to be subject *as to the Lord*, how said He that they must depart from them for the Lord's sake?

Yet their duty indeed it is, their bounden duty. But the word "as" is not necessarily and universally expressive of exact equality. He either means this, "as" "as knowing that you are servants to the Lord"; which, by the way, is what he says elsewhere, that, even though they do it not for the husband's sake, yet must they primarily for the Lord's sake or else he means, *when you obey your husband, do so, as serving the Lord.*[k] For if he who resists these external authorities, those of governments, I mean, *withstands the ordinance of God* much more so does she who submits not herself to her husband. Such was God's will from the beginning.

Let us take as our fundamental position, then, that the husband occupies the place of the "head," and the wife the place of the "body."[3] Then, he proceeds with arguments and says that *the husband is the head of the wife, as Christ also is the head of the Church, being Himself the Savior of the body.*[l]...He had already laid down beforehand for man and wife, the ground and provision of their love, assigning to each their proper role, to the one that of authority and provision, to the other that of submission.

On the Epistle to the Ephesians, c. V, Hom. XX, 1; PG 62, 135-136; NPNF

---

[i] Col 3:18   [j] Lk 14:33   [k] Rm 13:2   [l] Eph 5:23

[3] The thematic developed here turns up frequently in Chrysostom's reflections on matrimony. Cf. *On the Gospel of Matthew*, Hom. XVII, 2 , PG 57, coll. 256-257; *On the Gospel of John*, Hom. LXI, 3 , PG 61, coll. 211-217. On this see C. Militello, *op. cit.*, 178 and C. Scaglione, *op. cit.*, 315-345.

THE TWO MADE ONE: THE STRENGTH OF THE CONJUGAL UNION

39

What? Is marriage[1] a theater? It is a mystery and a type of a mighty reality; and even if you do not reverence it, reverence that whose type it is. *This mystery, said he, is great, but I speak in regard of Christ and of the Church.*[a] It is a type of the Church, and of Christ, and do you introduce harlots at it? If then, someone objects, neither virgins dance, nor the married, who is to dance? No one; for what need is there of dancing? In the Greek mysteries there is dancing, but in ours, silence and decency, modesty and reserve. A great mystery is being celebrated; out with the harlots! out with the profane! How is it a mystery? "They come together, and the two make one. Wherefore is it that at his entrance,[2] indeed, there was no dancing, no cymbals, but great silence, great stillness, but when they come together, making, not a lifeless image, nor yet the image of anything upon earth, but of God Himself, and after his likeness, you introduce so great an uproar, and disturb those that are there, and put the soul to shame, and confound it? They come, about to be made one body.

See again a mystery of love! If the two become not one, so long as they continue two, they make not many, but when they are come into oneness, then they make many. What do we learn from this? That great is the power of union. The wise counsel of God at the beginning divided the one into two, and being desirous of showing

---

[a] Eph 5:32

[1] Chrysostom, having discussed the value and lessons of the chains and tears of Paul and of Christ, reprimands the faithful for seeking joy by every means. Even when marriage is being celebrated amusement is sought by every means, and, with no respect for the great and arcane mystery of which it is the image, they resort even to harlots. Starting from these considerations Chrysostom teaches what are the constituents of a true Christian marriage. On this theme cf. *Because of Fornication*, 2-3, PG 51, 211-213.

[2] The verb *eiseimi*, "I enter, I am present" according to C. Piazzino, *op. cit.*, 444, n.1 [=p. 379, n. 8], refers to the bride who enters the new residence of her husband. The same verb is used in classical Greek in a technical sense of an actor in an entrance scene; therefore, given the contrasting parallelism proposed by the author between theatrical spectacles and matrimony, it seems more likely that it is a reference to an actor; if, in fact, his entrance on the scene is not accompanied by dances and songs why should that ever happen at a matrimonial union between a man and a woman?

that even after division it remains still one, He did not allow that the one should of itself be enough for procreation. For he is not one who is not yet [united], but the half of one, and it is evident from this that he begets no offspring, as was the case also previously.

Do you see then the mystery of marriage? He made of one, one; and again, having made these two, one, He so makes one, so that now also man is produced of one. For man and wife are not two persons, but one. And this may be confirmed from many sources; for instance, from James, from Mary,[3] the Mother of Christ, from the words: *He made them male and female.*[b] If he be the head, and she the body,[c] how are they two? Therefore the one holds the rank of a disciple, the other of a teacher, the one of a ruler, the other of a subject.

Moreover, from the very fashioning of her body, one may see that they are one, for she was made from his side,[d] and they are, as it were, two halves. For this cause He also calls her a help[e] to show that they are one; for this cause He honors their cohabitation away from both father and mother, to show that they are one. And in like manner a father rejoices both when son and daughter marry, as though the body were hastening to join a member of its own; and though so great a charge and expenditure of money is incurred, still he cannot bear with indifference to see her unmarried. For as though her own flesh itself were severed from her, each one separately is imperfect for the procreation of children, each one is imperfect as regards the constitution of this present life. Wherefore also the Prophet said, *the residue of your spirit.*[f]

And how do they become one flesh? As if you should take away the purest part of gold, and mingle it with other gold; so in truth here also the woman, as it were, receiving the richest part fused by pleasure, nourishes it and cherishes it, and contributing her own share, restores it back a man.

And the child is a sort of bridge, so that the three become one

---

[b] Gn 1:27   [c] cf. 1 Cor 11:3; Eph 5:23   [d] cf. Gn 2:21   [e] cf. Gn 2:18   [f] Ml 2:15

[3] The references to James (erroneously translated as Jacob in Piazzino, *op. cit.*, [p. 379, n. 8] 444) and to Mary are unclear.

flesh, the child connecting, on either side, each to the other. For just as two cities, which a river divides throughout, become one, if a bridge connect them on both sides, so is it in this case; and yet even more so, when the very bridge in this case is formed of the substance of each, so the body and the head are one body; for they are divided by the neck, but not so much divided as connected, for it, lying between them, brings together each with the other. And it is the same as if a chorus that had been separated should, by taking one part of itself from this quarter, and the other again from the right, make one — or as these when they come into close rank, and extending hands, become one, for the hands extended admit not of their being two.

Therefore He said with accuracy of expression, not "they shall be one flesh" but joined together *into one flesh*[g] namely, that of the child. What then? When there is no child, will they not be two? No, for their coming together has this effect, it diffuses and commingles the bodies of both. And as one who has cast ointment into oil has made the whole one, so in truth is it likewise here.

On the Epistle to the Colossians, Hom. XII, 5; PG 62, 387-388; NPNF

40

3. Even if you should say that your wife is incurably ill, and after receiving much care still behaves in her own fashion, still you must not cast her out.[1] The limb with an incurable disease is not amputated. She also is your limb, for it is written, *The two shall become one flesh.*[a] Besides, with the limb, we receive no benefit from the treatment when the illness turns out to be incurable; but with a wife, even if she remains incurably ill, we will receive a great reward

---

g cf. Gn 2:24   a cf. Gn 1:24

[1] The theme of this treatise, dedicated to Maximus, a colleague of Chrysostom in his evangelizing activity, is to give instructions concerning a prudent and carefully considered choice of marriage partner. In fact the divine law prohibits sending away one's wife, at least if she has not been caught in flagrant adultery (cf. *Elogium Maximi* 1: PG 51, col. 225; C. Roth, Ital. tr., DiNola, *op. cit.*, p. 91; *On the First Epistle to the Corinthians*, Hom. XIX, 2, PG 61, col. 153). On the controverted and complex problem of divorce cf. H. Crouzel, *L'Église primitive face au divorce* (Théologie historique, 13), Paris, 1971 (with regard to Chrysostom, 177-207).

for our attempts to teach and educate her. Even if she does not benefit at all from our teaching, we will receive a great reward from God for our patience, because we have shown so much forbearance through fear of Him. We have endured her evil ways with gentleness and have kept our member. For a wife is a member which is related to us, and because of this we especially ought to love her.

This is just what Paul was teaching when he said, *Even so husbands should love their wives as their own bodies. For no man ever hates his own flesh, but nourishes and cherishes it, as Christ does the Church, because we are members of His body, made from His flesh and His bones.*[b] Just as Eve came from the side of Adam, he says, so we come from the side of Christ. This is what he means when he says, *made from His flesh and His bones.*[c]

We all know that Eve came from the side of Adam himself; Scripture has told this plainly, that God put Adam into a deep sleep and took one of his ribs, and fashioned the woman.[d] ...We must love our wife not only because she is a part of ourselves and had the beginning of her creation from us, but also because God made a law about this when He said, *For this reason a man shall leave his father and his mother, and shall cleave to his wife, and the two shall become one flesh.*[e]

Paul reads us this law in order to surround us and drive us toward this love.[2] Consider the wisdom of the Apostle. He does not lead us to the love of our wives by divine laws only, or by human reasoning only, but by interchanging them he makes a combination of both. In this way the wiser and higher-minded may be led by the heavenly arguments, while the weaker may be led to love by the natural and earthly arguments. This is why he begins with Christ's righteous acts, and introduces his exhortation by saying, *Love your wives as Christ loved the Church.*[f] Then again from human experience: *Husbands ought to love their wives as their own bodies.*[g] Then again from Christ: *Because we are members of His body, made from His flesh and*

---

[b] cf. Eph 5:28-30   [c] Eph 5:30   [d] cf. Gn 1:21-22   [e] Gn 2:24   [f] Eph 5:25   [g] Eph 5:28

[2] On the theme of *agape* (=love), a presupposition and foundation of the relationship of the couple, cf. C. Scaglioni, *op. cit.*, 310-315.

His bones.[h] Then again from humanity: *For this reason a man shall leave his father and his mother, and shall cleave to his wife.*[i] After reading this law Paul says, *This is a great mystery.*[j]

Tell me, how is it *a great mystery?* Because the girl who has always been kept at home and has never seen her bridegroom, from the first day loves and cherishes him as her own body. Again, the husband, who has never seen her, never shared even the fellowship of speech with her, from the first day prefers her to everyone, to his friends, his relatives, even his parents. The parents in turn, if they are deprived of their money for another reason, will complain, grieve, and take the perpetrators to court. Yet they entrust to a man, whom often they have never seen before or come to know at all, both their own daughter and a large sum as dowry. They rejoice as they do this and do not consider it a loss. As they see their daughter led away, they do not bring to mind their closeness, they do not grieve or complain, but instead they give thanks. They consider it an answer to their prayers when they see their daughter led away from their home taking a large sum of money with her.

Paul had all this in mind, how the couple leave their parents and bind themselves to each other, and how the new relationship becomes more powerful than the long sojourn with their families.[3]

---

[h] Eph 5:30   [i] Eph 5:31   [j] Eph 5:32

---

[3] This notion also recurs in other works of Chrysostom. See, for example, *Baptismal Instructions*, I, 26-27, where the author develops the nuptial symbolism in relation to the theme of baptism, emphasizing how this rite implies a break with the modality of one's earlier life. The same occurs on the occasion of marriage when the spouses put distance between themselves and their families. He goes on to declare: "It is altogether impossible that the inexperienced bride be united to a husband unless she has forgotten her parents and those who reared her and unless she has given over her will, whole and entire, to him who will be joined to her as her bridegroom. What human reckoning will be able to grasp the nature of what takes place in marriage when one considers that the young wife, who has been nourished with her mother's milk, and kept at home, and judged worthy by her parents of such upbringing, suddenly, in a single moment, when she comes to the hour of marriage, forgets her mother's labor pains, and all her other care, forgets her family life, the bonds of love, and in a word forgets everything and gives over her whole will to that man whom she never saw before that night? Her life is so completely changed that thereafter that man is everything to her; she holds him to be her father, her mother, her husband, and every relative that one could mention. No longer does she remember those who took care of her for so many years. So intimate is the union of these two that thereafter they are not two but one," *Baptismal Cat. instr.*, I, 11-12, SC éd., A. Wenger, 114-115; Engl. tr., *St. John Chrysostom, Baptismal Instructions*, ACW 31, Westminster, MD, 1963, 26-27, tr. P.W. Harkins.

He saw that this was not a human accomplishment. It is God who sows these loves in men and women. He causes both those who give in marriage and those who are married to do this with joy. Therefore Paul said, *This is a great mystery.*[k]

Just as in the case of children, the baby which is born immediately from the first sight recognizes its parents without being able to speak, so also the hearts of the bride and bridegroom are entwined together at the first sight without anyone to introduce them, to advise them, or to counsel them, immediately from the first sight are united to one another.[4]

Even for men it is a great event, but when I observe that it happens equally through Christ and the Church, then I remain spellbound and marvelling. For this reason, after saying, *this is a great mystery,*[l] it is added, *I mean that it refers to Christ and the Church.*[m]

In Praise of Maximus, 3; PG 51, 228-230

41

For this cause shall a man leave his father and mother, and shall cleave to his wife, and the two shall become one flesh.[a] Behold again a third ground of obligation[1] for he shows that a man leaving them that begot him, and from whom he was born, is knit to his wife and that then the one flesh is father, and mother and the child, from the substance of the two commingled. For indeed by the commingling of their seeds is the child produced, so that the three are one flesh. Thus then are we in relation to Christ; we become one flesh by participation, and we much more than the child. And why and how so? Because so it has been from the beginning.

Tell me not that such and such things are so. Do you not see that we have in our own flesh itself many defects? For one man, for

---

[k] Eph 5:32   [l] Eph 5:32   [m] Eph 5:32   [a] Gn 2:24

[4] To support his own statements the author inserts at this point a christological argument which represents an important theological opening in the discussion relative to the mysterious reality of the conjugal union. With regard to the ecclesial symbolism of marriage cf. G. Oggioni, *op.cit.,* 265-272.

[1] The motives previously illustrated, both borrowed from Paul, are examples of the matrimonial union of Christ and the Church and the fact that the woman — as is read in Genesis — is bone and flesh of Adam (cf. no. 46).

instance, is lame, another has his feet distorted, another his hands withered, another some other member weak; and yet nevertheless he does not grieve at it, nor cut it off, but oftentimes prefers it even to the other. Naturally enough; for it is part of himself. As great love as each entertains towards himself, so great he would have us enter-tain towards a wife. Not because we partake of the same nature, no, this ground of duty towards a wife is far greater than that; it is that there are not two bodies but one; he the head, she the body. And how said he elsewhere: *and the Head of Christ is God?*[b]

This I too say, that as we are one body, so also are Christ and the Father one. And thus then is the Father also found to be our Head. He sets down two examples, that of the natural body and that of Christ's body. And hence he further adds, *This mystery is great but I speak in regard of Christ and of the Church.*[c]

Why does he call it a great mystery? That it was something great and wonderful, the blessed Moses, or rather God intimated. For the present, however, said he, I speak regarding Christ,[d] that having left the Father, He came down, and came to the Bride, and became one Spirit. *For he that is joined unto the Lord is one Spirit.*[e]

And well said he, *it is a great mystery.*[f] And then, as though he were saying, "But still nevertheless the allegory does not destroy af-fection," he adds, *Nevertheless, do you also love each one his own wife, even as himself; and let the wife see that she fear her husband.*[g] For in-deed, in very deed, a mystery it is, yes, a great mystery, that a man should leave him that gave him being, him that begot him, and that brought him up, and her that travailed with him and had sorrow, those that have bestowed upon him so many and great benefits, those with whom he has been in familiar intercourse, and be joined to one who was never even seen by him and who has nothing in common with him, and should honor her before all others.

A mystery it is indeed. And yet are parents not distressed when these events take place, but rather, when they do not take place — and are delighted when their wealth is spent and lavished upon it. A great mystery indeed! And one that contains some hidden wis-dom.

---

[b] 1 Cor 11:3   [c] Eph 5:32   [d] Eph 5:32   [e] 1 Cor 6:17   [f] Eph 5:32   [g] Eph 5:33

Such Moses prophetically showed it to be from the very first; such now also Paul proclaims it, where he said, *concerning Christ and the Church*.[h] However not for the husband's sake alone it is thus said, but for the wife's sake also, that he cherish her as his own flesh, as Christ also the Church, and, *that the wife fear her husband*.[i] He is no longer setting down the duties of love only, but what? *But that she fear her husband*.[j]

The wife is a secondary authority. Let her not then demand equality, for in fact she is subjected to the head; nor let him despise her as being in subjection, for she is the body — and if the head despises the body, it will itself also perish. But let him bring in love, on his part, as a counterpoise to obedience on her part. For example, let the hands and the feet, and all the rest of the members, be given up for service to the head, but let the head provide for the body, seeing it contains every sense in itself. Nothing can be better than this union. And yet how can there ever be love, one may say, where there is fear? It will exist there, I say, preeminently. For she that fears and reverences, also loves; and she that loves, fears and reverences him as being the head, and loves him as being a member, since the head itself is a member of the body at large.[2] Hence he places the one in subjection, and the other in authority, that there may be peace; for where there is equal authority there can never be peace — neither where a house is a democracy, nor where all are rulers; but the ruling power must of necessity be one. And this is universally the case with matters referring to the body, inasmuch as when men are spiritual, there will be peace. There were five thousand souls, and not one of them said, *that any of the things which he possessed was his own*,[k] but they were subject one to another;[3] this is an indication of wisdom, and of the fear of God. The principle of love he explains; that of fear he does not.

On the Epistle to the Ephesians, c. V, Hom. XX, 4; PG 62, 139-141; NPNF

---

[h] Eph 5:32 [i] Eph 5:33 [j] Eph 5:33 [k] Ac 4:32

---

[2] The dialectic "love" — "fear" recurs also in *Comm. on Ep. to Colossians*, Hom. X, 1: PG 62, col. 365 in the perspective of the complementarity of roles. Cf. further C. Scaglioni, *op. cit.*, 334-345.

[3] This is a reference to the situation described in Acts 4:31-37, concerning the first Christians who lived in perfect and admirable union, realizing human solidarity to the full.

THE HARMONY AND HAPPINESS OF THE SPOUSES

| 42 |

5. This is a true relationship,[1] this is the duty of a husband, while not taking too much account of his wife's words but making allowance for female frailty[2] to make it his one concern to keep her free from anguish and tighten the bonds of peace and harmony.

Let husbands take heed and imitate the restraint of this just man[3] in according their wives such great respect and regard and making allowances for them as the frailer vessel[a] so that the bonds of harmony may be tightened. This, you see, is real wealth, this is the greatest prosperity, when a husband is not at odds with his wife but rather they are joined together like one body — *the two will come to be one flesh,*[b] Scripture says.

Such couples, even though they are in poverty, even in low estate, they would be more blessed than all the rest, enjoying true delight and living in unbroken tranquility just as those who don't enjoy this have to put up with jealousy and lose the advantage of peace. Even should they abound in wealth, have luxurious tables and happen to live in the glare of publicity, they still live a more miserable life than anyone, day in and day out experiencing troubles and disturbances, suspecting one another, unable to have any joy as the conflict within them causes total confusion and creates complete disgust between them.[4]

---

[a] cf 1 P 3:7   [b] Gn 2:24

[1] Chrysostom is illustrating the figure of the patriarch Abraham who, together with his wife Sarah, is often pointed to as a model of correct behavior in marriage.

[2] It is opportune to point out how, notwithstanding the fact that Chrysostom tries hard to safeguard the dignity of the woman, created to be a "helper" of man and who is assigned a specific role in the context of the family, in his arguments the theme of "weakness" of the nature of the female constantly re-emerges. Therefore, for him the harmonious living together of the Christian couple is founded not on a relationship of parity but rather on substantial disparity not only of roles, but even of capability, in that the wife is considered, in the wake of the affirmation in 1 P 3:1-7, a fragile and weak human being.

[3] In other contexts Chrysostom returns to the Abraham-Sarah couple as an example of perfect conjugal harmony. Cf. *On Genesis*, Homily XXXII,5: PG 53, col. 512; Homily XLV,2, PG 54, col. 413; *Comm. On Ep. 1 to the Cor.*, Homily XXV1,6: PG 61, col. 221.

[4] A line of argument follows in which Chrysostom repeats the harmonious relationship between Abraham and Sarah, which not even cohabiting with Hagar was able to corrode. Therefore the author takes the occasion to affirm that right behavior can gain numerous benefits and to exhort the faithful not to lose heart in misfortune but to endure it with a serene spirit (5-6).

7. ...Let us learn to be restrained and gentle with everyone, especially our wives and take particular care not to be too demanding even if they chide us, rightly or wrongly but rather make it our sole concern to remove the cause of sadness and bring about a deep sense of peace at home so that the wife's attention may be devoted to her husband[c] and he may be able to find refuge in her, as in a port from all external confusion and disturbance and find there utter consolation.

The wife, after all, is given by way of assistance[d] so that the husband, strengthened by her support may succeed in withstanding assaults against him. You see, if she is discreet and restrained, not only will she provide her husband with comfort from their association but in all other respects as well she will give evidence of her great usefulness, rendering everything light and easy for him, not allowing him to find difficulty either in external matters or indeed in the problems that arise at home. Instead like a skilled pilot she will transform the storm into calm, by means of her particular wisdom, and by the understanding she shows she will provide him with deep comfort.

Nothing of the affairs of this life, in fact, will succeed any longer in worrying people bound together in this manner, nor in undermining their contentment. You see, wherever there is harmony and peace, and a loving relationship between wife and husband, all good things come together there and the couple will be safe from any stratagem, protected as they are by some wonderfully impregnable rampart, namely their harmony, in God's sight.

This renders them stronger than steel, this makes them firmer than iron, this contributes to them more than all wealth and prosperity, this conducts them to glory on high, this also wins for them favor from God in generous measure.

Accordingly, I beseech you, far from prizing anything more highly than this, let us move might and main to have peace and harmony in our family life. Then, you see, the children born of such union will follow the virtue of their parents, the servants will imi-

---

[c] cf. Gn 3:16   [d] cf. Gn 2:18

tate them in every respect, the household will advance in virtue and there will be great prosperity in our affairs. After all, when we give pride of place to God's concerns, all other things will be given to us as well, since God's goodness is supplying us with everything in generous measure.

In order, therefore, that we too may conduct this present life free from distress and may win favor from the Lord to a greater degree, let us hold fast to virtue, make it our concern to introduce harmony and peace into our home, attend to the orderly behavior of our children and give thought to the conduct of the servants, so that after receiving rewards to an extent beyond all others we may also be found worthy of those promised good things, thanks to the grace and loving kindness of our Lord Jesus Christ, to whom with the Father, and the Holy Spirit be glory, power and honor, now and forever, for ages of ages. Amen.

On Genesis, Hom. XXXVIII, 5 and 7; PG 53 357-359;
FOTC 82, 366-367, 371-372, tr. R.C. Hill

MUTUAL RESPECT AND TOLERANCE BETWEEN SPOUSES

43

6. And I say these things, not to encourage husbands to be harsh; but to persuade wives to put up even with churlishness in their husbands.[1] Because, when each is careful to fulfil his own duty, his neighbor's part will also quickly follow: as when the wife is prepared even to put up with churlish behavior on the part of the husband, and the husband refrains from abusing her in her angry mood, then calm will prevail everywhere and a harbor free from waves.

7. So also was it with those in olden times. Each was employed in fulfilling his own duty, not in exacting that of his neighbor. Thus,

---

[1] In this homily some arguments already treated turn up again. After illustrating the head/body theme Chrysostom goes on to speak of subjection on the part of the wife as a consequence of sin and then passes on to illustrate the proper behavior for a Christian wife which also applies equally to the husband. At this point the example of Sarah is invoked once more as one who in every circumstance demonstrated patience and condescension toward her own spouse.

if you notice, when Abraham took his brother's son,[a] his wife found no fault with him. He commanded her to travel a long journey; she did not complain even about this, but followed along.[b] Again, after those many tribulations and labors and toils, having become lord of all, he yielded the precedency to Lot.[c] And, far from Sarah being offended at this, she did not even open her mouth, nor utter anything like what many of the women of the present day say, when they see their own husbands coming off inferior in such allotments and especially in dealing with inferiors, reproaching them, and calling them fools and senseless and unmanly and traitors and stupid. No such thing did she say or think, but was pleased with all things that were done by him.

And here is another and an even better example: after Lot had the choice placed in his power, and had thrown the inferior part upon his uncle a great danger fell upon him. The patriarch, hearing of this, armed all his people, and set himself against the whole Persian army with his own servants,[d] and not even then did she detain him, nor say, as was likely, "O man, where are you going, thrusting yourself over precipices, and exposing yourself to such great hazards; for one who wronged you and seized on all that was yours, shedding your blood? Yes, and even if you make light of yourself, still have pity on me who have left home, and country, and friends, and kindred, and have followed you in such a long pilgrimage; and do not involve me in widowhood, and in the miseries of widowhood."

She did not say or think any of these things, but endured all in silence. After this, her womb remained barren, and she herself did not suffer the usual grief of women or lament: however Abraham complained though not to his wife, but to God. And see how each preserves his own appropriate role: for he neither despised Sarah as childless nor reproached her with any such thing: and she again was anxious to devise some consolation to him for her childlessness by means of the handmaid.[e] For that sort of thing had not yet been forbidden at that time as it is now. For now it is neither lawful for women to indulge their husbands in such behavior, nor for the men with-

---

[a] cf. Gn 11:31   [b] cf. Gn 12:1-5   [c] cf. Gn 13:5-12   [d] cf. Gn 14:1-6   [e] cf. Gn 16:2

out the wife's knowledge to form such connections, even though the grief of their childlessness should infinitely harass them: since they also shall hear the sentence, *their worm shall not die, neither shall their fire be quenched.*[f] For at the present time it is not permitted, but at that time it had not been forbidden. Therefore both his wife commanded this, and he obeyed, yet not even thus for pleasure's sake. But behold, it will be said, how he cast Hagar out again at her bidding.[g] Well, this is what I want to point out, that both he obeyed her in all things, and she him.

Do not you give heed to these things only, but examine, you who urge this plea, into what had gone before also, Hagar's insulting her, boasting herself against her mistress than which what can be more vexatious to a free and honorable woman?

8. Let not then the wife tarry for the virtue of the husband and then show her own, for this is nothing unusual nor, on the other hand, the husband, for the obedience of the wife and then exercise self-command; for neither would this any more be his own well-doing; but let each, as I said, furnish his own share first. For if to the Gentiles smiting us on the right, we must turn the other cheek; much more ought one to put up with harsh behavior in a husband. And I do not say this so that a wife may be beaten; far from it: for this is the most extreme affront, not just to the one that is beaten, but to him who does the beating. But even if by some misfortune you have such a partner allotted to you, do not take it badly, woman, considering the reward which is laid up for such things and their praise too in this present life.

And to you husbands also I say this: make it a rule that there can be no such offence as to bring you under the necessity of striking a wife. And why do I say "a wife"? since not even upon his handmaiden should a free man endure to inflict blows and lay violent hands. But if the shame be great for a man to beat a maidservant, much more so is it to stretch forth the right hand against her that is free. And one might see this even in pagan legislation which no longer compels the one so treated to live with him that beat her, as being unworthy of her fellowship.

[f] Mk 9:45 [g] cf. Gn 16:5-6

For surely it is a sign of extreme lawlessness when your life partner, she who in the most intimate relations and in the highest degree, is united with you, when she, like a lowly slave, is dishonored by you. Therefore also such a man, if indeed one may call him a man and not rather a wild beast, I should say, was like a parricide and a murderer of his mother. For if for a wife's sake we were commanded to leave even father and mother, not wronging them but fulfilling a divine law; and a law so gratifying to our parents themselves that even they, the very persons whom we are leaving, are thankful, and bring it about with great eagerness; what but extreme frenzy can it be to insult her for whose sake God bade us leave even our parents?

But we may well ask, Is it only madness? There is the shame too: I would like to know who can endure it. And what description can set it before us; when shrieks and wailings are borne along the alleys, and there is a running to the house of him that is so disgracing himself, both of the neighbors and the passersby, as though some wild beast were ravaging within? Better were it that the earth should open up and swallow one so frantic, than that he should be seen at all in the forum after it.

"But the woman is insolent," says he. Consider nonetheless that she is a woman, the weaker vessel,[h] whereas you are a man. For this reason were you ordained to be ruler; and were assigned to her in place of a head,[i] that you might bear with the weakness of her that is set under you. Make then your rule glorious. And glorious it will be when the subject of it meets with no dishonor from you. And as the monarch will appear so much the more dignified, as he manifests more dignity in the officer under him but if he dishonor and depreciate the greatness of that rank, he is indirectly cutting off no small portion of his own glory likewise: so also, if you dishonor her who governs next to yourself, will in no ordinary degree mar the honor of your governance.

Considering, therefore, all these things, command yourself: and withal think also of that evening on which the father having called you, handed over to you his daughter as a kind of deposit, and hav-

---

[h] cf. 1 P 3:7   [i] cf. 1 Cor 11:3; Eph 5:23

ing separated her from all, from her mother, from himself, from the family, entrusted her entire guardianship to your right hand. Consider that (under God) through her you have children and have become a father, and be you also on that account gentle towards her.

8. Do you not see husbandmen, how they tend the earth, once it has received the seed, with all the various methods of cultivation though it have innumerable disadvantages for instance, though it be an unkindly soil, or bear ill weeds, or though it be vexed with excessive rain through the nature of its location? This also you should do. For in this way you shall be first to enjoy both the fruit and the calm, since your wife is to you both a harbor, and a potent healing charm to rejoice your heart. Well then: if you shall free your harbor from winds and waves, you shall enjoy much tranquility on your return from the marketplace: but if you fill it with clamor and tumult, you only prepare for yourself a more grievous shipwreck.

In order, then, to prevent this, let my advice be carried out. When any thing uncomfortable happens in the household, if she be in the wrong, console her and do not aggravate the discomfort. For even if you should lose all, nothing is more grievous than to have a wife without good-will sharing your abode. And whatever offence you can mention, you will tell me of nothing quite so painful as being at strife with her. So that, if only for such reasons as these, let her love be more precious than all things. For if one another's burdens are to be borne, much more so the burdens of one's own wife. Though she be poor do not upbraid her; though she be foolish, do not trample on her, but train her rather: because she is a member of your very self, and you are become one flesh.[j]

"But she is trifling and drunken and passionate." You ought then to grieve over these things, not to be angry; and to beseech God, and exhort her and give her advice, and do every thing to remove the evil. But if you strike her, you aggravate the disease: for fierceness is removed by moderation, not by recrimination.

With these things bear in mind also the reward from God: that when you are permitted to cut her off, and you do not do so for fear

---

[j] cf. Gn 2:24

of God, but put up with such great defects, fearing the law appointed in such matters which forbids to put away a wife whatsoever disease she may have, you shall receive an indescribable reward. Yes, and before the reward you shall be a very great gainer, both rendering her more obedient and becoming yourself more gentle thereby. It is said, for instance, that one of the heathen philosophers, who had a bad wife, a trifler and a brawler, when asked, "Why, having such an one, he endured her"; made reply, "That I might have in my house a school and training-place of philosophy. For I shall be to all the rest meeker," said he, "being at home disciplined every day."

Did you utter a great shout? Why, I at this moment am greatly mourning, when pagans prove better lovers of wisdom than we; we who are commanded to imitate angels, nay rather who are commanded to emulate God Himself[k] in respect of gentleness. But to proceed: it is said that for this reason the philosopher having a bad wife, cast her not out; and some say that this very thing was the reason of his marrying her. But I, because many men have dispositions not exactly reasonable, advise that at first they do all they can, and be careful that they take a suitable partner and one full of all virtue.

Should it happen, however, that they fail in their endeavor, and she whom they have brought into the house prove no good or tolerable bride, then I would have them at any rate try to be like this philosopher, and train her in every way, and consider nothing more important than this. Since neither will a merchant, until he have made a compact with his partner capable of procuring peace, launch the vessel into the deep, nor apply himself to the rest of the transaction.

And let us then use every effort that she who is our partner in the business of life and in this our vessel, may be kept in all peace within. For thus shall our other affairs too remain all in calm, and with tranquility shall we run our course through the ocean of the present life.

On the First Epistle to the Corinthians, Hom. XXVI, 6-8;
PG 61, 221-223; NPNF 12, 155-157

---

[k] cf. Mt 5:48; Lk 6:36

44

6. So then, you wives, do everything *as in obedience to the Lord*,[a] and as doing everything for His sake. This is enough to induce and to persuade us, and not to allow that there should be any teasing and dissension. Let none be believed when slandering the husband to his wife; no, nor let the husband believe anything at random against the wife, nor let the wife be without reason inquisitive about his goings out and his comings in. No, nor on any account let the husband ever leave himself open to any suspicion whatever.

For what, tell me, what if you shall all day be at the disposal of your friends, and give the evening to your wife, and not even thus be able to content her, and place her out of reach of suspicion?

Though your wife complain, yet be not annoyed; it is prompted by her love, not her folly; they are the complaints of fervent attachment, and burning affection, and fear. Yes, she is afraid lest any one have stolen her marriage bed; lest any one have injured her in that which is the summit of her blessings, lest anyone have taken away from her him who is her head, lest any one have broken into her marriage chamber.[1]

7. Let us then imitate him ourselves. Let no one reproach his neighbor with his poverty; let no one be in love with money; and then all difficulties will be at an end. Neither let a wife say to her husband, "Unmanly coward that you are, full of sluggishness and dullness, and fast asleep! here is such a one, a low man, and of low parentage, who runs his risks, and makes his voyages, and has made a good fortune and his wife wears her jewels, and goes out with her pair of milk-white mules, and rides around everywhere; she has troops of slaves, and a swarm of eunuchs, but you have cowered down and live to no purpose." Let a wife say none of these things, nor anything like them. For she as the body is not to dictate to the head, but to be submissive and obey.

---

[a] Eph 5:22

[1] Chrysostom at this point recommends to spouses not to demand more of their servants than is their due. To show that benevolence toward his wife ought to be the principal preoccupation of the husband, he introduces the example of Abraham with regard to the episode with Hagar. According to the biblical account (cf. Gn 16:1-16), Abraham, although he had a son by a maidservant, did not hesitate to repudiate her so as not to cause Sarah to suffer, demonstrating in this way that he placed the love of his wife before everything else (cf. n. 43).

"But how," some one will say, "is she to endure poverty? Where is she to look for consolation?" Let her select and compare herself with those who are even more poor. Let her again consider how many noble and high-born young women have not only received nothing of their husbands, but have even given dowries to them and have spent their all upon them. Let her reflect on the perils which arise from such riches, and she will cling to this quiet life. In short, if she is affectionately disposed towards her husband, she will utter nothing of the sort. No, she will rather choose to have him near her, though gaining nothing, than gaining ten thousand talents of gold, accompanied with that care and anxiety which always arise to wives from those distant voyages.

Neither, however, let the husband, when he hears these things, on the score of his having the supreme authority, resort to revilings and to blows; but let him exhort, let him admonish her, as being less perfect, let him persuade her with arguments. Let him never once lift his hand — far be this from a noble spirit, no, nor give expression to insults, or taunts, or revilings; but let him regulate and direct her as being wanting in wisdom.[2]

Yet how shall this be done? If she be instructed in the true riches, in the heavenly philosophy,[3] she will make no complaints like these. Let him teach her, then, that poverty is no evil. Let him teach her, not by what he says only, but also by what he does. Let him teach her to despise glory; and then his wife will speak of nothing, and will desire nothing of the kind.

On the Epistle to the Ephesians, c.V, Hom. XX, 6-7;
PG 62, 144-145; NPNF 13, 149-150

---

[2] We have already emphasized how Chrysostom substantially accepted these notions which were firmly consolidated in the patristic tradition (cf. n. 42).

[3] The Chrysostom text carries the term *ano philosophia* which, as already noted, designates "the search for Christian perfection with the intervention of contempt for the present life and especially of riches." Cf. C. Scaglioni, *op. cit.*, 338-339.

THE VALUES OF THE LIFE OF THE COUPLE

45

3. ... Since you know then how great a mystery marriage is and how great a reality it configures,[1] do not consider marriage lightly or casually. In particular, you must not seek money when you are about to take a wife.[2] You must consider that marriage is not a commercial venture but a fellowship for life.

4. I hear many of you saying, "So and so got rich from his marriage, although he was poor beforehand. Since he took a rich wife, he enjoys wealth and luxury now." What are you saying, man? Do you desire to make a profit from your wife? Aren't you ashamed? Don't you blush? Why don't you sink into the ground, if you seek to better yourself in such a way? What kind of talk is this for a husband?

A wife has only one duty: to preserve what we have accumulated, to protect our income, to take care of our household.[3] After all, God gave her to us for this purpose, to be our helper[a] in these matters as well as in everything else. In general our life is made up of two spheres of activity, the public and the private. When God separated these two He assigned the management of the household

---

[a] cf. Gn 2:18

[1] The discourse developed here recalls what has been said in n. 40. After having illustrated the characteristics of Christian matrimony modulated on the edifying example of the union of Christ and the Church, Chrysostom passes on to give practical counsels on the criteria which should guide the choice of a partner in matrimony.

[2] The polemic against riches occupies a position of importance in the works of Chrysostom and is inserted in the picture of the program of moral renewal of the clergy (cf. S. Zincone, *Ricchezza e povertà nelle Omelie di Giovanni Crisostomo*, L'Aquila, 1973). With regard more specifically to matrimony, our author repeatedly exhorts the faithful, men and women, to seek out partners of equal economic conditions to avoid creating disparity and disagreeable disequilibrium in marriage relations. If, in fact, a poor man should marry a rich woman he would risk seeing his family order upset and the roles proper to each interchanged; besides, the wife being certainly bad-tempered and despotic, he would have difficulty making her recognize him as head and submitting to him as body (cf. *On the Gospel of Matthew*, Homily LXXIII,1: PG 58, coll. 677-678). But also the woman who would marry a richer man would find herself in an embarrassing situation by becoming a slave instead of a free person, and would be constrained to accept arrogant, and sometimes even depraved, behavior from her husband (cf. *On virginity*, LV: PG 48, coll. 576-577; SC éd. H. Musurillo-B. Grillet, *op. cit.*, 302-305). On the theme of the annoyances deriving from riches in matrimony cf. C. Militello, *op. cit.*, 223-229.

[3] Note here the persistence of a notion of the female role, "naturally" restricted to domestic chores, already clearly illustrated in Xenophon's *Oeconomicus*. See General Introduction, pp. 42-44.

to the woman, but to the men He assigned all political affairs, all the business of the marketplace, the courts, the council-chambers, armies, and everything else.

A woman cannot throw a spear or hurl a javelin, but she can take up the distaff, weave cloth, and manage well all the other household affairs. She cannot give an opinion in the council, but she can give her opinion in the household. Often, indeed, whatever her husband knows of household matters, she knows better. She cannot manage the affairs of the city well, but she can raise children well, which are the greatest of treasures. She can discover the misbehavior of the maids and oversee the virtue of the servants. She can free her husband from all cares and worries for the house, the store-rooms, the woolworking, the preparation of meals, the maintenance of the wardrobe. She takes care of all the other matters which it is not fitting or easy for a man to undertake no matter how competitive he might be.

After all, this is the work of God's generosity and wisdom, that he who is good at the more important matters is inferior and quite useless in lesser matters, so that the help of a woman is necessary to him. If God had made man competent in both areas, it would have been easy for men to despise womankind. If, on the other hand, God had assigned a greater and more important role to woman, He would have filled women with presumption. For this reason He did not give both spheres to one sex, lest the other might seem inferior and superfluous.

Neither did He assign both spheres to each sex equally, lest there should arise strife and contention from equality of honor, if women strove to be counted worthy of the same precedence as their husbands. God provided for peace by reserving a suitable position for each. He divided our life into these two parts, and gave the more necessary and important to the man, but the lesser and inferior part to the woman. In this way He arranged that we should admire the man more because we need his service more, and that because the woman has a humbler form of service she would not rebel against her husband.

Since we know all this, let us seek just one thing in a wife, virtue of soul and nobility of character, so that we may enjoy tranquility, so that we may luxuriate in harmony and lasting love.

The man who takes a rich wife takes a boss rather than a wife. If, even without wealth, women are filled with pride and prone to the love of fame, if they had wealth in addition, how would their husbands be able to put up with them? The man, however, who takes a wife of equal position or poorer than himself takes a helper and ally, and brings every blessing into his house. Her own poverty forces her to care for her husband with great concern, to yield to him and obey him in everything. It removes every occasion for strife, battle, presumption, and pride. It binds the couple in peace, harmony, love, and concord. Let us not, therefore, seek to have money, but to have peace, in order to enjoy happiness.

Marriage does not exist to fill our houses with war and battles, to give us strife and contention, to pit us against each other and make our life unlivable. It exists in order that we may enjoy one another's help, that we may have a harbor and a refuge, and a consolation in the troubles which hang over us, and that we may converse happily with our wife. How many wealthy men who have taken rich wives and increased their worth have yet destroyed their happiness and harmony, as they contend in daily battles at table?

How many poor men who have taken poorer wives, now enjoy peace and look upon each day's sun with joy? Rich men, even though they are surrounded by luxury, have often on account of their wives prayed to die and be relieved of the present life. Thus money is of no use when we do not have a partner with a good soul.

Besides, why should I speak of peace and harmony? Even in the acquisition of money we are often hindered by taking a rich wife. When a man has reckoned all his profits to the account of the dowry, if an untimely death occurs, he is forced to pay the whole amount to his in-laws. Like someone who has suffered shipwreck on the sea and saved only his body, so this man comes forth from a storm of contention, strife, insolent acts, and law-suits only barely keeping his body free.

Just as insatiable merchants, by filling their ship with innumerable wares and loading it with an excessive cargo, have often sunk their goods and lost everything, so these men have incurred over-burdensome marriages, thinking that they will collect a greater fortune through their wives, and have lost even what they had. Just as on the sea the sudden shock of a wave falls on the vessel and sinks it, so here an untimely death falls upon him and takes away all his possessions along with his wife.

5. Since we are aware of all this, let us investigate, not our bride's money, but the gentleness of her character and her piety and chastity. A wife who is chaste, gentle, and moderate, even if she is poor, can make poverty better than wealth. Likewise a wife who is corrupt, undisciplined, and contentious, even if she has immeasurable treasure stored away, blows it away more quickly than any wind and surrounds her husband with innumerable misfortunes along with poverty. So let us not seek a wealthy wife, but rather one who will use well what we have.

You must first learn what the purpose of marriage is, and why it was introduced into our life. Ask nothing else. What, then, is the reason for marriage, and why did God give it to us? Listen to what Paul says: *Because of the temptation to immorality let each man have his own wife.*[b] He does not say, "Because of relief from poverty," or "Because of the acquisition of wealth," but what? Because of the temptation to fornication, to restrain our lust, to practise chastity, and be well pleasing to God by being satisfied with our own wife: this is the gift of marriage, this is its fruit, this is its profit.

Do not, therefore, neglect the greater benefit and seek the lesser. Wealth is far inferior to chastity. We should seek a wife for this reason only, in order to avoid sin, to be freed from all immorality. To this end every marriage should be set up so that it may work together with us for chastity. This will be the case if we marry such brides as are able to bring great piety, chastity, and goodness to us. Bodily beauty, if it is not joined with virtue of the soul, will be able to hold on to a husband for twenty or thirty days, but will go no farther before it shows its wickedness and destroys all its attractiveness.

As for those who radiate beauty of soul, the longer time elapses and tests their proper nobility, the warmer they make their husband's love and the more they strengthen their affection for him. Since this is so, and since a warm and genuine friendship holds between them,

---

[b] 1 Cor 7:2

every kind of immorality is driven out. Not even any thought of wantonness ever enters the mind of the man who truly loves his own wife, but he continues always content with her. By his chastity he attracts the good will and protection of God for his whole household. This is how the good men of ancient times used to take wives, seeking nobility of soul rather than monetary wealth.

In Praise of Maximus 3-5; PG 51, 230-233

THE HUSBAND TO EXERCISE AUTHORITY "WITH LOVE";
THE WIFE TO SUBMIT "IN FEAR."

46

2. As the Church is submissive to Christ[a] so should be husbands and wives; that is to say, you *wives be submissive to your husbands, as unto God. Husbands, love your wives, even as Christ also loved the Church.*[b]

You have heard how great the submission; you have extolled and marvelled at Paul, how, like an admirable and spiritual man, he welds together our whole life. You did well, but now hear what he also requires from you, for again he employs the same example: *Husbands*, said he, *love your wives, even as Christ also loved the Church.*[c]

Have you seen the measure of obedience? Hear also the measure of love. Do you wish to have your wife obedient unto you, as the Church is to Christ? Make then the same provision for her; take care of her, as Christ takes of the Church. Yes, even if it shall be needful for you to give your life for her, yes, and to be cut into pieces countless times, yes, and to endure and undergo any suffering whatever, do not refuse it. Though you should undergo all this, yet you have not, no, not even then, have done anything like Christ. For you indeed are doing it for one to whom you are already closeknit; but He for one who turned her back on Him and hated Him. In the same way then as He laid at His feet her who turned her back on Him, who hated, and spurned, and disdained Him, not by menaces,

---

[a] cf. Eph 5:22-23   [b] Eph 5:22-25   [c] cf. Eph 5:25

nor by violence, nor by terror, nor by anything else of the kind, but by His affection, so also do you behave yourself toward your wife. Yes, though you see her looking down upon you, and disdaining, and scorning you, yet by your great thoughtfulness for her, by affection, by kindness, you will be able to win her over. For there is nothing more powerful to sway than those bonds, and especially for husband and wife. A servant, indeed, one will be able, perhaps, to hold down by fear; nay not even him, for he will soon take off and be gone. But the partner of one's life, the mother of one's children, the foundation of one's every joy, one ought never to chain down by fear and menaces, but by love and even temper.

For, what sort of union is that, where the wife trembles at her husband? And what sort of pleasure will the husband himself enjoy, if he dwells with his wife as with a slave, and not as with a freewoman? Yes, though you should suffer something on her account, do not upbraid her; neither did Christ do this. *He gave Himself up*, Scripture says, *for it, that He might sanctify and cleanse it.*[d] So then she was unclean! So then she had blemishes, so then she was unsightly, so then she was worthless! Whatsoever kind of wife you shall take, yet shall you never take such a bride as the Church, when Christ took her, nor one so far removed from you as the Church was from Christ. And yet for all that, He did not abhor her, nor loathe her for her surpassing deformity.[1]

Seek, then, for beauty of soul. Imitate the bridegroom of the Church. External beauty is full of conceit and great license, and throws men into jealousy, and the thing often makes you suspect monstrous things.[2] But at least it has some pleasure? For the first month or two, perhaps, or at most for a year: but then no longer; the admiration through familiarity wastes away. Meanwhile the evils which arose from the beauty still abide, the pride, the folly, the contemptuousness. In one who is not such, there is nothing of this kind.

---

[d] Eph 5:25-26

[1] In the section omitted Chrysostom repeats the same concepts expressed in the preceding argumentation.

[2] The polemic variously motivated against female beauty and external jewelry is a constant refrain in the works of Chrysostom. The theme is discussed at length in Militello, *op. cit.*, 197-222.

But the love having been run on just grounds, still continues ardent, since its object is beauty of soul, and not of body.

3. What, tell me, is better than heaven? What better than the stars? Tell me of what body you will, yet there is none so fair. Tell me of what eyes you will, yet there are none so sparkling. When these were created, the very angels gazed with wonder, and we gaze with wonder now — yet not in the same degree as at first. Such is familiarity; things do not strike us in the same degree. How much more in the case of a wife! And if moreover disease come too, all is at once fled.

Let us seek in a wife an affectionate nature, modest-mindedness, gentleness: these are the characteristics of beauty. But shapeliness of person let us not seek, nor upbraid her upon these points, over which she has no power, no, rather, let us not upbraid at all (that would be rude), nor let us be impatient, nor sullen. Do you not see how many, after living with beautiful wives, have ended their lives pitiable, and how many, who have lived with those of no great beauty, have run on to extreme old age with great enjoyment.

Let us wipe off the "spot" that is within, let us smooth the "wrinkles" that are within, let us do away with the "blemishes" that are on the soul. Such is the beauty that God requires. Let us make her fair in God's sight, not in our own. Let us not look for wealth, nor for that lofty birth which is outward, but for that true nobility which is in the soul. Let no one endure to get rich by a wife for such riches are base and disgraceful, no, by no means let any one seek to get rich from that source. *For they who desire to be rich, fall into a temptation and a snare, and many foolish and hurtful lusts, and into destruction and perdition.*[e]

Seek not, therefore, in your wife abundance of wealth, and you shall find everything else go well. Who, tell me, would overlook the most important things, to attend to those which are less so? And yet, alas, this is in every case our experience. Yes, if we have a son, we concern ourselves, not how he may be made virtuous, but how we may find him a rich wife; not how he may be well-mannered, but

---

well-monied; if we follow a business, we enquire, not how it may be clear of sin, but how the income will be most profitable. And everything has become money and thus is everything corrupted and ruined, because that passion possesses us.

Even so ought husbands love their own wives, said he, *as their own bodies*.[f] What, again, does this mean? To how much greater, a similitude, and stronger example has he come; and not only so, but also to one now much nearer and clearer, and to a fresh obligation. For that other one was of no very constraining force, for He was Christ, and was God, and gave Himself.

For the rest, he treats this same theme methodically elsewhere, saying: *Thus they must* is not, in fact, a favor, but an obligation. After having said, *as their own bodies*,[g] he adds: *For no one hates his own flesh, but rather nourishes and cherishes it.*[h] That is, he takes care of it with great solicitude. And in what way is she his own flesh? Let us listen. *This one, at last* — Scripture says — *is bone of my bones and flesh of my flesh.*[i] And not only that, but also: *They are one flesh.*[j] *Even as Christ loved the Church.*[k]

He has come back to the first example. For we are members of his body, of his flesh and bone.[l] In what way? He is, in fact, made up of our matter, as Eve is flesh of the flesh of Adam. It was opportune that he mentions flesh and bone: in fact, these are the most important elements in our makeup, flesh and bones; the one is cast in the role of holding up the structure, the other gives it its shape. But, in that case it is clear; in this, how is it possible? As there is a great closeness in the one, so — he says — also here.

What does *of his flesh* mean? This: legitimately from him....[3]

On the Epistle to the Ephesians, c. 5 Homily XX, 2-3;
PG 62 136-139; NPNF 13, 144-145

---

[f] Eph 5:28 [g] Eph 5:28 [h] Eph 5:29 [i] Gn 2:25 [j] Gn 2:24 [k] Eph 5:31 [l] cf. Gn 2:24

[3] In the concluding section the author inserts an interesting christological argument which proceeds from the theme of relations between spouses to the broader theme of the bond between the entire community of the faithful and Christ.

47

5. And mark, how he expands on the arguments based on love, stating the arguments relating to Christ and those relating to one's own flesh, the words, *For this cause shall a man leave his father and mother*.[a] Whereas upon those arguments drawn from fear he forbears to enlarge. And why so? Because he would rather that this principle prevail, this, namely, of love; for where this exists, everything else follows in due course, but where the other exists, not necessarily for the man who loves his wife, even though she be not a very obedient one, still will bear with everything. So difficult and impracticable is unanimity, where persons are not bound together by that love which is founded in supreme authority at all events, fear will not necessarily effect this. Accordingly, he dwells the more upon this, which is the strong tie. And the wife, though seeming to be the loser in that she was charged to fear, is the gainer, because the principal duty, love, is charged upon the husband. "But what," one may say, "if a wife reverence me not?" Never mind, you are to love, fulfill your own duty. For though that which is due from others may not follow, we ought of course to do our duty. This is an example of what I mean. He says, *submitting yourselves one to another in the fear of Christ*.[b]

And what then if another submit not himself? Still, obey the law of God. Just so, I say, is it also here. Let the wife at least, though she be not loved, still reverence notwithstanding, that nothing may lie at her door and let the husband, though his wife reverence him not, still show her love notwithstanding, that he himself be not wanting in any point. For each has received his own. This then is marriage when it takes place, according to Christ, spiritual marriage, and spiritual birth, not of blood, nor of travail, nor of the will of the flesh. Such was the birth of Christ, not of blood, nor of travail. Such also was that of Isaac. Hear how the Scripture said, *And it ceased to be with Sarah after the manner of women*.[c]

Yes, a marriage it is, not of passion, nor of the flesh, but wholly spiritual, the soul being united to God by a union unspeakable, and which He alone knows. Therefore he said, *He that is joined unto the Lord is one spirit*.[d]

---

[a] Gn 2:24   [b] Eph 5:21   [c] Gn 18:11   [d] 1 Cor 6:17

Mark how earnestly he endeavors to unite, flesh with flesh, and spirit with spirit. And where are the heretics? Never surely, if marriage were a thing to be condemned, would he have called Christ and the Church a bride and bridegroom; never would he have brought forward by way of exhortation the words, *A man shall leave his father and his mother;*[e] and again have added, that it was spoken *in regard of Christ and of the Church.*[f] For of her it is that the Psalmist also said, *Hearken, O daughter, and consider, and incline your ear; forget also your own people, and your father's house. So shall the king desire your beauty.*[g] For this reason, therefore, also Christ said, *I came out from the Father, and am come.*[h]

Now why did he not say of the wife also, "She shall be joined unto her husband"? Why, I say, is this? Because he was discoursing concerning love, and was discoursing to the husband. For to her indeed he discourses concerning reverence, and says, *the husband is the head of the wife,*[i] and again, *Christ is the Head of the Church.*[j] Whereas to him he discourses concerning love, and commits to him this province of love, and declares to him that which pertains to love, thus binding him and cementing him to her.

For the man that leaves his father for the sake of his wife, and then again, leaves this very wife herself and abandons her, what forbearance can he deserve? What then, a man may say, if our duty is done, and yet she does not follow the example? Yet if the unbelieving depart, let him depart[k] — the brother or the sister is not under bondage in such circumstances. However, when you hear mention of "fear," demand that fear which is appropriate to a free woman, not as though you were exacting it from a slave. For she is your own body; and if you do this, you reproach yourself in dishonoring your own body.

And of what nature is this "fear"? It is the not contradicting, the not rebelling, the not being fond of preeminence. It is enough that fear be kept within these bounds. But if you love, as you are commanded, you will make it yet greater. Or rather it will not be any

---

e Gn 2:24   f Eph 5:32   g Ps 44:11   h Jn:16:28   i Eph 5:23   j Eph 5:23   k 1 Cor 7:15

longer by fear that you will be doing this, but love itself will have its effect.

The sex is said to be weaker, and in need of much support, much condescension.

But what will they say, who are knit together, in second marriages? I speak not at all in condemnation of them — God forbid — for the Apostle himself permits them, though indeed by way of concession. Supply her with everything. Do everything and endure trouble for her sake. Necessity is laid upon you.

Here he does not think it right to introduce his counsel, as he in many cases does, with examples from them that are without. The word of God, so great and forcible, is by itself sufficient; and more especially as regards the argument of subjection. *A man shall leave,* he quotes, *his father and mother.*[l] Behold, this then is from without — But he does not say, and "shall dwell with," but *shall cleave unto,*[m] thus showing the closeness of the union, and the fervent love. Indeed, he is not content with this, but further by what he adds, he explains the subjection in such a way as that the two appear no longer two. He does not say, "one spirit," he does not say, "one soul" (for that is manifest, and is possible to any one), but so as to be *one flesh.*[n]

6. She is a secondary authority, possessing indeed an authority, and a considerable duality of dignity but at the same time the husband has something of an advantage. In this consists most especially the well-being of the house. For he took that former argument, the example of Christ, to show that we ought not only to love, but also to govern; *that she may be,* it says, *holy and without blemish.*[o] But the word "flesh" has reference to love — and the words "shall cleave" have in like manner reference to love. For if you shall make her *holy and without blemish,* everything else will follow.

Seek the things which are of God, and those which are of man will follow readily enough. Govern your wife, and thus the whole house will be in harmony. Hear what Paul says: *And if they would learn anything, let them ask their own husbands at home.*[p] If we thus regulate our own houses, we shall be also fit for the management of the

---

[l] Gn 2:24; Eph 5:31   [m] Gn 2:24   [n] Gn 2:24   [o] Eph 5:27   [p] 1 Cor 14:35

Church. For indeed a house is a miniature Church.[1] For it is possible for us by becoming good husbands and wives, to surpass all others.

Consider Abraham, and Sarah, and Isaac, and the three hundred and eighteen born in their house. How the whole house was harmoniously knit together, how the whole was full of piety and fulfilled the Apostolic injunction. She also *reverenced her husband*, for hear her own words, *It has not yet happened unto me even now, and my lord is old also*.[q]

And he again so loved her, that in all things he obeyed her commands. And the young child was virtuous, and the servants born in the house were so excellent that they refused not even to hazard their lives with their master; they delayed not, nor asked the reason. Nay, one of them, the chief, was so admirable, that he was even entrusted with the marriage of the only-begotten child, and with a journey into a foreign country.[2]

For just as with a general, when his soldiers also are well organized, the enemy has no quarter to attack; so, I say, is it also here; when husband and wife and children and servants are all interested in the same things, great is the harmony of the house. Since where this is not the case, the whole is often overthrown and broken up by one bad servant — and that single one will often mar and utterly destroy the whole. So then be very thoughtful both for our wives, and children, and servants; knowing that we shall thus be establishing for ourselves an easy government, and shall have our dealings with them be gentle and lenient, and say, *Behold I, and the children whom God has given me*.[r] If the husband command respect, and the head be honorable, then the rest of the body will sustain no violence.

---

q Gn 18:12   r Is 8:18

[1] The harmony begun between the spouses has also the effect of realizing in the heart of the family a small ecclesial community. On this recurring theme in Chrysostom (cf. *On the First Epistle to Timothy*, Hom. X, 2, PG 62, 549; *On Genesis*, Hom. II, 4, PG 53, 31; *On Genesis*, Disc. VI, 2, PG 54, 607; Disc. VII, 1, PG 54, 608; Disc. VIII, 2, PG 54, 619-620; *On the Epistle to the Ephesians*, Hom. XX, 8, PG 62, 147) see E. Lodi, 'Famiglia-chiesa domestica nella tradizione patristica,' *Rivista di pastorale liturgica* 18 (1980), 19-24.

[2] The servant in question is Eliezer, a man of Damascus (cf. Gn 15:2). The entire event is described at length in *In Praise of Maximus*, 5-9, PG 51, 232-242; Ital. tr. DiNola, *op. cit.*, 108-128.

Now what is to be the wife's fitting behavior, and what the husband's, the Apostle states accurately, charging her to reverence him as the head, and him to love her as a wife; but how, it may be asked, can these things be? That they ought indeed so to be, he has proved. But how they can be so, I will tell you. They will be so, if we will despise money, if we will look but to one thing only, excellence of soul, if we will keep the fear of God before our eyes. For what he says in his discourse to servants, *Whatsoever any man does, whether it be good or evil, the same shall he receive of the Lord;*[s] this is also the case here. Love her therefore, not for her sake so much as for Christ's sake. This, at least, he as much as intimates, in saying, *as unto the Lord.*[t]

On the Epistle to the Ephesians, c. 5, Homily XX, 5-6;
PG 62, 141-143; NPNF 13, 147f.

RECIPROCAL "EDUCATION" OF THE SPOUSES

A. *The Man as "Master"*

48

7. Let him, as if he had an image given into his hands to mould, let him, from that very evening on which he first receives her into the bridal chamber, teach her temperance, gentleness, and how to live, casting out the love of money at once from the outset, and from the very threshold. Let him discipline her in wisdom, and advise her never to have pendants of gold hanging from her ears, and down her cheeks, and laid round about her neck, nor laid up about her boudoir, nor golden and costly garments stored up. But let her room be handsome; still let not what is handsome degenerate into gaudiness. Leave such things to the people of the theater.

Adorn your house yourself with all possible neatness, so as rather to breathe an air of sobriety than much perfume. For from that two or three good results will arise. First, then, the bride will not be

---

[s] Eph 6:8   [t] Eph 5:22

grieved, when after the wedding feast, the garments, and the golden ornaments, and silver vessels, are sent back to their respective owners. Second, the bridegroom will have no anxiety about the loss, nor for the security of the accumulated treasures. Thirdly again, in addition to this, which is the crown of all these benefits, by these very points he will be showing his own judgment, that indeed he derives no pleasure from any of these things, and that he will moreover put an end to everything else in keeping with them, and will never so much as allow the existence either of dances or of indecent songs.[1]

What then do I say is our duty? Take away from marriage all those shameful, those Satanic, those immodest songs, those parties of profligate young people, and this will avail to chasten the spirit of your bride. For she will at once thus reason with herself: "Wonderful! What a philosopher this man is! He regards the present life as nothing; he has brought me here into his house, to be a mother, to bring up his children, to manage his household affairs."

"Yes, but these things are distasteful to a bride"? Just for the first or second day but not afterwards; no, she will even reap from them the greatest delight, and relieve herself of all suspicion. For a man who can endure neither flute players, nor dissolute songs, and that too at the very time of his wedding, such a one will scarcely endure ever to do or say anything shameful.

And then after this, when you have divested the marriage of all these things, then take her, and form and mould her carefully, encouraging her bashfulness, for a considerable length of time, and not destroying it suddenly. For even if the young woman be very bold, yet for a time she will keep silence out of reverence for her husband, and feeling herself a novice in the circumstances. You then break not off this reserve too hastily, as unchaste husbands do, but encourage it for a long time. For this will be a great advantage to you.

Meanwhile she will not complain, she will not find fault with any laws you may frame for her. During that time therefore, during which shame, like a sort of bridle laid upon the soul, does not allow

---

[1] There follows a short argument of a parenetic character by which the author proposes to convince his hearers of the opportunity to follow his advice.

her to make any murmur, nor to complain about what is done, lay down all your laws. For as soon as ever she acquires boldness, she will overturn and confound everything without any sense of fear. When is there a better time for moulding a wife than that during which she reverences her husband, and is still timid, and still shy? Then lay down all your laws for her and, willing or unwilling, she will certainly obey them.

But how shall you avoid spoiling her modesty? By showing her that you yourself are no less modest than she, addressing to her but few words, and those too with great gravity and collectedness. Then entrust her with the discourses of wisdom, for her soul will receive them. And establish her in that loveliest habit, I mean modesty.

I will also tell you, if you wish, by way of example, what sort of language should be addressed to her. For if Paul did not shrink from saying, *do not defraud one another,*[a] and spoke the language of a bridesmaid, or rather, not of a bridesmaid, but of a spiritual soul, much more should we not shrink from speaking.

What then is the language we ought to address to the wife? With great delicacy then we may say to her, "I have taken you, my child, to be partner of my life, and have brought you in to share with me in the closest and most honorable ties, in my children, and the superintendence of my house. And what advice then shall I now recommend you?" Or rather, first talk with her of your love for her; for there is nothing that so contributes to persuade a hearer to admit sincerely the things that are said, as to be assured that they are said with heartfelt affection. How then are you to show that affection? By saying, "When it was within my power to take many to wife, both ones with better dowries and of noble family, I did not so choose, but I was enamored of you, and your beautiful life, your modesty, your gentleness, and sobriety of mind."

Then immediately from these beginnings open the way to your discourse on true wisdom, and with some circumlocution make a protest against riches. For if you direct your argument at once against riches, you will come down too heavily upon her; but if you do it by

---

[a] 1 Cor 7:5

taking an occasion, you will succeed entirely. For you will appear to be doing it by way of apology, not as a morose sort of person, and ungracious, and over-nice about trifles. But when you take occasion from what relates to herself, she will be even pleased. You will say then (for I must return to the point I was making) that, "Whereas I might have married a rich woman, and one with good dowry, I could not endure it. And why so? Not out of caprice and without reason; but I was taught well and truly, that money is no real possession, but a most despicable thing, a thing which moreover belongs as well to thieves, and to harlots, and to tomb-robbers. So I gave up these things, and went on till I encountered the excellence of your soul, which I value above all gold. For a young maiden who is discreet and ingenuous, and whose heart is set on piety, is worth the whole world. For these reasons then, I courted you, and I love you, and prefer you to my own soul. For the present life is nothing. And I pray, and beseech, and do all I can, that we may be counted worthy so to live this present life, that we may be able also then in the world to come to be united to one another in perfect security. For our time here is brief and fleeting. But if we shall be counted worthy by having pleased God to so exchange this life for the next one, then we shall forever be both with Christ and with each other, with more abundant pleasure. I value your affection above everything, and nothing is so bitter or so painful to me, as ever to be at variance with you. Yes, though it should be my lot to lose my all, and to become poorer than Irus,[2] and undergo the most extreme hazards, and suffer any pain whatsoever, all will be tolerable and endurable, so long as your feelings remain true towards me. And then will my children be most dear to me, while you are affectionately disposed towards me. But you must do these duties too."

Then mingle also with your discourse the Apostle's words, that thus God would have our affections blended together; for listen to the Scripture, which says, *For this cause shall a man leave his father and mother, and cleave to his wife*.[b] Let us have no pretext for narrow-

---

[b] Gn 2:24; Eph 5:31

---

[2] Irus is the nickname of Arnaios, a beggar in Homer's *Odyssey*. He lived in Ithaca, the fatherland of Odysseus, where the latter had an angry altercation with him on his return: *Odyssey*, XVIII, vv. 1-136.

minded jealousy. Perish riches, and a retinue of slaves, and all that outward pomp. "For me this is more valuable than all."

What weight of gold, what amount of treasure, is so dear to a wife as these words? Have no fear that because she is beloved she will ever rave against you. But confess that you love her. For courtesans indeed, who attach themselves now to one and now to another, would naturally enough feel contempt towards their lovers, should they hear such expressions as these, but a free-born wife or a noble young woman would never be so affected with such words; no, she will be so much the more submissive.

Tell her too, that you set a high value on her company, and that you are more desirous to be at home for her sake, than in the marketplace. And esteem her before all your friends, and above the children that are born of her, and let these very children be beloved by you for her sake. If she does any good act, praise and admire it; if she does anything foolish, and such as young ladies may happen to do, advise her and remind her. Condemn outright all riches and extravagance, and gently point out the ornament that there is in neatness and in modesty, and be continually teaching her the things that are profitable.

9. Say your prayers in common. Let each go to church and let the husband ask his wife at home, and she in turn ask her husband, to give an account of the things which were said and read there.[3] If any poverty should overtake you, quote the case of those holy men, Paul and Peter, who were more honored than any emperors or rich men and yet how they spent their lives in hunger and in thirst. Teach her that there is nothing in life that is to be feared, only offending against God. If a man marry thus, with these views, he will be but little inferior to monks; the married will be little below the unmarried.

If you have a mind to give dinners, and to entertain, let there be nothing immodest, nothing disorderly. If you should find any poor

---

[3] There emerges here the datum, according to which the religious aspect integrates the portrait of a Christian marriage. The spouses are nourished in church on the word of God and at home they reserve a period of time for prayer which not even the smallest of the children should miss; cf. *Hom. on Acts*, XXVI, 3-4, PG 60, coll. 202-204; *On Genesis*, Disc. IV, 2, PG 54, 607.

saint able to bless your house, able just by setting his foot in it to bring in the whole blessing of God, invite him.

And may I say one more thing? Let no one of you make it his endeavor to marry a rich woman, but much rather a poor one. When someone rich becomes a bride, she will not bring so great source of pleasure from her riches, as she will annoyance from her taunts, from her demanding more than she brought, from her insolence, her extravagance, her vexatious language.

For she will say perhaps, "I have not yet spent anything of yours, I am still wearing my own clothes, bought with what my parents settled upon me." What are you saying, woman? Still wearing your own! And what can be more miserable than such language? Why, you have no longer a body of your own, and have you money of your own? After marriage you are no longer two, but are become one flesh. Are, then, your possessions twofold, and not one? Oh! this love of money! You both are become one person, one living creature; and do you still say "my own"? Cursed and abominable word that it is, it was introduced by the devil.

Things far nearer and dearer to us than these has God made all common to us, and are these then not common? We cannot say, "my own light, my own sun, my own water." All our greater blessings are in common, and are riches not common? Perish riches ten thousand times over! Or rather not riches, but those dispositions of mind which know not how to make use of riches, but esteem them above all things.[4]

Teach her these lessons also with the rest, but with much graciousness. For since the recommendation of virtue has in itself much that is stern, and especially to a young and tender maiden whenever discourses on true wisdom are to be made, contrive that your manner be full of graciousness and kindness. And above all banish this notion from her soul, of "mine" and "yours."

---

[4] This is a theme which is ever present to Chrysostom, one to which he frequently returns in his parenesis to his people. It is also developed in relation to the well-known Gospel parable of the rich young man (Mt 19:16-30; Mk 10:17-31; Lk 18:18-30) on which see C. Scaglioni, 'La proposta pastorale di san Giovanni Crisostomo tra rigore e condiscendenza,' in AA. vv., *Per foramen acus. Il cristianesimo antico di fronte alla pericope evangelica del "giovanne ricco,"* (SPM 14) Milan, 1986, 329-360.

If she says the word "mine," say to her, "What things do you call yours? For in truth I know not; I for my part have nothing of my own. How then can you speak of 'mine' when all that is mine is yours?"

Freely grant her the word. Do you not perceive that such is our practice with children? When, while we are holding something, a child snatches it, and wishes again to get hold of some other thing, we allow it, and say, "Yes, and this is yours, and that is yours." The same also let us do with a wife; for her temperament is more or less like that of a child;[5] and if she says "mine," say, "Why, everything is yours, and I am yours." Nor is the expression one of flattery, but of exceeding wisdom. In this way you will be able to abate her wrath, and put an end to her disappointment. For it is flattery when a man does an unworthy act with an evil object: whereas this is the highest philosophy.

Say then, "Even I am yours, my child; this advice Paul gives me where he says, *the husband has not power over his own body, but the wife.*[c] If I have no power over my body, but you have, much more have you over my possessions." By saying these things you will have quieted her, you will have quenched the fire, you will have shamed the devil, you will have made her more your slave than one bought with money, with this language you will have bound her fast. Thus then, by your own language, teach her never to speak of "mine and yours."

And again, never call her simply by her name, but with terms of endearment, with honor, with much love. Honor her, and she will not need honor from others; she will not want the glory that comes from others, if she enjoys that which comes from you. Prefer her before all on every account, both for her beauty and her discernment, and praise her. You will thus persuade her to give heed to none that are without, but to scorn all the world except yourself. Teach her the fear of God, and all good things will flow from this as from a fountain, and the house will be full of ten thousand blessings. If we seek

---

[c] 1 Cor 7:4

[5] We have already had occasion to underline the frequency of this theme in the works of Chrysostom (cf. no. 44, n. 2).

the things that are incorruptible, these corruptible things will follow. *For,* said He, *seek first His kingdom, and all these things shall be
added unto you.*[d]

What sort of persons, think you, must the children of such
parents be? What the servants of such masters? What all others who
come near them? Will not they too eventually be loaded with innumerable blessings? For generally the servants also have their characters formed after their master's, and are fashioned after their humors,
love the same objects, which they have been taught to love, speak
the same language, and engage with them in the same pursuits. If
we regulate ourselves in this way, and attentively study the Scriptures, in most things we shall derive instruction from them. And thus
shall we be able to please God, and to pass through the whole of the
present life virtuously, and to attain those blessings which are promised to those that love Him, of which God grant that we may all be
counted worthy, through the grace and loving kindness of our Lord
Jesus Christ, with Whom, together with the Holy Spirit, be unto the
Father, glory, power, and honor, now, and ever, through all ages.
Amen.

On the Epistle to the Ephesians, c.V, Homily XX,7-9; PG 62, 145-149

B. *The Wife A Wise Educator*

49

3. Do you perceive how much profit the Apostles got from their
stay in this place, and from their isolation from wicked men?[1] Because of this He repeatedly led them apart and brought them away
from evil companionship. And therefore He appeared to do this also
in the Old Law, for He separated the Jews from the Egyptians, far
away in the desert, and gave them instruction in all things.[2]

---

[d] Mt 6:33

---

[1] The discussion turns to the advantages enjoyed by a serene soul, like that of a wife who
spends all of her time in domestic quiet.

[2] The reference is to the providential intervention of God which continued to happen for the
Jews during their flight from Egypt.

Moreover, He urged us to do this, bidding us to shun market-places and noisy confusion and to pray in our room in secret. And He gave this advice, for a ship sails prosperously, if untroubled by a storm; and a soul likewise, if it is free from worldly cares, remains in a state of tranquility. Therefore, too, women ought to be better able to live a truly Christian life since they remain, for the most part, closely secluded at home. It was thus, in fact, that Jacob[3] was a plain man, since he dwelt at home and was not involved in the troubles of public life. And so, not without reason Scripture says: *he kept to his tent.*[a]

"But" you will say, "there is much confusion at home, also." Yes, when you wish it so, and attract around yourself a host of anxieties. For the man who is greatly preoccupied with the affairs of the market-place and the law-court is completely swamped by worldly cares, as if by a kind of turbulent sea. Since woman, on the contrary, remains at home, as if in some school of asceticism, by keeping her thoughts recollected she will be able to fix her attention on prayer and reading, and the other practices of the Christian way of life. Further, just as those who dwell in the desert have no one to bother them, so also, because she is always within the house, she can continually enjoy peace and calm. If it should ever be necessary for her to go out, not even then will there be cause for disturbance on her part — indeed, there are necessary occasions for women to go abroad, whether for the sake of coming to church here or when the needs of the body must be cared for in the bath. However, she spends the bulk of her time at home, and so it is possible for her both to live as a good Christian herself, and, on welcoming her husband home, to soothe his cares, to mold his character, to cause him to cease from useless or angry thoughts. Thus, she can send him forth again, completely rid of whatever evil effects he had acquired from the market-place, and carrying with him the virtues he has learned at home.

Indeed, nothing — nothing, I repeat — is more potent than a

---

[a] cf. Gn 25:27

[3] The third Patriarch of the Old Testament after Abraham and Isaac; he was the son of Isaac and Rebekah and the twin brother of Esau. By a stratagem and the favor of his mother he deprived his brother of his birthright in exchange for a stew of lentils (cf. Gn 25:19-34).

good and prudent woman in molding a man and shaping his soul in whatever way she desires. For he will not listen to friends, or teachers, or magistrates in the same way as with his wife, when she admonishes and advises him. Her admonition, in fact, carries with it a kind of pleasure, because of his very great love of the one who is admonishing him. Moreover, I could mention many men, formerly harsh and stubborn, who have become more tractable by this means. She shares with him his table and couch, the procreating of his children, his spoken words and secret thoughts, his comings and goings, and a great many other things as well. She is devoted to him in all things and as closely bound to him as the body is fastened to the head. If she chances to be prudent and diligent, she will surpass and excel all in her solicitude for her husband.

4. Therefore, I beseech women to carry this out in practice, and to give their husbands only the proper advice. For, just as a woman has great power for good, so also she has it for evil. A woman destroyed Absalom[b]; a woman destroyed Amnon[c]; a woman would have destroyed Job[d]; a woman saved Nabal[e] from being murdered; a woman saved an entire nation. Furthermore, Deborah[f] and Judith[g] and innumerable other women directed the success of men who were generals.[4] And that is why Paul said: *For how do you know, O wife, whether you will save your husband.*[h] In his day, too, we see Persis and Mary and Priscilla[5] sharing in the Apostle's difficult trials. You also ought to imitate these women, and mold the character of your husbands, not only by your words but also by your example.

"But how shall we teach them by our example?" When your husband sees that you are not an evil woman, or a busybody and fashion conscious, and that you do not demand an extravagant expenditure of money but are content with what you have, then, indeed,

---

[b] 2 S 17:15-20 [c] 2 S 13:1-9 [d] Jb 2:9-10 [e] 1 S 25:2-42 [f] Jg 4:1-5 [g] Jdt 7:1-15 [h] 1 Cor 7:16

[4] On the typology of the strong woman — the *mulier fortis* — cf. U. Mattioli, *Astheneia e andreia. Aspetti della femminilità nella letteratura classica, biblica e cristiana*, Rome, 1983, 87-161. [Engl. tr. Add: K. Aspegren, *The Male Woman: a Feminine Ideal in the Early Church*, Stockholm, 1990.]

[5] Three female figures are actively engaged in the mission of the Pauline church. Cf. Rm 16:3 and 12 (Priscilla, *synergos*, collaborator; Mary and Persis, *kopiosai*, who worked hard for the Lord).

he will bear with you even when you give him advice. If, on the contrary, you show true wisdom in your words, while you do the opposite in practice, he will find fault with you for your very foolish talk.

But when you provide him with instruction, not only by your words but also by your example, then he will both show approval of you and be the more effectively convinced. For example, when you do not look for gold, or pearls, or a very extensive wardrobe, but seek in their stead modest and decorous behavior, and kindness, you both display these qualities in your own character, and in return receive them from his.

If, indeed, you must do something to please your husband, you ought to adorn your soul rather than to deck out — or rather, corrupt — your body. For golden raiment will not make you as lovable and desirable to him as decorum, and tenderness toward him, and willingness to give up your life for him. These are things that more surely captivate your husbands' hearts. In fact, that other kind of adornment is even a source of displeasure to him, since it depletes his wealth and causes him a great deal of expense and worry, while the things I have mentioned, on the contrary, cause the husband to become firmly attached to his wife. Love and affection and mutual attachment do not give rise to worry, nor do they make for expense, but quite the opposite. Further, that other kind of adornment begins to pall as it becomes familiar, while that of the soul grows more beautiful day by day, and enkindles a still greater flame of love.

Homily on the Gospel of John LXI, 3-4; PG 59, 340-341; FOTC 41, 159-163

This book was designed and published by St. Pauls/Alba House, the publishing arm of the Society of St. Paul, an international religious congregation of priests and brothers dedicated to serving the Church through the communications media. For information regarding this and associated ministries of the Pauline Family of Congregations, write to the Vocation Director, Society of St. Paul, 7050 Pinehurst, Dearborn, Michigan 48126 or check our internet site, www.albahouse.org